*Guide to American Literature
from its Beginnings
through Walt Whitman*

About the Authors

James T. Callow is Professor of American Literature at the University of Detroit, where he also directs the Computerized Folklore Archive. He holds a B.S.S. from John Carroll University, an M.A. from the University of Toledo, and a Ph.D. from Western Reserve University. His book *Kindred Spirits* (1967) treats the affinities between American writers and artists, as does his work on the (Old New York) Sketch Club, a project supported by the National Endowment for the Humanities. Since 1964 Dr. Callow has served on the American Literature Bibliography Committee of the Modern Language Association.

R. J. Reilly is Professor of American Literature and Literary Criticism at the University of Detroit. He holds the Ph.B. and M.A. degrees from the University of Detroit and the Ph.D. degree from Michigan State University. His essay "Henry James and the Morality of Fiction" won the Norman Foerster Award as the best essay to appear in *American Literature* in 1967, and his book *Romantic Religion* (1971) was selected by the Modern Language Association for inclusion in its Scholar's Library.

Guide to American Literature from its Beginnings through Walt Whitman

by

James T. Callow and Robert J. Reilly

BARNES & NOBLE BOOKS

A DIVISION OF HARPER & ROW, PUBLISHERS

New York, Hagerstown, San Francisco, London

To Pat and Kathy Callow, George H. Orians,
and Lyon N. Richardson

First BARNES & NOBLE BOOKS edition published 1976

LIBRARY OF CONGRESS CATALOG CARD NUMBER: 75–29621

PAPERBACK ISBN: 0-06-460165-X
HARDBOUND ISBN: 0-06-480132-2
78 79 80 5 4 3 2

Contents

Abbreviations   vii
Introduction   xi
  1. Earliest American Writing   1
  2. Puritans and Non-Puritans in New England   5
  3. Later Puritans   23
  4. Diarists   33
  5. Essayists, Statesmen, and Propagandists   41
  6. Neoclassic Poets   53
  7. Preromantics   61
  8. Early Fiction and Drama   67
  9. The Knickerbockers   75
10. The Transcendentalists   91
11. Hawthorne, Poe, and Melville   104
12. New England Poets   123
13. Humorists, Wits, and Informal Essayists   138
14. Writers in the Civil War   151
15. Walt Whitman   160
16. Compiling and Updating Your Own
     Bibliography   167
General Bibliography   172
Chapter-by-Chapter Bibliographies   183
Index   235

Abbreviations

AACS   American Authors and Critics Series
AH   *American Heritage*
AI   *American Imago*
AL   *American Literature: A Journal of Literary History, Biography, Criticism, and Bibliography*
ALR   *American Literary Realism*
ALS   *American Literary Scholarship*
AN&Q   *American Notes and Queries*
AQ   *American Quarterly*
AS   *American Speech*
ASch   *American Scholar*
Atl   *Atlantic Monthly*
ATQ   *American Transcendental Quarterly*
AWS   American Writers Series
BAL   Jacob Blanck, *Bibliography of American Literature*
BB   *Bulletin of Bibliography*
BNYPL   *Bulletin of the New York Public Library*
BPLQ   *Boston Public Library Quarterly*
BuR   *Bucknell Review*
BUSE   *Boston University Studies in English*
CairoSE   *Cairo Studies in English*
CCC   *College Composition and Communication*
CE   *College English*
CEA   *CEA Critic*
CEAA   Center for Editions of American Authors
CHAL   *Cambridge History of American Literature*
CJF   *Chicago Jewish Forum*
CL   *Comparative Literature*
CLAJour   *College Language Association Journal*

CritQ	*Critical Quarterly*
DA	*Dissertation Abstracts*
DAB	*Dictionary of American Biography* (See chap. 16.)
DAI	*Dissertation Abstracts International*
EAL	*Early American Literature*
EALN	*Early American Literature Newsletter* (original title of *EAL*)
EJ	*English Journal*
ELH	*Journal of English Literary History*
ELN	*English Language Notes*
ES	*English Studies*
ESQ	*Emerson Society Quarterly*
EUQ	*Emory University Quarterly*
Expl	*Explicator*
Expl Cyc	*The Explicator Cyclopedia*
GaR	*Georgia Review*
GB	General Bibliography (of this book)
HLB	*Harvard Library Bulletin*
HLQ	*Huntington Library Quarterly*
HudR	*Hudson Review*
JA	*Jahrbuch für Amerikastudien*
JAAC	*Journal of Aesthetics and Art Criticism*
JAF	*Journal of American Folklore*
JAH	*Journal of American History*
JAmS	*Journal of American Studies*
JEGP	*Journal of English and Germanic Philology*
JHI	*Journal of the History of Ideas*
JQ	*Journalism Quarterly*
JSH	*Journal of Southern History*
KFQ	*Keystone Folklore Quarterly*
KFR	*Kentucky Folklore Record*
KR	*Kenyon Review*
Leary	Lewis Leary, *Articles on American Literature* (See chap. 16.)
LHUS	Robert E. Spiller and others, *Literary History of the United States*
Lud	Richard M. Ludwig, ed., *Literary History of the United States: Bibliography Supplement* (See chap. 16.)
MASJ	*Midcontinent American Studies Journal*
MFS	*Modern Fiction Studies*
MissQ	*Mississippi Quarterly*
MLN	*Modern Language Notes*
MLQ	*Modern Language Quarterly*
MLR	*Modern Language Review*

MP	*Modern Philology*
MR	*Massachusetts Review*
MS	manuscript
MTJ	*Mark Twain Journal*
MuK	*Maske und Kothurn* (Graz-Wien)
n.	note
N&Q	*Notes and Queries*
NCF	*Nineteenth-Century Fiction*
NEQ	*New England Quarterly*
NS	*Die Neueren Sprachen*
n.s.	new series
NYFQ	*New York Folklore Quarterly*
NYH	*New York History*
NYTBR	*New York Times Book Review*
PAPS	*Proceedings of the American Philosophical Society*
PBSA	*Papers of the Bibliographical Society of America*
PLL	*Papers on Language and Literature*
PMASAL	*Papers of the Michigan Academy of Science, Arts, and Letters*
PMLA	*Publications of the Modern Language Association of America*
PN	*Poe Newsletter*
PNJHS	*Proceedings of the New Jersey Historical Society*
PQ	*Philological Quarterly*
PW	*Publishers Weekly*
QJS	*Quarterly Journal of Speech*
QQ	*Queen's Quarterly*
RivEd	Riverside Editions
RLV	*Revue des Langues Vivantes* (Bruxelles)
RS	*Research Studies* (Washington State University)
SA	*Studi Americani*
SAQ	*South Atlantic Quarterly*
SB	*Studies in Bibliography*
SCB	*South Central Bulletin*
SDR	*South Dakota Review*
SFQ	*Southern Folklore Quarterly*
Sig	Signet
SIR	*Studies in Romanticism*
SLJ	*Southern Literary Journal*
SN	*Studia Neophilologica*
SNNTS	*Studies in the Novel* (North Texas State University)
SoQ	*The Southern Quarterly*
SoR	*Southern Review*
SoWS	Southern Writers Series

SP	*Studies in Philology*
SR	*Sewanee Review*
SSF	*Studies in Short Fiction*
SUS	*Susquehanna University Studies*
SWR	*Southwest Review*
TCL	*Twentieth Century Literature*
TCV	Twentieth Century Views
TSE	*Tulane Studies in English*
TSL	*Tennessee Studies in Literature*
TSLL	*Texas Studies in Literature and Language*
TUSAS	Twayne's United States Authors Series
TWA	*Transactions of the Wisconsin Academy of Science, Arts, and Letters*
UKCR	*University of Kansas City Review*
UMPAW	University of Minnesota Pamphlets on American Writers
UMSE	*University of Mississippi Studies in English*
UR	*University Review*
UTQ	*University of Toronto Quarterly*
UTSE	*University of Texas Studies in English*
VMHB	*Virginia Magazine of History and Biography*
VQR	*Virginia Quarterly Review*
w.	written (Dates without w. are dates of publication.)
WAL	*Western American Literature*
WF	*Western Folklore*
WHR	*Western Humanities Review*
WMQ	*William and Mary Quarterly*
WPHM	*Western Pennsylvania Historical Magazine*
WWR	*Walt Whitman Review*
XUS	*Xavier University Studies*
YR	*Yale Review*

Introduction

This outline covers approximately the first 250 years of American literature, from the seventeenth to the mid-nineteenth century. Our story starts with Captain John Smith and his Elizabethan contemporaries, then concentrates on the New England Puritans. As we move into the eighteenth century, we discuss the literary accomplishments of such famous statesmen as Franklin and Jefferson and of lesser-known figures like poet Philip Freneau and Gothic novelist Charles Brockden Brown. Next, in the nineteenth century, we find those standard authors whose names are so familiar: Irving, Cooper, and Bryant; Emerson and Thoreau; Hawthorne, Poe, and Melville; Whittier, Lowell, and Holmes. From the Knickerbockers and transcendentalists in New York and New England we turn to the dialect humorists of the antebellum South. The volume ends with the writers of the Civil War, the greatest of whom was Walt Whitman.

American literature may be analyzed in many ways. We have adopted the traditional chronological approach. For an overview of the history covered by this volume let us consider each century, describing it in terms of the status of its writers, the intellectual currents that influenced them, and the literary genres they best employed.

The seventeenth century

A) Writers: Explorers, settlers, and colonials, they took up the pen for utilitarian purposes. They had no intention of creating a native literature, nor did they regard themselves as professional authors.

B) Intellectual currents: Puritanism dominated New England. Anglicanism, Separatism, Catholicism, and Quakerism influenced the various colonies.

C) Genres: Travel literature, histories, diaries, and poetry constituted the best writing of this century.

The eighteenth century

A) Writers: Though still not professional authors, they became more and more American as the century progressed, until the Revolutionary War ended their colonial status.

B) Intellectual currents: Deism, rationalism, and neoclassicism flourished. Signs of preromanticism were evident even before midcentury.

C) Genres: In addition to histories, diaries, religious and political essays, there were poems, satires, short moralistic tales, and (toward the end of the century) novels and plays.

The nineteenth century

A) Writers: It was now possible to make a living as a professional author, though many writers still regarded literature as an avocation.

B) Intellectual currents: Predominant in this period of *isms* were nationalism, romanticism, transcendentalism, realism, regionalism, and (by the end of the century) naturalism.

C) Genres: The so-called American Renaissance produced classic examples of belles-lettres in the form of fiction and poetry. Dialect humor and local-color stories reached their peak.

1
Earliest American Writing

American literature began in the 1600s as an obscure offshoot of the English Renaissance. Gradually growing out of its provincial status, it underwent its own Renaissance in the nineteenth century and in the twentieth century achieved international recognition.

THE LANGUAGE OF THE EARLY PERIOD

The birth of American literature coincided with that of the modern English language; the earliest American writers are therefore not nearly so difficult to read as the earliest English writers. Nevertheless, the Elizabethan English of early American literature does differ noticeably from present-day English.[1] There are some completely strange words, while seemingly familiar words have different meanings. (The student can find these early meanings in the *Oxford English Dictionary*.) There is also a great freedom in Elizabethan English: Not only are sentences long, loose, and disjointed, but there are many instances of double negation and functional change (verbs used as nouns, adjectives used as adverbs, and so on), freedoms still to be found in the dialects of Appalachia and the Ozarks.

EXPLORATION AND SETTLEMENT

American literature was born out of English explorations and settlements. The Elizabethan and Jacobean periods produced a host of adventurers, cartographers, artists, sea dogs, and professional soldiers. These included men who, eager to best Spain, sailed off to a strange and exciting New

---

1. We tend to exaggerate this difference by mispronouncing "ye" and "eth." "Ye" should be pronounced "the," and in most cases "eth" (as in "maketh" or "holdeth") should be pronounced "s" or "z" (as in "makes" and "holds"). See McKerrow (GB), p. 322, n. 1; Marckwardt (GB), pp. 16–17.

1

World. The queen herself was very much interested in their activities, and so was the reading public. As a result, the list of English travel books began to grow. Some of these writings, among them Thomas Hariot's *A Briefe and True Report of the New Found Land of Virginia* (1588) and Richard Hakluyt's famous anthology *The Principall Navigations, Traffiques, Voiages, and Discoveries of the English Nation* (1589, enlarged 1598–1600), were issued in the sixteenth century. The early seventeenth century saw the publication of works by Captain John Smith, the writer who contributed most to beginning American literature.

CAPTAIN JOHN SMITH (1579/80–1631)

Although he has been called a liar and a fraud, Captain John Smith was really a genuine adventurer with a penchant for bragging and a talent for making himself into a legend. If his writings and his character have been vigorously attacked, they have been more convincingly defended (see Bibliography).

Life. Born in England, the son of a well-to-do farmer, Smith in his youth read many chivalric romances and under their influence embraced the military life. His autobiography, *The True Travels, Adventures, and Observations of Captain John Smith* (1630), tells of his fighting with the Christian forces in Hungary and beheading three Turks in single combat. Later wounded and sold into slavery by the Moslems, he managed to escape by braining his master with a threshing bat.

Continuing his adventures, Smith arrived in Virginia in 1607 to help found Jamestown, the first permanent English settlement in the New World. He became president of the colony (1608–1609), and during his years there he established a firm, realistic Indian policy, did some vital exploring, and showed his yeoman origins by urging the daintiest males among the company to dirty their hands with manual labor. When the Virginia Company decided to send Lord De La Warr to rule Jamestown, Smith, a commoner, left for London. But in 1614 he was back in America on a five-month voyage along the coast of New England (a place name of his own invention). In 1615 he again sailed for New England but was captured at sea by the French before being able to land. After this, although he tried several times, he never returned to America. Instead he lived quietly in England writing of past adventures in some half-dozen books.

Style. Smith's style, like that of most Elizabethan prose writers, is irritating and pleasing at the same time. He refers to himself in the third person; he punctuates erratically; his predicates sometimes disagree with their subjects; he confuses *then* and *than;* and his vocabulary is occasionally unfamiliar to us. On the other hand, he is a master of antithesis. For example, he contrasts the early Romans, who "by their pain and vertues became Lords of the world," with the late Romans, who "by their ease and vices became slaues to their seruants" (1:209).[2] Metaphor, too, he handled deftly, as for example in his dedication of *The Generall Historie of Virginia:* "This History . . . might and ought to haue beene clad in better robes then my rude military hand can cut out in Paper Ornaments" (1:275). He could be euphuistic at one time, straightforward at another. Finally, with the simple device of word piling he achieved very persuasive effects. When he tells us that a colony needs "Carpenters, Masons, Fishers, Fowlers, Gardiners, Husbandmen, Sawyers, Smiths, Spinsters, Taylors, [and] Weauers" (1:214), we are convinced that he knows what he is talking about.

Representative Works

A True Relation of . . . Virginia (1608). According to Tyler (GB:1878), "unquestionably the earliest book in American literature" (1:21). Published in London without Smith's knowledge, it was an abridgment of a letter he had written to a friend in England concerning the first few months of the Jamestown settlement. Possibly in order to avoid scaring off potential colonizers, Smith pictured Powhatan as curious but kindly and made no mention of being rescued by Pocahontas.

A Description of New England (1616). Based on Smith's two voyages to New England (1614, 1615), this is an excellent sample of promotional literature. Smith employs all kinds of psychological appeals to persuade his readers to settle in the New World. He argues from the example of antiquity and the promise of posterity; he cites patriotic as well as religious motives. He also inventories the abundant "commodities" or natural resources of New England and disparages his critics as caviling misfits. This small book, with its map carefully prepared by Smith, proved useful to the Pilgrims when they settled the area in 1620.

The Generall Historie of Virginia, New England, and the Summer Isles (1624). Smith's longest book and the first comprehensive history of the English settlements in America. It is an anthology as well as an original treatise, reprinting not only accounts by Hariot, John Pory, John White, Edward Winslow, and others but also works by Smith. A great part of the *Generall Historie* narrates Smith's own exploits and attempts to justify them. Here is his Pocahontas story, which led his critics to accuse him of capitalizing on the popular interest aroused by her visit to England (1616–1617) and his defenders to see this book as his first real chance to tell all that had happened to him in Virginia. Other sensational material in the *Generall Historie* includes accounts of rat plagues and cannibalism during the "Starving Time" at Jamestown.

Significance. In his life and in his works that told of it, Smith qualifies as

2. Quotations are from *Travels and Works of Captain John Smith,* ed. Edward Arber, new. ed. (Edinburgh: John Grant, 1910).

the traditional character type that folklorists call the unpromising hero.[3] A farmer's son, he had the adventures of a medieval knight, mixed with people of high social status, and did not hesitate to call himself "Admiral of New England." His friends, patrons, and rescuers were noble ladies: Princess Pocahontas of Attanoughkomouch, Lady Tragabigzanda of Istanbul, and the Duchess of Richmond and Lennox. Although he never married any of them and never became Sir John, he did rise well above his original position and gave American literature its first success story.

Smith established or excelled in several literary genres. He was America's first important historian. Unlike the typical armchair history, Smith's books were on-the-spot reports by a man who was often in the midst of the action. True, they were loosely structured and heavily weighted with borrowings from many authors, but Smith's egocentricity actually compensated for these defects by changing the historic into the heroic. Besides, he displayed a talent for reporting sensational events in a day when neither the novel nor the newspaper had truly emerged. As a master of promotional writing, Smith had the imagination to see America as a land of unlimited potential and thus began a tradition of boosting that includes such diverse writers as Crèvecoeur, Irving, Twain, Sandburg, and the anonymous authors of real estate advertisements and travel folders.[4] The Indian captivity narrative was another genre that Smith established. Hundreds of such accounts have been written since, but Smith's Powhatan-Pocahontas story remains the best known.

OTHER WRITERS IN THE SOUTH

"Bacons Epitaph, Made by His Man" (1676), a poem on the leader of Bacon's Rebellion, has been attributed to John Cotton of Queen's Creek, Virginia. *A Character of the Province of Mary-Land* (1666), by George Alsop (1638–?), is a lively prose treatise, remarkable for its humor, occasional poetry, and Edenic images.

3. See motifs L100 to L199 in Thompson (GB), 5:8–16.
4. For manifestations of this booster complex on the popular level, see Botkin, ed. (GB), pp. 276–308.

2
Puritans and Non-Puritans in New England

Most of the authors discussed in this chapter were born in England, came to the New World in their youth, and spent the rest of their lives in either religious or civil positions. Writing was not their profession. Some were busy pioneers; yet life on the frontier, instead of frustrating their literary impulses, actually seemed to stimulate them.

PURITAN DOCTRINE AND LITERATURE

To explain the Puritanism that dominated New England and its literature during the seventeenth century it is necessary to distinguish between the founders of Plymouth Colony and the founders of Massachusetts Bay. The latter were true Puritans, wealthy, well-educated, and intent on purifying the Church of England of its popish customs and festivals. The former—the Pilgrims—were Separatists; they believed the Church of England was beyond reform and therefore disassociated themselves from it. They were poor and less educated than their Massachusetts neighbors.

Both groups accepted the main doctrines of Calvinism:

1. Natural depravity. All men are born in original sin and can do nothing to save themselves.

2. Unconditional election. God, in his absolute sovereignty, saves some and damns others as he pleases.

3. Predestination. God knows from the beginning who has been elected.

4. Irresistible grace. Man cannot earn this saving grace, nor can he refuse it. The step-by-step process of realizing and accepting grace, and the sense of rebirth resulting from it, was called regeneration or sanctification.

Both groups also held that

5

1. God continuously directs the affairs of men. A thriving business, for example, might very well indicate divine favor and approval.

2. The Bible was the guide for virtually all aspects of life. Thus the Puritan theocracy was modeled on the covenant between God and man in the Old Testament, and persecution of nonbelievers was justified by scriptural example.

In this culture the purposes of literature were utilitarian. Religion was foremost, and all things were made to serve it.

The genres favored by Puritan writers demonstrate this love of the useful. Sermons, theological treatises, dialogues, debates, biographies, and histories were most popular, for they best served a didactic purpose. But there were no short stories, novels, or plays. Poetry flourished, however, although this also had its practical uses.

The subject matter of the Puritans' writing was dictated by the primacy of religion in their lives. Thorny theological problems turned up everywhere, even in ballad meter. To any Puritan the most important religious topic was his own spiritual journey out of Original Sin through the complicated process of regeneration; and stages of this journey were carefully analyzed in poems as well as in diaries. The religious progress of entire communities was similarly traced in various histories. Outside the Puritan theocracy were Quakers, Anglicans, Seekers, Dutchmen, Indians, and other aliens or renegades. These people the Puritan also wrote about, if only to denounce them, so that, though obviously biased, his work was broader than might be expected.

The Puritan's writing style was also influenced by religion. Believing that God ordered all events, he tended to treat the things of everyday life as allegories and symbols; and thinking that God had directed the Puritan exodus to the New World, he wrote seriously and dramatically about this great topic. Because the Bible dominated all his affairs, he filled his writing with biblical allusions, imagery, and figures of speech. Finally, because he advocated simplified rituals, he sometimes aimed for a plain writing style.

PURITAN PROSE WRITERS

Prose style varied widely among the Puritans. On the one hand, there was the plain style with its loose (nonperiodic) sentences and simple diction. Such were Samuel Sewall's *Diary,* Jonathan Edwards's philosophical treatises, and Mary Rowlandson's narrative of her captivity among the Indians.[1] On the other hand, there was Cotton Mather's elaborate style, replete with foreign quotations, polysyllabic words, and typographical

1. *The Sovereignty & Goodness of God* (1682), conveniently reprinted in *Narratives of the Indian Wars, 1675–1699,* ed. C. H. Lincoln, Original Narratives of Early American History (New York: Scribner, 1913. Reprinted by Barnes & Noble).

devices, and the prose of Nathaniel Ward, whose *Simple Cobler of Aggawam* (1647) is lavishly splashed with inkhorn terms and witty phrases. Apropos of clothes-conscious women, he observed: "When I heare a nugiperous Gentledame inquire what dresse the Queen is in this week: what the nudiustertian fashion of the Court; I meane the very newest: with egge to be in it in all haste, what ever it be; I look at her as the very gizzard of a trifle, the product of a quarter of a cypher, the epitome of nothing, fitter to be kickt, if shee were of a kickable substance, than either honour'd or humour'd."[2]

William Bradford (1590–1657). William Bradford, whose style, like seventeenth-century architecture, lies somewhere between the extremes of simple and ornate, was one of the most important Puritan prose writers.

LIFE. The only son of a well-to-do yeoman, Bradford grew up in southern Yorkshire. When he was about twelve, he was greatly affected by the Bible and joined the Separatists (the group wanting to leave the Church of England) in his neighborhood. At the age of eighteen, with other members of the Scrooby congregation, he left England, where persecution of Separatists had become intolerable. With the congregation, he lived first in Amsterdam and then in Leyden. There he married, worked as a weaver, became a guild member, and (apparently with no formal education) stored up the learning that he later poured into his prose.

In 1620 Bradford and his fellow Pilgrims made their famous exodus to the New World on the *Mayflower*. They settled in Plymouth, and in 1621 Bradford was elected their governor, a post to which he was reelected almost continually until his death. Bradford revealed little of himself in his writings; yet he obviously had no small role in the life at Plymouth Colony. Dealings with the London financiers, the neighboring Dutch colonists, and the Indians were under his supervision; and it was he who extended the hospitality of the so-called old comers to later arrivals. He also assigned jobs, settled disputes, meted out punishments, and kept official records of marriages, inventories, deeds, and wills.

Of Plymouth Plantation. Bradford's masterpiece, *Of Plymouth Plantation,* was written for the most part between 1630 and 1646 but not published until 1856. Meanwhile, however, it had circulated in manuscript on both sides of the Atlantic and had been freely incorporated into the histories of Nathaniel Morton, Cotton Mather, Thomas Prince, Thomas Hutchinson, and others. As a historical document, *Of Plymouth Plantation* has proved extremely useful.

Book I, comprising about one-fifth of the document, starts with the Protestant Reformation and ends with the first days at Plymouth. As Bradford reverently recalls the arduous voyage on the *Mayflower* and the arrival

2. Nathaniel Ward, *The Simple Cobler of Aggawam in America,* ed. David Pulsifer (Boston: James Munroe, 1843), p. 26.

at Cape Cod, he echoes so many biblical passages that the book sounds almost like Exodus. He treats his material dramatically, as befits a reenactment of the crossing of the Red Sea, but does not mention the legendary landing at Plymouth Rock (probably because it never happened in the way tradition relates).

In Book I Bradford had varied the range of his chapters so that one covered nearly six decades, others less than a year. Perhaps because he was writing Book I in 1630, at least ten years later than most events recorded in it, he could see things in perspective, skipping over scenes of little importance and dwelling on others. Yet by the end of Book I, apparently because such an approach seemed too ambitious or awkward, he announced that, "for brevitis sake," he would handle Book II "by way of annalls, noteing only the heads of principall things, and passages as they fell in order of time" (1:187).[3] This book, which comprises four-fifths of the history, is organized by years rather than chapters. Of course, it is sketchier than Book I, and it notes many events that Bradford undoubtedly would have interwoven had he given more sustained attention to the book.

Besides recording such historical events as the Mayflower Compact and the first Thanksgiving (the latter very briefly), Book II contains two large clusters of topics: (1) relations with outsiders and (2) internal affairs.

The Pilgrims and the Indians, for example, enjoyed a friendly relationship. Squanto was especially helpful, teaching the Pilgrims how to plant corn; and the Indian chiefs turned white miscreants over to the whites for trial rather than meting out their own justice. Bradford's attitude toward the Indians was realistic, conditioned not only by his religion but also by his frontier environment. He could call the surprise attack in which the Pilgrims and their Narragansett allies killed some 400 Pequots "a sweete sacrifice" (2:250), yet he could also censure those colonists who thought that Arthur Peach and others should not be executed for murdering an Indian brave. (For the Plymouth Colony's troubles with Thomas Morton and Roger Williams, see pp. 17–20, 20–22.)

The internal affairs of Plymouth occupy the bulk of Book II. Plagues and starvation, quite realistically portrayed, comprise some of the most moving episodes. An outbreak of bestiality and other sexual sins is also frankly recounted. In general, the book records obstacles overcome and is basically optimistic. But toward the end, an unrelieved gloomy note is struck when it becomes apparent to Bradford that Plymouth is a doomed colony: Its members have grown out of their simple primitive state; they have accumulated worldly goods; and many have decided to move away to other settlements.

STYLE. Bradford's style, like John Smith's, can simultaneously puzzle and please. He used the third-person point of view for events in which he was

3. The quotations are from William Bradford, *History of Plymouth Plantation, 1620–1647* (Boston: Massachusetts Historical Society, 1912).

the chief actor, as when he wrote: "Shortly after [the death of Carver] William Bradford was chosen Gove[rno]r in his stead" (1:216). This device may serve to convey a certain objectivity, but no such compensation can be found in Bradford's habit of using pronouns without clear antecedents.

Nevertheless, Bradford's style strikes a nice balance between the plain and the ornate. He himself announced that he was going to write plainly (1:1), but we must not ignore his artful use of alliteration, litotes, antithesis, allusion, and other traditional devices. Perhaps he is most easily identified for his pairing words as in "grow and increse," "an humble and modest mind," "rested and refreshte," "scofes and scorns" (2:247, 350, 249, 56). Despite the redundance, the effect is pleasing in its rhythm and useful in its emphasis. Bradford was also able to achieve a dramatic tone by stopping to reflect on present, past, and future events. Thus, having told of the Pilgrims' sojourn in Holland, their voyage to America, and their arrival at Cape Cod, he could "stay and make a pause, and stand half amazed at this poore peoples presente condition" (1:155). Several hundred words later he moved forward to the descendants of the Pilgrims and turned around to look back from that vantage point. Another merit in Bradford's style is his sense of irony, apparent, for example, in his account of the "very profane yonge" seaman who, having told the Pilgrims he hoped "to cast halfe of them over board before they came to their journeys end," was filled with "a greeveous disease" and therefore "was him selfe the first that was throwne overbord" (1:149).

SIGNIFICANCE. Bradford demonstrated the versatility that was to characterize later American statesmen such as Jefferson; he could write as well as govern. Moreover, he was a self-made man like Ben Franklin, John Smith, and many another unpromising American hero. In his writing Bradford proved that an artful prose could come from the frontier. *Of Plymouth Plantation* is not only an important historical document—our chief source for the history of the Pilgrims—but also an important literary document.

Samuel Sewall (1652–1730). Another prose writer whose most famous work was kept as a private record of events in which he played a major role was Samuel Sewall of Boston.

LIFE. Born in England, Sewall was only nine when he crossed the Atlantic, and for the rest of his life he was completely a New Englander. He studied divinity at Harvard but chose business as his profession. He imported various manufactured goods and raw materials while exporting fish, oil, pork, and turpentine to the West Indies, the South Seas, and England. Yet it was his marriage to Hannah Hull, daughter of the mintmaster for the Massachusetts Colony, that made him a rich man. Able to live like a Puritan aristocrat, Sewall gave some fifty years to public service. In 1692 he was a commissioner in the special court that tried the Salem witchcraft cases. Five years later, in a statement read to the congregation of Boston's Old South Church, he publicly confessed shame for his part in this episode. From 1718 to 1728 Sewall was Chief Justice of Massachusetts.

He was thrice married. Hannah, having borne fourteen children, only five of whom outlived her, died in 1717. In 1719, after unsuccessfully courting a Madam Denison, Sewall married the widow Abigail Tilley; but within seven months she suddenly died. He next offered marriage to Madam Katherine Winthrop, the widow of his longtime friend and fellow justice. When this courtship failed, Sewall proposed to Mrs. Mary Gibbs of Newtown, and they were married in 1722.

Diary. Sewall's *Diary,* covering the years 1673 to 1678/9[4] and 1685 to 1729, is one of the most interesting of all personal records from the seventeenth and eighteenth centuries. Its thousands of entries form three large mosaics: one of Puritanism, one of New England, and one of Sewall himself.

Puritanism determined the subject matter and tone of these entries. Like other Puritans, Sewall kept a diary as a running analysis of his spiritual state, a means of confession, a form of prayer, and a record of God's treatment of him. His diary-confessions were sometimes copies of notes or bills he had asked to be read or posted in church (for example, his recantation of his part in the Salem trials). His diary-prayers fall into two types: those composed before being entered into the diary and, a more important type, those that were part of the very act of diary writing. Some are as short as "Help Lord" (7:146)[5] while others are long and complex, even involving puns and alliteration.

Sewall's picture of New England has the breadth to be expected of a judge who not only lived in the best Boston society but also rode a circuit that included such places as Plymouth, Ipswich, and Springfield. Though himself godly, he saw much of the ungodly, so that sin and crime are as likely to be noticed in his diary as a good sermon: A mother beats her son, then chokes to death; a Maypole is erected; drunkards abuse their neighbors; first cousins marry; a woman murders her illegitimate child, and Sewall sentences her; rioters profane the Sabbath—the record goes on and on.

From these pages we also get a clear picture of Sewall himself—a pious and humane man with strong likes and dislikes. He had a talent for allegorizing and could extract spiritual truths from almost any event. The diary

4. Since under the Old Style calendar the year began on March 25 and under the New Style on January 1, the period from January 1 through March 24 was assigned both years by Sewall, who was living in an era of calendar reform. However, Sewall still numbered his months according to the Old Style. March was therefore the first month, February the twelfth month. An entry dated 11. 23, 1678/9 would then be January 23, 1679 according to the modern calendar. Sewall also sometimes assigned numbers to the days of the week, Sunday being the first day, Saturday the seventh day, and so on.

5. *Diary of Samuel Sewall,* vols. 5–7, 5th ser. of the Coll. Mass. Hist. Soc. (Boston: Massachusetts Historical Society, 1878–1882).

shows him working on behalf of Indians and Negroes; he also wrote a pioneering antislavery tract, *The Selling of Joseph* (1700). We see too that he relished the pleasures of the senses, especially music and food. Just as interesting were the things that irritated him; for example, the celebration of festivals like Christmas, April Fools' Day, and St. George's Day. He disliked periwigs, and his refusal to wear them helped ruin his courtship of Madam Winthrop.

While the diary understandably lacks polish and proportion, it does have some artistic merit. Sewall obviously prided himself on saying things in an artful way. He often noted his bons mots, as when he recalled trying to remove Madam Winthrop's glove by noting the great difference "between handling a dead Goat, and a living Lady" (7:267). Even material written directly in the diary (some prayers, for example) displays such embellishments as alliteration and metaphor.

PURITAN POETS

The poetry of the Puritans, partly because of the considerable variety of its audience, ranged from the complex to the simple. Edward Taylor, writing only for the eyes of his God, could afford to indulge in a complicated syntax and private diction that would have puzzled his contemporaries almost as much as it does us. *The New-England Primer* (ca. 1683), on the other hand, was a highly popular text designed for Puritan children, and its verses were pious but simple. Its alphabet-rhymes have the easy intelligibility of proverbs:

In *Adam's* Fall	A *Dog* will bite
We Sinned all.	A Thief at night.
Thy Life to Mend,	An *Eagles* flight
This *Book* Attend.	Is out of sight.
The *Cat* doth play,	The Idle *Fool*
And after slay.	Is whipt at School.[6]

Between these extremes was not only the work of Anne Bradstreet and Michael Wigglesworth but also the *Bay Psalm Book* (1640), the attempt of a group under Richard Mather, Thomas Welde, and John Eliot to translate the Psalms into hymns. Even with its infamous rendition of the Twenty-third Psalm—"The Lord to mee a shepheard is, want therefore shall not I"—this

6. *The New-England Primer Enlarged* (Boston: Kneeland and Green, 1727, p. [8]). A reprint of this earliest known edition is *The New-England Primer,* ed. with a fifty-three-page introduction by Paul Leicester Ford, Classics in Education, No. 13 (New York: Teachers College, Columbia University, 1962).

book was no worse than similar attempts and was actually more artful than its critics have been willing to admit.[7]

Anne Bradstreet (1612–1672). Long considered America's leading colonial poet, Anne Bradstreet lost this distinction to Edward Taylor after his poetry was discovered by the twentieth century. Her craftsmanship was nonetheless genuine, and she had a gift for humor and a definite charm missing in Taylor and other Puritan poets. She is, moreover, the first important female poet in American literature.

LIFE AND POETIC DEVELOPMENT. Anne Bradstreet's early years were spent in her native England where, as the daughter of Thomas Dudley, the Earl of Lincoln's steward, she was well educated. In 1628 she married Simon Bradstreet, a graduate of Cambridge, who had succeeded Dudley as steward. In 1630 her family immigrated with John Winthrop's party to Massachusetts Bay. For the rest of their lives—spent successively in Salem, Boston, Cambridge, Ipswich, and Andover—the Dudleys and the Bradstreets were prominent New Englanders. Both Thomas and Simon became governors of the Massachusetts Colony. Anne, despite almost continual ill health, the demands of a growing family (she bore eight children), and the rigors of a colonial environment, managed to write poetry that gave her a transatlantic reputation. Her verse was first published in England; without her consent, it was given the title *The Tenth Muse Lately Sprung up in America* (1650). Embarrassed by the amateurishness of these poems and the extravagance of their billing, she began to cleanse her style of euphuisms and to abandon such encyclopedic topics as "The Four Ages of Man." Instead she wrote simply of things in her own daily life: her spiritual temptations, her illnesses and her recoveries, her musings on walks along the Merrimack, her devotion to her husband and her children. Unfortunately she did not live to see the fruition of her efforts, the publication of a revised, enlarged edition of her work, this time with a somewhat less pretentious title: *Several Poems Compiled with Great Variety of Wit and Learning* (1678).

Representative Poems

"Contemplations" (1678). Often considered her most mature work, despite some awkward lines, this long meditative lyric contrasts nature and God, antediluvian man and modern man, man and nature. (One of the earliest American landscape poems, it anticipates Emily Dickinson in depicting such humble creatures as the grasshopper and the cricket.) Philosophical messages, proclaiming that God is glorious and that man is immortal, appear in stanzas 2, 7, 20, and 33 as logical conclusions to various sections of the poem. Among the traditional stylistic ingredients of "Contemplations" are apostrophes (addresses to the oak, sun, and so on) and

7. *The Whole Booke of Psalmes* ([Cambridge, Mass.: Stephen Daye] 1640), p. [34].

poetic diction (the nightingale is called "sweet-tongu'd Philomel").[8] Perhaps influenced by Edmund Spenser or his follower Giles Fletcher, Bradstreet ends her stanzas with alexandrines.

"The Flesh and the Spirit" (1678). A poetic debate between twin sisters. After refuting Flesh point by point, Spirit presents a vision of the Heavenly City (ll. 85–106). Both the debate and the vision were medieval survivals in seventeenth-century literature.

"To My Dear and Loving Husband" (1678). A twelve-line lyric analyzing Bradstreet's love for her husband and recalling the spiritual purpose of their marriage. The poem develops with no poetic diction, few figures of speech, and only slight alliteration; yet it displays a quiet art. The opening and closing lines, with their paradoxes and iterations, are nearly identical. But within this framework the sentences progress in gentle movements from plural to singular pronouns and back again. As the reader begins to feel these progressions, he also senses the contrasts they involve, so that he stresses such words as "My" in line 7 and "Thy" in line 9. This rhetorical stress alters the metrical regularity. Instead of a strictly iambic pattern in line 7, for example, we now have a welcome variation: ◡ ◡ ◡ ◡ ◡ ◡ ◡ ◡ ◡ ◡.

"The Author to Her Book" (1678). Clever, humorous, and modest twenty-four line commentary on her verse; an extended personification in iambic pentameter couplets. Perhaps imitating a metaphor in Sidney's sonnet "Loving in Truth," Bradstreet addressed her poems as "Thou ill-form'd offspring of my feeble brain." Her attempts to revise them, especially in meter, she regarded as futile: "I stretch thy joints to make thee even feet, / Yet still thou run'st more hobling then is meet."

Michael Wigglesworth (1631–1705). A versifier of decidedly less merit than Anne Bradstreet, Michael Wigglesworth wrote New England Puritanism's most notorious poem, *The Day of Doom.*

Wigglesworth was born in Yorkshire, England. In 1638 his Puritan family moved to New England, settling in New Haven. Michael graduated from Harvard in 1651 and stayed on for three more years as a teaching fellow. After a period of guest preaching, he accepted charge of the congregation at Malden, Massachusetts, where he was ordained, probably in the spring of 1657. However, when a chronic throat ailment kept him out of the pulpit, he took up the pen. The tremendous sales of his versified sermons must have been welcome to Wigglesworth, for during this time he apparently received little or nothing from his congregation and had taken up the study and practice of medicine to make a modest living. During the last twenty years of his life, however, his health improved; and he became a truly active minister, gaining the esteem and support of his church.

Wigglesworth's poem on the Last Judgment, *The Day of Doom* (1662),

---

8. Line 178. Quotations are from *Several Poems Compiled with Great Variety of Wit and Learning* (Boston: John Foster, 1678).

was a colonial best seller. Its first edition, running to some 1,800 copies (one copy for every thirty-five people in New England), was sold out within a year. By 1778 the poem had gone through at least ten American and two English editions. It was also printed as a broadside ballad and hawked on the streets. Perhaps only the Bible surpassed it in popularity with the colonists.

Orthodox Calvinism appears throughout *The Day of Doom* but most of all in the many lines devoted to predestination. Christ justifies this doctrine in stanza 43 and reverts to it later when answering the sinners whom he has ordered to speak in their own behalf (see especially stanza 147). Even infants are consigned to hell, although it is "the easi[e]st room" there.[9]

The poem's faults outweigh its merits. Its stanzaic pattern, essentially that of a ballad, ill suits the many argumentative passages. Nor do the quickly recurring rhymes and the monotonous meter convey the dignity required by the subject. On the other hand, Wigglesworth displayed better-than-average imaginative powers in this work; and while his imagery and figures of speech were borrowed wholesale from the Bible, he did think his scenes through to some ultimate ironies as in stanzas 4 and 50. Finally, such artistic devices as parallelism (stanzas 202–203, 209–210) and chiasmus (stanza 210) are not lacking in Wigglesworth's avowedly plain style.

The Day of Doom is however a significant poem. First, it demonstrates the polemical use to which the Puritans could put their verses. Second, it is a seventeenth-century representative of a long artistic tradition devoted to doomsday; as such, it is related to the medieval hymn "Dies Irae," to many paintings of the Last Judgment, and even to London Bridge and similar games in which there is a final separation of saints and sinners.[10] Third, it is an embryo of gothic literature, whose native beginnings are usually attributed to such late-eighteenth-century writers as Philip Freneau and Charles Brockden Brown.

Edward Taylor (ca. 1642–1729). When Anne Bradstreet and Michael Wigglesworth had already gained contemporary fame, Edward Taylor was quietly, secretly writing poems that would ultimately earn him a reputation far greater than theirs.

LIFE. Taylor was the son of a moderately prosperous but uneducated farmer. The early years in his native England were untroubled; he was a Puritan living during the Protectorate. After 1660, however, with the restoration of monarchy and Anglicanism, he "conscientiously scrupl'd," as his obituary puts it, to "take the Oaths [of conformity] then requir'd,"[11] and in 1668 he immigrated to New England. He spent the next three years at Harvard, rooming with Samuel Sewall, who became his lifelong friend. Shortly

9. *The Day of Doom,* 5th ed. (Boston: Benjamin Eliot, 1701), stanza 181.

10. See William Wells Newell, *Games and Songs of American Children* (New York: Dover, 1963), pp. 204–215.

11. *Weekly News-Letter* (Boston, Aug. 7, 1729).

after his graduation, Taylor became minister to the Congregational Church of Westfield, Massachusetts, a frontier outpost of some thirty families. "He was eminently holy in Life, and very painful and laborious in his Work," continues his obituary, obviously written by a Westfield citizen. Fifty-four years Taylor gave to his job, relinquishing it in 1725 only when he was almost completely incapacitated. A true man of parts, he also worked as a physician and farmer. He was twice married and had fourteen children, of whom only six survived him.

DISCOVERY AND REPUTATION. Although Taylor's literary fame was slow in coming, he is now regarded as a major American poet. Except for two stanzas printed in 1689, his work remained in manuscript until tracked down and edited by Thomas Johnson in the 1930s. Subsequently it was printed in various anthologies, but it was not until 1960 that *The Poems of Edward Taylor,*[12] edited by Donald Stanford, made the bulk of Taylor's verse available.

Characteristics of Taylor's Poetry

1. Craftsmanship and careful revision.

2. Subject matter limited to the relationship between God and man.

3. Sensuous imagery prompted by a religious desire to see, hear, smell, taste, and feel doctrine. Memorable examples of olfactory imagery occur in Meditations Three (First Series) and Sixty-Three (Second Series), tactile imagery in "Upon a Wasp Chilled with Cold," and visual imagery in "The Preface" of *God's Determinations.*

4. Homely comparisons. Sin is a spider's bite that so swells man up he can't get through Heaven's gates; Taylor's soul is a thicket in need of clearing; angels are waiters; God is the master craftsman.

5. Unconfined diction. Because he had no audience but himself and God, Taylor could use his whole vocabulary. No word was too technical, too local, or (considering his coinages) too personal. In words like "glore," "fet," "Sprindge," "tweedle," and "bibble" (pp. 1, 388, 15, 18, 13) we see a foreshadowing of the modern idea that all language may be the stuff of poetry.

6. Puns. Two favorites are the sun and the rose of Sharon, both doubling as the rising or risen Christ.

7. Reiteration. Sometimes a word is repeated with only a change in syntactic function, e.g., "As Justice justice evermore must doe: / So Mercy Mercy evermore must show" (p. 391). At other times only the root of the word is repeated, e.g., "lovely Love" (p. 400) or "bright brightness" (p. 26).

8. Compression. Elisions and contractions abound, often requiring a good imagination and nimble tongue: "yets" (yet his), "t'catch" (to

---

12. *The Poems of Edward Taylor,* ed. Donald Stanford (New Haven: Yale University Press, 1960). All quotations are from this edition.

catch), "He'th" (He hath) (pp. 394, 40, 394). Taylor sometimes eliminated conjunctions and prepositions and frequently jammed words together in heavy spondaic lines.

These and other characteristics place Taylor among the English metaphysical poets as their last significant member. They too coupled the abstract with the earthy, concocted word play, and habitually roughened up their lines. Taylor, however, went even further in the exploitation of non-poetic language.

REPRESENTATIVE POEMS. With the exception of "Huswifery," each poem analyzed here comes from one of two groups: (1) *Preparatory Meditations,* also called *Sacramental Meditations,* 217 lyrics composed at approximately six-week intervals from 1682 to 1725 on the doctrine of the sermons preached on sacrament days; these comprise Taylor's best work; (2) *God's Determinations* (written ca. 1685), a combination morality play and verse-sermon embodying thirty-five separate poems in various verse forms.

God's Determinations (undated). "The Preface," the first of these poems, depicts God as creator and potential destroyer and man as the fa-vored creature who lost all through sin. In a subsequent poem of *God's De-terminations,* God's Mercy and Justice decide the fate of fallen man. The rest of the poems show how these determinations are carried out to the ulti-mate salvation of the elect. "The Preface" has a strong chantlike tone, achieved largely through parallel questions and reiteration, especially of the words "nothing" and "all." Note the chiasmic complexity of line 28: "Root up the rocks and rock the hills by th' roots." This poem is characteristic of Taylor's work in its use of paradox and homely, anthropomorphic meta-phors.

"Meditation Six" (First Series) (undated). After questioning whether he is of real worth to the Lord, Taylor hopes that God will designate him as one of the elect. A basic coin metaphor is used to develop these ideas. The "Plate" of line 13 and the "Angell" of line 18 are both words for coin, the latter also becoming a pun on the idea of an angel as a heavenly being and, in one of its seventeenth-century meanings, as the pastor of a church.

"Meditation Eight" (First Series) (dated June 8, 1684). A lyric celebrating the Eucharist as true nourishment for the soul ("this Bird of Paradise," l. 7). The difficult first sentence is clarified if one considers "Divine" a verb rather than an adjective. Thus the poet, preparing to partake of the Lord's Supper (l. 6), discovers the mysterious means (l. 3) by which God communi-cates with man. He reflects that through Original Sin (l. 9) man lost the heavenly nourishment that the world can never provide (l. 17), but in sub-sequent stanzas he consoles himself by meditating on man's new spiritual food—God's own Son served to man in the eucharistic feast. The final cou-plet—"This Bread of Life dropt in thy mouth, doth Cry, / Eate, Eate me, Soul, and thou shalt never dy"—recalls not only the scriptural saying head-ing the poem ("I am the Living Bread") but also the many utopias, variously known as Schlaraffenland, Lubberland, and Cockayne, where roasted animals beg to be eaten. Note the spondee-filled line (34), with the compound-epithet "whelm'd-down," and the unusual ending that has neither request nor bribe.

"The Experience" (undated). One of the unnumbered *Preparatory Meditations*. Essentially, this lyric celebrates an occasion on which Taylor, partaking of the Lord's Supper, felt united to God. He asks (l. 30) to possess forever the experience he once possessed momentarily. The idea that on occasions like these man can unite to God better than angels can (see stanza 4) provides welcome relief from the traditional Puritan emphasis on depravity.

"Huswifery" (undated). Taylor's best-known work. Although it is one of his miscellaneous poems, "Huswifery" resembles Taylor's preparatory meditations in subject matter and rhyme scheme. Here the poet, asking to be "Cloathd in Holy robes for glory," is in fact requesting that he may be prepared to receive the Eucharist. This represents a reply to the Reverend Solomon Stoddard, who advocated administering the Sacrament even to so-called unconverted persons (i.e., church members who had accepted the articles of faith but were as yet unable to make a public "relation" that they had experienced saving grace). In Taylor's orthodox Puritan view, no one should be admitted to the Lord's Supper without a visible sign that God himself had prepared him for this sacrament. The singleness of the spinning-wheel conceit developed in "Huswifery" is welcome to readers perplexed by the multiple and sometimes unrelated conceits of other Taylor poems.

NON-PURITANS

The Puritan Commonwealth, composed of people who not only considered themselves elected to salvation but also claimed to have the divine stamp of approval on their doctrines and government, was not prone to tolerate dissent. But, of course, this theocracy was threatened time and again; the most vigorous attacks came from the religious protest of Roger Williams and the satire of Thomas Morton.

Roger Williams (ca. 1603–1683). In some ways Williams represented a threat from within, for he began his career in New England as an unbending Separatist.

LIFE. Williams's early life had been filled with distinct advantages. As a young man he found a patron in the famous English jurist, Sir Edward Coke. Williams was graduated from Cambridge in 1627 and stayed on for eighteen months to study divinity. Then for a short time he was the chaplain in the household of a Puritan country gentleman. In 1630, now married, Williams sailed to Massachusetts. There he served as minister or teacher (a minister not officially ordained) in the Massachusetts Bay Colony and in Plymouth. In each place he alarmed the magistrates by falling, as Governor William

Bradford noted, "into some strang[e] opinions."[13] In 1635 Williams was sentenced to banishment by the General Court of Massachusetts Bay. After fleeing to the wilderness, where he spent the winter among Indians, he founded Providence in 1636 with a small band of followers. This settlement was unlike its Puritan neighbors. Not only had its land been purchased from the Indians rather than the king, but it was open to settlers of all beliefs, promising tolerance and separation of church and state. In 1644 Williams succeeded in getting a parliamentary charter for this first Rhode Island colony. To procure the charter and later to renew it (1689), Williams traveled to England twice (1643–1644, 1651–1654). During his later life he was president of the Rhode Island colony (1654–1657) and engaged in debate with the Quakers (his arguments were published in 1676 as *George Fox Digg'd out of His Burrowes*).

PHILOSOPHY. Williams was inescapably a man of his time, and even his radical ideas developed from his orthodox Calvinistic beliefs.

1. He preached that the New England churches should announce their secession from the Church of England. At the time he advocated this Separatist doctrine it was especially repugnant to the New England Puritans, who were trying to prove themselves free of sedition in the eyes of the mother country.

2. He declared himself a Seeker, meaning that although God had shown him the corruption of some churches, He had not yet revealed to him the true Church.

3. He advocated freedom of worship, basing it particularly on the doctrine of election rather than on any idea of equality. When God denies his saving grace to some and grants it to others, he himself creates inequality and no one must tamper with his plan. Man must be left free—if a pagan, to live in the natural state that God has decreed for him and if a Christian, to seek the true Church.

4. He conceived of the church solely as a religious body and denied it the physical means of enforcing orthodoxy. Central to this idea was his insistence that the Old Testament, with its accounts of wars on disbelievers, cannot be a model for the church established by the New Testament. The older book is rather an allegory of the new church, which should translate the physical force of David and Solomon into spiritual weapons. Thus Williams modified the typological reading of the Bible practiced by his contemporaries.

5. He conceived of the state as a nonspiritual body separate from the church and therefore denied it the right to meddle in spiritual matters or to punish religious offenses. Specifically he argued against its enforcement of the first table of the Decalogue, i.e., those commandments that concern

13. *History of Plymouth Plantation* (Boston: Massachusetts Historical Society, 1912), 2:162.

man's relationship with God. Witchcraft, swearing, and Sabbath breaking were sins that Puritan magistrates punished with great severity, and to deny that they had the right to do so was equivalent to striking at the very root of their commonwealth.

6. His concept of the source and purpose of civil government was essentially democratic; he considered the state a functional agent predestined by God but originating in, empowered by, and administering to the people. As such, it was severely limited; for while "a People may erect and establish what *forme* of *Government* seemes to them most meete for their *civill condition* . . . such *Governments* as are by them erected and established, have no more *power,* nor for no longer time, then the *civill power* or people consenting and agreeing shall betrust them with" (3:249–250).[14]

7. Perhaps his most radical belief was that the Indians were the true owners of American lands; that the king of England had no right to these lands; that the Massachusetts Bay patent, coming from the king, was therefore invalid; and that the colonists should deal directly with the Indians.

Representative Works

A Key into the Language of America (1643). An authentic and readable phrase book of the Narragansett Indian tongue. The translations are enlivened by frequent comments on native culture and by several poems of quiet dignity but unassuming form—e.g., *"Boast not proud English, of thy birth & blood, / Thy brother* Indian *is by birth as Good"* (1:81).

The Bloudy Tenent of Persecution (1644). One of the weapons in a ten-year controversy between John Cotton and Williams, it argues for freedom of worship and against *"Persecution* for cause of *Conscience"* (3:425). Presented as a sustained dialogue between the personifications Truth and Peace, the 247 pages of argumentation are disorderly, prolix, and tedious. Nevertheless, they contain such quotable aphorisms as "Having bought Truth deare, we must not sell it cheape" (3:13). Considered seditious, *The Bloudy Tenent* was ordered by the House of Commons to be publicly burned.

The Bloody Tenent Yet More Bloody (1652). A later document in the Cotton-Williams controversy, it too argues against persecution and has the form of a dialogue between Peace and Truth.

"A Letter to the Town of Providence" (dated January 1654/55). Argues that, while enjoying freedom of worship, man is not completely free in civil matters. The state may require him, for example, to obey laws promoting "common peace or preservation" and to contribute "in person or purse" to the country's defense (6:279). In addition, the state may lawfully punish sedition and insurrection. As in *The Bloudy Tenent,* Williams uses a ship-of-

14. Quotations are from *The Writings of Roger Williams* (Providence: Narragansett Club, 1866–1874).

state metaphor to develop his idea, but the style here is plain and terse in contrast with that of the earlier writings.

STYLE. Roger Williams's style was an inadequate vehicle for his noble thought. His sentences were usually wordy and awkward, even ungrammatical. On the other hand, his style had moments of dignity; such works as the "Letter to the Town of Providence" demonstrate that he could be simple and forceful. Then, too, whether it was his intention or not, he helped create a public image of himself through his writing, so that at least in some of his works we perceive not only the ideas but also the man who conveys them and the setting in which he does so.

Thomas Morton (ca. 1579–1647). Thomas Morton belongs in several literary traditions. He qualifies above all as one of the earliest American humorists, and in his quixotic satirical method he anticipates Brackenridge and Irving. As a spinner of tall tales, he should be associated with John Smith and the travel writers. He also belongs with the English Cavalier authors, not just because he was a swashbuckling monarchist who fought Puritans but also because he was lighthearted and witty and fond of clever allusions to Latin classics.

LIFE. From what little we know of him, Morton was a gentleman of some education who had followed the law, for he signed himself as "of Cliffords Inne gent" (p. 107).[15] In 1624 he came to New England as a member of the party that founded Mount Wollaston (renamed Ma-re-Mount, or Merry Mount, by Morton, and later forming part of Quincy, Massachusetts). When Captain Wollaston left the settlement, Morton took over and soon angered Plymouth neighbors by trading with the Indians and serving as "lord of misrule" at decidedly non-Puritan revels. According to William Bradford, the Merrymounters "set up a May-pole," took Indian women "for their consorts," and began "dancing and frisking" with them as if to revive "the feasts of the Roman Goddes Flora, or the beasly practieses of the madd Bacchinalians."[16] The Maypole was torn down, and in 1628 Morton was deported to London, charged with trafficking in firearms and keeping a house for disreputable people. In 1629 he returned to New England. This time he was set in the stocks and in 1630 was again deported. The next dozen years he seems to have spent in London, promoting schemes to establish Cavalier settlements in New England. During this period he wrote *The New English Canaan* (1637), the main reason for his being remembered today. This book, composed several years before its publication, forcefully supported monarchy and Anglicanism, but it was no sooner published than monarchy and Anglicanism started to topple and Morton's fortunes with them. In 1643, after the Civil War began, Morton returned to New England,

15. Quotations are from *The New English Canaan,* ed. Charles Francis Adams, Jr. (Boston: Prince Society, 1883).

16. *History of Plymouth Plantation* (Boston: Massachusetts Historical Society, 1912), 2:48–49.

obviously a broken man. He was again arrested but released after about a year in the Boston jail. Within two years (ca. 1647) he died.

The New English Canaan (1637). Morton's *New English Canaan* is divided into three books. The first serves to arouse interest by discussing America's chief curiosity, the Indians. Morton fancies their descent from the Trojans, tells tall tales about their physical powers, and remarks on their mythology and magic. Above all, he makes his book a prime example of primitivism by contrasting the Indians with the Christians, in particular with the New England Puritans. He had been criticized for consorting with Indians; he replied that the Indians had more humanity than his accusers. Finally, we are told the Indian has few wants and "being voyde of care, which torments the mindes of so many Christians," he "leades the more happy and freer life" (p. 177).

The second book was obviously intended as a promotional tract to entice non-Puritans to the region. Its thesis is that New England equals and in some cases surpasses the Promised Land of the Jews. This new land far exceeds Canaan in the "plenty of [its] birds, beasts and Fish" (p. 230), for example. At times fish are so thick in the water that it is possible to "goe over their backs drishod" (p. 222). One tall tale or curious bit of lore soon leads Morton into another: The beaver keeps his tail in the water so it won't "over heate and rot off" (p. 204); rattlesnake bite is cured by drinking a "saucer of Salet oyle" (p. 213); "No man living . . . [in New England] was ever knowne to be troubled with a cold, a cough, or a murre; but many men, coming sick out of Virginea to New Canaan have instantly recovered with the helpe of the purity of that aire" (pp. 231–232). Morton even pictured a utopia within a utopia, a "Lake of Erocoise" (Iroquois, i.e., Lake Champlain) that, lying to the westward (as utopias generally do), is replete with naiads and fabulous beasts. Throughout the book there is a great amount of folklore and New World boasting; also apparent is a kind of early regionalism, as Morton praises New England at the expense of Virginia.

The third book of *The New English Canaan* is the best known; for it deals with Morton's Maypole at Merry Mount, a topic that inspired a short story by Hawthorne and a novel by John Lothrop Motley (1814–1877). It is also the most irreverent, obscure, and humorous of the three books. From beginning to end Morton attacks the Puritans who had deported him, and on the final pages, confident that the Massachusetts Bay patent is about to be voided, he assumes the "posture" of Jonah, warns them that their luck has run out, and jeers at them in their own biblical language: "Repent you cruell Schismaticks, repent" (p. 344). Morton makes many charges against these Puritans, from being dense and illiterate to praying overly long; but most of all he accuses them of inhumanity—not only toward himself but toward all outsiders, especially including the Indians. He uses a variety of weapons, the best of which are humorous. There are comic names: Miles Standish is "Captain Shrimpe"; Governor John Winthrop is "Josua Temperwell";

Morton himself is "mine Host." And there are comic similes, notably those that link the Puritans with such animals as geese, colts, and rams. Finally, there is a quixotic strain, reminding us that scarcely a generation separated the first publication of *Don Quixote* (1605) and *The New English Canaan* (1637). Not only is Don Quixote mentioned several times, but a mock-heroic tone permeates the entire Maypole episode.

3
Later Puritans

The principals of this chapter, Cotton Mather and Jonathan Edwards, were unlike in many ways, but both devoted their lives to the same task—saving Puritanism from decay. Mather, a third-generation Puritan, worked in the late seventeenth and early eighteenth centuries, when Puritanism was just beginning to lose its bloom. Edwards, forty years younger, wrote in the mid-eighteenth century, when Puritanism had noticeably withered.

DECLINE OF PURITANISM

This decay had both external and internal causes. New England Puritans never represented more than a small fraction of the early American colonists, and this fraction became even smaller in the wake of increased wealth. Many later Puritans found it difficult to work in the world yet remain unworldly, to keep their piety apace with their prosperity, to attribute this prosperity to Providence instead of their own abilities, and to live in luxurious homes but worship in plain meetinghouses. Those who did not actually leave the church often remained "halfway" members, without giving evidence of their election or conversion. Others, not born to Puritanism, never joined because they saw only its worst side, those aspects made notorious by the Salem witchcraft trials, writings like Wigglesworth's *Day of Doom,* and hellfire sermons, such as those of Edwards. Dissatisfaction with monarchial government increased; the idea of God as Absolute Sovereign—the crux of Calvinism—also proved unattractive. Finally, Puritanism declined because of such opposing philosophies as the Antinomianism of Anne Hutchinson, which postulated private, immediate revelation from the Holy Spirit, and Arminianism, which attacked the Calvinist doctrines of unconditional election and irresistible grace.

23

COTTON MATHER (1663–1728)

Cotton Mather failed to save Puritanism but did extend the fame of the Mather dynasty, which included such illustrious New England divines as his grandfathers, John Cotton and Richard Mather, and his father, Increase Mather.

Life. Cotton Mather was only eleven when he entered Harvard, where before he was twenty he had taken a bachelor's degree (1678) and a master's (1681). Ordained in 1685, he spent the rest of his life as minister to Boston's Second (Old North) Church, sharing this post with his father until the latter's death in 1723. We learn from Cotton Mather's diaries that he kept hundreds of fasts and vigils; yet for all this private asceticism, his ministry was a public one, and he devoted enormous energy to maintaining his family's accustomed control over the affairs of men. He helped lead the Massachusetts colony in rebellion against its governor, Sir Edmund Andros. Later, under the governorship of Sir William Phips, Mather wielded considerable political influence. In education the Mathers lost control when Increase was forced out of the presidency of Harvard and Cotton relinquished his fellowship there, but Cotton then helped the cause of orthodoxy by transferring his support to the newly founded Connecticut College (Yale). Mather was deeply interested in science. The Royal Society, to which he sent over fifty letters on scientific matters, elected him to membership in 1713. Equally significant was his spirited advocacy of inoculation, even though public and professional opinion was against its use. His recommendations, including those in his *Account . . . of Inoculating the Small-Pox* (1722), helped save the town; but Mather himself was nearly killed by a grenade that some malcontent threw into his house with this scribbled curse: " *'Cotton Mather, you Dog; Dam you: I'l enoculate you with this, with a pox to you.'* "[1] As he got older and his popularity seemed to wane, Mather was also beset with family tragedies. His first wife died, then his second; his third went insane. Thirteen of his fifteen children predeceased him, and his son Increase disgraced him by leading a dissolute life.

Representative Works

Wonders of the Invisible World (1693). A treatise (combining argument and narrative) on Salem witchcraft that was written to inform readers in England, assail the devil in Massachusetts, and befriend if not vindicate the judges at the Salem trials. Its argument was basically millenarian. The devil, knowing that he had but a short time before the millennium, was redoubling his efforts. He had long regarded America as his own territory, and when

1. Quoted in Barrett Wendell, *Cotton Mather: The Puritan Priest* (New York: Dodd Mead [1891]), p. 280.

the Puritans began to intrude upon his reign, he directed his wrath against them in the form of Indian raids, war with France, religious dissensions and, of course, witchcraft. Mather, a true man of his times, never doubted the existence of devils and witches; but he did question the condemnation of witches on the sole basis of spectral evidence (testimony by the afflicted that they were victimized by the specter or shape of the accused). Like his father, he contended that devils could wreak their mischief in the shapes of innocent people. Cotton seemed to think that the Salem trials had been just, but he recommended other means of combatting witchcraft, such as prayer, visiting by ministers, and greater pity for the afflicted. After making these suggestions Mather presented his major narratives. Summarizing and quoting from court records, he carefully reconstructed the testimony against five of the twenty persons executed in the Salem purge. The accusations against them were drawn from stock beliefs, the traditional nature of which can be authenticated through Stith Thompson's *Motif Index of Folk-Literature*. According to the accusers, puny George Burroughs could lift heavy objects with the ease of a giant (see motif G221.3 in Thompson's index); Bridget Bishop had a disappearing supernumerary nipple; Susanna Martin could travel in a storm without getting wet (motif D1840); Martha Carrier disenchanted her victims by touching them (D782); and Elizabeth How worked her charms with magic apples (D981.1). They were also supposedly overlookers and shapeshifters: i.e., they could torment others with the evil eye and change themselves into such things as a moving light, a black cloud, and various animals (G211). Their accusers complained of bewitched cattle (G265.6.2); of horses with bridle marks burned in their hides (G265.3); of objects flying through the room; of themselves or their children being thrown about or sat upon, or pinched, bitten, and choked (G263) by tormentors who were sometimes invisible; and even of deaths caused by the accused (G262), the ghosts of the victims occasionally making an appearance to reveal their murderers (E231).

Magnalia Christi Americana: or, The Ecclesiastical History of New-England, from Its First Planting in the Year 1620 . . . unto the Year . . . 1698 (1702). Mather's magnum opus and in some ways the culmination of his earlier writings, many of which it reprints with slight changes. It embodies several genres: prose-epic, history (based on oral as well as written materials), jeremiad (Mather denounces his contemporaries for straying from the ideals of primitive Christianity), biography and hagiography (he almost always narrated history in terms of idealized saints' lives), prose character (like the creations of John Earle and other seventeenth-century character writers, Mather's saints are in many ways static types rather than individuals). A huge work—larger than the *Iliad,* the *Odyssey,* or *Paradise Lost*—it comprises more than 1,200 pages and is divided into seven books. Although the *Magnalia* is seldom today read in its entirety, certain parts still hold considerable interest. The "General Introduction" sounds more like an epic than do other sections, perhaps because it was written expressly for the *Magnalia* rather than adapted from Mather's earlier works. Besides the echoes of Virgil's *Aeneid,* there are such general epic characteristics as the formal statement of theme and purpose, frequent expressions of patriotism, long catalogs, worldwide perspective, and the invocation of the muse (here changed to a dedication to Jesus). Of the biographies in the *Magnalia,* those of William Bradford, John Eliot, and William Phips are still read not only as informative historical documents but also as examples of Mather's hagiographic formula. The four-page chapter on his first New England saint, Plymouth's Governor Bradford, contains several typical ingredients: the opening foreign quotation, biblical figures to whom the saint might be favorably compared (Bradford is the Moses of his people), the saint's scholarly achievements (Bradford's mastery of languages and theology), the saint's dying words, and the concluding epitaph. Also typifying Mather's biographical technique is the forty-one-page section on John Eliot, with its idealized picture of family life, stress on the subject's preaching ability, and frequent use of supporting documents (in this case, letters from Increase Mather and Richard Baxter). The longest and liveliest biography is the life of Sir William Phips. It tells of sunken pirate vessels, of pieces of eight recovered by the bushel, of mutinies, wars, cannibalisms, and witchcrafts. But this adventurous material never dominates, for throughout the *Magnalia* Mather's intent is didactic. In fact, he defines biography as the art of reviving "our Departed *Friends* . . . [in order to] bring to a fresh View, what was *Memorable* and *Imitable* in them" (Bk. 2, p. 37).[2]

Bonifacius (1710). Often known as *Essays to Do Good.* The first third of this book establishes the philosophical basis for doing good; the rest offers practical advice to various groups, such as doctors, tutors, rich men, and magistrates. Benjamin Franklin was influenced by the *Essays to Do Good* and called some of his own essays the "Dogood Papers."

Manuductio ad Ministerium: Directions for a Candidate of the Ministry (1726). A handbook for prospective ministers. Writing directly and plainly, Mather gives advice on a wide range of topics, from how to prepare a sermon to how to cure a cold. In its de-emphasis of logic, rhetoric, and harsh Calvinistic doctrines, this book represents an unofficial modernization of Puritanism. But in its preference for vocal over instrumental music, its insistence on an educated clergy, and its spirited defense of Mather's own anachronistic style, it looked back to earlier values. The *Manuductio* is noteworthy for its qualified approval of poetry. Although unable to condone the debasement of the gods and the supremacy of fate in Homer and Virgil, Mather grudgingly recommended their works as models of the epic form; and he even advised candidates to write verse of their own occasionally in

2. Quotations throughout are from the first edition of *Magnalia Christi Americana* (London: Thomas Parkhurst, 1702).

order to improve their style "for more important Performances." "Let not what should be *Sauce* rather than *Food* for you, Engross all your Application," he counseled.[3]

Style. Desiring above all the *"Easy Conveyance"* (*Manuductio,* p. 46) of ideas, Mather thought that style should always fit the audience and praised John Eliot's plain sermons to the Indians. But otherwise he thought that everyone should be free to develop his own style, as peculiar to himself as his way of walking.

Mather's own style was both ornate and plain, or rather, ornate and less ornate, for it seldom reached the simplicity of Woolman or Edwards. He seems to have controlled two styles at once. In the *Magnalia,* for example, the "General Introduction" is one of the most ornate things he ever wrote; the life of Bradford that follows close upon it is one of the simplest.

Certain defects and merits appear in both styles. Perhaps the modern reader will be most irritated with the abundance of italics and capitals in Mather's prose, or with the many quotations, often in foreign languages. Flashy wordplay and pedantic vocabulary add to the impression that Mather is showing off his learning and wit. Even for today's reader, however, Mather's style is sometimes impressive. Its very pedantry serves to steer it clear of provincialism and to give a universal meaning to New England and its religion. There is, too, something arresting in his style. "We have in our Hands a Letter from our Ascended Lord in Heaven," he once announced (*Wonders,* 1:50). Few writers could open a paragraph with anything better than that. Mather also handled metaphors with ease (see, for example, the fire conceit at the beginning of his life of Bradford).

His ornateness is based largely on repetitions of syntax and sound in a variety of units, large and small.

1. Paragraphs: See the first five paragraphs of the *Magnalia*'s "General Introduction." Each begins with the word "I" and has the same subject-predicate-object construction.

2. Phrases: Mather creates refrains by repeating phrases like the "voice of the glorious God in the thunder," which rumbles through chapter 3 of the *Magnalia*'s sixth book.

3. Words repeated without change: "It was not on the *Lord's Day* only, but *every Day,* that this good Man [Jonathan Burr] was usually, *In the Fear of the Lord all the Day long"* (*Magnalia,* bk. 3, p. 79).

4. Words repeated with change (a device called *polyptoton*): "Eminent . . . eminently" (*Wonders,* 1:71).

5. Syllables: *"Numbers . . . Measures"*;[4] *"unseasonable . . . unreasonable"* (*Magnalia,* bk. 2, p. 14).

3. [Cotton Mather], *Manuductio ad Ministerium* (Boston: Thomas Hancock, 1726), p. 42.

4. *Psalterium Americanum* (Boston: B. Eliot, S. Gerrish, D. Henchman, and J. Edwards, 1718), p. vii.

6. Alliteration, which frequently betrayed him into wordiness: "many *particular Persons* among the People of *New-England*" (*Magnalia*, p. [1] of "A General Introduction").

JONATHAN EDWARDS (1703–1758)

A much simpler style, closer to eighteenth-century literary ideals, was cultivated by Jonathan Edwards as he too attempted to arrest the decay of Puritanism.

Life. Edwards was born at East Windsor, Connecticut. A precocious child, he was graduated from Yale before he was seventeen. After spending two more years there as a theology student, he became a minister in New York City and then a tutor at Yale. In 1727 he married Sarah Pierrepont and brought her to Northampton, Massachusetts, where he had been elected assistant minister to his grandfather, Solomon Stoddard. Upon Stoddard's death in 1729, he became full minister. In 1735 Edwards conducted a successful revival at Northampton, following the example of his grandfather, who had reaped five such "harvests." Edwards's harvest included a four-year-old girl, and he carefully described this conversion along with others in *A Faithful Narrative of the Surprising Work of God* (1737). This book and the conversions that prompted it represent an early phase of the Great Awakening, a period of religious fervor that spread throughout New England and into the middle and southern colonies during the 1730s and 1740s. Edwards was not only the leader of this revival but its apologist as well. In addition to fanning its fires with such terror-sermons as *Sinners in the Hands of an Angry God,* he answered Charles Chauncy and other rationalists who objected to the emotionalism of the awakening by writing *A Treatise Concerning Religious Affections* (1746). Solomon Stoddard had extended full church membership, including admittance to the Lord's Supper, even to those who had not gone through the formal process of regeneration. His grandson reversed this policy and was dismissed by his congregation, already irritated by his austere manner. In 1751 Edwards became missionary to the Indians at Stockbridge, Massachusetts, a frontier settlement. Here he composed *Freedom of the Will,* his most ambitious work. In January 1758 he became president of the College of New Jersey (Princeton) but two months later died from smallpox inoculation.

Representative Works

"Sarah Pierrepont" (written 1723).[5] Edwards apparently composed this 277-word prose description of his future wife on a blank page in a book he

---

5. Quoted here from [Sereno E. Dwight], *Life of President Edwards* (New-York: S. Converse, 1829), pp. 114–115.

was reading at the time, four years before their marriage, when Sarah was only thirteen and Edwards twenty. "Sarah Pierrepont" makes a pleasing contrast to the stress on a terrifying Deity in some of Edwards's other works. The "Great Being" is seen, not as the Absolute Sovereign in his judgment seat, but as Sarah's divine companion, who "comes to her and fills her mind with exceeding sweet delight."

A Divine and Supernatural Light, Immediately Imparted to the Soul by the Spirit of God, Shown to Be Both a Scriptural and Rational Doctrine (1734). One of Edwards's best tranquil sermons, it combines Calvinistic theology, biblical authority, and Lockean psychology to analyze the redemptive process. Neither revelation nor reason had the most important role in the drama of redemption as Edwards saw it. True, their roles are indispensable, just as eyes are indispensable for perceiving light, but above them is the light itself, the divine and supernatural light of saving grace, "a true sense of the divine excellency of the things revealed in the word of God, and a conviction of the truth and reality of them thence arising" (8:8).[6] Revelation furnished doctrine, reason agreed to it; but the divine light embraced it as superlatively excellent. The divine light was a religious affection stirred up by the Holy Spirit. Moreover, the divine light was imparted immediately by God and was seen, not through "a long and subtile train of reasoning" (8:18), but as directly as light itself. By recognizing the key functions of emotion and illumination in the redemptive process, Edwards was perhaps opening the door for Antinomianism, revivalism, transcendentalism, and a religion of feeling; but he himself did not step through that door. Insisting on the importance, indeed the necessity, of reason and revelation in conversion, he remained true to orthodox Calvinism. At the same time, however, he adapted the new psychology of John Locke by carefully examining the internal processes of the mind and by implying that seeing, feeling, and willing can comprise a single act of faith rather than three separate operations of the intellect and will.

This sermon functions as excellent background for Edwards's other writings. It defines the "new sense of things" that he himself experienced and wrote about in *Personal Narrative,* and it explains the motives for human volition that are stressed in his *Freedom of the Will.* There men are said always to choose the highest apparent good. Here that good among regenerate men is shown to be the divine excellencies that delight their hearts.

The imagery of *A Divine and Supernatural Light* deserves more attention than its doctrine-reasons-uses structure, which was common to most Puritan sermons. Some of the best images are gustatory. For example, a man with mere speculative knowledge is compared with a person who knows

---

6. Unless otherwise noted, all quotations in this section are taken from *The Works of President Edwards* ("A New Edition"; London: James Black and Son, 1817).

about the sweetness of honey only through hearsay, but a man with a sense of the heart is compared with a person who has actually experienced the sweetness of honey by tasting it. As might be expected of a sermon that equates grace with light, visual imagery also appears to advantage here.

Personal Narrative (1765). A spiritual autobiography designed to analyze the author's religious affections and separate the true from the false. *Personal Narrative* was a case history of Edwards's own conversion. The story spanned over twenty years of his life; yet with the aid of his diary he was able to trace every important step in remarkably fresh detail. As the opening sentence implies, Edwards experienced several spiritual relapses and recoveries and was often in doubt as to the genuineness of his personal "awakenings." Certain feelings on which he first prided himself later turned out to be false. Having mistaken these signs for grace, he became "self-righteous" (1:28) and even self-reliant (i.e., not sufficiently convinced of his spiritual depravity and of the fact that salvation is God's work, not man's). In contrast with these false feelings were the true religious affections that gave Edwards a new sense of "divine glory, in almost every thing" (1:31). His newfound delight in thunderstorms (which he had dreaded before his conversion) anticipated the love of the picturesque exhibited by early romantic writers and painters. New meanings now began to appear in the Bible, and on numerous occasions he had powerful visions of God as excellent, glorious, lovely, holy, or merciful. In these passages there is the essence of mysticism—a God-man union the human partner calls ineffable but may nevertheless attempt to describe in erotic metaphors. Like other mystics, Edwards thought of God as the active partner in this love union and of himself as the passive one panting "to be full of Christ alone" (1:39). Eventually he even took pleasure in Calvinism's harshest doctrine: that God orders all things, "choosing whom he would to eternal life and rejecting whom he pleased" (1:29). As if to compensate for these delights, Edwards's conversion brought with it a greater conviction of sin. Nevertheless, the overall tone of this autobiography lacks the penetrating gloom of *Sinners in the Hands of an Angry God.*

The form of *Personal Narrative,* its chief claim to be literature, is an interesting blend of contrasting elements. Unlike Edwards's other case histories, this story is told in the first person but with a clinical objectivity and honesty seldom attained in autobiographies. Edwards's relentless probings led him into many psychological and theological complexities that he refused to evade. At times, however, he attempted to simplify them. For example, when he wrote of God's "majestic meekness" (1:31) he crammed a massive theological paradox into brief oxymorons. He depicted spiritual processes in an emotive, sensual language. The word "sweet" appears in phrase after phrase, including such synesthesias as "a sweet burning in my heart" (1:31). The Christian's reception of grace he compares to a flower "peacefully and lovingly" baring its bosom "to receive the pleasant beams of the sun's glory" (1:34).

Sinners in the Hands of an Angry God (first preached and published in 1741). Edwards's most notorious work; the best example of his terrifying sermons, but hardly representative of his sermons as a whole. It was composed to persuade his listeners to seek personal conversion rather than to claim church membership (as compromises like the Half-Way Covenant of 1662 allowed them to do) solely on the basis that their parents and grandparents were members. Edwards tried to begin their regeneration with the traditional first step, a conviction of sin, and stressed the precariousness of their position. Apparently his effort was met with instantaneous success; as one listener recalled, "There was such a breathing of distress, and weeping" that Edwards "was obliged to speak to the people and desire silence, that he might be heard."[7]

The emotional force of this sermon derives largely from Edwards's artistic use of the familiar and the sensual in simply stated figures of comparison. In one metaphor God has bent his bow and aimed the arrow at the listener's heart; in another he dangles the listener "over the pit of hell, much as one holds a spider, or some loathsome insect over the fire" (6:458). As Edwin Cady has pointed out, this sermon contains an unusual abundance of tactile imagery. References to the fires of hell are addressed to the thermal sense, while the spider figure just mentioned and the comparison of the listener with a man standing on "slippery declining ground" (6:451) are forms of kinesthetic terror. Believing with Locke that ideas are formed through sense experience, Edwards was titillating the senses of his listeners so they might attain a better notion of hell.

Freedom of the Will (1754). Edwards's most ambitious philosophical treatise, an attack on Arminianism, a defense of Calvinism. Although his complex arguments defy summarizing, it is clear that he limits rather than denies freedom of the will. On the one hand, man is free to *do* what he wills: i.e., to act upon his choices. This is the highest kind of liberty. On the other hand, the will is not free, for it must choose the strongest motive that man's "whole faculty of perception," not just his reason, presents to him (1:138). It cannot resist the greatest apparent good. Moreover, since God has predestined all events and since every human volition is a link in a universal chain of cause and effect, man's choices are ultimately determined. These precariously balanced conclusions allowed Edwards to retain the sovereign, foreordaining God of Calvinism and still assign some responsibility to man for his acts, this latter in refutation of Arminianism, which held that without freedom of the will man could hardly be thought to sin. In Edwards's philosophy, the Supreme Ruler treats men "as moral agents, making them the objects of his commands, counsels, calls, warnings, expostulation[s], promises, threatenings, rewards and punishments" (1:417). However, as a Calvinist, Edwards denied that the good works of these moral agents can earn salvation. God alone dispenses that, and then only to his elect.

7. Benjamin Trumbull, *Complete History of Connecticut,* 2 vols. (New Haven: Maltby, Goldsmith and Co., and Samuel Wadsworth, 1818), 2:145.

Style. If the writings of Jonathan Edwards are difficult to comprehend, it is because of their matter, not their manner; for in the history to date of American literature few writers have achieved a plainer style than he. As already noted, Edwards used familiar comparisons, paradox, sense appeal, and emotive language. But he never let such literary devices call attention to themselves. In fact, throughout his career he kept to an early resolution "not [to] look as if I was much *read*, or was conversant with books, or with the learned world."[8] Quotations are therefore almost completely absent from his work. When Edwards's treatises were polemic—and almost all were—he used the conventional types of argument, including analogy, appeal to common sense, and appeal to authority. One of his specialties, the *reductio ad absurdum*, proved an especially devastating weapon. He used it memorably in *Freedom of the Will* when, to show the inconsistencies in his opponents' idea of free will, he compares it with a fabulous animal

that begat and brought forth itself, and yet had a sire and dam distinct from itself; . . . that his master, who led him, and governed him at his pleasure, was always governed by him, and driven by him where he pleased; that when he moved, he always took a step before the first step; that he went with his head first, and yet always went tail foremost; and this, though he had neither head nor tail.

(1:328–329)

Curiously, for all his serious intent, Edwards was here indulging in a form of folk humor sometimes known as *tangletalk*.[9]

Edwards's sermons were not only plainly written but also plainly delivered, partly because he was habitually austere in public and partly because he wanted nothing to get in the way of his thought. Contemporaries remembered him speaking solemnly in distinct but undramatic tones, without gestures, looking straight ahead.

8. Dwight, *Life of President Edwards*, pp. 702–703.
9. See Iona and Peter Opie, *The Lore & Language of Schoolchildren* (London: Oxford University Press, 1959), pp. 24–26; Aarne and Thompson (GB), under types 2014 and 2335.

4
Diarists

There were many diarists and journal writers in the eighteenth century; three of the most important were Sarah Kemble Knight, William Byrd, and John Woolman. Knight (a New England businesswoman) and Byrd (a Virginia aristocrat) gave early American literature some of its richest humor. Both authors often treated their materials satirically, reflecting their awareness of class distinctions, their sense of their own superiority, and their part in the growth of eighteenth-century neoclassicism. In marked contrast with this approach was the gentle humanitarianism and modest bearing of New Jersey Quaker John Woolman.

SARAH KEMBLE KNIGHT (1666–1727)

We know less about Sarah Kemble Knight than about any of the authors in this chapter. Even the barest facts tell us, however, that for her time she was a remarkable woman, one blessed with large shares of domestic, legal, and literary talents.

She seems quite self-reliant and apparently kept a boardinghouse, a shop, and a writing school that numbered Ben Franklin among its pupils. Moreover, she frequently served as business manager, legal adviser, and notary public, which is clearly evident in the many surviving documents that bear her name. No doubt it was to act in these capacities that she rode horseback from Boston to New Haven and New York in 1704–1705, the round trip described in her journal, the only extant example of her literary accomplishment. A native and longtime resident of Boston, Madam Knight spent the last years of her life in Norwich and New London, Connecticut, where she acquired considerable property.

The Journal of Madam Knight (w. 1704–1705) seems to be a reworking of notes made daily on her trip. The notes have been lost, and we can only suspect that such things as the poems, the literary allusions, and the mock-epic tone were additions to this original account. For over a century the journal remained in manuscript. When it was published in 1825, the press on both sides of the Atlantic hailed it as a great discovery.

The *Journal* may be read profitably as history and local color, as imaginative experience, and as humor and satire, although none of these aspects predominates.

Certainly the *Journal's* historical value arises in large part from its authentic picture of backwoods America at the beginning of the eighteenth century. First of all, the route from Boston to New York—some 270 miles—was hazardous for anyone, let alone a thirty-eight-year-old woman. Crossing swollen or ice-filled streams was especially dangerous, and the terrors of creeping over a broken bridge were excelled only by a canoe ride of such precarious balance that Madam Knight remembers "not daring so much as to lodg my tongue a hair's breadth more on one side of my mouth then tother" for fear of upsetting the craft (p. 969).[1] Where the country was wild the people were uncouth, with manners at worst cruel, at best awkward. For example, Madam Knight tells of a man forcing his daughter to ride bareback and, when she complained, purposely kicking the horse to make it "Jolt ten times harder" (p. 972). Less harsh but better known is her description of Bumpkin Simpers, who "advanc't to the midle of the Room . . . spitting a Large deal of Aromatic Tincture . . . gave a scrape with his shovel like shoo . . . [and] Stood staring rown'd him, like a Catt let out of a Baskett" (p. 975). While she seems rather tolerant of these manners and admits that such bumpkins sometimes have more "mother witt" than cityfolk, she nevertheless hopes that they will "leave such follies," which she blames on the lamentable lack of "Education and Conversation" in the backwoods (p. 975). Also of historical value are the various short descriptions of Indians, Negroes, and Quakers, and a substantial section on New York City, whose inhabitants proved neat and sociable and quite exact in business matters.

Besides this narrative account of towns and back country, the *Journal* contains a dream world produced by Madam Knight's imagination working upon actual experience. Her own words indicate an intentional subjectivity: On one occasion she writes of "composing my Resentments" (p. 971) and on another of slipping away "to enter my mind in my Jornal" (p. 971). Sometimes this mind allowed her to escape from reality, as when, during a moonlit ride in the New England wilderness, she was filled with "pleasent delusions" of looking upon "a Sumpteous [Old-World] city" with churches, a castle, and various "famous Buildings" (p. 970); at other times it served only to deform reality. During an earlier ride, for example, every

1. Quotations are from "The Private Journal Kept by Madam Knight," *Littell's Living Age* 57 (1858): 967–980.

tree trunk, "with its shatter'd Limbs, appear'd an Armed Enymie; and every little stump like a Ravenous devourer" (p. 969). In passages such as these there is a merging of factual and psychological truth, Madam Knight's fantasies representing the terrors that her contemporaries experienced in the wilderness and the nightmares that everyone experiences in dreams.

As suggested by these passages, Madam Knight had the ability to see comedy even in the harsh realities of the frontier. This, together with her keen ear for dialect, anticipates the local-color humor of the nineteenth century. In its mock-epic satire, on the other hand, the *Journal* came midway between Thomas Morton's *New English Canaan* and the work of the Connecticut Wits. Some eighty years earlier than Trumbull and Barlow, Madam Knight was cleverly using poetic diction and heroic allusions for comic distortion. Tavern patrons drinking silently out of their mugs are said to be "tyed by the Lipps to a pewter engine" (p. 968); one of Madam Knight's guides talks so much like characters in sixteenth- and seventeenth-century romances that she fancies him a possible "Prince disguis'd" (p. 968); and she herself is a female Ulysses in a frontier odyssey. Even the supernaturalism of epics is used satirically when she depicts her brief stop with a family named Devil as a visit to the underworld.

WILLIAM BYRD II (1674–1744)

Another diarist who described the backwoods with memorable humor was William Byrd II, an imposing figure from the southern colonies.

Life. Born in Virginia, Byrd was educated abroad, receiving his legal training in London. He returned several times to England as an agent of the colony and in all spent about half his life in the Old World. Byrd was one of Virginia's wealthiest planters, ultimately owning some 186,000 acres; his library was among the largest in the colonies. He was at various times a member of the Virginia House of Burgesses, commander-in-chief of local militia, and receiver-general of revenues. From 1709 to 1744, he was a member of the Supreme Council (the upper house of the Virginia Assembly) and became its president in the last year of his life. Westover, his mansion on the James River, is one of the finest examples of Georgian architecture in America.

None of Byrd's major writings was published during his lifetime, although he did circulate some in manuscript. He apparently never considered them finished enough for print.

Representative Works

The Secret Diary of William Byrd of Westover, 1709–1712 (1941). Five hundred ninety-one pages recording both his public and private life, including entries on his relationship with Governor Spotswood, his unsuccessful attempt to become governor himself, his work with the militia, and his attendance at raucous council meetings in Williamsburg. Equally interesting are his business and domestic affairs. We see him hiring workmen, looking after his slaves, checking on shipments, writing to his overseers, and otherwise tending his estate. Seldom, however, did he allow these matters to cut short his morning routine, which included reading Greek or Hebrew, doing his dance (probably daily exercises), and saying his prayers. Later in the day there would be other respite from business. The diary mentions a range of diversions definitely wider than that enjoyed by Byrd's middle-class Puritan or Quaker contemporaries: not only ice skating, hunting, billiards, ninepins, and cricket but also cards, dice, and dancing. Nevertheless, life was not always merry at Westover, for Byrd often quarreled with Lucy, his irascible first wife. Accounts of their relations make up this diary's most intimate entries.

The London Diary, 1717–1721 (1958). Clearly reveals London society and Byrd's passionate but religious nature. Occasionally mentioned are such important literary acquaintances as William Wycherley, William Congreve, and Nicholas Rowe. Many more entries allude to the earls and dukes who were Byrd's lifelong friends. While Byrd moved in this high society he was seeking a wife, Lucy having died in 1716. Besides courting aristocrats, he was involved with housemaids, prostitutes, and other women. These numerous amours were generally recorded with expressions of repentance.

The Secret History of the Line (1929). A lively narrative of a survey made in 1728 to determine the boundary between Virginia and North Carolina.

History of the Dividing Line betwixt Virginia and North Carolina Run in the Year of Our Lord 1728 (1841). Byrd's most important literary work. Apparently intended for publication, it covers the same survey as *The Secret History* but has more topographical, botanical, and zoological descriptions; fewer references to manners and morals among the surveying party; harsher treatment of North Carolinians; and a more urbane style.

Nature and people are the two main topics of this book, where folklore and fact often rub elbows. A louse placed on a piece of paper is said to have located north as accurately as a compass, while an alligator can supposedly kill a cow by swallowing stones and then dragging her under water.

Byrd was deeply conscious of national and regional differences. He noticed, for example, that the French had promoted Catholicism in America by intermarrying with the Indians; and he half-seriously recommended that Englishmen use the same means to promote their own religion and colonies. He himself was quite interested in the religions of the Indians; several pages of *The History* explain the mythological beliefs of Bearskin, the surveying party's Indian guide. Byrd's best-remembered group portrait is of certain North Carolina males who, living in Lubberland (a land of plenty), felt little need to work themselves but "impose[d] all the Work upon the poor

Women."[2] This description is now recognized as one of the earliest literary treatments of the southern "poor white." It also smacks of regionalism (a Virginian looking down upon North Carolinians), while in other passages there is even a form of sectionalism as Byrd expresses dislike of New Englanders by charging them with mistreating their government officials, overapplying Sabbath laws, and selling inferior rum to the South.

In the *History,* Byrd demonstrates that he knew the value of a humorous outlook as a means of enduring frontier discomforts, and he was quick to praise his men for turning bad situations into merriment. Furthermore, his satires of various people show that although he considered himself above them, he could tolerate them if allowed a few chuckles at their expense.

Byrd's style was usually descriptive and allusive, often ironic and exaggerative. As his sketch of a border hermit and his concubine proves, Byrd could select (or invent) details to create a memorable picture:

Like the Ravens, he neither plow'd nor sow'd, but Subsisted chiefly upon Oysters, which his Handmaid made a Shift to gather from the Adjacent Rocks. Sometimes, too, for Change of Dyet, he sent her to drive up the Neighbour's Cows, to moisten their Mouths with a little Milk. But as for raiment, he depended mostly upon his Length of Beard, and She upon her Length of Hair, part of which she brought decently forward, and the rest dangled behind quite down to her Rump, like one of the Herodotus's East Indian Pigmies.

Thus did these Wretches live in a dirty State of Nature, and were mere Adamites, Innocence only excepted.

(p. 37)

Byrd could cram a great amount of irony into single words (e.g., "Handmaid" and "decently" in the passage above) or into short phrases like "the honest Dutch" (p. 15) and "the Saints of New England" (p. 32). Also successful were his exaggerations. Apropos of the supposed aphrodisiac properties of bear meat, which had constituted the bulk of the surveying party's diet, he joked: "All the Marryed men of our Company were joyful Fathers within forty weeks after they got Home, and most of the Single men had children sworn to them within the same time, our chaplain always excepted, who, with much ado, made a shift to cast out that importunate kind of Devil, by Dint of Fasting and Prayer" (p. 190).

Byrd's style is also quite allusive. Writing with a London audience in mind, he probably felt a need to justify his subject, which was after all extremely narrow. Therefore, in accordance with eighteenth-century critical standards, he enriched, broadened, and universalized it by connecting it geographically and chronologically to other cultures. The boundary

2. *The Writings of Colonel William Byrd of Westover in Virginia Esqr,* ed. John S. Bassett (New York: Doubleday, Page, 1901), pp. 75–76.

expedition surveyed some 241 miles; the similes used to describe it span much of the world and its peoples. Dutchmen, Frenchmen, Spaniards, Italians, Lithuanians, Muscovites, Tartars, Hottentots, and other faraway folk are carefully linked to the Indians, whites, and Negroes of North Carolina and Virginia. Byrd often used alliteration to emphasize contrasts and key words, as in his observation that Indians, like "the wild Irish . . . would rather want than Work" (pp. 200–201). His historical allusions usually come from biblical and classical eras, although a few were drawn from the Middle Ages.

JOHN WOOLMAN (1720–1772)

The first significant American Quaker writer was John Woolman. Heretofore authors including Samuel Sewall, Sarah Knight, and the otherwise tolerant Roger Williams had written disparagingly of this sect not only in disagreement with many of its beliefs but also in fear of those earlier members who had groaned and quaked, poured ashes over their heads, broken into Puritan meetings, or walked naked through the streets. The gentle but effective humanitarianism of John Woolman represented Quakerism's nobler aspects.

Although Woolman gained some reputation during his life, he lived humbly. He grew up on the family farm in New Jersey and had the brief country-schoolhouse education common among Quakers; he extended it by reading widely on his own. When he was twenty-one, he moved five miles away to Mount Holly, where he worked as a clerk and bookkeeper, performed such legal services as drawing up wills and conveying property, and finally settled upon tailoring as his life's work. In 1849 he married Sarah Ellis, "a well-inclined damsel" (p. 78)[3] who bore but one child, a daughter, to survive infancy. Woolman was deeply moved by the plight of humanity— the sick, bereaved, poor, dispossessed, enslaved—and in their service was often away from home. For thirty years he was an itinerant minister, traveling from New England to North Carolina, to the interior of Pennsylvania, and ultimately to England, where he died of smallpox.

Most of Woolman's works were issued during his lifetime; the *Journal* (1774), his best-known book, was published posthumously.

The *Journal* should be considered an autobiography. Although its sections are dated like diary-entries, its final coherent form could have been achieved only by retrospective composition. The work clearly reveals four interrelated aspects of Woolman's character: Quakerism, mysticism, humanitarianism, and primitivism.

In numerous passages he refers to the influence of the Holy Spirit, which

3. Quotations are from *The Journal of John Woolman, with an Introduction by John G. Whittier* (Boston: James R. Osgood, 1871).

whispered to his "inward ear" (p. 98), stirred him to mystical ecstasies, gave him love and pity for all God's creatures, set "right bounds" on his earthly desires (p. 94), and enabled the Indians to understand him. This, too, is the spirit that moves men to do their duty and to use God's "gifts . . . [as] they were intended" (p. 94). The *Journal* also mentions occasions when, like other Quakers, Woolman was led by the Spirit to break the silence of their meetings to make a short speech. Nonsectarianism is another aspect of the Quaker religion brought out in the *Journal*. Because he believed that God accepts all "sincere, upright-hearted people, in every society" (p. 58), Woolman had no trouble welcoming Presbyterians into his group, saying good things of Mennonites and Nicholites, and working as an Indian missionary side by side with a Moravian.

Woolman's mysticism is revealed in that he often sought solitude and sometimes experienced trances, visions, or dreams in which he was closely united to God. The climax of these events—and, indeed, the goal of Woolman's life—was a complete submission to God's will. Thus he tells of lying sick and hearing an angel say, "John Woolman is dead," words that sorely puzzled him until he realized they "meant no more than the death of my own will" (p. 265). Like most mystics, he could "find no language equal to convey[ing] . . . a clear idea" of such experiences (p. 58). Characteristic of mysticism, too, was his overwhelming love, "not only toward all men, but also toward the brute creatures" (p. 58), a theme introduced at the beginning of the *Journal* as he recalls his guilt over having killed a robin and her young.

Woolman's great humanitarianism is apparent on nearly every page. Above all, he worked for the abolition of slavery. He refused to make out wills for slaveholders, to use sugar produced by slave labor, and to lodge free at the homes of Quakers who were exploiting their Negroes. But he visited these Quakers, north and south, and calmly urged them to free their slaves, and he spoke to this effect at Quaker meetings throughout the colonies. He also wrote about the problem in *Some Considerations on the Keeping of Negroes,* published in two parts (1754 and 1762), and of course in the *Journal* itself. Chapter 4 has probably the most detailed arguments, but Chapter 2, with its picture of slavery as a "dark gloominess hanging over the land" (p. 72), is equally effective. Woolman's humanitarianism grew to embrace many other groups, including Indians, coachmen, sailors, and—most important—the poor, whose plight he thought could be ameliorated if all classes would cease striving after creature comforts.

The *Journal* reveals Woolman as a chronological primitivist. For him the "golden age" was the first period of Christianity, when the "primitive followers of Jesus Christ" (pp. 156–157), who was the very essence of "simplicity" (p. 230), were dedicated to a life of "ardent love and heavenly-mindedness" (p. 156). Woolman advised his fellow men to rid themselves of the world's "superfluities" (pp. 180, 262, 263) and "conveniences" (p. 88) and become "content with a plain way of life" (p. 172), even to the point of discontinuing all businesses that did not employ people in genuinely "useful" labor (p. 179). He himself was the best model of eighteenth-century simplicity. When his retail trade showed signs of growing into a "large business," he gave it up to follow the uncluttered life of a tailor without even an apprentice. Unlike his contemporary Ben Franklin, who was a model of Yankee shrewdness, Woolman learned "to be a fool . . . to worldly wisdom" (p. 96).

Considered as a work of art, the *Journal* is uneven. Its pictures of the world outside Woolman's soul are sometimes fuzzy and generalized, a drawback to be expected of spiritual autobiographies. Less tolerable are tedious itineraries of Woolman's missionary trips. Modern readers may lack the enthusiasm of Henry Crabb Robinson, who thought that Woolman wrote with "exquisite purity and grace" (p. 3); yet they must admit that Woolman's style is a fine example of Quaker austerity. His writing does not call attention to itself, and only occasionally are we aware of the sensory images or of the metaphors derived from early Quaker books and, of course, from the Bible. Even the mystical episodes in Woolman's *Journal* are rather plainly described, in contrast with the erotic passages common in Edward Taylor, Jonathan Edwards, and other religious writers.

5

Essayists, Statesmen, and Propagandists

Some of the best eighteenth-century prose was written by the Founding Fathers—statesmen associated with the Revolutionary War and the making of the Constitution. Although their work comprises a variety of genres, it exhibits an unmistakably homogeneous outlook, reflecting the scientific rationalism of the time.

THE ENLIGHTENMENT

Glimmerings of this rationalism had appeared in the Renaissance and even earlier, but the most intense illumination burst forth in the eighteenth century—for Americans, particularly during its latter half. This was the Enlightenment, also known as the Age of Reason and the neoclassic age. It produced great and sometimes violent changes as, for example, the American and French revolutions. It also produced great names: Voltaire and Rousseau in France; Lessing, Herder, and Mendelssohn in Germany; and Franklin and Jefferson in America.

Essentially, the Enlightenment represented a shift from supernaturalism to rationalism in attitudes toward nature, man, and God. Science, as the analysis of nature, advanced significantly after Isaac Newton's formulation of the mechanistic laws governing the universe. Scientific advances often served to undermine the literal interpretation of Genesis and other parts of the Bible. These challenges to orthodoxy met with various reactions from American authors, who were generally close observers of nature, anxious to record and communicate their discoveries. Cotton Mather, Jonathan Edwards, and William Byrd all engaged in scientific pursuits without leaving their Puritan or Anglican faiths; but most of the authors discussed in the present chapter gave up orthodoxy. They and their enlightened fellows became less concerned with natural wonders and remarkable providences, the extraordinary aspects of nature that had awed the seventeenth century, and more concerned with its ordinary and orderly aspects, which revealed a universe operating by scientific laws rather than supernatural intervention.

Deism, as the religion of nature, developed out of this change in attitude. The deists believed in God, but an impersonal God. To them, God was the Prime Mover, the divine clockwinder who set the universe in motion and let it run without interference. He was no longer directly concerned with the affairs of men, if indeed he had ever been. Only through natural laws did he manifest himself, and only through reason could man understand him. In general, the deists distrusted the Bible and the clergy, denied the divinity of Christ and the concept of grace, and deplored all forms of organized religion. Instead they put their faith in reason and science, believed in an innate moral sense, and advocated a life of virtue. Like the English deists, whom they followed, they displayed significant differences among themselves, not only over such ideas as eternal rewards and punishments, but also over the desirability of proselytizing. Franklin and Jefferson were loath to publicize their deistic opinions. The militant deists, on the other hand, wrote books on the subject. Ethan Allen's *Reason, the Only Oracle of Man* (1784) and Tom Paine's *Age of Reason* earned their authors many an enemy among the orthodox.

The shift from supernaturalism to rationalism also appeared in the new attitude toward man. During the Enlightenment, man's reason reigned supreme. With it he could learn the laws of nature and place himself in harmony with the universe, thus fulfilling his purpose. He was no longer considered a victim of original sin; hence his reason could operate without aid from the Bible or the clergy.

Man was also the source and object of government. According to the theory developed by Dutch jurist Hugo Grotius and reaching Americans via English philosopher John Locke, man is born with such natural rights as those to life, liberty, and property. He forms governments and chooses rulers, not to surrender his rights, but to delegate to his rulers the power to protect them. Thus the source of government is the people rather than God, and the divine right theory was replaced with Locke's compact or contract theory. American patriots eagerly adopted it to justify the Revolutionary War, contending that if man could form governments he could also dissolve them.

This was not the first adaptation of the natural rights concept to native surroundings. John Wise, a brilliant New England minister, had applied it to church government early in the eighteenth century. With *The Churches' Quarrel Espoused* (1710) and *Vindication of the Government of New-England Churches* (1717), he attempted to stop the Mathers from subjecting the Puritan churches to an oligarchic system. In the process he struck some early blows for democracy, which he considered a reasonable government for both church and state. One of his sentences in particular summarizes the natural rights philosophy that he derived from Samuel Pufendorf rather than Locke: "The End of all good Government is to Cultivate Humanity, and Promote the happiness of all, and the good of every Man in all his Rights, his Life, Liberty, Estate, Honour, &c. without injury or abuse done to any."[1] This passage clearly anticipates the Declaration of Independence.

Every man might have inalienable rights, the faculty of reason, and an almost unlimited potential for progress; yet the writer-statesmen of the period were pessimistic enough about human nature in the aggregate to propose an elaborate system of checks and balances to control factions and modify the power of government. Having installed this self-corrective system in the Constitution of 1787, the Founding Fathers were optimistic enough to believe it would work, representing the triumph of human reason over human passion.

The literature that conveyed these new attitudes toward nature, God, and man was essentially utilitarian. In Europe and America, wherever the Enlightenment spread, men wrote to make other men use their reason (sometimes called "common sense"). But they wrote in a variety of ways, ranging from the sober frankness of the *Federalist* essays to the humorous indirections of Franklin's satires.

BENJAMIN FRANKLIN (1706–1790)

Of all the statesmen of the Englightenment, the versatile Benjamin Franklin was the most literary. From the time he began to improve his prose by imitating *The Spectator* papers, he developed a great concern for style. Ultimately he achieved several styles of his own and became a master of indirection, able easily to assume any number of roles and to use irony with consummate skill.

Franklin's total output was large; yet all his important writings except the *Autobiography* were short. Two groups of works are notable—the satires and the bagatelles. His best satires were hoaxes in which his fictions seemed to be historical or legal documents. These include the *Edict* and *Rules* (see pp. 44–45), *The Speech of Polly Baker*, and *The Sale of the Hessians*, both of uncertain date. His bagatelles (Italian for trifles) were usually written as letters to the Parisian ladies with whom he flirted while serving as American representative to France (1776–1785). "The Ephemera" (see p. 45), "To Madame Helvetius" (1779), "The Whistle" (1779), and "Dialogue between Franklin and the Gout" (1780) are the most popular. As shaped by Franklin, this form could turn into humor and the familiar essay.

1. John Wise, *A Vindication of the Government of New-England Churches* (Boston: N. Boone, 1717), p. 61.

Representative Works

Poor Richard's Almanack (issued annually 1732–1757, for the years 1733–1758; the title after 1747 was *Poor Richard Improved*). A popular series compiled, written, and published by Franklin. He borrowed heavily from many sources but created a semioriginal persona in Richard Saunders—a money-minded stargazer, practical joker, and victim of "petticoat government." In later issues this comic figure was converted into a true philosopher-moralist, becoming more respectable but less entertaining. Franklin crammed his almanac with quotations. Literature provided him with aphorisms and poems; folk tradition, with proverbs. These proverbs—anonymous, pithy statements of observation and advice—range widely in subject and sometimes offer several views of the same problem (see numbers 1 and 2 in the group quoted below). Many appeal because of their humorous tone (3, 4, 9) and forceful style, which could be anticlimactic (4), chiasmic (6), antithetic (10), assonant (3, 7, 13), alliterative (9), rhymed (8, 11), symbolic (12), metaphoric (5), and literal (11, 13). Franklin did not originate these proverbs (almost all have been found in earlier collections), but he gave them currency and sometimes improved them.

(1) He that takes a wife, takes care. (2) He that has not got a Wife, is not yet a compleat Man. (3) Three may keep a Secret, if two of them are dead. (4) Let thy maid-servant be faithful, strong, and homely. (5) Experience keeps a dear school, yet Fools will learn in no other. (6) As Charms are nonsence, Nonsence is a Charm. (7) Fish and Visitors stink in 3 days. (8) Little Strokes, / Fell great Oaks. (9) Men and Melons are hard to know. (10) A fat kitchin, a lean Will. (11) Early to bed and early to rise, makes a man healthy [,] wealthy and wise. (12) An empty Bag cannot stand upright. (13) Three Removes is as bad as a Fire.[2]

The Way to Wealth (published in 1757 as the preface to *Poor Richard Improved* for 1758). So frequently reprinted and widely translated as to be termed "the most famous piece of literature the colonies produced,"[3] it consists mostly of sayings on thrift, industry, and prudence that Franklin reworked from his previous almanacs. Richard Saunders remains as persona, but most of the piece is given over to a new character, Father Abraham, who harangues the crowd outside an auction. The narrative framework ends in irony, as the people proceed to waste their money despite his praise of thrift.

Rules by Which a Great Empire May be Reduced to a Small One (1773). A satire-hoax which, like Swift's *Modest Proposal,* ironically recommends measures—in this case, of British colonial policy—that the writer is in fact condemning.

2. *Poor Richard* for 1736, 1744, 1735, 1736, 1743, 1734, 1736, 1750, 1733, 1733, 1735, 1740, 1758.

3. John Bach McMaster, *Benjamin Franklin as a Man of Letters* (Boston: Houghton Mifflin, 1887), p. 129.

An Edict by the King of Prussia (1773). A satire on England's treatment of its American colonies. Franklin quotes and paraphrases various parliamentary acts respecting America in the guise of a proclamation issued by Prussia to lay claim to England.

The Ephemera (w. 1778). A bagatelle for Mme Brillon. Franklin hears a group of ephemerae (mayflies) arguing over the talents of two musicians (representing the musical partisanship then prevalent in Paris). Turning from this frivolous dispute, he listens to the soliloquy of an old philosopher-ephemera who predicts the impending destruction of the world and hence the futility of all human endeavor. The ephemera (obviously Franklin himself) is now plunged into sadness at seeing the meaning gone out of his long hours (years) of political and scientific effort; but he can still reflect on his good intentions and enjoy the companionship of such female ephemerae as Brillante (Mme Brillon). Here we have a rare view of Franklin as a melancholy stoic. But *The Ephemera* is indirect and complex, revealing in addition Franklin the humorist, the gallant, and the satirist. While he draws forth smiles at the miniperspective of emphemerae who reach old age in seven hours, he indulges in subtle compliments to Mme Brillon and gentle mockery of himself, Parisian society, and all humans.

Autobiography (the four parts were written respectively in 1771, 1784, 1788, 1789–1790). Though a genuine classic, *The Autobiography* is fragmentary, loosely structured, and sometimes inaccurate. The narrative stops at 1758, leaving more than one-third of Franklin's life unwritten. We must rely on other sources for information about his scientific activities and honors, his part in the Revolution, his diplomatic service, his popularity in France, and his help to the new American nation. The inaccuracies (many of which are corrected in the footnotes of the Yale edition) resulted from Franklin's not having his private papers with him as he wrote. The loose structure is typical of the genre. Franklin achieved a degree of unity by creating prediction-fulfillment patterns or by sustaining his imagery, as when in Part 1 he repeatedly refers to various actions as the "errata" of his life; but the four parts of the book remain disparate.

Yet the work is memorable. The old motifs of success stories and folktales grace its pages, giving them the appeal of tradition. Franklin is the clever youngest son who, cruelly treated, runs away from home and finds a job. While his employer stares in amazement, he is visited by a great personage (Governor Keith). Soon after, the youth visits home and, to show off, buys drinks for his former fellow workers. Back at his job he works hard and saves his money so that, fulfilling the prophecy of an old man, he is able to surpass his employer. Franklin created sharp, clear, and memorable images, for example, of his swimming over three miles, to the astonishment of English acquaintances, and of his walking through the streets of Philadelphia with threepenny worth of rolls.

When he began this book, Franklin had only his own descendants in mind, but he later directed it to a wider audience. At the beginning of Part 3, for instance, he not only converts various stories from his life into exempla for printers, schoolgirls, educators, parents, business managers, and business partners, but also proposes uniting the good people of the entire world into an international party for virtue. Neither his advice nor those classes to whom he addressed it would be considered out of date today. It is this universality that makes his plan for eliminating vice and acquiring virtue so widely anthologized. Then, too, the story of his rise from obscurity to fame is ever appropriate in a country that prides itself on self-improvement and vertical mobility. Franklin is eminently interesting in his own right, but he appeals to us even more as a symbol of the unpromising hero, the rising middle class, and America itself, whose fortune was intertwined with his own.

"Letter to Ezra Stiles" (March 9, 1790). Written the month before Franklin's death, it summarizes his mature religious beliefs. Although he was a deist, he tolerated all sects, and he regarded good deeds as the best means of worshipping God.

THOMAS PAINE (1737–1809)

With ideas akin to Franklin's but with methods far more direct and bold, Thomas Paine became one of the world's great propagandists. His style was clear, direct, and forceful, his ideas apparently flowing easily into words (for his manuscripts show only slight revision). As a phrasemaker he had few peers.

The first real test of Paine's persuasive powers was provided by the Revolutionary War. After spending half of his life rather aimlessly in his native England, Paine came to America in 1774 and soon threw himself behind the patriot cause. He not only served in Washington's army but, more important, wrote *Common Sense* and *The Crisis* papers, which proved extremely useful in the fight for independence. After the war, Paine returned to Europe and spent fifteen years supporting the French Revolution. He served the radical cause so well with his *Rights of Man* that England exiled him for sedition. Conversely, although he was elected to the French Assembly, some Frenchmen thought him too conservative and he was imprisoned for ten months after he opposed the execution of Louis XVI. With his next book, *The Age of Reason,* Paine tried to teach deism, but was accused of fostering atheism. Returning to America in 1802, he spent his last years as the subject of much abuse.

Representative Works

Common Sense (January 10, 1776). A political pamphlet advocating the immediate separation of the colonies from England. Writing after the

Boston Tea Party, the battles of Lexington and Concord, and the convening of the Second Continental Congress, Paine obviously was not initiating revolutionary ideas. But he did restate these ideas with vigor and, at just the right time, he carried them to the masses. (Other pamphleteers, including John Dickinson and James Otis, were less bold and wrote primarily for the educated.) Although the American sales of *Common Sense* may not have been so high as the 150,000 copies its author claimed, it was undeniably popular and influential. Most important, it helped bring about the Declaration of Independence.

Some ideas in *Common Sense* were not original with Paine, deriving from Thomas Hobbes, John Milton, and John Locke, but Paine pressed them into unique service. He began by declaring that, although government is necessary, it should be as simple as possible. He then attacked the British government, finding it not only too complex but also tyrannical in its very origins. Going farther than his fellow colonists, he denounced the king as well as Parliament and characterized attempts at reconciliation as folly. Then, he proposed ways to implement a new American government and develop a navy. Finally, he argued for a declaration of independence. Of the four sections in *Common Sense,* the third, "Thoughts on the Present State of American Affairs," has been most often anthologized. It stresses the colonists' duty to their posterity; views America as an asylum for the persecuted; insists on the worldwide aspects of the problem; and traces the influences of reason, emotions, and imagination on man's actions.

The Crisis (published irregularly from December 1776, to December 1783). Sixteen papers issued to boost morale at critical times during the Revolution. Number 1, the most famous of these successful essays, demonstrates their use and technique. According to legend, Paine wrote it on a drumhead; and Washington, in near despair after defeat in the Battle of Long Island, had it read to his troops. It was a masterpiece both of good writing and of propaganda, and Washington's subsequent victory at Trenton has been attributed partly to its influence. It opens with those bold and alliterative statements: "THESE are the times that try men's souls: The summer soldier and the sunshine patriot will, in this crisis, shrink from the service of his country" (p. 1).[4] In almost everything that follows—in such capitalized words as "FREEDOM" (p. 1) and "NOW" (p. 1), in rhetorical questions, interjections, and curses—there is obvious emotionalism. Paine resorts to invective, linking the British in one typical metaphor with the "cunning of the fox" and "the violence of the wolfe" (p. 7). At the end, an absolute volley of propaganda devices bursts before our eyes. The two closing sentences contain scare techniques, a forced dilemma, an apostrophe, and a curse:

4. *The American Crisis. Number I. By the Author of Common Sense* ([Philadelphia: Melchior Steiner and Charles Cist, 1776]).

By perseverance and fortitude we have the prospect of a glorious issue; by cowardice and submission, the sad choice of a variety of evils—a ravaged country—a depopulated city—habitations without safety, and slavery without hope—our homes turned into barracks and baudy-houses for Hessians—and a future race to provide for whose fathers we shall doubt of. Look on this picture, and weep over it!—and if there yet remains one thoughtless wretch who believes it not, let him suffer it unlamented.

(p. 8)

Even in this essay, however, emotionalism does not hold complete sway. Many balanced sentences remind us that Paine was well in control of his thought and his prose, and there is a definite appeal to the ideals of the Enlightenment in his signature—COMMON SENSE.

The Rights of Man (part 1, 1791; part 2, 1792). Part 1 primarily attacks Edmund Burke's conservative *Reflections on the Revolution in France* (1790). Part 2 primarily explains Paine's own theories of government, expressed in *Common Sense*.

The Age of Reason (w. ca. 1793–1795). A two-part book defending deism and attacking the Bible. Paine's immediate purpose was to quell atheism in France, but the distribution and influence of his work went far beyond this motive. It was widely published not only in France but also in England, Ireland, and America. Through large, cheap printings it reached the common man, and Americans called it the "frontier Bible." In this work Paine argued that the Bible is neither divine in origin nor morally healthy; its stories and characters are actually reworkings of Greek myths. For true revelation, man must study nature. Thus, while undermining Christianity and other traditional faiths, Paine helped popularize science and anticipated the comparative and anthropological study of religions.

THOMAS JEFFERSON (1743–1826)

The third and probably the most versatile president of the United States, Thomas Jefferson, was interested in aesthetics, music, gardening, and other arts but excelled in architecture and literature. A conscious stylist, he reportedly considered himself second only to Tom Paine among contemporary American authors. Fellow patriots were well aware of Jefferson's literary prowess when they asked him to draft the Declaration of Independence, the document that ensures his enduring reputation as a writer just as Monticello, the Virginia State Capitol, and the University of Virginia ensure his enduring reputation as an architect.

Representative Works

The Declaration of Independence (adopted July 4, 1776). When Jefferson composed this classic document, he was acting as a member of the five-man committee appointed for that purpose by the Second Continental Congress on June 11, 1776. (The other members were Benjamin Franklin, John Adams, Roger Sherman, and Robert R. Livingston.) He made no attempt to be original; instead he built upon such well-known ideas as John Locke's compact theory of government. Moveover, he used phrases from the Virginia Bill of Rights (the work of George Mason) and the preamble to the Virginia Constitution (his own work). As the Declaration progressed from Jefferson's original draft to its final form, it went through some eighty-six revisions, by Jefferson, the rest of the drafting committee, and Congress. The purpose of the Declaration was not only to declare independence (which Congress accomplished by adopting it on July 2) but also to enlist the support of foreign countries by justifying this action. The logic and style of the document suit its purpose admirably. With one graceful opening sentence, Jefferson named his audience—all mankind—and stated his subject. He then began his argument as far back as possible, with "self-evident" truths—ideas that, requiring no proof, left him free to proceed to the main argument without fear of begging the question. This argument may be reduced to a syllogism:

Major premise: A tyrannized people have the right to form a new government.
Minor premise: The United States of America are a tyrannized people.
Conclusion: Therefore the United States of America have the right to form a new government.

To reinforce the minor premise, Jefferson concentrated on George III, charging him with a long list of abuses, each laid squarely on his shoulders by a clause opening with the words "He has"—a formula repeated no less than eighteen times. Jefferson skillfully paired this picture of a cruel king with one of a long-suffering people. In a document of this sort one might expect bombast; instead, the language is solemn, and throughout there is a tone of thoughtful finality.

Notes on the State of Virginia (1785). Jefferson's only full-length book. Its title is overmodest, for its twenty-three copiously documented chapters are essays rather than notes, and the opinions they express often apply to the nation, not only to Virginia. Jefferson discussed slavery, which he deplored as corruptive of whites and blacks alike; he examined the culture of American Indians, including their oratory, their treatment of their wives, and their methods of birth control; he argued for the superiority of brick over plank buildings and lamented the scarcity of architects; he rejected the theory of a universal deluge (this earned him much criticism); he proposed for the United States a basically agrarian economy and warned against the evils of large cities. Discussions of such regional matters as the beauty of the Natural Bridge are intermingled with debate on such topics as the supposed degeneracy of the New World (Jefferson debunked Count Buffon's theory that in Europe animals are larger and exhibit more species than in America).

First Inaugural Address (delivered March 4, 1801). Although Jefferson's voice and temperament made him a poor orator, he gave this speech in person. Modest in tone, it was meant to conciliate as power shifted from North to South and from Federalists to Republicans after a hotly contested election. Thus governmental economy, religious and political toleration, and other Jeffersonian ideals were tempered here with various compliments and pledges to the losers. Throughout the address Jefferson's literary talents are evident, especially in such famous slogans as "A rising nation" (p. 12),[5] "WE ARE ALL REPUBLICANS; WE ARE ALL FEDER-ALISTS" (p. 15), "peace, commerce, and honest friendship with all nations, entangling alliances with none" (p. 19).

Letter to Dr. Benjamin Rush (April 21, 1803). A succinct explanation of Jefferson's deistic beliefs, which were derived from close study of classical writers. Jefferson accepted Christ's teachings as the best moral system of all time, but he thought they had been corrupted by evangelists, theologians, and clergymen.

Letter to John Adams (October 28, 1813). Probably the best-known of the more than 300 letters in the Jefferson-Adams correspondence, it explains Jefferson's concept of natural aristocracy. The elections of 1796 and 1800 had estranged the two Founding Fathers, and not until 1812 did they resume their correspondence. With increasing eagerness they now began to explore thoroughly the similarities and differences in their views. Adams had claimed, with characteristic skepticism, that the true aristocrat in the state is beautiful, wealthy, and wellborn rather than talented and virtuous. Jefferson, replying with characteristic optimism, explained his program for nurturing and selecting natural aristocrats (leaders of genius and virtue). First, he would destroy hereditary wealth and any church-state connection. Then he would educate the electorate by providing free schools at all levels and by introducing a system of self-governing townships or wards. Adams, still convinced that both aristocrat and electorate were corruptible, saw hope only in a government of checks and balances.

Letter to Dr. Walter Jones (January 2, 1814). Jefferson's realistic evaluation of George Washington as slow to adjust, cold, and naturally ill-tempered, but also noble in appearance, prudent, sound of judgment, fearless, honest, just, and self-controlled. According to Jefferson, Washington's reading was narrow, his conversation mediocre, but his writing facile.

THE FEDERALIST (1787–1788) AND ITS AUTHORS

Although *The Federalist* papers were propaganda pieces written to serve the needs of the moment, their scope is so great, their matter so relevant,

5. *Speech of Thomas Jefferson . . . March 4, 1801* (Philadelphia: Mathew Carey, 1801).

and their style so fitting that they have endured as classics of political literature. The authors of these eighty-five essays are familiar names in American history. Alexander Hamilton (1757–1804), who wrote fifty-one, would become secretary of the treasury under Washington. James Madison (1751–1836), who wrote twenty-nine (three possibly with help from Hamilton), was a Virginia statesman destined for the presidency. John Jay (1745–1829), who wrote five, would be appointed the nation's first chief justice. Their collaboration came about when it seemed doubtful that the Constitution would be ratified by the necessary nine out of thirteen states, because the aim of the framers of the Constitution to provide a strong central government was opposed by various states'-rights advocates. New York, led by Governor George Clinton, seemed especially loath to ratify. Hamilton, Jay, and Madison therefore addressed themselves to its citizens in a series of essays printed in local newspapers over the signature of Publius and published in book form even before the last eight installments had appeared. Although these essays had a common purpose—defense of the new Constitution—there was some overlapping and contradiction. Much of the work was impromptu and hasty. Hamilton was prone to grant the federal government far more power than was Madison. Still, the work had a general plan: Number 1 announced the series; Numbers 2 through 14 discussed the merits of strengthening the union of states and the disadvantages of weakening or dissolving it; Numbers 15 through 22 laid bare the defects in the Articles of Confederation; Numbers 23 through 85 explained the principles, powers, and mechanics of the projected new government. The still-relevant question of federalism in relation to the rights of states and individuals is discussed objectively in a calm, dignified style that befits the subject.

In Number 10, his first and most important contribution to *The Federalist,* Madison argued convincingly that the large size of the proposed American republic would help it control inevitable factions. This view echoed the Scottish social scientist David Hume but contradicted Aristotle and Montesquieu, who favored small governments. It even contradicted Madison's coauthor. In Number 9 Hamilton had proposed a stronger government that could control factions with force; in Number 10 Madison also proposed a stronger government, but one that could control factions without force. Madison's paper is especially well constructed. The opening sentence, in words remarkable for clarity and precision, previews his entire argument; eight sentences develop the importance of the topic; and a one-sentence paragraph defines faction. These preliminaries over, Madison shows the impossibility of removing the causes of faction by destroying liberty or by trying to make men uniform in opinions, passions, and interests. Instead, he contends, government should control the effects of faction. If the faction is a minority, it is kept in check by the votes of the majority. If the faction is a majority, it is restrained in a large republic by three factors. First, factions are unlikely to achieve a majority where there are many interests and many parties. Second, when majority factions do develop in such a government, their efforts will be less concerted and their power consequently slighter than in smaller territories. Third, a republic can "refine and enlarge the public views, by passing them through the medium of a chosen body of citizens, whose wisdom may best discern the true interest of their country, and whose patriotism and love of justice, will be least likely to sacrifice it to temporary or partial considerations" (1:58).[6]

In Number 23 Hamilton argues from a self-evident premise that the new government should have powers equal to its purposes. This essay pleads especially for strong military powers.

6. *The Federalist: A Collection of Essays,* 2 vols. (New York: J. and A. McLean, 1788).

6
Neoclassic Poets

Like the prose works discussed in chapter 5, American poems of the Enlightenment era were often political in content, satiric in tone, and didactic in purpose. Neoclassical might be the best label for them since it indicates their close resemblance to English poems of the period. Imitation, to the eighteenth-century neoclassicist, was not the ugly word it would be to the nineteenth-century romantics. The British neoclassicists imitated the writers of ancient Greece and Rome; the American neoclassicists imitated the writers of ancient Greece and Rome and their British imitators. However, imitation often resulted in adaptation as American poetry, like American architecture, mixed the classical with the indigenous.

NEOCLASSICAL POETRY

The neoclassical poetry of America and that of England resembled each other in three important aspects:

1. The couplet form. This was the preferred form. The couplets could be open or closed, pentameter or tetrameter. Occasionally, writers even experimented with blank verse, Spenserian stanza, and other kinds of meter and rhyme.

2. Poetic diction. Words like "blade" and "steed" were considered more appropriate to poetry than were words like "knife" and "horse." American applications of this theory sometimes appear absurd, as when a farmer is called a "shepherd" or a panther a "tiger." Because the neoclassicists used generalized diction in striving for universality, they also overworked the device of personification. Eighteenth-century iconography shows the same tendency in medals, wallpaper, engravings, and other objects that represent such topics as America Guided by Wisdom or Liberty Triumphant over Oppression.

3. Satire. The neoclassicists favored satire because it seemed an effective way to bring about the rule of reason. These writers excelled in working with ideas, in explaining and arguing, in exposing vice and folly. When they tried to wax lyrical, however, they often failed.

SATIRE AND NATIONALISM IN EIGHTEENTH-CENTURY AMERICA

Satirical poetry appeared early in the eighteenth century. Chief among the satirists was Ebenezer Cook (or Cooke), who viciously but amusingly attacked the life of colonial Maryland in a long poem called *The Sot-Weed Factor* (1708).[1]

A great impetus to satire came from the nationalism of the Revolutionary War and the Federalist era. As might be expected of those heated times, the writers pulled few punches and often hit below the belt. For example, in "The Battle of the Kegs" (1778), a ballad by Francis Hopkinson (1737–1791), one stanza refers pointedly to a scandal involving General William Howe and Mrs. Joshua Loring:

> Sir William he, snug as a flea,
>   Lay all this time a snoring,
> Nor dream'd of harm as he lay warm,
>   In bed with Mrs. Loring.[2]

Whatever their subjects, American satirists wrote with the idea of cleansing the New World of Old World impurities. They attacked England's government, politics, and army, the ethics of Lord Chesterfield, the infidelity of Voltaire, and any other threat from abroad to the paradisiacal purity of America.

THE CONNECTICUT WITS

The most important group of poets during this period of intense nationalism were known as the Connecticut or Hartford Wits: John Trumbull, Timothy Dwight, Joel Barlow, Richard Alsop (1751–1816), David Humphreys (1753–1818), and several others, almost all associated with Yale College. Their individual works—and such joint efforts as *The Anarchiad* (1786–1787) by Humphreys, Barlow, Trumbull, and Dr. Lemuel Hopkins (1750–1801)—reveal indebtedness to Samuel Butler's *Hudibras,* Alexander Pope's *Dunciad,* and various other British satires. Even when the Wits turned from neoclassicism to experiment briefly with the ideas and tech-

1. For comment and bibliography, see Hubbell (1954), pp. 63–65, 926.
2. *Pennsylvania Packet,* March 4, 1778.

niques of romanticism, they borrowed from such Old World authors as Milton and Goldsmith.

Despite their imitativeness, the Wits had religious and political ties that clearly distinguished them from their British counterparts. For example, as Calvinists, they could hardly subscribe to the deism Pope expounded in *The Essay on Man*. During the Revolutionary War, moreover, they actually became a new kind of writer—not Tory, but Whig; not colonial, but American—yet not radical either, for their conservative outlook kept them from sympathizing with the French Revolution, democracy, or Jeffersonianism. Federalists and Calvinists they remained throughout their lives, Barlow proving a notable exception.

In subject matter as well as outlook, their work was distinctive and, at times, even original. Trumbull satirized education at Yale; Dwight analyzed the various levels of society in Connecticut; and Barlow extracted poetry from a bowl of mush. Previous American writers had also found their subjects in the life around them but had never approached these themes with such patriotism.

John Trumbull (1750–1831). Of the three major Connecticut Wits, John Trumbull wrote the best satire, although he had a shorter literary career than the others.

Trumbull passed the entrance examination for Yale at the age of seven but waited until he was thirteen to enter the college. Throughout his nine years' stay at Yale, where he received a bachelor's and a master's degree, he distinguished himself as both student and tutor. After criticizing the college curriculum in a long, satirical poem, *The Progress of Dulness,* he moved to Boston (1773), studied law for a year in John Adams's office, and familiarized himself with the material that would make up *M'Fingal,* his verse-satire on the Revolutionary War. These poems earned him an enduring reputation, but he could not match them in his later work and his literary career gradually gave way to a legal one. A staunch Federalist, he served his native state as both legislator and judge.

Representative Works

The Progress of Dulness (Part I, 1772; Parts II and III, 1773). A long narrative verse-satire on contemporary education. Part I criticizes college and ministry, blaming the dullness of the latter on the poor curriculum of the former. Part II satirizes the fop whose college career consists of learning to be a freethinker and a seducer. Part III deals with another universal type, the coquette, and advocates reform in the education of women. In their story line the parts are interlinked. Tom Brainless, the "hero" of Part I, goes to college, becomes a minister, and ultimately marries Harriet Simper, the "hero" of Part III, who is rebounding from an affair with Dick Hairbrain, the "hero" of Part II. An amusing passage, describing a prevalent academic disease that seizes Tom Brainless, is typical of the octosyllabic couplets throughout:

> Thĕn év'rў bóok, whĭch óught tŏ pléase,
> Stĭrs úp thĕ séeds ŏf díre dĭséase;
> Gréek spòils hĭs éyes, thĕ prínt's sŏ fíne,
> Grŏwn dím wĭth stúdў, ór wĭth wíne;
> Ŏf *Túllў's* látĭn múch ăfráid,
> Ĕach páge, hĕ cálls thĕ dóctŏr's áid;
> Whĭle gĕómĕtrý, wĭth línes sŏ cróokĕd,
> Sprăins áll hĭs wíts tŏ óvĕrlóok ĭt.[3]

(Pt. I, ll. 97–104)

There are occasional mock-heroic descriptions; for example, a "squadron" of coquettes prepares to conquer the eligible males at Sunday meeting (Part II, l. 273).

M'Fingal (Canto I, which later became Cantos I and II, was published in 1776 but dated 1775; the complete poem, in four cantos, was first published in 1782). The cornerstone of Trumbull's reputation; a mock epic of 3,282 lines. The story is set in a small Massachusetts town during the Revolutionary War. Honorius (a Whig) and M'Fingal (a Tory squire) debate at morning and afternoon sessions of a town meeting (Cantos I and II). When M'Fingal is tarred and feathered for trying to cut down a Whig liberty pole (Canto III), he realizes the futility of the Tory cause. At a clandestine gathering of fellow Tories, he describes gloomy visions of British defeats. The Whigs break up the meeting, and M'Fingal heads for Boston (Canto IV). We must not overestimate the patriotic sentiments of the poem, which aims to satirize bombastic oratory and demagoguery, no matter what their side.

While the subject matter of *M'Fingal* is indigenous, its style derives from Old World satirists and epic writers. The strained rhymes resemble those in Samuel Butler's *Hudibras,* and the swiftly moving octosyllabic meter imitates the work of Charles Churchill. Mock-epic elements include the hero's genealogy, the long speeches, battles of armies and single combatants, the intervention of the gods in these battles (Canto II, ll. 779–787; Canto III, ll. 349–362), the descent to the underworld (in this case, M'Fingal's cellar), visions of the future (Cantos II, IV), and various catalogues (for example, of British abuses, Tory writers, and Whig demagogues). In mock-epic irony, the English are praised for bravely conquering such formidable foes as beetles, mosquitoes, oxen, geese, and half-starved prisoners. Nevertheless, Trumbull apparently intended *M'Fingal* as

---

3. *The Poetical Works of John Trumbull,* 2 vols. (Hartford: Samuel G. Goodrich, 1820). The second and eighth lines of the quoted passage also scan well with reversed initial feet: "Stírs ŭp" and "Spráins ăll."

something more than a pure mock epic: He subtitled it "A Modern Epic Poem," cast it in an untraditional number of cantos, and dealt with a subject of great import and seriousness.

Timothy Dwight (1752–1817). The most militantly orthodox and least poetically gifted of the three major Connecticut Wits was Jonathan Edwards's grandson Timothy Dwight.

Dwight entered Yale at the age of thirteen, graduated with highest honors in 1769, and tutored there from 1771 to 1777. After serving as chaplain in the Continental Army (1777–1779), he became pastor of a Congregational church at Greenfield Hill, Connecticut (1783–1795), where he also established and conducted a coeducational school. In 1795 he was elected president of Yale. During his twenty-two years in office he modernized the college administration and curriculum without compromising his orthodox principles. Throughout his life he showed a remarkable talent for self-discipline. Sometimes this had ill effects, as when he damaged his health with such ascetic habits as studying fourteen hours a day and limiting his dinners to only a dozen mouthfuls.

Dwight wrote some fifteen volumes of prose and poetry, but almost none of it has been reprinted. Usually recalled by title alone are his *Conquest of Canaan* (1785), a biblical epic in heroic couplets, and *The Triumph of Infidelity* (1788), a verse-satire on deism, universalism, and contemporary clergy.

Representative Works

"Columbia, Columbia, to Glory Arise" (written ca. 1778). A popular patriotic song Dwight composed when he was a chaplain.

Greenfield Hill (1794). A 4,337-line poem divided into seven parts.[4] Dwight wrote it to convince his readers of both the actual and potential superiority of the New World to the Old. He accused Europe of fostering poverty, luxury, irreligion, and war. Its art he labeled shockingly corrupt, and he even censured that paragon of English neoclassicism, Alexander Pope, for "obscene" lines (p. 181). Adopting the microcosmic viewpoint of the local-colorist, he glorified his country by glorifying his region.

The landscape of Greenfield Hill afforded him a panoramic prospect, and his imagination stimulated him to an even more far-reaching vision. What he saw was an American utopia—everywhere godliness, happiness, competence, and the "golden mean" between poverty and luxury (p. 17).

In contrast with such visions are the pragmatic aspects of Parts V and VI, which Dwight devoted to various kinds of advice. In fact, Part VI in particular serves as a verse-parallel to *Poor Richard*. Here Dwight ranged widely in his aphorisms, proffering amazingly practical advice on agriculture, education, and other topics. In all, *Greenfield Hill* must be regarded as a handbook for the new Adam in his new Eden. It boosted his morale,

4. Quoted here from the first edition (New York: Childs and Swaine, 1794).

taught him how to live, and in Part VII tendered him a vision of a worldwide utopia in which an already perfected West renews the jaded East.

On the whole, Dwight's techniques in this poem fail to convey his ideas artistically. True, the panoramic views are interesting, and he achieved some metrical diversity by writing Part I in blank verse, Part IV in Spenserian stanzas, and the other parts in octosyllabic and heroic couplets. Still, the poem was an imitative exercise. For example, the overall plan with its hill perspective was probably derived from John Denham's *Cooper's Hill,* while Part II was modeled on Goldsmith's *Deserted Village.* Actually Dwight's adaptations from British poets serve to bolster the central theme of *Greenfield Hill*—the Old World–New World contrast. Less excusable are the poem's fuzzy images and pervadingly abstract language. A single passage of eight lines (Part II, ll. 109–116) contains no less than seven personifications.

Travels in New England and New York (1821–1822). The best of Dwight's prose. Four volumes of travel letters recording his observations when he took to walking and riding long distances for his health. Letter 8, on the residents of the Connecticut Valley, parallels his enthusiasm in *Greenfield Hill.*

Joel Barlow (1754–1812). Although in his youth Joel Barlow was one of the Connecticut Wits, he ultimately differed from them in his thinking, if not in his writing style. Philosophically he belongs with Paine, Jefferson, and other eighteenth-century liberals.

Barlow was born and raised in rural Connecticut and educated at Yale, where he took his B.A. in 1778 and did postgraduate work. From Timothy Dwight, one of his tutors, he received some instruction in composing poetry, and he later helped write *The Anarchiad,* a serialized satire on democratic liberalism. At the same time, he proved himself as ambitious, verbose, and patriotic as the other wits by composing *The Vision of Columbus* (1787), an epic-length poem in nine books which he later expanded into *The Columbiad* (1807). In 1788 Barlow went to Europe as an agent of the Scioto Land Company, and during his seventeen years' stay there he became a democrat rather than a Federalist. In France he consorted with revolutionaries and was made a French citizen. In England he got to know Tom Paine and under his influence attacked monarchy and conservatism by writing *The Conspiracy of Kings* (1792) and *Advice to the Privileged Orders* (1792, 1793). *The Hasty Pudding,* a less serious work but one of more literary interest, also dates from this time. It was occasioned by Barlow's memories of home when he came upon this Yankee dish in Savoy.

Barlow served as American consul to Algiers (1795–1797). Not until 1805 did he return to the States, and in 1811 he was back in Europe as minister to France. A year later he died in Poland, where he had gone in an attempt to arrange a treaty with Napoleon.

Representative Works

Advice to the Privileged Orders. A defense in clear, reasoned prose of the principles behind the American and French revolutions and an attack on crown, church, and army as harmful survivals of feudalism. Published less than one year after Paine's *Rights of Man, Part I,* Barlow's treatise represents a second major salvo against Edmund Burke's conservatism.

The Hasty Pudding (w. 1793). A seriocomic poem in praise of cornmeal mush. Its charm, complex tone, and interesting mixture of neoclassic and romantic elements make it one of the best American poems of the eighteenth century. Barlow establishes the seriocomic tone at the very beginning, first by the academic joke of mistranslating a Latin epigraph and then by a serious "Preface" that explains his purpose—to show Americans the worth of a simple diet.

This variation places *The Hasty Pudding* in several genres. It belongs to local-color literature, as it carefully portrays the regional folkways of New England. From it one learns, for example, the ritual of the husking bee, an important pioneer custom. In its serious aspects, as an extension of two strains in English literature, the poem might even be called a pastoral. Like Alexander Pope and the followers of Theocritus and Virgil, Barlow waxed nostalgic over rural simplicity, while, like the followers of Edmund Spenser, he strove to depict rural life with realism. In its comic aspects, *The Hasty Pudding* belongs to a popular neoclassic genre—the mock-epic or mock-heroic poem, which lavishes a lofty style on a trivial subject. Poetic diction abounds: There are wights, swains, maids, and nymphs; a bird is called a "feather'd robber"; a scarecrow a "man of straw" (ll. 204–205).[5] Periphrasis, or roundabout statement, appears in the superbly comic directions for eating mush:

> First in your bowl the milk abundant take,
> Then drop with care along the silver lake
> Your flakes of pudding; these at first will hide
> Their little bulk beneath the swelling tide;
> But when their growing mass no more can sink,
> When the soft island looms above the brink,
> Then check your hand; you've got the portion due,
> So taught our sires, and what they taught is true.
>
> (ll. 332–339)

Also part of this lofty manner are numerous inversions, apostrophes, and classical allusions. Barlow addresses one verse paragraph to a cow and in another invokes mush instead of his muse. Other epic conventions adapted for the poem include games (the husking bee), genealogies (the ancestry of

5. Joel Barlow, *The Hasty Pudding* (New York: Fellows & Adam, 1796).

mush), catalogues (the various regional names of mush), and wandering heroes (mush migrates to Savoy, where the author, also a wanderer, finds it). Last, although the poem is written in couplets and cantos, Barlow treats these structural devices with a freedom more akin to romanticism than to neoclassicism. The couplets are not closed and the cantos, despite a seasonal progression, are loosely organized.

"Advice to a Raven in Russia" (w. December 1812). A denunciation, in iambic pentameter couplets, of Napoleon. Composed in the last month of Barlow's life, the poem expresses gothic horror through an ironic apostrophe to a raven in search of carrion.

PHILLIS WHEATLEY (1754?–1784)

Also writing in the neoclassical mode was early America's foremost black poet, African-born Phillis Wheatley. She was transported to America in 1761. Though technically a slave in the household of John Wheatley, a Boston merchant, she was treated like one of the family and in 1771 received her freedom. Encouraged in her learning, she achieved considerable reputation both as scholar and poet, not only in Boston but also in London, which she visited in 1773. Her *Poems on Various Subjects, Religious and Moral* (1773) may well be the first book by an Afro-American. The heroic couplets, poetic diction, Christian imagery, and literary allusions that abound in her poetry place it among the other neoclassic works discussed in this chapter. However, in "On Being Brought from Africa to America," "To the University of Cambridge, in New-England," and "To S. M. a Young African Painter, On Seeing His Works," a new note is struck as the poet identifies with her people.

7
Preromantics

In eighteenth-century America, as in eighteenth-century England, the dominant literary spirit was neoclassical; the recessive literary spirit, romantic. During the first half of the nineteenth century, romanticism dominated the literature of both countries.

ROMANTICISM

Although romanticism was not always a conscious revolt against neoclassicism, it did replace the neoclassic emphasis on reason with its own emphasis on the imagination and emotions, and the neoclassic emphasis on authority with an emphasis on individuality. Remoteness and strangeness are also often cited as clues to romanticism. Linked to these qualities are other romantic traits:

Mysticism, pantheism, and transcendentalism

Sentimentalism, sensibility, and melancholy

Gothicism (both gothic horror and Gothic architecture)

Humanitarianism and democracy

Love of nature, animals, plants, wild (picturesque) scenery, and rural life

Primitivism (belief in the superiority of the simple life, often of a society remote in time or place)

Antiquarianism (interest in the prehistoric, medieval, and recent pasts as well as the classical past; interest in the early Celts, Scandinavians, Amerinds, and so on, as well as in the Greeks and Romans)

More freedom in poetry: greater use of lyrics (sonnets, elegies, odes, and other vehicles of emotion), narratives (ballads, metrical romances), and verse forms other than the heroic couplet (blank verse, Spenserian stanza, and—in the nineteenth century—free verse); less use of "poetic" diction

The personal or informal essay: This genre, popular in both the eighteenth and nineteenth centuries, often displayed a willingness to sacrifice strict form and logic to wit, humor, and the expression of individuality.

America had its counterparts to Gray, Goldsmith, and the other English preromantics. None of these writers was completely romantic, but all possessed some aspects of the romantic spirit. Even Barlow and Dwight, whom we have discussed as neoclassicists, had their romantic side. Other eighteenth-century preromantics include gothic novelist Charles Brockden Brown (1771–1810); nature writers Alexander Wilson (1766–1813), John Bartram (1699–1777), and his son William Bartram (1739–1823); poet Nathaniel Evans (1742–1767); essayists Joseph Dennie (1768–1812) and Francis Hopkinson (1737–1791) (Hopkinson's "On White-Washing" [1785] is a charming example of the informal essay); and the principals of the present chapter—Crèvecoeur and Freneau.

ST. JOHN DE CRÈVECOEUR (1735–1813), "AN AMERICAN FARMER"

Rural life, one of the prime love interests of romantic authors, enjoyed no better champion than St. John de Crèvecoeur, "the American Farmer."

Life. Crèvecoeur led a more complex and varied life than his appellation—derived from the title of his famous *Letters from an American Farmer*—would indicate. By birth and upbringing he was a Norman aristocrat, born Michel-Guillaume Jean de Crèvecoeur. He attended the Collège du Mont in his native Caen and perhaps continued his education in England, where he lived with distant relatives. In 1755 Crèvecoeur migrated to America, where he traveled widely. During the French and Indian War, he served with the French militia in Canada as a surveyor-cartographer and later as a second lieutenant in the regular army. After the war he began life anew under the name of James Hector St. John. He worked as a trader and surveyor in New York and Vermont (1764), traveled south to Virginia (1766), west to Detroit and the Great Lakes country (1767), became a naturalized citizen of New York (1765), married Mehitable Tippet (1769), and, buying 120 acres of land in Orange County, assumed the role he would soon depict in his first and best book. At his farm, Pine Hill, life was idyllic until the Revolutionary War, when it changed into a nightmare.

Unsympathetic to the Patriots and perhaps desirous of establishing claim to his father's estate, Crèvecoeur returned to the Old World with his firstborn son, leaving his wife with the other two children at Pine Hill. Before he embarked from New York (1780), however, the British imprisoned him for several months as a spy—a traumatic experience that must have soured his earlier satisfaction with their "mild" rule. Still, it was to a London publisher that he sold the manuscript of his *Letters from an*

American Farmer, written at Pine Hill. This edition (1782) was followed by Irish, Dutch, and German editions; and Crèvecoeur himself radically revised and enlarged it into several French editions (1784, 1787). Meanwhile, chiefly through the patronage of Madame d'Houdetot, he found himself lionized by French society.

In 1783 Crèvecoeur returned to America as French consul to find that Pine Hill had been burned in an Indian raid and his wife had died. He served with distinction as consul until the French Revolution. After 1790 he lived in Europe.

Letters from an American Farmer (1782). This book, consisting of twelve essays on the British colonies in North America, was probably the first such work written from direct observation by an American settler. Although Crèvecoeur accomplished much of this social analysis through expository writing, the character, moods, circumstances, and vicissitudes of his persona are so thoroughly developed that the work verges on being a novel. Romantic elements—primitivism, nature worship, sentimentalism, humanitarianism, and gothicism—abound here but are uniquely shaped and sometimes contradicted by Crèvecoeur's personality and experience. The persona himself assumes a kind of primitivistic pose. He lives close to nature, knows little of reading or writing, considers himself a provincial alien to the sophistication of Europe, and in Letter XII, facing the violence of the Revolutionary War, even resolves to live in an Indian village. Yet he shudders at the possibility of his children marrying these Indians or becoming hunters instead of farmers. In his treatment of nature, he carried on the tradition fostered by John Smith and William Byrd of recounting natural wonders (his tale of the boy killed by snake fangs embedded in his father's boots was old when he told it and even today survives on the oral level). As a preromantic, Crèvecoeur anticipated Bryant's druidism; Dwight's, Barlow's, and Whittier's bucolic scenes; Coleridge's and Thoreau's reverence for animal life. Like the best romantic nature writers, he knew how to fuse close observation with symbolic meaning. But unlike many of his contemporaries, he occasionally viewed nature as harmful and even vicious. His habitual sentimentalism often proves irritating, but it also has its better moments. In one powerful passage it is combined with humanitarianism and gothic horror in depicting a caged Negro whose eyes have been pecked out by birds. In the book's closing letter, as the persona finds his idyll shattered by the Revolutionary War, the tragedy becomes national as well as personal: Crèvecoeur stands for all Americans whose dreams have failed.

Letter III ("What Is an American?") is notable for its idealization of America and its optimistic tone. Throughout this often-quoted chapter Crèvecoeur stressed the metamorphosis undergone by immigrants to the new country, and he clearly prefigured the melting-pot image when he noted that "here individuals of all nations are melted into a new race of men" (pp.

54–55).[1] The idea of America as an asylum for Europe's poor he borrowed from Abbé Raynal (the historian-philosopher to whom he dedicated the *Letters*), but the concept was no doubt confirmed by his own experience. In this early letter optimism predominates, and even Crèvecoeur's low opinion of the frontiersman is modified when he reminds us that frontiers are inevitably purged by "prosperity," "law," and shifts in population (p. 60).

PHILIP FRENEAU (1752–1832)

As a nature poet, Philip Freneau stands chronologically between Bradstreet and Bryant; as a gothicist, between Wigglesworth and Poe; as a primitivist, between Morton and Cooper.

Life. Freneau was born in New York City. After graduation from Princeton, he became known as a patriotic and satiric writer. From 1776 to 1779 he spent much of his time in the West Indies before enlisting in the New Jersey militia. In 1780 he was captured as a privateer and held for six weeks in New York harbor—an experience recorded in his satire *The British Prison-Ship*. From 1778 to 1807 he sailed as supercargo, master, or captain of many a merchant vessel; his sea poems were thus authentic. With characteristic passion he also pursued a career of journalism. As Jeffersonian editor of the *National Gazette,* he attacked Hamiltonian Federalism with such venom that Washington reportedly called him "that rascal Freneau." In 1807 Freneau retired from the sea but continued to write. He was much given to revising his work, and he supervised collections of it in 1809 and 1815. Poor, neglected, anachronistic, Freneau lived well into the Knickerbocker period.

Freneau as a Transitional Poet. In some ways Freneau's poetry was neoclassical; in others, romantic. Such pieces as *The British Prison-Ship* and "To Sir Toby" are linked to neoclassicism not only through their satire but also through their heroic couplets. Also, like many neoclassicists, Freneau espoused deism and even wrote doctrinal verse on the subject ("On the Religion of Nature," "On the Uniformity and Perfection of Nature," "On the Universality and Other Attributes of the God of Nature"). But romantic elements are in greater abundance in Freneau's work. In many poems he let fancy or imagination dominate reason or gave vent to emotions in scenes of gothic horror and in melancholy musings over mutability, his favorite theme. Such meditations worked best when poets could philosophize on some kind of symbol, for example, the ruins of a castle. Freneau found indigenous counterparts for these traditional antiquities and thus helped create a New World symbology with poems like "The Deserted Farm-House" and "The Indian Burying Ground." He also exploited primitivism

1. *Letters from an American Farmer . . . Reprinted from the Original Edition* (New York: Fox, Duffield, 1904).

("The Indian Student") and nature, including gothic scenes from his own life ("The Hurricane"). And to give his poems a truly American flavor, he habitually cited native flora and fauna.

Representative Works[2]

"The Power of Fancy" (w. 1770). Describes the exercise of Fancy as a cosmic trip through space and time to the remote places for which the romantic spirit yearns. If the poem suffers from erratic shifts of person (sometimes speaking *to* Fancy and sometimes *about* her), it pleases with its panoramic imagery, clipped iambic tetrameter ($\prime \smile \prime \smile \prime \smile \prime$), and rich allusiveness. There are echoes of the deists, Milton, James Macpherson, and Joseph Warton.

"The House of Night: A Vision" (1779). Freneau's most ambitious gothic and graveyard poem; 136 quatrains describing the death of Death. In true romantic vein, the narrator attributes this vision to Fancy, who works during our sleep "when Reason holds no sway" (1786 ed., p. 102, stanza 6). With remarkably sensuous detail, Freneau pictures the midnight hour, the gloomy landscape, and the hideous figure of Death. Here he clearly anticipates Poe.

"The Vanity of Existence" (1781). Melancholy lyric in elegiac rhyme with realistic nautical imagery.

"To the Memory of the Brave Americans" (1781). Also known as "Eutaw Springs"; a patriotic lyric in elegiac rhyme. Here Freneau achieved emotion without bombast or invective, but he confused the effect by addressing at least five audiences.

"To Sir Toby" (w. 1784). A scathing denunciation of slavery in Jamaica. Neoclassic in its allusions, satire, and couplets; romantic in its humanitarianism and gothicism.

"The Wild Honey Suckle" (w. 1786). A nature lyric on the mutability of flowers. Unlike most romantic poets, Freneau leaves to his readers the extension of the symbol's meaning and its application to man. His choice of flower places him with poets who celebrated nature in its humble and familiar aspects—poets like Blake, Wordsworth, and Burns (whose "To a Mountain Daisy" was also written in 1786). The last six lines of "The Wild Honey Suckle," which employ iambic tetrameter in a Venus and Adonis rhyme scheme *(a b a b c c),* are frequently praised and quoted.

"The Indian Burying Ground" (1787). Probably Freneau's finest lyric.

2. Quotations are from the following editions: *The Poems of Philip Freneau* (Philadelphia: Printed by Francis Bailey, 1786); *The Miscellaneous Works of Mr. Philip Freneau* (Philadelphia: Printed by Francis Bailey, 1788); *Poems Written . . . by Philip Freneau, of New Jersey* (Mount Pleasant: Printed at the Press of the Author, 1795); *A Collection of Poems . . . by Philip Freneau,* 2 vols. (New York: David Longworth, 1815).

Exemplifying the shift from neoclassicism to romanticism, it begins in the tone of calm argument, with the abstract language typical of neoclassic poets. But as early as the second stanza, romanticism begins to take over. Instead of arguing from the authority of Greece and Rome, the poet turns to the "ancients of these lands" (1788 ed., p. 188). He not only muses in the manner of the preromantic graveyard poets but also proves himself an early primitivist by positing the superiority of the noble savage to the white man. He praises the Indians, not for believing in an active afterlife, but for translating this belief into their burial customs. Thus when he writes, "They do not *lie,* but here they *sit*" (p. 188), *lie* could mean action as well as position, indicating that the Indians, unlike the whites, pointed in their burying ground to the truth about their beliefs. Next, as the poet shows the reader visions of Indian children, an Indian queen, and an Indian hunter, the imagination sensualizes the ideas presented earlier. When Freneau concludes that reason must now "bow the knee" to "shadows and delusions" (p. 189), he clearly summarizes this movement from the neoclassic to the romantic. Yet we are left with some ambiguity. Do the "shadows and delusions" connote skepticism about immortality? Do they connote the actual superiority of reason?

"Ode: God Save the Rights of Man" (1793). A patriotic piece sung to the tune of "God Save the King" and undoubtedly alluding to Tom Paine's *Rights of Man.*

"To an Author" (first published 1788 as "An Author's Soliloquy"). Iambic tetrameter couplets expressing the discontent of a romanticist and would-be professional with the American literary climate. Only satire, the "least engaging" type of poetry, survives "where rigid Reason reigns, alone, / Where flowery Fancy has no sway" (1795 ed., p. 327).

"On a Honey Bee Drinking from a Glass of Wine and Drowned Therein" (1797). Humorous lyric; Freneau's light verse at its best. Venus and Adonis rhyme is adapted to iambic trimeter and tetrameter: a^4b^3 (or ^{4})a^4b^3 (or ^{4})c^4c^4. The insect-questioning device appears also in "To a Caty-Did."

"To a Caty-Did" (first known publication 1815). A seriocomic lyric that at first seems nothing more than light verse. The refrain sounds like pure nonsense, while the manipulation of "Caty-did" into "Caty do" and "Caty not" (1815 ed., pp. 35–36) must be classified as wordplay. Moreover, the lines are short and clipped (´ ˘ ´ ˘ ´ ˘ ´), moving with a quickness by no means contemplative. Behind all this pleasantry, however, Freneau manages to work with ideas, including death, mutability, and tenderness for the lower forms of life. The Caty of line 30 is a new Caty, a human Caty, perhaps, as Theodore Hornberger suggests, Freneau's daughter Catherine. With charming obliqueness the poet chides her for her mistreatment of Caty-did. The poem concludes with a moral that recalls Pope's *Essay on Man* (1733) and Burns's "To a Mouse" (1786). If children cannot see even so far as the coming winter, adults cannot peer into the afterlife; hence the fate of Caty-did, who may represent all creation, remains unknown.

8
Early Fiction and Drama

The colonists got along for nearly two centuries without indigenous novels and plays. Then, just as their new nation came into being, they began to develop these forms and to argue over their validity. English drama had already accumulated an impressive history, culminating in the glorious age of Shakespeare. Novel writing, however, was a new art; its American practitioners lagged only a few years behind its English practitioners. Both these forms were used to express the nationalistic spirit that dominated the new republic.

EARLY FICTION

Developing in a culture that sometimes frowned upon it, American fiction tended to be documentary, moralistic, and either sentimental or satirical. In the late eighteenth and early nineteenth centuries, because many descendants of the Puritans regarded novels as a pack of lies and a source of vice, some authors wrote prose fiction anonymously, and readers often perused it in secrecy. To counteract such attitudes, novelists tried to prove their work beneficial. They chose actual people and events for their subjects; if this was impossible, they at least claimed to have so chosen. Many a novel of this period bears the subtitle "A Tale of Truth" or contains statements of its veracity in preface, text, or footnotes. The first American novel, William Hill Brown's *The Power of Sympathy* (1789), was suppressed after publication because its sensational plot, which involves seduction, near incest, and suicide, was easily recognized as depicting an actual situation. Frequent moralizing was employed to help upgrade fiction, and authors seldom hesitated to call themselves moralists rather than fictionists. All this, of course, irritates modern readers as does the sentimentalism. However, there was always an antidote to sentimentalism in satire. During the early days of the Republic, readers who cried over the ever-popular

Charlotte Temple (1791) by Mrs. Susanna Haswell Rowson could turn for laughs to such fiction as Brackenridge's *Modern Chivalry,* Tabitha Tenney's *Female Quixotism* (1801), and Royall Tyler's *Algerine Captive* (1797), where they might find satire on all manner of things, including literature.

Especially popular were three types of novels: epistolary, seduction, and gothic. (Some books, like Charles Brockden Brown's *Wieland,* encompassed all three types.) The epistolary novel, which owed its popularity to Samuel Richardson's *Pamela,* was employed in various ways. An entire novel might be written as a single letter, or it might contain a number of letters, perhaps fifty, by several characters. With multiple correspondents, an author could achieve multiple viewpoints and an accompanying psychological richness (see, for example, Hannah Foster's *Coquette* [1797] and the novels of Charles Brockden Brown). The seduction theme not only attracted readers but also provided opportunity for moralizing. In William Hill Brown's *Power of Sympathy* this element supplies essential background, and in Mrs. Rowson's *Charlotte Temple* it is central to the plot. Again, the influence of Samuel Richardson, the supreme moralist among English novelists, can be seen.

All the best-known early American gothic novels were written by one author, Charles Brockden Brown. Actually, the gothic form had a rather limited vogue in America and, as employed by Brown, was radically altered from the English model.

Hugh Henry Brackenridge (1748–1816). The earliest American author to write satirical prose fiction that effectively dealt with the country's emerging democracy was Hugh Henry Brackenridge, a colorful figure from the Pennsylvania frontier.

Brackenridge received a master's degree from Princeton (1774), served as chaplain in Washington's army (1776–1778), and edited the *United States Magazine* at Philadelphia (1779). In 1781 he moved to Pittsburgh, then a frontier village. There and in Carlisle, Pennsylvania, he spent the rest of his life pursuing the law, politics, and literature with the assurance and zeal of a classicist bent on the intellectual salvation of the Wild West. He was elected to the Pennsylvania State Assembly in 1786 and appointed to the Pennsylvania Supreme Court in 1799. He helped establish the University of Pittsburgh and also Pittsburgh's first bookstore and newspaper. Yet the public remembered him equally well as an eccentric who once rode naked in a rainstorm to save the clothing he had tucked under the saddle.

Brackenridge's most important work, *Modern Chivalry,* was issued piecemeal between 1792 and 1815; the 1815 edition not only added new material but incorporated the previous five installments. The overall purpose of this huge book was to explain democracy to Americans, and each installment had its own theme toward this aim.

A difficult work to classify, *Modern Chivalry* lacks the sexuality of a picaresque romance but has wanderers, rogues, and episodic structure. It also comes close at times to Swift's *Tale of a Tub* and to Cervantes's *Don Quixote,* but its mood is not so harsh as Swift's, and its principal character (Captain John Farrago) is only occasionally quixotic. Satirical prose narrative seems the best label for it. As satire, few works have been so comprehensive. Brackenridge laughs at religious, national, and racial groups (Quakers, Scotch Presbyters, Irish, French, Indians), societies (The Order of the Cincinnati, The American Philosophical Society), occupations (fortune-telling, journalism, criticism, education, medicine, law, religion), and customs (dueling, slavery, treaty making). All these targets he regarded as either abuses or abusers of democracy. Democracy itself he never satirized because he considered it a desirable and workable system of government. But with the realism and fear of excess that characterized the eighteenth-century neoclassicists, he maintained that men must be kept out of offices for which they are unqualified. To demonstrate this lesson, Brackenridge used the characters of Captain Farrago and his illiterate servant Teague O'Regan. Teague strives to hold political office, to join the American Philosophical Society, and to become a minister, a lawyer, and a lady's man. Sometimes Farrago dissuades him from social climbing; on other occasions Teague must learn from experience. The abundant humor in the book often takes the form of artistic indirection, employed even in the purportedly serious essay-chapters that come between episodes. Irony appears, for example, in the author's avowal that his book was intended only as an example of style and would therefore be completely devoid of "thought, or the smallest degree of sense" (1: 9).[1] In some aspects, *Modern Chivalry* anticipates the work of Irving, Longstreet, and other nineteenth-century writers. It mixes fantasy with realism and the sophisticated with the uncouth. Brackenridge can describe the exotic sights in a petrified cave on one page, a bit of homely local color on another. However, despite its historical significance and its intrinsic merit as comedy, *Modern Chivalry* suffers from the limitations of its episodic structure and from awkward dialogue.

Charles Brockden Brown (1771–1810). America's most important early novelist was Charles Brockden Brown. In its gothic and psychological aspects, his work foreshadows Cooper, Poe, Hawthorne, and even James. In addition to this significance, it possesses undeniable literary merit and force of its own.

LIFE. Brown's "natal soil"[2] was Philadelphia. His Quaker parents sent him to the Friends' Latin School, and in 1787 he was apprenticed to a Philadelphia lawyer. Brown soon, however, gave up law for literature. During the yellow fever epidemic of 1798 he contracted the disease but eventually recovered. This very year marks the beginning of an amazing

1. H. H. Brackenridge, *Modern Chivalry* (Philadelphia: John M'Culloch, 1792).

2. A characteristically fancy phrase from Brown's *Arthur Mervyn* (Philadelphia: H. Maxwell, 1799).

two-year period in which were published all four of the books that made his reputation. Throughout the rest of his life, he continued to write copiously, rapidly, compulsively; but even though he engaged in journalistic work and became a partner in his brothers' mercantile firm, he found it difficult to support his wife and four children. At the age of thirty-nine he died of consumption.

ACHIEVEMENT. Despite his frenzied and slipshod methods of composition, Brown exhibited great emotional power and intensity, created a New World form of the gothic novel, outdistanced every American novelist before Cooper, and was the first native novelist to achieve a transatlantic reputation. His emotional impact comes not only from his first-person narration but also from his tone. He wrote, observed a shrewd critic, like someone who "believes every word of his own story" and is "telling you of it—with his face flushed."[3] But Brown vowed not to fill his stories with the *"peurile [sic] superstition and exploded manners, Gothic castles and chimeras"* used by Mrs. Radcliffe and other Old World romancers. Instead he set himself the task of *"calling forth the passions and engaging the sympathy of the reader, by means hitherto unemployed by preceding authors"* (1: 4).[4] Ventriloquism, spontaneous combustion, and sleepwalking were among the devices Brown originated for this purpose. Still, the artistic appeal of his novels lies less in these inventions than in his ability to plumb complex states of mind. Here he anticipates Hawthorne and James.

Although Brown wrote enough reviews to be considered by some as the founder of American literary criticism, he earned his lasting reputation mainly with his novels.

Representative Works

Wieland; or, The Transformation: An American Tale (1798). Brown's best-known work; a combination psychological novel and gothic romance. Ventriloquism, human spontaneous combustion, and murder constitute its three main terror ingredients. Since the first two were quite unusual, Brown took pains to authenticate them in footnotes referring to scientific sources. (Later novels that employed the device of spontaneous combustion include Dickens's *Bleak House* and Melville's *Redburn*.) The plot traces the transformation of Theodore Wieland, Jr., into a religious maniac who carries out an imagined command from Heaven to murder his wife and children. But Wieland seems to go through several transformations, and the theme also applies to his sister Clara, their friend Pleyel, and the villainous ventriloquist Carwin. In fact, Wieland finally takes his own life because in a

---

3. X. Y. Z. [John Neal], "American Writers," *Blackwood's Edinburgh Magazine* 16 (1824): 421.

4. Charles Brockden Brown, *Edgar Huntly*, 3 vols. (Philadelphia: Thomas Dobson and Asbury Dickins, 1799).

momentary return to sanity he sees the naked horror of his deeds and is "transformed at once" into a *"man of sorrows"* (p. 281).[5] Instead of stopping this story with Wieland's suicide, Brown tacked on a conventional happy ending in which Clara regains her equanimity and marries Pleyel. Critics disagree on the artistic merit of this ending, just as they disagree on the function of the Maxwell-Stuart subplot, the degree of Carwin's villainy, and Brown's attitude toward heredity and psychology. All seem to agree that the book's faults include wordiness, stuffy diction, and contradictory details (the result of Brown's habitual neglect of revision). Its indisputable merits include unusual terror devices; effective use of light and sound; multiple points of view; its swift, suspenseful plot; its intensity and power; and its penetration into the inner mind of its characters. Some of these merits are well illustrated in the scene where Wieland recalls the supreme joy that came upon him after he killed his wife (Chapter 19). According to Whittier, there was "no more thrilling passage" than this in "the entire range of English literature."[6]

Ormond (1799). Combination gothic, education, and seduction novel. The villain Ormond pursues and is killed by Constantia Dudley, a heroine educated to a life guided by reason. The yellow-fever plague, which Brown knew at first hand, supplied him with material for gothic scenes.

Arthur Mervyn; or, Memoirs of the Year 1793 (Part I, 1799; Part II, 1800). Realistic novel combining initiation, success-story, and gothic motifs. Much of the plot takes place in Philadelphia, where Mervyn, an uneducated rural youth, is befriended and betrayed by various people, including the kindly Dr. Stevens and the villain Welbeck. Here too he experiences the myriad degrees of selflessness and selfishness that yellow fever evokes in the population. The plague scenes, purportedly written to enlist the charity of readers "able to afford relief" (p. vi), qualify not only as history but as American gothic at its goriest. The book is almost hopelessly complicated in plot, but the characterization of Mervyn, whose life mixes benevolence with opportunism, benefits from this complexity.

Edgar Huntly; or, Memoirs of a Sleep-Walker (1799). Gothic-psychological-epistolary-initiation novel that achieves terror through wilderness settings, the bloody enmity between Indians and frontiersmen, and the insanity of Huntly (the narrator) and Clithero, both of whom are sleepwalkers. In its most memorable scene Huntly awakens in the total darkness of a cave, tomahawks a panther, and then rescues a girl from her Indian captors.

5. *Wieland; or The Transformation: An American Tale* (New-York: H. Caritat, 1798).

6. *The Works of John Greenleaf Whittier,* Standard Library Ed. (Boston: Houghton Mifflin [1892]), 7: 393.

EARLY DRAMA

American drama, like American fiction, grew out of unfavorable circumstances and even attempts to suppress it into something at once imitative and nationalistic.

In the sixteenth and seventeenth centuries French and Spanish Catholic priests had used drama for missionary work among the Indians, but in the English colonies its growth was slow. The Puritans, Quakers, and other Protestant groups of New England and the middle colonies echoed the thinking of those who had closed the English theaters from 1642 to 1660. Not only did drama resemble fiction in corrupting the mind, sapping moral energy, and alienating people from the business of everyday life, but it had additional inherent disadvantages: The playhouses provided districts for harlots; acting fostered effeminacy and homosexuality; and stage pageantry represented the pretentiousness that the Puritans and Quakers had kept out of their churches. In the Southern colonies, where gentry like William Byrd shared the tastes of those who had restored the English theater, there were few such objections, and Williamsburg, Virginia, boasted what was probably America's first playhouse.

Of course, most of the early drama was imported from England. British companies performed plays of Congreve, Otway, Gay, Farquhar, and others in Williamsburg, Charleston, New York, Philadelphia, and elsewhere. Native dramatists, with only foreign works for their models, naturally stuck to traditional techniques.

Some dramatists exploited foreign subjects. Among them were Thomas Godfrey, whose *Prince of Parthia* (1767) is considered the first play by an American to be professionally produced; John Howard Payne, whose *Clari, or the Maid of Milan* (1823) contained the song "Home, Sweet Home"; and George Henry Boker, whose *Francesca da Rimini* (1855) took its theme from Dante.

Most American dramatists, however, became quite nationalistic in subject matter and message. They wrote plays about Indians (Major Robert Rogers's *Ponteach,* 1766; James Nelson Barker's *The Indian Princess,* 1808; John Augustus Stone's *Metamora, or The Last of the Wampanoags,* 1829); New England witchcraft (James Nelson Barker's *Superstition,* 1824); the fate of a British spy (William Dunlap's *André,* 1798); and New York social climbers (Anna Cora Mowatt's *Fashion,* 1845).

During the Revolutionary War, dramas championed both sides of the struggle. The English general Burgoyne wrote plays in support of the Loyalists; *The Blockade* was performed in Boston while the British occupied the city. Hugh Henry Brackenridge and Mrs. Mercy Otis Warren wrote on behalf of the Patriots. Following independence, as the nationalistic spirit grew, plays incorporated spread-eagle speeches or confrontations between native and foreign character types.

Royall Tyler (1757–1826). A good specimen of early American drama is *The Contrast,* the most famous work of Royall Tyler, who, typically, was not a professional playwright.

A native of Boston, Tyler earned two degrees from Harvard. His youth was notoriously dissipated, but he eventually settled down and became a successful lawyer. Already known as a wit, he achieved literary fame in a very short time. In March 1787 he paid his first visit to New York City, where he very likely saw Sheridan's *School for Scandal,* which was performed on March 21 of that year. It is quite possible that he had never before seen an actual dramatic performance. Yet, less than three months later, the city was lionizing him for two plays of his own: *The Contrast* and *May Day in Town,* a comic opera (now lost). From this time on Tyler's career was divided between law and literature. He served as judge of the Vermont Supreme Court (1801–1813) and as professor of jurisprudence at the University of Vermont (1811–1814). As a writer he was versatile. His works include *The Algerine Captive* (a novel, 1797), *The Yankey in London* (outlander letters, 1809), the "Colon & Spondee" essays (with Joseph Dennie as coauthor), several plays that never reached the boards, many poems, and reports of Vermont supreme court cases. Tyler's income waned in his latter years, and he died impoverished, leaving his author-wife (Mary Palmer) and ten children.

Initially performed in New York on April 16, 1787, *The Contrast* is distinguished both as the first professionally produced American comedy and as a memorable (though not the earliest) presentation of the stage Yankee, or Jonathan-character. It is also worth noting that the play uses native characters, settings, and themes. For example, opposition to the American theater is satirized when Jonathan, learning that he has visited a playhouse, not a private home, admits that he enjoyed himself but is sure that the candles burned blue and "it smelt tarnally of brimstone" (p. 57).[7] In its main plot, *The Contrast* is imitative of the *School for Scandal* and other English plays. Billy Dimple, though betrothed to Maria Van Rough, tries to seduce Charlotte Manly and marry her friend Letitia. His duplicity is foiled, and he is shown to be a fop poisoned by continental travel and an overdose of Lord Chesterfield's *Letters.* The two coquettes, Charlotte and Letitia, vow to reform. The heroine, Maria, becomes engaged to Charlotte's brother, Colonel Manly, a noble, patriotic sentimentalist given to grandiloquence. Out of this plot comes the contrast promised in the play's title. Dimple represents the affected manners and corrupt morals of the Old World, while Manly represents the simple manners and innocent virtues of the New. Supplementary contrasts are frequent. Dimple's recklessness with money clashes with the practicality of Mr. Van Rough (Maria's father). Letitia and Charlotte admire European values, while Maria cherishes American values.

7. *The Contrast* (New York: Dunlap Society, 1887).

Especially effective contrasts appear between Dimple's servant Jessamy and Manly's servant Jonathan. Jessamy, who considers himself "courtly and accomplished" (p. 45), appears to be city-bred and therefore well at home in New York, where the play is set. Jonathan, however, is a bumpkin, an outlander sent by his father "to see the world" (p. 35). Thus *The Contrast* becomes an initiation story in which Jonathan eagerly seeks new experience, learns about playhouses and brothels, and yet retains his virtue. Still another deft contrast is the urban world Jonathan sees pitted against the rural world he recalls.

Jonathan's significance lies in his character. He is young, curious, and adaptable; rustic, naive, and, in his distrust of drama, puritanic; he is usually self-confident, though awkward with women; uneducated but salty in his speech, given to colorful exclamations and occasional malapropisms; patriotic, democratic, and impatient with affectation and social distinctions. Perhaps no stock character better represents the diverse and often contradictory facets of American society. Jonathan above all is a genuinely comic figure—one who appeals nearly as much today as when Tyler created him.

9
The Knickerbockers

During the early nineteenth century, New York City became the literary capital of America. Its writers were called the *Knickerbockers,* from Washington Irving's pseudonym, Diedrich Knickerbocker. Ironically, of the three major Knickerbockers, only Irving was a native of New York City. James Fenimore Cooper came from New Jersey, William Cullen Bryant from Massachusetts. Other members of the group included James Kirke Paulding (1778–1860), Clement Clarke Moore (1779–1863), Samuel Woodworth (1784–1842), Fitz-Greene Halleck (1790–1867), John Howard Payne (1791–1852), Joseph Rodman Drake (1795–1820), M'Donald Clarke, known as "The Mad Poet of Broadway" (1798–1842), William Leggett (1801–1839), George Pope Morris (1802–1864), Nathaniel Parker Willis (1806–1867), and Charles Fenno Hoffman (1806–1884).

Their literature was a popular art. They wrote to entertain and did their best work in belles-lettres—poetry, fiction, the informal essay. Nevertheless, their work has survived, sometimes outlasting the fame of the writers. Although we may be able to name the authors of "Rip Van Winkle," *The Last of the Mohicans,* and "Thanatopsis," we may not remember that "A Visit from St. Nicholas," "The Old Oaken Bucket," "Home, Sweet Home," and "Woodman, Spare that Tree!" are respectively by Moore, Woodworth, Payne, and Morris.

Romanticism (see chapter 7), which had appeared earlier in the writings of Freneau, Crèvecoeur, and others, continued in the literature of the Knickerbockers. Especially significant was the appreciation of nature manifested by Bryant and Cooper, since it emerged almost simultaneously with America's first group of landscape painters, the Hudson River school, whose members were not only contemporaries of the Knickerbockers but their friends as well.

WASHINGTON IRVING (1783–1859)

While the Knickerbockers became leading romanticists, they also revealed certain neoclassic leanings. Washington Irving excelled in both traditions. His *History of New York* (1809), in its exuberance, scope, and satiric art surpassing anything by his New World predecessors, is the peak of neoclassical satire in America. *The Sketch Book,* written a decade later, showed that Irving had gradually become a romanticist. He specialized in two romantic genres, the familiar essay and the gothic tale, sometimes giving a native twist to the latter by suspending its tone in the world of half-belief. He had already pioneered in the history of his own city; now he turned to such faraway places as England, Spain, and the American West. Ruined castles, specters, and Indians filled his work as he replaced satire with sentiment and humor with melancholy. In the romantic area of folklore or popular antiquities he also made important contributions, not only by perpetuating various Old World legends, but also by finding others for the New World and thus enhancing it with "associations."

Life. Irving was born and brought up in New York City, the eleventh child of a well-to-do merchant. From 1799 to 1804 he read law and in 1806 was admitted to the bar. Meanwhile, he contributed "The Letters of Jonathan Oldstyle, Gent." (1802–1803) to a daily paper edited by his brother Peter. His brothers, hoping to better his delicate health, sent him on a grand tour of Europe (1804–1806) during which he scrupulously pursued the habit of journal writing, for he now apparently saw himself as at least a part-time author. Upon his return, he joined his brother William and his brother-in-law James K. Paulding in composing *Salmagundi* (1807–1808), a series of satirical pamphlets that captivated the town. Under the name Diedrich Knickerbocker, he also wrote his comic *History of New York* (1809), finishing it, ironically, during the sad days immediately following the death of his fiancée, Matilda Hoffman.

In 1815 Irving began a seventeen-year sojourn abroad, at first to help conduct the family business; but when this business failed in 1818 he resolved to live by writing. He visited Scott at Abbotsford, and their celebrated friendship exerted an important influence on Irving by directing him to folk materials. He soon began producing a fairly steady stream of works: *The Sketch Book* (1819–1820), *Bracebridge Hall* (1822), *Tales of a Traveller* (1824), *Life and Voyages of Christopher Columbus* (1828), *Conquest of Granada* (1829), *Voyages of the Companions of Columbus* (1831), and *The Alhambra* (1832). During this time he lived in Birmingham, Paris, Dresden, London, Madrid, and Seville. In 1829 he left Spain to become secretary of the U.S. legation in London, where he had been lionized since publication of *The Sketch Book.* When in 1832 he returned to America, he received a hero's welcome. Intent on native themes now, he traveled to the West and the South, replenished his notebook, and wrote *A Tour on the*

Prairies (1835), *Astoria* (1836), and *The Adventures of Captain Bonneville, U. S. A.* (1837). Although he had achieved the status of a literary leader to whom younger authors made pilgrimages, he left Sunnyside (his romantic snuggery on the Hudson) to become American minister to Spain (1842–1845). Now a confirmed biographer, he wrote *Oliver Goldsmith* (1849); *Mahomet and His Successors* (1849–1850); *Wolfert's Roost* (1855), a miscellany; and his five-volume *Life of Washington* (1855–1859). The last thirteen years of his life were spent at Sunnyside.

Irving and the Short Story. Literary historians sometimes credit Irving with writing the first modern short stories. Certainly he popularized this genre and improved it with his own peculiar emphasis on setting, tone, and finish. Yet his introductions and conclusions, usually devoted to landscape and legend, are overly long by modern standards, and he used little dialogue. In his work, the short story still resembles the essay.

Style. Irving has always been praised for his style, and rightly so. Few American authors labored so hard polishing their works, and few achieved such a high finish. His style is usually urbane, charming, graceful, witty, and melodious, although there are exceptions; *Knickerbocker's History,* for example, reveals more youthful zest than urbanity.

Representative Works

A History of New York, from the Beginning of the World to the End of the Dutch Dynasty . . . by Diedrich Knickerbocker (1809; revised several times, most significantly in 1812, 1819, and 1848, this last "author's revised edition" becoming the best known). A comic masterpiece; Irving's greatest satirical work. He and his brother Peter began it as a parody of a handbook called *A Picture of New York;* when Peter had to leave for Europe, Washington finished the *History* himself. To promote his book, he inserted in the newspaper various notices reporting first the disappearance of an old gentleman named Diedrich Knickerbocker, then the discovery of his manuscript, and finally the publication of it. This clever hoax aroused interest in the work.

Divided into seven books, the *History* treats the creation of the world (Book 1), the settlement of New Netherlands (Book 2), and the reigns of three Dutch governors—Wouter van Twiller (Book 3), William Kieft (Book 4), and Peter Stuyvesant (Books 5–7). Although it stimulated a great deal of interest in local history among later writers, the book should not be regarded as a historical model. Entertainment was its primary goal; humor, its primary tone. Diedrich Knickerbocker himself, with his addled wits and pompous manner, not only conveys humor but embodies it. As a satire this work cut a wide swath, ridiculing the Dutch, Puritan, and Swedish settlers and, at the same time, Irving's contemporaries. The section on Governor Kieft (William the Testy), portraying him as an irascible quack inventor and superficial scholar who tries to govern by proclamation and economy, actually satirizes Thomas Jefferson. Mock-epic devices abound: bloated chapter headings, lofty speeches, catalogues, extended similes, inversions, and several battles (including a mosquito war). All these ingredients—plus a good many others—appear in the uproarious account of "the most horrible battle ever recorded." The world stops revolving to watch the contest (hyperbole); the Dutch, whose names are catalogued with an admixture of puns, prove themselves "brimful of wrath and cabbage" as they face the Swedes (zeugma); the gods intervene in the fray, and when Peter Stuyvesant falls on a cushion left by "Minerva, or St. Nicholas, or some kindly cow" he is able to bean the Swedish commander with a liquor bottle.[1] Despite all the violence, this combat ends without one casualty (anticlimax).

Here was a book that America could be proud of, for it displayed an unusual degree of artistry and achieved universality with indigenous materials. Irving borrowed freely from world literature, drawing upon, alluding to, and sometimes parodying Cervantes, Rabelais, Homer, Charlevoix, Shakespeare, Dryden, Smollett, Sterne, Fielding, Swift, Malory, and numerous others. He portrayed contemporaries as colonials (Yankees as Puritans, Southerners as Swedes), but above all his characters represent humanity itself—the hypocrites, dullards, dabblers, fake intellectuals, gossips, gluttons, and blowhards of all ages and places.

"The Author's Account of Himself" (preface to *The Sketch Book,* 1819). A tactful explanation of why Irving went abroad. Without depreciating America, he displays a romantic interest in the civilization of the Old World.

"Rip Van Winkle" (first published 1819 as part of *The Sketch Book*). One of the best-known American short stories. When Scott urged him to seek out materials in German folklore, Irving began learning the German language. He read the tale of Peter Klaus, a goatherd who enters a cave, acts as pinsetter for twelve knightly bowlers, drinks some wine from an inexhaustible tankard, awakens twenty years later minus his goats and dog but with a foot-longer beard, and looks for family and friends in a village he hardly recognizes. Indeed, Rip Van Winkle resembled Peter Klaus so clearly that some critics accused Irving of plagiarism. Irving answered as Chaucer, Shakespeare, and many another author would have—that folktales are common property.[2] Besides, he had personalized and localized his version, giv-

---

1. *A History of New York,* 2 vols. (New York: Inskeep & Bradford, 1809), bk. 6, chap. 7.

2. This tale in particular has been known for centuries and widely distributed. The Aarne-Thompson *Types of the Folktale* includes it under Type 766 (The Seven Sleepers). In Thompson's *Motif Index* we find several motifs that appear in Irving's version, among them E577.3 (Dead Persons Bowling), E541.4 (Revenants Drinking), D2011 (Years Thought Days). A close reading of both "Rip Van Winkle" and "Peter Klaus" reveals that neither hero is plied with drink but that they quaff their potions without invitation. Perhaps a drinking taboo (motif C250) is implied here.

ing it a Diedrich Knickerbocker framework, a Hudson River setting, and New World Dutch characters. In Rip, a careerless dreamer, he must have seen himself; and in Rip's return he may have foreshadowed his own return from Europe to a changed America that had already forgotten him. Ironically, this story more than any other work has kept Irving's reputation alive. Proof of the tale's wide appeal is the variety of criticism surrounding it. To one critic (Martin), Rip represents the imagination in a distrustful society; to another (Le Fevre) an Edenic dislike of work and civilization; to a third (Young) an arrested ego partaking in a pagan ritual; a fourth interpreter (Heiman) sees the story as revealing the author's ambivalent feelings toward his father and mother.

"The Legend of Sleepy Hollow" (first published 1820 as part of *The Sketch Book*). Irving's other short-story classic. Ichabod Crane elicits our laughter and derision but also our sympathy and admiration. A comic figure who is compared to a grasshopper, a crane, and a scarecrow, he not only swallows everything in hearing or sight—folktales as well as food—but an overactive imagination feeds his insatiable appetite from within. He represents the greed and superstition that have been proverbially charged against the Yankee character. Yet we sympathize with his efforts to bring culture to the frontier; we accept his ambition and speculative vision as American traits; and we admire his versatility, self-reliance, shrewdness, and adaptability, seeing them as the better side of the Yankee folk type. Brom Bones embodies far different qualities: brawn instead of wit, daring instead of shrewdness, practicality instead of imagination. Bones's conflict with Ichabod exemplifies the Yorker-versus-Yankee stories that apparently were already circulating orally and were soon to get printed in the magazines. His antics parallel those of frontier tricksters like Mike Fink and anticipate those of Sut Lovingood and other characters in Southwestern humor. Irving's tale has none of the dialect of these stories, but it has a remarkable fullness of detail—gustatory, auditory, and especially visual (it was depicted by a number of American artists, including John Quidor, Henry Inman, and Felix O. C. Darley). Besides being a notable early example of local color, the tale deserves recognition for its delicious humor. Note, for instance, the culinary images used to describe Katrina, the Cervantine touches, and the non sequitur moralizing in the postscript.

"The Adventures of the German Student" (published in *Tales of a Traveller,* 1824). A more somber gothic story than was usual with Irving. The morning after the student takes a beautiful woman home, he finds her dead. When he removes the black band around her neck, her head falls off; she has been guillotined. The tale still survives on the oral level and has turned up in the folklore archives of various universities.[3]

---

3. B801 in Jan H. Brunvand, "A Classification for Shaggy Dog Stories," *JAF* 76 (1963): 42–68.

JAMES FENIMORE COOPER (1789–1851)

The historical and literary accomplishments of James Fenimore Cooper were impressive indeed. Although he was probably not the first professional man of letters in America, he did write the nation's first significant utopian novel, historical romances, international novels, frontier novels, and sea novels. American romanticism owed much of its progress to his efforts. He contributed memorable primitivistic portraits of Indians, frontiersmen, and old salts. Carrying on the work of Brockden Brown, he created gothic scenes with such indigenous terror ingredients as scalping. He excelled in using nature as a vehicle for thought and as panoramic background for sweeping action. He has even been called America's first literary conservationist because as early as *The Pioneers* (1823) he expressed a deep concern for the preservation of the environment. His influence on later fiction was pervasive. Many commonplace ingredients of Western stories and movies, in fact, were either invented or first used effectively by Cooper. He also influenced a number of his novelist-contemporaries, especially John Neal (1793–1876), Catharine Maria Sedgwick (1789–1867), William Gilmore Simms (1806–1870), Timothy Flint (1780–1840), Caroline Matilda Kirkland (1801–1864), John Pendleton Kennedy (1795–1870), and Robert Montgomery Bird (1806–1854).

Life. Cooper's father, Judge William Cooper, founded the Cooperstown area in central New York and wrote *A Guide in the Wilderness* (1810). James, the twelfth of thirteen children, was born in Burlington, New Jersey, but brought up in Cooperstown, where the family moved in 1790. Here he could share the frontiersmen's closeness to nature and still enjoy the luxuries made possible by his father's wealth and power. Cooper showed no great promise in his youth. Yale College, which he entered in 1803, expelled him in 1805 as an incurable prankster, and his father sent him off to sea. He visited England as a common sailor on a merchantman (1806–1807), but during the next three years, as a midshipman in the U.S. Navy, he was usually shorebound in Oswego and New York City. After marrying Susan De Lancey in 1811, he became a gentleman farmer and entered into various business ventures with the hope of reducing his mounting debts.

Only gradually did Cooper come to rely on literature for his livelihood. As a boy, he had composed impromptu romances for his schoolmates. Then in 1820, on a dare from his wife and her cousin, he began to write a moral tale, destroyed it when it reached an awkward length, and instead wrote a novel of manners, published as *Precaution* (1820). This was followed by *The Spy* (1821), which was a great success. Already at work on a third novel, Cooper moved his family to New York City (1822) and decided to become a professional writer. He was plagued with financial instability and personal tragedies (including the death of his son Fenimore), but his books nearly always met with an enthusiastic reception. In the early 1820s he founded the

Bread and Cheese Club, a convivial group of merchants, doctors, and other professional men. From 1826 to 1833 he lived abroad. There he made the acquaintance of Walter Scott and grew especially close to Lafayette and the American artists William Dunlap, Horatio Greenough, and Samuel F. B. Morse. Europe changed some of his thinking, as can be seen in the difference between his *Notions of the Americans* (1828) and his later travel books (1836–1838). Although *Notions* declares a lack of native materials for literature, it otherwise praises America at every turn. The European travel books reveal Cooper's growing dissatisfaction with his countrymen but not with the true principles of democracy.

Cooper's outspokenness made him many enemies, so that soon after his return he retreated from New York City to Cooperstown, there to live at Otsego Hall, his Gothic mansion. He continued to provoke criticism, not only with his novels, but even with his meticulously researched and coolly written *History of the Navy of the United States of America* (1839), still considered a standard work. When the reviewers became libelous in their denunciations of him, Cooper won lawsuit after lawsuit against them. He died at Cooperstown on September 14, 1851.

Style and Techniques. Cooper's writings usually displayed more imagination than polish. His novels get off to a slow start. They typically have a polemical preface, and the chapters are headed with epigraphs from Shakespeare, Scott, and other favorite authors. In creating magnificent backdrops for his characters, Cooper had few rivals. He often presented his landscapes as panoramas and then gradually narrowed the focus to a small group or a solitary figure. Like paintings, his scenes sometimes portrayed the symbolic ruins of an old fort or an ancient tree, and he knew how to use chiaroscuro (dramatic lighting). The speech of his genteel characters seems stilted. Happily, he did much better with lower classes. He had, in fact, a fine ear for dialects and was fond of salting them with proverbs. Although he could not resist digressing occasionally, even when the narrative was well on its way, he nevertheless created exciting scenes with varying combinations of attack, massacre, torture, flight, pursuit, capture, rescue, and escape. Like any good gothic writer, he delighted in gory details.

Sociopolitical Books. In both his fictional and nonfictional works Cooper's theories of society and government rest on certain basic ideas. Democracy, he believed, was preferable to monarchy and aristocracy, for it best served to elevate the greatest number of people. Yet he saw democracy's weaknesses: its tendency to replace law with public opinion and sentiment, its approval of mediocrity, its baneful effect on the independent thinker, and, most important, its susceptibility to demagoguery. To guard against these weaknesses, Cooper thought that Americans should seek the leadership of the few who may rightfully claim superior intelligence, education, achievement, and responsibility.

The American Democrat (1838). Elucidates the principles noted above and discusses such topics as freedom of the press, property, slavery, and politics. Its quiet tone, simple language, and short chapters hint that Cooper wrote it for use in schools.

TRAVEL BOOKS. *Sketches of Switzerland* (1836); *Gleanings in Europe: France* (1837), *England* (1837), *Italy* (1838).

OTHER NONFICTIONAL WORKS. *Notions of the Americans* (1828), *A Letter to His Countrymen* (1834).

NOVELS WITH EUROPEAN SETTINGS. *The Bravo* (1831), *The Heidenmauer* (1832), *The Headsman* (1833). Set respectively in Venice during the Renaissance, Bavaria during the Reformation, and Switzerland during the early eighteenth century. Written to show Americans the evils of oligarchies.

Home as Found (1838). Speaking through the Effinghams, who represent the Coopers newly returned from Europe, the author discusses his homeland, criticizing a variety of topics from white-painted houses to newspaper editors.

The Littlepage Manuscripts: *Satanstoe* (1845), *The Chainbearer* (1845), *The Redskins* (1846). A series of novels attacking the Antirent movement. Several generations of the Littlepage family are traced, in order to demonstrate the merits of the landowner system. *Satanstoe*, the best of the trilogy, is set in the New York area of the mid-eighteenth century and combines history, adventure, and local color. In some of the more memorable scenes pranksters steal the mayor's supper, Negroes celebrate Pinkster holiday, and characters race over thawing ice.

The Crater (1847). A cycle-of-nations novel depicting the rise and fall of a Pacific colony. The prose counterpart of Thomas Cole's "Course of Empire," a series of paintings Cooper greatly admired.

OTHER SOCIOPOLITICAL NOVELS. *The Monikins* (1835), *The Ways of the Hour* (1850).

Indians and Other Characters. In his thirty-two novels Cooper created a great variety of characters. The high characters (historical personages, sensitive young women, and so-called dummy, puppet, or technical heroes) hold little interest for us. But Cooper's low characters comprise a fascinating gallery of types made human: Yankees, old salts, Negroes, Indians, and frontiersmen. Yankees seldom fared well in his fiction. He made David Gamut as awkward as the typical Down Easter of folklore, and in the hypocrite Jason Newcome, the villainous editor Steadfast Dodge, and other despicable characters, he went beyond the folk stereotype of the Yankee trickster. Yet his Yankee seamen like Captain Truck and Long Tom Coffin were pictured respectfully. Cooper's old salts regarded the ocean as Edenic and land as an inferior world of great discomfort. Cooper's Negroes range in character from comic, childlike dependents to mature, brave Neb, whom Miles Wallingford loves like a brother.

The Indians in Cooper's novels are essentially of two kinds, embodying on the one hand the cult of the noble savage and on the other the fearful image of frontier massacres and captivities. (This dichotomy was suggested in his chief source, a book by the Moravian missionary John Heckewelder.) Cooper made good Indians out of the Delaware and bad Indians out of the Iroquois or Mingoes, later drawing the same distinction between the Pawnee and the Sioux. His good Indians are loyal, altruistic, and affectionate. His bad Indians are vengeful, treacherous, and brutal. Both groups are eloquent, stoic, and brave. They function in various ways: for example, as agents of gothic terror (even the good Indians indulge in scalping) and as New World ruins, far more expressive of mutability than are decayed trees and deserted farmhouses. Thus, in *The Last of the Mohicans,* Uncas symbolizes the cyclical theory of history, the rise and fall of nations, and he also serves to warn all races of their impending extinction.

Cooper's frontiersmen display a similar range. On the bad side are the renegade Ishmael Bush, the land-despoiler Billy Kirby, the squatter Aaron Thousandacres, the Indian-haters Hurry Harry and Thomas Hutter. On the good side are the bee-hunters Paul Hover and Ben Boden and the most memorable frontiersman of all—Leatherstocking.

The Leatherstocking and Other Wilderness Novels. The immensely popular Leatherstocking Tales have come to be called an American epic, and their internationally known hero—Leatherstocking, or Natty Bumppo (to mention only two of his names)—is now considered a mythic figure. As epic, the series deals with a dramatic period of history—the westward movement of civilization; it copes with a national issue—the race conflict between red and white; and it places its actors in a vast, almost transcontinental setting. Leatherstocking himself embodies national, even universal traits and ideals: (1) Everyman's dream of living primitivistically, (2) the white man's ambivalent attitudes toward the red men, (3) fear of despoiling the environment, (4) the American admiration for skilled marksmanship. Possible prototypes of Leatherstocking were Daniel Boone, Nat Foster, and other legendary frontiersmen Cooper had met or heard about. If we read the Leatherstocking Tales in the order of Natty's life story (*Deerslayer, Mohicans, Pathfinder, Pioneers, Prairie*), we find Natty at his most heroic in *The Deerslayer* (where he is youngest) and at his least heroic in, perhaps, *The Pioneers* (where Cooper not only makes him toothless and uncouth but also subjects him to punishment in the stocks). Since *The Pioneers* was the first novel in the series and the *Deerslayer* the last, it is obvious that Cooper conceived Leatherstocking without fully realizing his heroic potential. But even in *The Pioneers* Natty shows heroism.

The Pioneers (1823). A Northern plantation novel, picturing life at Cooperstown, here called Templeton. Judge Temple, principal landowner, is based on Cooper's father. The story takes place in the decade after the Revolution; has a seasonal pattern; and involves interesting minor characters, including well-drawn foreign types. The Indian Chingachgook

(John Mohegan), though addicted to drink and fallen from his noble state, dies stoically, reverting to paganism. Natty and the judge argue over the need for law in a frontier community, but both decry the despoliation of nature. Memorable scenes include rescues from a panther and a forest fire, a turkey shoot, a pigeon massacre, and a night of fishing. This diversity shows Cooper creatively blending adventure, history, and manners into a genre that in the book's subtitle he called *A Descriptive Tale*.

The Last of the Mohicans (1826). One of the world's most famous novels; a primary source for the foreign image of America. The plot involves the French and Indian siege of Fort William Henry, on Lake George (1757). The story moves in an exciting rhythm of flight, capture, and rescue, begun when the heroines, Alice and Cora Munroe, attempt to make their way to their father, who is the fort's commander. For gothic horror this book has few equals; note especially chapter 17, which pictures the massacre at the fort. In chapters 13 and 19 the ruins of blockhouse and fort serve to reinforce the mutability theme that gives the book its title. Above all, Cooper pictures the world of the Indian with its strong contrasts—its profound silence, its eloquent oratory, its cruelty toward the enemy, its respect for the aged and imbecilic. Magua, the diabolical Huron, opposes and finally kills the Mohican Uncas, the last of his line, who in the second half of the story replaces Leatherstocking as hero.

The Prairie (1827). Now in his eighties, Leatherstocking uses his head rather than his legs or rifle to solve problems. Cooper treats him reverently here, refining his speech of much of its dialect, dramatically transfiguring him with a flood of fiery sunlight in the opening chapter, linking him with Moses as he guides the emigrant train, and making his simple faith and familiarity with nature conquer the science of the pedantic Dr. Obed Bat. All this takes place on prairies as spaciously rendered as the ocean to which Cooper, never having visited the Western plains, compared them. Ishmael Bush represents the patriarchal stage of civilization, and his hanging of his wife's brother betokens the introduction of law, however primitive, to these grim successors of Leatherstocking in the westward movement. The final chapter tenderly pictures Leatherstocking's death.

The Pathfinder (1840). The novel in which Leatherstocking almost marries Mabel Dunham but finally decides to remain true to his gifts. By setting the story in the Lake Ontario area, Cooper combined his two fortes—the wilderness and the water—with firsthand knowledge, for this was where he had been stationed in 1808–1809.

The Deerslayer (1841). The most idyllic novel of the series; set near Lake Otsego around 1740. Leatherstocking, now in his early twenties and named Deerslayer, undergoes symbolic initiation as he kills his first Indian and receives a new name, Hawkeye. In his essential goodness he contrasts with the Indian-haters Hurry Harry and Thomas Hutter and with Judith Hutter, whom Deerslayer cannot reform and will not marry. Also in contrast with these fallen characters are Chingachgook and Hist, whose tender courtship portrays Indian life at its noblest.

OTHER WILDERNESS NOVELS. *Wyandotté* (1843), *The Oak Openings* (1848).

Historical Novels. Cooper's success with the historical romance stems from the strong influence of Walter Scott, who not only created a market for this genre but also provided a formula Cooper could adapt to the New World.

The Spy (1821). America's first impressive historical novel. Set in Westchester during the Revolution, it concentrates on the divided loyalties of a family, a plot often used by later novelists. Although George Washington makes an incognito appearance in this novel, more interest attaches to his spy, Harvey Birch, whose history had been told to Cooper by John Jay.

OTHER HISTORICAL NOVELS: *Lionel Lincoln* (1825), *The Wept of Wish-ton-Wish* (1829), and several of the books included under other categories, e.g., the Leatherstocking Tales, the European novels, and *Satanstoe*.

Sea Novels. Cooper originated the nautical novel. He not only placed more action on the water than had his predecessors, but he also envisioned the sea as symbol, thus anticipating Melville. Romanticism and realism flow together through his work. Moody seascapes, mysterious vessels, exotic heroes, and exciting episodes constitute romantic currents. Realism, the product of Cooper's firsthand acquaintance with the sea, appears in his careful reproduction of the sailors' speech, his inclusion of technical terms, and his attention to the actual workings of ships.

The Pilot (1823). Cooper's first sea novel, set during the Revolutionary War. The pilot, called Mr. Gray, is obviously John Paul Jones. More impressive is Long Tom Coffin, an ideal sailor, moral, brave, patriotic, given to salty speech, a Natty Bumppo of the sea.

The Red Rover (1828). The Rover himself is a mixture of good and bad, a Byronic hero who is a pirate but also a patriot. Numerous hidden identities extend even to the Rover's ship, which is linked by the sailors to the phantom *Flying Dutchman*. By including such folk superstitions, Cooper romanticized his story without implying that reader or author believed them.

OTHER SEA NOVELS. *The Water-Witch* (1831), *Homeward Bound* (1838), *Mercedes of Castile* (1840), *The Two Admirals* (1842), *The Wing-and-Wing* (1842), *Afloat and Ashore* (1842), *Miles Wallingford* (1842), *Jack Tier* (1848), *The Sea Lions* (1849).

WILLIAM CULLEN BRYANT (1794–1878)

The most versatile of the major Knickerbockers, William Cullen Bryant is best known for his poetry, but he also made significant contributions to journalism and literary criticism.

Life. Bryant was born and grew up in Cummington, Massachusetts, spent a year at Williams College (1810–1811), and practiced law in Great Barrington (1816–1825). He took an early interest in writing. *The Embargo* (1808), a verse-satire on Thomas Jefferson, was written when he was only thirteen. But it was "Thanatopsis," published in the *North American Review* for September 1817, that revealed Bryant as a true poet. In 1825 he moved to New York, and literature now wooed him away from the law. He coedited the short-lived *New-York Review* (1825–1826) and gave two series of lectures—one on poetry, the other on Greco-Roman mythology. It was journalism, however, rather than literature that eventually made him a rich man. In 1827 he began work as assistant editor of the *Evening Post.* Shortly thereafter he became editor-in-chief (1829) and part owner. Fifty-two years he labored on the *Post,* relieving the daily grind with weekends at his Long Island home and frequent trips to Europe. Though a shy man, Bryant was one of New York's most respected citizens and, known as "the old man eloquent," was much sought after to give speeches.

Bryant and American Artists. Throughout his life, Bryant was closely associated with American artists. For some forty years he attended the weekly meetings of the Sketch Club, a convivial society of New York artists, writers, and patrons. Two of the members, Thomas Cole and Asher Durand, were America's foremost landscape painters, and Bryant delighted in accompanying them on their rambles. Durand's famous painting *Kindred Spirits,* depicting Bryant and Cole amidst a spectacular mountain landscape, serves well to symbolize not only such artist-writer friendship but also the intense devotion to nature manifested by both groups during the romantic period. Another reminder of this affinity is Bryant's sonnet "To Cole, the Painter, on His Departure for Europe" (1829). Bryant also served various art organizations. He was professor of mythology at the National Academy of Design, a president of the American Art-Union, and a vice-president of the Metropolitan Museum of Art.

Bryant as Journalist. During his long career as a journalist, Bryant applied high principles in a style remarkable for clarity and simplicity. Journalists, he thought, should dedicate themselves to serving mankind, form their opinions reasonably and independently, avoid quarreling with each other, and write in simple, honest English. He himself outgrew the Federalism of his youth and became a genuine liberal whose editorials supported free trade, free labor, free speech, and free press. Alexander Hamilton had in fact founded the *Post* on Federalist principles; Bryant turned it into an organ for Jacksonian Democracy. It took him until the 1860s to become an abolitionist, but in the meantime he insisted on the right of the abolitionist press to speak freely and sided with them in denouncing such proslavery measures as the annexation of Texas. In 1856 he joined the new Republican party. Although he had introduced Lincoln at the Cooper Union speech and endorsed him for the presidency, he soon chafed at Lincoln's slowness in prosecuting the war and emancipating the slaves. Later, during the Grant administration, Bryant helped break the hold of the corrupt Tweed Ring on New York City. In addition, he made and supported such diverse proposals as international copyright, rapid transit, a paid fire department, police uniforms, street-cleaning machines, cheaper postage, and a central park. Especially bold were his editorials upholding workingmen's right to organize, bargain collectively, and strike.

Bryant as Literary Critic. Bryant's reviews, essays, and speeches on literary matters, like his editorials, combined good sense with romantic liberalism. For six decades he formulated and applied his literary theories, but most of his key ideas date from his early years. In 1818 he advocated the free substitution of trisyllabic feet in duple meters. His own poetry abounds in these substitutions, one example of which appears in the second line of "Thanatopsis":

$$\text{Cŏmmú} \mid \text{niŏn wìth} \mid \text{hĕr vís} \mid \text{ĭblĕ fórms,} \mid \text{shĕ spéaks}$$
$$(3:17)[4]$$

By advocating and practicing this metrical freedom, Bryant led American literature into the romantic revolt against neoclassic restraints. Like the romantics Coleridge and Poe, he favored short poems. In general, he was optimistic. Unlike some critics, he saw a future for poetry even in an age of advancing science and materialism, and he thought of America as fertile ground for cultivating an indigenous novel of manners. He believed, however, that Americans should not strive to be completely original in their literature but that they should creatively imitate and selectively borrow from writers of other nations and ages.

Bryant and Nature. Bryant was one of America's greatest nature poets. Throughout his life he communed with nature and could express his ardor in concrete images based on a thorough knowledge of botany. He was fond of addressing his subjects in lyrics such as "The Yellow Violet" and "To the Fringed Gentian," which ended, like the poetic apostrophes of Burns and Wordsworth, with a stanza or two of moralizing. At other times Bryant described panoramic views that paralleled (and often anticipated) the landscape paintings of the Hudson River school.

However, Bryant's view of nature was more than pictorial. He believed in nature therapy as a cure for the evils of civilization, and in fact he seemed to regard nature as the repository of the pleasures of the golden age. He was not a pantheist (although he came close to pantheism in "A Forest Hymn") but a druid who advocated outdoor worship. Then, too, in such poems as "The Prairies," "Earth," and "The Flood of Years," he fancied nature as a

---

4. All quotations are from *The Life and Works of William Cullen Bryant,* ed. Parke Godwin, 6 vols. (New York: Appleton, 1883–1884).

symbol of time and used it with motifs like the cyclical theory of history and
the idea of progress.

Bryant's Style. Although some critics find fault with his diction and accuse him of coldness, sentimentality, and dullness, Bryant was an able poet
whose work still rightly commands our attention. In his best poems he
achieved intensity of emotion, loftiness of vision, and soundness of structure. America's first significant prosodist, he broke away from the heroic
couplet and, in the spirit of the English romantics, looked for forms that
would better suit his subjects. As a result he became a master of blank
verse. Thomas Godfrey and Philip Freneau had used this form before him,
and others were to follow him throughout the nineteenth century, but none
surpassed the dignified sonority of his lines. Bryant's was a highly finished
art, akin to that of Irving's prose.

Representative Works

"To a Waterfowl" (written at Bridgewater, July 1815; first published
1818). A frequently anthologized lyric. It has been praised for the gliding effect of its unusual stanzaic form, which arranges three- and five-stress lines
in a chiasmic pattern: $a^3b^5a^5b^3$. Its didacticism is an organic part of the
poem and, though concentrated in stanzas 4 and 8, seems by no means ob-
trusive. The final stanza, in fact, has been prepared for at the very beginning
of the poem. Here the poet asks the question that is repeated in stanza 3 and
answered in stanza 6, which portrays the poet like the bird as being guided
by a heavenly power.

"Thanatopsis" (written ca. autumn of 1815 [not 1811, the date generally
given]; first published September 1817 in the *North American Review;* later
expanded for the 1821 collection of Bryant's work). One of the most famous
blank verse poems in American literature; ultraromantic in its employment
of this metrical form, in its mingling of nature and melancholy, and in its
literary origins (Bryant was influenced by Robert Southey, William
Cowper, and various so-called graveyard poets). The title means in its
Greek derivation "view of death," and the poem offers consolation to all
who fear the annihilation that death will bring to their "individual being" (l.
25). In the expanded version of 1821[5] this comfort is provided not by the
voice of the poet but by the "still voice" of Nature (l. 17), which has power
to match our gaiety and heal our melancholy. Whether lines 73–81 are
spoken by Nature or by the voice who had introduced it is not clear, but in
any case this concluding section shows the application of the message. Un-
ceasingly egalitarian, Nature brings death to all men everywhere and then
assimilates them in its being. This process, as natural as sleep, should be ac-

5. The version published in 1817 began with "Yet a few days" and ended with
"make their bed with thee!" The version published in 1821 added seventeen lines at
the beginning and sixteen lines at the end.

cepted with stoic resignation and (by implication) with a deistic awareness of the grand design. In harmony with this universal subject is the panoramic sweep of the images, which move through time as well as space. Temporally we are taken back to "the infant world" (l. 34) and forward to our own death. Spatially we stride the surface of the earth (ll. 37–43); we enter the cosmos (ll. 17–19, 45–47) where we peer down on "the great tomb of man" (ll. 18, 45); and we find ourselves underneath the ground, our beings "mix[ed] for ever with the elements," our "mould" pierced by the roots of the oak (ll. 26, 30). Contrasting with the consoling wide-angle view are the "sad images" of confinement—"Of the stern agony, and shroud, and pall, / And breathless darkness, and the narrow house" (ll. 11–12). Bryant heightens this contrast by skillful manipulation of pauses: Such panoramic lines as 16, 37–41, 43–48 are never interrupted by more than a caesura, while the quoted lines are sectioned by commas into short units suggesting confinement. Also distinctive is the poem's hushed mood. Even such action verbs as "glides" and "steals away" (ll. 5, 7) connote a minimum of sound in keeping with Nature's "still voice" (l. 17).

"Inscription for the Entrance to a Wood" (w. 1815). A blank verse tribute to Nature's therapeutic power. The mood throughout is joyous, for Nature has escaped the full brunt of the "primal curse" visited upon sinful man and can still offer "abodes of gladness" (ll. 11–15).

"A Winter Piece" (w. 1820). An autobiographical landscape poem in blank verse. It is obvious from the wealth of detail here that Bryant communed with Nature even in the dead of winter.

"A Forest Hymn" (1825). A blank verse tribute to Nature. The opening verse paragraph begins with exposition and argumentation but ends with the subjective strain that will dominate the rest of the poem. Bryant first argues that modern man should return to the communion with Nature of prehistoric people. From the second paragraph on, however, the landscape is no longer part of the dead past but a living presence infused with the breath of the Creator. The poet learns to read Nature's symbols (ll. 52–68); he views the paradox of life following death (ll. 69–89); he fears Nature's "sterner aspects" and prays to be brought to virtue in a gentler way (ll. 101–118). Note the stress on Nature as teacher.

"Oh Fairest of the Rural Maids" (1826). A love poem addressed to Bryant's wife, the former Frances Fairchild, on whose name he puns by describing her as a "fair child" of Nature.

"The Prairies" (1833). A fanciful landscape poem in blank verse. The poet, on horseback, views the spatial panorama before him until his imagination conceives a temporal panorama: the prairies inhabited successively by the Mound Builders, the later Indians, the animals, and the white men. One of the best nationalistic poems of the period, "The Prairies" stresses the unique beauty of this landscape (ll. 3, 33–34) and the antiquity of its civilizations (ll. 45–50). To those in search of indigenous symbols, Bryant could point not simply to "the mighty mounds" but, more important, to the Mound Builders themselves, one of whom he pictured as the last of his tribe (ll. 75–85). Although some details of Mound Builder culture probably came to Bryant via the archaeological writings of his day, he had seen the prairies on a visit to Illinois in 1832 and had then thought of "the fields of a race which had passed away" (1:286). Moreover, the graveyard and druidic themes of the poem were favorites of his. What makes this one of his greatest works, however, is the skillful handling of images. The cycle-of-nations theme is prefigured in the undulations of the landscape in the first verse paragraph and is then carefully developed through auditory imagery. Just as the poet realizes that the landscape continually fluctuates the reader must realize that all races, including his own, are destined to vanish from the earth.

"The Battle-Field" (1837). Famous for the line "Truth, crushed to earth, shall rise again."

"The Death of Lincoln" (w. 1865). Opens with a memorable alliterative line: "Oh, slow to smite and swift to spare."

10
The Transcendentalists

Emerson and Thoreau, the principal subjects of this chapter, were both New England transcendentalists. In Europe transcendentalism had been a philosophy only, but in America it took on some of the characteristics of a social movement.

⌐Transcendentalism is a form of idealism that encompasses belief in intuitive (nonsensory) knowledge, the indwelling of divinity in man and nature, and the consequent inalienable worth of man. It stresses the unity of being—viewing God, man, and nature as sharers in a universal soul, which Emerson called the Oversoul. In order to feel the divine flowing through him, the transcendentalist turned to nature, seeking it in solitude. He had little use for religion in the traditional sense. His was a religion of nature, and he served as his own priest. (Transcendentalism tended to be nonsectarian and at times anti-Christian.) In nature he not only worshiped but also learned, seeing even the smallest element of nature as a microcosm of the universe containing all its laws and meanings. With its emphasis on the individual, nature, and solitude, transcendentalism qualified as an important branch of romanticism. ⌐

SOURCES AND ANALOGUES

In its various stages, transcendentalism was a reaction against (*a*) John Locke's empirical philosophy, (*b*) materialism, and (*c*) traditional religion, particularly Calvinism with its concepts of human depravity and a punitive God. (Also see Unitarianism below.)

In forming their philosophy, the American transcendentalists turned to an unusually wide range of sources:

1. German idealism: Kant (the father of transcendentalism), Fichte, Schelling, and Hegel (whose dialectic method of thesis, antithesis, and synthesis was used at times by Emerson).

2. French writings: Madame de Staël and Victor Cousin.

3. English literature: some seventeenth-century authors but especiall\
Wordsworth (in whom the transcendentalists found a congenial pantheism), Coleridge and Carlyle (from whom they learned much about
German thought, including the distinction between reason and the understanding that Emerson got from Coleridge).

4. Plato, the Neoplatonists, and the Cambridge Platonists.

5. Oriental literature: the *Sayings of Confucius,* the Hindu *Bhagavad
Gita,* and the *Upanishads.*

6. Quakerism: for the concept of the inner light, which easily
translates into transcendental intuition.

7. Deism: for its devotion to nature.

8. Swedenborgianism: for mysticism and the doctrine of cor-
respondences.

9. The frontier spirit: for optimism, individualism, and antitradi-
tionalism (traits that qualified the transcendentalists as spiritual
pioneers).

10. Unitarianism: for anti-Trinitarianism, antisectarianism, and anti-
Calvinism, although transcendentalists did not follow Unitarian forma-
lism and emphasis on the mind to the exclusion of the religious affections.
Some of the most prominent transcendentalists had been trained as Unitarian ministers, and transcendentalism is sometimes regarded as an out-
growth of Unitarianism.

DEVELOPMENT IN NEW ENGLAND

American transcendentalism, which centered in Concord, Massachusetts, began in the 1830s and ended around the time of the Civil War. Its
chief exponents, besides Emerson and Thoreau, were Amos Bronson Alcott
(1799–1888), George Ripley (1802–1880), Orestes A. Brownson (1803–1876),
Elizabeth Palmer Peabody (1804–1894), Frederick Henry Hedge (1805–
1890), Margaret Fuller (1810–1850), Theodore Parker (1810–1860), James
Freeman Clarke (1810–1888), Jones Very (1813–1880), Christopher Pearse
Cranch (1813–1892), and William Ellery Channing (1818–1901). At one time
or another all of them attended the informal meetings of the so-called
Transcendental Club formed in 1836. Sylvester Judd (1813–1853) and
Frederick Goddard Tuckerman (1821–1873) were also transcendentalists
though not members of the club.

These transcendentalists found various outlets for their ideas. Emerson
and Thoreau gave Lyceum lectures; Fuller and Alcott conducted discussion
groups. Of the several magazines which published their work, the most influential was *The Dial* (1840–1844), edited first by Margaret Fuller and then
by Emerson with the help of Thoreau. Some of the transcendentalists even

experimented with community living, which was seemingly inconsistent with their allegiance to individualism. Brook Farm, founded in 1841, lasted only five years. A brave attempt to combine self-culture, group culture, and agriculture, it was joined by several notables, including Hawthorne. In addition to this official activity, the transcendentalists joined the incredibly numerous reform movements of the day. Margaret Fuller worked for women's rights; Brownson for the labor movement; and nearly all of the group, even the nonjoiner Thoreau, for abolition of slavery.

The greatest literary accomplishments of the transcendentalists were the works of Emerson and Thoreau. We should also mention the poems of Jones Very and Frederick Goddard Tuckerman, and Sylvester Judd's *Margaret* (1845), an early local-color novel, which was apparently the only genuine piece of fiction to come out of the movement. Transcendentalism also influenced a number of later writers, including Walt Whitman.

RALPH WALDO EMERSON (1803–1882)

Ralph Waldo Emerson holds one of the highest positions among American authors, and his influence has been worldwide. As an essayist he ranks with Montaigne and Bacon. As a poet he stands on a lower plane, but a few of his poems, including "Days" and "Brahma," are memorable, and his poetic theory was embodied in the chants of Walt Whitman. Whether working in verse or prose (and his prose was actually poetic prose), Emerson gave his sentences such a jewellike polish that many have come down to us as epigrams, and he remains one of the most quoted authors of all time. His optimism has sometimes been contrasted with the so-called darker visions of Hawthorne and Melville; yet Emerson too saw the evil in the world and knew tragedy first hand. His reaction differed from theirs, however, evolving into a personal philosophy of idealism, compensation,[1] and self-reliance.

Life. Emerson was born in Boston to a family well-stocked with ministers. He was only eight when his father died, and the family thereafter lived in straitened circumstances. Nevertheless, the four boys went to college. Ralph Waldo showed little promise, graduating below the middle of his class. In 1829 he was ordained a minister at Boston's Second (Unitarian) Church and was married to Ellen Tucker; but in 1831 Ellen died, and in 1832

---

1. In nature this is the law of polarity. Emerson saw it also as applying to man and in his essay "Compensation" cited it to contradict the traditional notion that men are rewarded and punished in the hereafter. Instead, he argued, this happens in the here and now: "Every sweet hath its sour; every evil its good. . . . For every thing you have missed, you have gained something else; and for every thing you gain, you lose something" (2:98). Quotations in this section are from the *Complete Works of Ralph Waldo Emerson,* Concord Ed., 12 vols. (Boston: Houghton Mifflin, 1904).

he resigned from his position, ostensibly out of reluctance to administer the Lord's Supper but probably also for other reasons, including a desire to find a more influential vocation. From 1832 to 1833 he traveled in Europe and looked up Thomas Carlyle, thus initiating their famous friendship. The year 1833 also marks the beginning of his long career as platform lecturer. Meanwhile he moved to Concord, Massachusetts (1834); married Lydia Jackson (1835); wrote *Nature* (1836), the seminal book of New England transcendentalism; and gave two lectures that met with vigorous receptions. One, an oration titled "The American Scholar" delivered in 1837 before the Harvard Phi Beta Kappa Society, proved of great influence (see below). The other, an address to the Harvard Divinity School in 1838, had little lasting effect but did provoke immediate criticism from the orthodox, who disliked its de-emphasis of historical Christianity. For more evidence of Emerson's emerging liberalism we may cite his endorsement of Walt Whitman's poetry and his friendship with such independent thinkers as Carlyle, Margaret Fuller, Bronson Alcott, and Thoreau, whose help he enlisted in editing *The Dial*. His lecturing carried him to the Western states, the Near East, and Europe.

Nature (1836). Emerson's first book, *Nature* is a forceful though sometimes confusing statement of romantic individualism. It places man over nature, identifies him with God, and designates him as "creator in the finite" (1:64). In the introduction Emerson notes that modern man should no longer look at nature through the eyes of past generations but should seek out "an original relation" to it (1:3). He proposes to use nature not only in the "philosophical sense" as "the NOT ME" (a term borrowed from Carlyle) but also in the "common sense" as "essences unchanged by man" (1:5). In chapter 1, drawing on his own experience, Emerson notes that even under unpromising urban conditions he has "enjoyed a perfect exhilaration" from nature (1:9). Additional poetic delights come in the fields and forests when man sees his kinship with the vegetable or with God. Here "I am become a transparent eyeball," Emerson wrote in a rapture of pantheism that foreshadowed his explanation of the Oversoul. "The currents of the Universal Being circulate through me. I am part or parcel of God" (1:10). Each of the next four chapters is devoted to a specific use of nature. As "commodity" (chapter 2), nature serves the senses but only as a means to a higher end. "A man is fed," for instance, "not that he may be fed, but that he may work" (1:14). Chapter 3 tells us that nature serves man's love of beauty, which his eye finds in skies, trees, and other natural forms; which his higher faculties find in virtue and thought; and which his art seeks to concentrate into new microcosms. Chapter 4 deals with nature as language, as "the vehicle of thought" and "the symbol of spirit" (1:25). Here Emerson broached the Swedenborgian idea of correspondence between the material and ideal worlds, maintaining that the laws of physics are also the laws of ethics. Chapter 5 sees nature as a discipline that teaches "intellectual truths" to the understanding and moral truths to the reason (1:36). Emerson next turned to the question of "whether nature outwardly exists" (1:47). His answer, explained in chapter 6 ("Idealism"), is No; it exists in the mind and is in fact subordinated to the mind. Nevertheless, Emerson continues in chapter 7, nature commands our reverence, for it is "the apparition of God" (1:62). When we stray from it (Emerson later rejected this theory of lapse), nature can show us our degeneracy and then "lead [us] back" to the "universal spirit" (1:62). The book concludes with a rhapsodic chapter called "Prospects." Here Emerson notes the limitations of empirical science and calls for greater reliance on guesses, glimpses, and dreams—in short, transcendental intuition. Intensifying the lyricism, he quotes an "Orphic poet," probably Emerson himself. In this visionary passage, which contains such epigrams as "A man is a god in ruins" (1:71), "Know then that the world exists for you" (1:76), and "Build therefore your own world" (1:76), the poet predicts limitless horizons if you will but "conform your life to the pure idea in your mind" (1:76). Although Emerson preached unity in *Nature*, the essay has been criticized for lack of it, and the author himself thought it disjointed. Still its style is forceful and its thought original.[2]

Essays and Addresses. The chief collections of Emerson's prose writings are *Essays* (1841); *Essays: Second Series* (1844); *Representative Men: Seven Lectures* (1850), including Plato, Swedenborg, Montaigne, Shakespeare, Napoleon, and Goethe; *English Traits* (1856); and *The Conduct of Life* (1860).[3]

"The American Scholar" (delivered August 31, 1837). Termed by Holmes "our intellectual Declaration of Independence"[4] because it proclaimed an end to foreign domination of thought and art in the New World. Many writers, including Paulding and Bryant, had called for a truly national literature, but Emerson's manifesto not only surpassed its predecessors in eloquence but was also more timely, for it both announced an actual American Renaissance and was itself a stirring example of what could be done. The title should not be taken too narrowly. *Scholar* here means "Man Thinking" (1:84)—not simply a philosopher, clergyman, teacher, or artist, but all these and more. Nor does *American* denote cultural isolationism. Emerson was trying to stimulate man to creativity; hence he minimized the influence of the past and relegated books to "the scholar's idle [uncreative] times" (1:91), but he did not banish them. Conversely, he stressed the im-

2. This in spite of such influences as Plato, Plotinus, Swedenborg, Berkeley, Coleridge, Wordsworth, Carlyle, and Alcott.

3. *Society and Solitude* (1870) is best remembered for one of its epigrams: "Hitch your wagon to a star" (7:30).

4. Oliver Wendell Holmes, *Ralph Waldo Emerson* (Boston: Houghton Mifflin, 1886), p. 115.

portance of self-reliance, which of course meant attention to transcendental intuitions.

"Self-Reliance" (1841). A memorable plea for romantic individualism. However, Emerson here is not preaching egocentricity. Rather he is equating self-reliance with reliance on the divinity in each man, envisioning a society of individuals made good through self-reform, providing a needed tonic to a culture just emerging from the dominance of Calvinism, and prescribing a far-from-easy obedience to conscience ("If any one imagines that this law is lax, let him keep its commandment one day" [2:74]). The essay depicts the strangling effect of society on the individual, then moves to the liberating effect of the individual on society. It abounds in quotable lines.

"Experience" (1844). One of Emerson's most difficult essays, more sober and less optimistic than such earlier pieces as "Self-Reliance." Here Emerson ʳhows a kinship with Poe, Melville, and the later Twain as he pictures a world where we are subject to illusion, temperament, subjectiveness, and other "lords of life"; where we accomplish little or nothing and know even less; where we sense our divinity only at very rare moments. The essay is developed dialectically and employs a journey motif.

Poetic Theory. "The Poet," which is one of Emerson's most famous essays, and several of his poems contain his chief ideas about poetry and art. (By *poet* he often meant artist.)[5]

1. The materials of poetry are limitless. "Thought makes everything fit for use"—even base, obscene, and ugly things, even "Bare lists of words" (3:17).

2. The form of a poem should grow out of its thought, which "like the spirit of a plant or an animal . . . has an architecture of its own" (3:9–10). This organic theory discourages poetic decoration; if a poet is truly inspired, the form will take care of itself. "He shall not his brain encumber / With the coil of rhythm and number" ("Merlin," ll. 29–30) (9:121).

3. The poet represents "the complete man" in a world of knowers, doers, and sayers, for he is the most adept at perception and expression (3:5). Divine inspiration (a Platonic as well as transcendental concept) comes to his aid, causing him to speak "somewhat wildly" (3:27). He should court this intoxication not with opium or wine but by living so simply that common things will excite him and by abandoning himself to "the ethereal tides" of the universe (3:26), which are best found in outdoor solitude. (See "Good-Bye" and "The Apology.")

4. The poet's powers include (a) reconciling nature's polarities, (b) penetrating spiritual essences and meanings, (c) announcing unity in variety, (d) conquering time and custom, (e) liberating men from old thoughts and inspiring them with new ones, (f) restoring them to lost knowledge, and

5. Unless otherwise noted, quotations in this section are from "The Poet."

(g) showing them their relation to the universe (see "The Sphinx" for *c*; "Merlin" for *a* and *d*; "Bacchus" for *b*, *d*, and *f*; "The Poet" for *e* and *g*).

5. America (itself a poem) needs a poet to celebrate its "incomparable" though "yet unsung" materials (3:37–38).

Poetic Practice. Emerson's poetic practice only partially fulfilled his poetic theory. His verse, usually grouped under four headings—nature, personal, public, and philosophic—reveals a wide range of subject; but his call for a poet who could celebrate humble things and elevate base ones was better answered by Whitman than himself. Emerson lacked the swing and sweep of Whitman; his utterance tended toward the gnomic. He was best at single, aphoristic lines. Nor did he strive or care for the musicality achieved by Poe. Instead he sometimes reached the opposite extreme (for example, in "Fable," a poem that sounds like prose). His insistence on organic form did not preclude the use of such structural and musical devices as stanza, rhyme, and meter. Yet in these matters he displayed a marked freedom. He moved early from the heroic couplet to blank verse, in keeping with the romantic tendency of the day. Soon four-stress meter became his favorite, but he frequently interspersed it with lines of fewer or more stresses, and he varied the number of unstressed syllables, creating a sprung rhythm just short of free verse. While some of his better poems (e.g., "The Apology") are in unvaried stanzas, many have irregular stanzas and rhyme schemes. His odes are of the loose Cowleyan type. His rhymes were notoriously inexact, anticipating Emily Dickinson's.

Chief Poems

"Grace" (w. ca. 1833). Shows a recessive strain in Emerson: conformity rather than self-reliance.

"The Rhodora" (w. 1834). A nature lyric, apostrophizing a native flower, on the theme that "Beauty is its own excuse for being" (9:38). The final line suggests the purpose of a directing power.

"Each and All" (w. ca. 1834). Analyzes the concept of totality: "All are needed by each one; / Nothing is fair or good alone." In frequently irregular octosyllabics and with increasing subjectivity, the poet explores the relationship first of each to each and then of each to all.

"The Snow-Storm" (w. 1834 or 1835). Portrays nature as a fierce artist who, though heedless of artistic rules, in a single night creates a wildly imaginative architecture that would take man "an age" to imitate. The people in this blank verse poem stand in quiet contrast to the storm.

"Concord Hymn: Sung at the Completion of the Battle Monument, July 4, 1837." A classic piece of public, occasional verse best remembered for the line "And fired the shot heard round the world." Cast in elegiac rhyme, it celebrates the battle of April 19, 1775, fought on land owned by Emerson's stepgrandfather. Much of the diction is trite though not inappropriate. (For example, the word *flood,* an eighteenth-century cliché for river, suits the outbreak recalled in the first stanza.) The poem also offers interesting contrasts (softness-hardness, sound-silence, motion-fixity) and effective aural devices (note the way alliteration reinforces the thought-connection between "deed redeem" and "dare / To die"). It was sung to the tune of "Old Hundred" (9:158–159).

"The Problem" (w. 1839). Develops a personal dilemma: Why should the poet so admire churchmen whose ranks he has declined to join? He reminds himself that religious expression was born "from the heart of nature" (l. 13), that some of its structures are as old as the mountains (ll. 41–44), and that indeed nature has welcomed this expression (stanza 4). Yet the poet himself would look behind the accomplishments of art and religion to "the vast soul" that planned the universe (l. 48) and behind their human agents—artists, priests, and prophets—to the divine inspiration. The "Holy Ghost" still "whispers" to any "willing mind" (l. 60) (9:6–9).

"Give All to Love" (1846). Urges total commitment to present love and yet a willingness if need be to relinquish it. Note the irregular meter, random rhymes, parallel commands, basic solar imagery.

"Ode: Inscribed to W. H. Channing" (w. 1846). Bitter satire combined with expression of faith in the doctrine of compensation through which the "over-god" will bring issues to solution despite the pettiness and folly of statesmen and reformers. Emerson criticizes not only that notorious compromiser Daniel Webster (ll. 6, 8–9, 12–15, 24–28, 34–35) but also his fellow transcendentalist and "glowing friend," William Henry Channing, who at the New England Antislavery Convention of 1846 had proposed dissolving the federal union (ll. 2, 5, 8–9, 36–43).

"Uriel" (from *Poems,* 1847). Variously interpreted as an illustration of Emerson's poetic theory, an allegory of the effect produced by his "Divinity School Address," and an assertion of the transcendental idea of circles (see his essay of that name) over the outmoded philosophies of his day (a conflict summarized in the archangel Uriel's treasonable speech, ll. 21–24).

"Hamatreya" (from *Poems,* 1847). A successful attempt to convey Hindu wisdom in a Yankee setting and experimental verse. Attacking the folly of avarice in the face of inevitable death, the poem develops a saying from the *Vishnu Purana:* "The words *I* and *mine* constitute ignorance," i.e., failure to see the unity of being behind the illusion (*maya*) of variety. Emerson depicted land-hungry New England farmers in contrast with the personified earth, who chides them for their possessiveness in her "Earth-Song." To intensify this effect, he cast the song in short, two-stress lines but the surrounding passages in longer lines, usually five-stress. These latter passages qualify as blank verse, but we must not ignore the prosodic freedom exercised throughout. For example, the catalogues in lines 1, 3, and 20 extend the meter to as many as eight stresses to achieve the author's purpose. Line 3 perfectly expresses human acquisitiveness, emphasizing each item separately with spondees that thud like full sacks thrown into storage.

"Days" (w. 1851). A blank verse masterpiece of compression, suggestiveness, and universality. It combines a Puritan warning against wasting time and oriental imagery inspired in part by Emerson's reading of the Persian poet Hafiz. The days, though rich in gifts, are "Muffled and dumb"; they cannot help man choose these gifts wisely.

"Brahma" (w. 1856). A distillation of Hindu ideas about Brahma or Brahman (the Oversoul). In quiet quatrains Brahma dispels the illusions of *maya* and expresses his own changeless, omnipresent nature. Stanza 1 denies the finality of death since the dead are reincarnated to begin a new cycle. Stanza 2 shows that opposites such as visibility and invisibility, good and evil are illusions.[6] Brahma comprehends them all and makes no distinctions. Stanza 3 asserts his pantheistic immanence. Brahma concludes by exhorting men to seek his own abode (Nirvana), which is higher than the "heaven" of the "strong gods" and which mortals reach better by striving for selflessness as "meek lover[s] of the good" than by practicing the showy asceticism of "the sacred Seven" (9:195).

"Terminus" (1867). A realistic acceptance of old age, written when Emerson was in his early sixties. Compare Tennyson's "Ulysses," Lowell's "Auspex," and Longfellow's "Morituri Salutamus."

HENRY DAVID THOREAU (1817–1862)

A unique embodiment of naturalist, philosopher, and verbal artist, Thoreau brought American transcendentalism to fruition and gave American literature one of its genuine classics.

Life. Thoreau spent most of his life in Concord, Massachusetts, his birthplace. He attended the Concord Academy and in 1833 entered Harvard, where he was a good student. After his graduation in 1837 he took up teaching, first in a Concord public school and then in a private school he and his brother John ran in their home from 1838 to 1841. Meanwhile a close friendship developed between Thoreau and Emerson, who had moved to Concord in 1834. For several years Thoreau actually lived in Emerson's house, serving as a handyman, helping with *The Dial,* and (while Emerson lectured in England) taking care of his friend's family. The famous Walden experiment was begun in 1845, when Thoreau started building his cabin on land recently purchased by Emerson. During his stay at Walden, which ended in 1847, he wrote both *A Week on the Concord and Merrimack Rivers* (1849), recording an excursion with his brother John, and the greater part of *Walden* (1854). His most famous essay, *Civil Disobedience,* inspired by his arrest for refusing to pay a poll tax to a government that carried on the Mexican War and supported slavery, also dates from this time. Besides writing, Thoreau gathered natural history specimens for Dr. Louis Agassiz at Harvard, worked as a surveyor, helped in the family business (pencil making), and

6. Also see Emerson's essay "Illusions."

served the Concord Lyceum as secretary, curator, and frequent lecturer. His various pursuits took him to the Maine woods, Cape Cod, Canada, Brooklyn (where he looked up Walt Whitman), the White Mountains, and Minnesota. A true nay-sayer, he refused to join organizations, including those he suspected like the church and those he sympathized with like the abolition societies,[7] and he never married. Although *A Week* . . . proved to be a financial fiasco,[8] *Walden* enjoyed some success, and Thoreau could even claim a few disciples. However, just as he approached contemporary fame, he succumbed to tuberculosis. Asked on his deathbed if he had made his peace with God, Thoreau replied, " ' I did not know we had ever quarrelled.' "[9]

Walden, or Life in the Woods (1854). Thoreau's masterpiece may be read in several ways:

1. As autobiography. Culled in large part from his journals, *Walden* records Thoreau's development specifically during the time spent at Walden Pond and indirectly during the later years when he readied the book for publication. He tells why he made the experiment of going to the woods, how he adjusted to a life in nature, and what spiritual enrichment he received from this experience.

2. As social criticism and satire. In the early chapters Thoreau spent more time tearing down the world from which he had withdrawn than building up his new world. He criticized the age for its materialism, its inhumanity toward the slave and the workingman, its political corruption, and its alienation from the organic life of nature.

3. As inspirational literature. *Walden* belongs with the youth's companions and self-help or self-culture types of books. A number of individuals have changed their lives after reading Thoreau's words, and as E. B. White has demonstrated in several essays, *Walden* remains supremely pertinent to modern situations. From first to last it breathes optimism. If, says Thoreau, a man will but discipline himself and spiritualize his life, he can achieve a private golden age.

4. As an expression of transcendentalism. The central concepts of individualism, idealism, and intuition appear throughout. One example is

---

7. But he helped in the latter without joining. In 1857 he met John Brown, and in 1859, following the Harpers Ferry raid, he gave two lectures defending the militant abolitionist: "A Plea for Captain John Brown" (before his execution) and "After the Death of John Brown."

8. One thousand copies were printed. When the publisher returned 706 copies unsold, Thoreau wryly observed in his journal: "I have now a library of nearly nine hundred volumes, over seven hundred of which I wrote myself" (5:459). Unless otherwise noted, quotations are from *The Writings of Henry D. Thoreau*, Walden Ed., 20 vols. (Boston and New York: Houghton Mifflin, 1906).

9. Edward Waldo Emerson, *Henry Thoreau as Remembered by a Young Friend* (Boston and New York: Houghton Mifflin, 1917), p. 118.

Thoreau's urging each man to live "in conformity to higher principles," not to "the arguments and customs of mankind," but to "the faintest but constant suggestions of his genius, which are certainly true" (2:239). *Walden* also contains such corollaries of transcendentalism as the microcosm, solitude, manual labor, and nature.

5. As a nature book. Thoreau treated nature on several levels. This can be seen in his famous descriptions of the deep-diving loon and the battling ants, which not only qualify as first-rate examples of descriptive writing but also have deeper meanings and functions. (As Charles R. Anderson observes on the "Brute Neighbors" chapter, the loon seems to embody Algonquin folk beliefs, while the ants, depicted in mock-epic imagery, serve to satirize the Mexican War.) To Thoreau it was a spiritual experience to adjust his life to the organic principle in nature, and he described his spiritual development in terms of nature's development from season to season, culminating during the spring thaw in the rebirth of nature and of his own psyche. However, there are signs (especially in the chapter "Higher Laws") that during the post-Walden years when he was still working on the book, Thoreau came to view nature with somewhat disenchanted eyes. He found himself more interested in recording than interpreting it; he feared that it nourished in man a wildness that could not always be eradicated by attention to higher laws; and he foresaw the end of the pastoral age in America.

6. As an artistic masterpiece. At first glance *Walden* may seem as simple and casual as a collection of informal essays, but it is actually a complex work of art, the result of nearly a decade of patient, thoughtful writing and rewriting (there are at least seven versions). Thoreau's artistry is especially apparent in *Walden*'s structure, imagery, indirections, and poetic prose. In order to focus the work, he adopted a seasonal framework and compressed his twenty-six-month stay at Walden into a single year beginning in March and ending the following spring. All units—sentences, paragraphs, and chapters—show evidence of careful planning and are linked by transitional devices. Contrast is enhanced by chapter sequence. "Visitors," for example, follows "Solitude" while "Brute Neighbors" follows "Higher Laws." Reinforcing the structure are numerous images drawn from myth and ritual. Thoreau refers throughout to the ancient gods and heroes of the oriental, Greco-Roman, and Scandinavian cultures; and his persona seems at various times to be a hermit at his meditations or a St. Francis conversing with the lesser creatures. The story itself is a reenactment of ancient purification-rebirth rituals.

Thoreau loved puns and delighted in using words in their etymological sense (see, for example, his play on *impertinent* and *extravagant* in the first and last chapters). Related to this was his practice of taking proverbs and other famous sayings in new, unaccepted ways. He often employed paradox, occasionally expressing it with a reversal technique called *antistrophe,* as in the sentence "We do not ride on the railroad; it rides upon us" (2:102). He used fables such as the forceful story of the bug that emerged from the old applewood table (chapter 18), and in the tradition of Sewall, Edwards, and Emerson, he habitually pointed to symbolic meanings. He saw many symbols as microcosms. Morning represented "the heroic ages" (2:98); a mosquito not only was an entire *Iliad* and *Odyssey* but also contained "the everlasting vigor and fertility of the world" (2:99), while an owl symbolized the "unsatisfied thoughts" of all men (2:139). Thoreau also employed various sound devices like onomatopoeia and reiteration, and it is even possible to break some of his passages into scannable verses—all of which helps to qualify *Walden* as a prose poem.

"**Civil Disobedience.**" The assertion of the individual conscience reached a peak in this memorable essay, first given as a lecture in 1848 and printed the following year. Not only did it preach highly individualistic ideas of government, but it also recorded Thoreau's own way of practicing what he preached. This method (as we have noted under "Life") was his refusal to pay the Massachusetts poll tax as a gesture of protest against the Mexican War. Someone secretly paid the tax for him, however, and he was released after spending one night in jail (probably July 23 or 24, 1846). Thoreau had been preceded in this form of civil disobedience by Bronson Alcott and Charles Lane, both of whom were also arrested (although only Lane was jailed).[10] In this way Thoreau waged a private, nonviolent war against the government. His night in jail Thoreau treated with noticeable humor in this essay, but the theories behind it he presented more seriously.[11] In the opening paragraph he declares, "That government is best which governs not at all" (4:356); and although he soon turns from this ideal to the practical consideration of immediately improving the present government, he advocates doing so not by voting but by denying its authority, breaking its laws (when he cannot in conscience obey them), and refusing to support it, even though "blood should flow" from this "peaceable revolution" (4:371). For such bold statements, Thoreau has been called a mystic, a liberal, an absolutist, and an anarchist. Conversely, he has been praised for his idealism, social consciousness, courage, and for the mystical vision that allowed him to recognize higher laws than those of government or religion. For half a century "Civil Disobedience" created no stir, but after 1900 it became one of the world's most influential writings. Among its admirers have been Leo Tolstoi, Upton Sinclair and Norman Thomas, Mahatma Gandhi, and Martin Luther King. It proved useful to Gandhi's passive resistance

10. In "Civil Disobedience" Thoreau notes that he has "paid no poll-tax for six years" (4:375), and readers frequently wonder why he spent only a single night in jail for these infractions. The answer, as was the case with Alcott, is that friends or relatives periodically paid the taxes for them well in advance.

11. These derived in part from Sophocles' *Antigone* and Emerson's essay "Politics."

movements in South Africa and India, to the Danish resistance during World War II, and to American pacifist groups.

Poetry. In his best poems Thoreau achieved the clear images that he found so admirable in classical Greek verse.

"The Inward Morning" (first printed in *The Dial,* October 1842). Written in common meter and concerned with such transcendental matters as intuitive knowledge, the microcosm, and the correspondence between the inner and outer worlds. Note Thoreau's characteristic use of matutinal imagery to express psychic renewal.

"Smoke" (first printed in *The Dial,* April 1843; reprinted in *Walden,* chapter 13). One of Thoreau's best and most famous poems; written in blank verse. The spare images capture the essence of smoke: its silence, its upward movement, its obscurant power, and its evanescence. The poem progresses from dawn to dark and dissolves the Icarian hope of the opening line into the "departing dream" of line 5. The last two lines have been taken as an expression of Thoreau's transcendental self-assurance. Perhaps, however, he means to propose the paradox that smoke can come from a "clear flame" (2:279).

"Haze" (1843). Approaches sprung rhythm in the unpredictable number of its unstressed syllables; approaches imagism in its sharp pictures, free of moralizing. Thoreau uses oxymoron ("aerial surf," "dry sea") and other contradictions to describe the haze as an exotic hybrid.[12]

"Inspiration" (pieced together from various fragments, including some printed as early as 1849). Defines the poet's inspiration, in the transcendental view, as an unearned gift from God, apprehended intuitively.

12. Quoted from *The Dial* 3 (1843): 506.

11
Hawthorne, Poe, and Melville

Turning to the fiction of the American Renaissance, we come upon three writers of the highest quality, artists who took their profession seriously and wrote genuine classics. They were not transcendentalists (although they did address themselves to ultimate meanings), nor did they share the optimism of the transcendentalists. Instead their fiction has a somber tone, and it raises more questions than it answers. It is, in fact, difficult and challenging—in part because of its many symbols (including the scarlet letter, house of Usher, and white whale). As a result, the critical interpretations prompted by this work have proliferated but have often proved contradictory. We have cited some representative interpretations in our text and bibliography, but the reader should remember that no interpretation of such classics as *Moby-Dick* and *The Scarlet Letter* can ever be definitive.

NATHANIEL HAWTHORNE (1804–1864)

Nathaniel Hawthorne was truly appreciated in his own day and has since been recognized as one of America's foremost writers.

Life. Hawthorne came from an old New England family, a fact that accounts for the strong sense of past and place in his work. While he took some pride in the accomplishments of his Puritan forebears, his writing also reveals an acute awareness of their misdeeds, including persecutions of Quakers and participation in the Salem witchcraft trials.

Salem, Massachusetts, was Hawthorne's birthplace and for many years his home. There he spent a family-centered but not unsocial boyhood. He read widely, but also enjoyed the outdoors, especially when the family lived in the wilderness-bordered settlement of Raymond, Maine. After graduating from Bowdoin College in 1825, he moved back to the family home in Salem and spent the next dozen years in serious pursuit of a literary career.

His novel *Fanshawe* was issued in 1828, and in 1837 his shorter narratives and sketches were collected in a volume called *Twice-Told Tales*. During 1839 and 1840 he worked as measurer of salt and coal in the Boston Custom House. In April 1841 he joined the transcendentalist community of Brook Farm but stayed only seven months. After he and Sophia Peabody were married (1842), they lived at the Old Manse, where two of their three children were born and where Hawthorne enjoyed the friendship of such literary figures as Emerson and Thoreau. From 1846 to 1849 Hawthorne was surveyor in the Salem Custom House.

He now turned to novels instead of the less profitable short stories. By working at *The Scarlet Letter* (1850) nine hours a day, he was able to finish it within six months. This accelerated pace continued after the Hawthornes moved to Lenox, Massachusetts, where Hawthorne wrote *The House of the Seven Gables* (1851) while enjoying frequent visits with his neighbor Herman Melville. Later the Hawthornes lived in West Newton and Concord, Massachusetts. From 1853 to 1857 Hawthorne served as U.S. Consul at Liverpool, a reward for writing the campaign biography of his old friend Franklin Pierce. He produced no important works during this time. From 1857 to 1859 he lived in Rome and Florence—a new, stimulating environment that gave him material for *The Marble Faun* (1860).

In 1860, the Hawthornes again settled in Concord, and Hawthorne wrote steadily in the ensuing years. *Our Old Home,* a collection of articles on England, was published in 1863, shortly before his death.

Subjects and Style. Hawthorne specialized in psychological topics (as did Henry James) and frequently dealt with morbid states of mind (as did Brockden Brown and Poe, although Hawthorne exploited the past more than they did). Sin and evil, ubiquitous in his work, are analyzed not as static abstractions but as they develop in the human psyche. This relentless probing of man's inner recesses produced enough horror and gloom to link Hawthorne with the preceding gothic novelists.

Hawthorne's complex techniques include symbolism, irony, and multiple choice. He was fond of color symbolism but achieved his best effects with chiaroscuro (the interplay of light and shade) used, for example, in the forest scene of *The Scarlet Letter* and in *The House of the Seven Gables* when a dark housefly alights on the dead, sunlit face of Judge Pyncheon. Hawthorne often offers the reader several interpretations of an element in a story. For example, the end of *The Scarlet Letter* provides three explanations for the *A* on Dimmesdale's breast, then follows these with the suggestion that there was no *A* on his breast (a possibility corresponding to the "none of these" answer on a multiple-choice test). Often these devices involve supernatural possibilities that the author may deride as rumors spun by superstitious old women, but that nevertheless place the story in the complex world of half-belief.

Tales. It is somewhat appropriate to refer to Hawthorne's brief narratives as tales rather than short stories. If his work does not have the loose structure implied by this term, it does have the subjective, chatty tone the tale inherited from the informal essay, another genre in which Hawthorne excelled; witness the various prefaces to his romances.

"My Kinsman, Major Molineux" (1832). Interpreted in many ways, for example, as a New World enactment of the deposition of the Royal Scapegoat, an ancient rite here used to represent the expulsion of British rule from the colonies (Hoffman);[1] as an allegory in which Robin personifies not young America but the governors of Massachusetts Bay Colony (Russell); as an initiation story in which Robin loses his bucolic innocence and learns that self-reliance has its limitations in the city of night (Gross); as a pessimistic initiation story in which Robin is introduced to the Seven Deadly Sins (the ferryman personifies avarice, the watchman sloth, and so on) and identifies himself with the forces of evil replacing the innocent Major (Broes); as a seriocomic moral tale that, through literary allusions, reveals Robin not only as a mock-heroic figure but also as an innocent turned into a Judas (Allison).

"Young Goodman Brown" (1835). Probably Hawthorne's best-known tale. In a dream or in reality Brown meets the devil and sees a witches' sabbath attended by respectable citizens, including his wife Faith. From then on he is a gloomy man, distrustful of humanity. According to various interpretations, Brown has been awakened to sex by his marriage and now attributes carnality to people he once admired (Robinson); justifies his own sinfulness by dreaming of sin in others (Hurley); has taken a chance with sin because Antinomianism has made him overconfident of salvation (Mathews); falls victim to specter evidence, deceptive images conjured up by the devil to convince him of universal depravity (Levin; see also chapter 3, under Mather's *Wonders,* one of Hawthorne's sources).

"The Minister's Black Veil" (1836). Here the ambiguities concern Mr. Hooper, the clergyman who insists on covering his face with a piece of crepe as a sign of secret sin. To some he seems noble, kindly, and self-sacrificing (Strandberg), successful in converting a knowledge of sin into salvation (Cochran). Another view is that his fate cannot be determined, that he might have been saved or damned (Walsh). To others he seems proud, cruel, and inhumane (Canaday); he preaches against hiding sins; yet, ironically, he hides a sin from himself—the sin of becoming obsessed to the point of inhumanity (Stibitz). Some critics, like Poe, would ascribe even another personal sin to the minister, accusing him, for example, of having caused the death of the young girl whose corpse shuddered as he bent over it (Wycherley). The veil itself belongs as a device to the gothic novel (Allen), but in meaning it harks back to the Old Testament, where it symbolizes the limits of man's knowledge on earth (Turner).

1. Names in parentheses refer to exponents of various interpretations. For fuller references to these scholars, see the bibliography for Hawthorne.

"The Maypole of Merry Mount" (1836). Shows that the revelers with their love and the Puritans with their seriousness complement each other. Readers may better appreciate the story by knowing about Thomas Morton (see page 20).

"The Celestial Railroad" (1843). A dream-satire of systems such as Unitarianism and transcendentalism that Hawthorne views as absurdly optimistic. An adaptation of Bunyan's *Pilgrim's Progress* in itinerary, language, and other elements, Hawthorne's allegory is told in the first person and abounds in irony.

"The Artist of the Beautiful" (1844). An allegorical tale. Steeped in the tradition of famous automata (Woodward, McCullen), Owen Warland creates a mechanical butterfly of great beauty. Although Hawthorne does not note this, its various attributes, including smallness and delicacy, belong to the definition of beauty in Edmund Burke's *On the Sublime,* a standard treatise on aesthetics (Delaune). Warland, like Hawthorne himself, must be regarded as one of those artists who achieve personal fulfillment (Yoder) and are ennobled while pursuing an art to which the practical, materialistic world will remain indifferent. Yet Hawthorne may not have been entirely sympathetic with such artists, for he saw them as presuming to improve upon God's work and as isolating themselves from their fellow men (Moore).

"Rappaccini's Daughter" (1844). One of Hawthorne's most provocative but obscure tales. Rappaccini has sinned by creating exotic hybrids, an act traditionally regarded as adulterous (Boewe). Besides, he cares not at all for mankind; and like other intellectuals in Hawthorne's stories, he exhibits a Faustian eagerness for knowledge at any price. His daughter Beatrice is essentially innocent, although her breath is poisoned by the plants (Rossky). Giovanni, her would-be lover, fails to recognize this innocence and therefore sins against it (Gwynn, Hovey). The mixed emotions that taint this first-time love affair (Crews) echo the hybridization and fallen-world themes introduced earlier. Other interpretations emphasize the role of Baglioni. Not only does he represent a view of science directly opposed to Rappaccini's (Rosenberry), but he could have purposely caused Beatrice's death (Gale).

"Ethan Brand" (1850). The story of a lime-burner who, after a long search, finds the Unpardonable Sin in his own heart and commits suicide. Chief sources of the tale are the Bible (White, Stock) and Hawthorne's notebooks (Brother Joseph). To emphasize the futility of Brand's quest, which ends where it began—in his own heart—the author uses circular structure and images, for example, the dog chasing his own tail (Vanderbilt). Various minor characters have functional roles. The German showman, a composite of Mephistopheles and the Wandering Jew (Herndon and Moss), serves as Brand's double (Sokoloff). The villagers are linked with Brand (and with hell) through fire imagery but are no more sympathetic with his plight than is Bartram (Davison). Only Joe exhibits the love that ennobles and saves. He functions, along with the brief description of the dawning day, as a glimmer of optimism in this dark story.

Romances. Instead of novels Hawthorne called his longer works *romances*. Explaining his choice in the preface to *The House of the Seven Gables,* he noted that the romance writer, unlike the novelist, may "mingle the Marvellous" in his stories (3:13).[2] This distinction places Hawthorne's romances somewhere between present-day fantasy and fiction.

The Scarlet Letter (1850). Hawthorne's most famous story and one of the world's classics. At its simplest level, *The Scarlet Letter* treats the effects of adultery on the Reverend Arthur Dimmesdale and Hester Prynne (the adulterers), Pearl (their child), and Roger Prynne (alias Chillingworth, Hester's cuckolded husband). But there are other themes: the paradoxical relationship between good and evil or, specifically, between passion and moral growth (Sandeen); the conflict between the individual and society (Male, Lewis); variations on the Christian process of sin-isolation-suffering-reunion (Roper); loss of position in the great chain of being (Mathews); the tragic irreconcilability of conflicting moral viewpoints (Gross); and the harshness of Puritanism (Woodberry).

Consideration of the major characters discloses more of the ambiguities. Hester has been called on the one hand a saint (Munger), on the other a female Faustus (Stein). She is the very essence of paradox—passionate yet controlled, isolated by the community yet devoted to serving it, unrepentant in the traditional sense yet hopeful of immortal life with her lover. A freethinker, a moral speculator, and therefore a kind of transcendentalist, she certainly was; but while one scholar (Sherman) sees this as an implied criticism of Puritanism, another (Carpenter) sees it as a criticism of transcendentalism. In the imagery that describes her Hester is also ambiguous, being linked with both flowers and weeds (Waggoner).

Another controversial character is Arthur Dimmesdale. Scholars concur that he embodies hypocrisy but argue over his ultimate fate, which Hawthorne left open to speculation. Some would have him saved (Van Doren, Stewart); others damned him (Nolte, Davidson). One (Abel) thinks that Hawthorne rescued Dimmesdale with a well-timed death. Of those who see him as damned, one (Nolte) finds him treated with loathing and irony by the author; another calls his confession morally insignificant since it did little toward his assuming responsibility for Pearl (Austin; cf. Baughman, Parcher); and still another (Schwartz) attributes his fate to the Puritan failure to envision a God of love.

As for Pearl, there is also diversity of opinion over her portrayal. In creating her, Hawthorne relied upon close observation of his daughter Una. The

2. Quotations in this section are from *The Complete Works of Nathaniel Hawthorne,* Riverside Ed., 12 vols. (Boston: Houghton Mifflin, 1883–1884).

result was curiously mixed—a real yet unreal child, a child too elflike for even a romance (Trollope) or so completely allegorical as to have no character at all (Julian Hawthorne). While the Puritans would have called her *natural* (Eisinger)—a term they used for pagans—she should be considered innocent rather than sinful, for according to the psychology of Hawthorne's day, she inherited Hester's sin but not her guilt (Garlitz). Pearl's function in the novel is important, in fact, crucial: Although coming from sinful parents, she must paradoxically lead these parents out of sin. At this point the critics split, some maintaining that she succeeds (Whalen, Abel, McNamara), others that she does not (these are especially the critics mentioned above who argue for Dimmesdale's damnation).

If Pearl qualifies as the kind of good angel one finds fighting for endangered souls in the morality plays, then Chillingworth, the least ambiguous of the characters, qualifies as a bad angel. Not only a Mephistopheles, he is also a Faustus seeking forbidden knowledge as he attempts to uncover Dimmesdale's secret guilt (Stein). Yet something good may be said even of him (Nolte). His earlier life had been "studious, thoughtful, quiet" and rather benevolent (5:208), so that like Milton's Satan (Vogel) he represents less the essence of evil than the loss of goodness (Abel). And, paradoxically, out of his moral degeneration comes the opportunity for moral progress in others (Male).

Symbolism dominates *The Scarlet Letter*. The chief symbol, the embroidered letter worn by Hester, is paralleled throughout. Pearl becomes its living embodiment, as does Dimmesdale. With this symbolism Hawthorne mixed a hint of the supernatural, suggesting that the letter *A* on Dimmesdale's chest was of necromantic or divine origin and that another letter *A*, a kind of portent, had once appeared emblazoned in the midnight sky. Henry James thought the first suggestion overworked, the second "superficial." Yet these supernatural possibilities were true to the atmosphere of the seventeenth-century New England setting. Scholars have found many other symbols in this novel. Some seem to polarize into those representing the harsh restrictions of society and its laws (the prison, the pillory, and the scaffold) and those representing the free world outside this society (the Indians, the sailors, the wild rosebush, and the forest) (Male). Multiple and even contradictory meanings sometimes occur. Thus the forest stands for escape, freedom, unlimited possibility, and the American dream, but also for evil, witchcraft, and moral bewilderment, depending on whether the point of view is from the romantic age of nature-sympathy in which Hawthorne was living or the Puritan age of nature-fear he wrote about (Lewis, Carpenter, Eisinger).

The Scarlet Letter has been deservedly praised for the symmetry of its structure, although critics vary in their analysis of this structure. One thinks it is divided into five acts like a play (Cowley); others suggest such structural units as epic quests (Maclean), journey motifs and metaphors

(Von Abele), and parts built around scaffold scenes (Schubert) or a single dominant character (Gerber, Roper).

The House of the Seven Gables (1851). A masterful mixture of humor and pathos (Whipple). To show that "the wrong-doing of one generation lives into the successive ones" (3:14), Hawthorne begins with two seventeenth-century Salemites, then portrays their nineteenth-century descendants. In the opening chapter Colonel Pyncheon obtains Matthew Maule's property by having him executed for witchcraft; the rest of the book traces the long-term effects of this sin and the greed that caused it. The villain of the piece is Judge Jaffrey Pyncheon, whom Hawthorne modeled on Charles W. Upham, chief among those who had caused his removal from the Salem Custom House. The Judge inherits the dominant vices of the Pyncheons but specializes in his own brand of hypocrisy. Although Hawthorne kills him off with obvious pleasure, extending his death through several chapters, few character portrayals have been more artistically controlled than this one (Duyckinck): Not until chapter 18 does Hawthorne cease to portray the Judge with the verbal irony that perfectly matches his hypocritical nature.

Hepzibah Pyncheon represents the ruined aristocrat, a character type indigenous to America, where class fluidity prevails. Hawthorne treats her with both satire and sympathy. Her brother Clifford, imbecilic but innocent, embodies the recessive traits of the Pyncheon family and is thus overpowered by Judge Pyncheon, who has him jailed for thirty years. Clifford and his sister enjoy no real link with humanity, having inherited, through a sin not their own, the terrible curse of isolation. In the midst of this gloom shines Phoebe, whom Hawthorne consistently describes with sun imagery (Von Abele). Her role is redemptive; she brings the gift of love to offset Judge Pyncheon's evil (Levy). Holgrave the daguerreotypist proves a descendant of the Maules but by no means a carbon copy of them. A much-criticized ironic reversal at the end of the story has him coming under Phoebe's influence and losing his radical, Emersonian ideas.

Scholars have interpreted the story as depicting the "interaction of past and present, heredity and environment," "evolution and regeneration" (Male); the struggle between the artist and antiartist in Hawthorne's life and the triumph of the imagination, represented by Clifford, over materialism, represented by the Judge (Marks), and of democracy, represented by the Maules, over aristocracy, represented by the Pyncheons (Hall).

The Blithedale Romance (1852). Based on Hawthorne's stay at Brook Farm (here called *Blithedale*). When critical of its subject, this romance belongs with various antireformist pieces by Carlyle, Paulding, and Emerson. But occasional passages reveal sympathy with the Blithedalers' experiment, for the author's personal feelings toward Brook Farm were ambivalent (Elliott). According to various suggestions, the narrator Miles Coverdale must be regarded as a dreamer (Griffith) and a failure (Smith) seeking to prove his innocence (Rose), although there are some who insist on the essential accuracy of his reporting (Hedges, Ragan). Less debatable is the technical attractiveness of his role as a pre-Jamesian narrator who learns as the story progresses (Crane). Other characters include Hollingsworth, the monomaniacal reformer; Priscilla, the seamstress; and Zenobia, an exotic woman modeled after Margaret Fuller (Stanton, Lefcowitz).

The Marble Faun; or, the Romance of Monte Beni (1860). A novel set in Rome and thus belonging with the fiction of the foreign scene written by Cooper and James. As a story with artists as central characters, it follows N. P. Willis's *Paul Fane* (1857) and anticipates the work of James. The plot involves Hawthorne's favorite topic, the consequences of sin, each character finding himself implicated when Donatello flings a mysterious stranger off the Tarpeian Rock. In theme, *The Marble Faun* defines the conflict between the ideal and the material (Schneider); denies the validity of cultural isolationism and Emersonian self-reliance (Goldfarb); reenacts the Garden of Eden story; and treats the idea of the fortunate Fall, which regards sin as the prelude to redemption (Schwartz, Beidler, Waggoner). Its characters have attracted much less critical comment than those in *The Scarlet Letter,* although the view of Donatello as an innocent has been challenged (Pattison) and the complexity of Miriam's personality reasserted (Guilds). Hilda, who qualifies as a pre-Jamesian international heroine, remains especially intriguing, for while Hawthorne modeled her after his wife, gave her ideal qualities, and explained her motives for refusing to help Miriam (Bercovitch, 1968), he also chided her Puritanism (Bercovitch, 1966) and even portrayed her as one of his proud "isolatoes" (Zivkovic).

EDGAR ALLAN POE (1809–1849)

In the writings and life of Edgar Allan Poe we see some of the farthest reaches of romanticism. Poe surpassed all his American predecessors in conceiving poetry as music. He rivaled the graveyard poets in melancholy and even declared that, of all possible topics, the death of a beautiful woman was the most poetic. His gothicism was no mere congeries of haunted castles, thirsty vampires, and persecuted heroines but the psychological illumination of the dark recesses of the mind. He yearned for supernal beauty and carried remoteness beyond Europe, beyond Arabia, to the very heavens. Surely he fitted the stereotype of the romantic solitary pining to escape from a world that rewarded him not. But he was far from being one of the demonic drug addicts pictured in his stories.

Life. After his actor-father deserted the family and his actress-mother died (1811), Poe was brought up, though never adopted, by John Allan, a merchant. In 1826 Poe attended the University of Virginia, where he won scholastic honors; but Allan refused to pay Poe's gambling debts and withdrew him from the university. He then enlisted in the army and later attended West Point (1830–1831), bringing about his own dismissal after Allan's second marriage spelled an obvious end to his support. Meanwhile, although three volumes of his poems were printed (1827, 1829, 1831) he had made little impression on the public. Then he turned to writing prose, won a prize for a story entitled "MS. Found in a Bottle," and edited several magazines, including the *Southern Literary Messenger* (1835–1837) and *The Broadway Journal* (1845–1846). Publication of "The Raven" (1845) finally brought him recognition as a poet, but his personal trials grew with his reputation. He was consistently underpaid, whether he worked in Baltimore, Philadelphia, or New York; and marriage (1836) to his young cousin Virginia Clemm merely intensified his poverty. During Virginia's five-year illness, which terminated in her death (1847), he not only starved himself to provide for her but also took to drink, even though the slightest bit of alcohol made him sick. Four days before his own death (October 7, 1849) he was found half-conscious in Baltimore, possibly in a diabetic coma.

Criticism. Poe did much to raise the standards of American criticism. True, he overpraised certain writers, usually women, and abused others for nonexistent plagiarisms and grammatical offenses. On the subject of versification, moreover, he was patently confused. But he was a fearless, dedicated critic who warred against puffery, evolved an aesthetic of his own, and demanded close attention to the text.[3]

Poetry he defined as *"The Rhythmical Creation of Beauty"* (14:275)[4] and, like Coleridge, insisted that this beauty, the taste that apprehends it, and the pleasure it produces are the chief business of the poet. Truth, intellect, morality must be subordinate concerns. His ideal poets glimpsed "Supernal Beauty" (14:290) and elevated the soul. His ideal poems were original, universal, melancholy, and suggestively indefinite in meaning.

To the short story or tale Poe contributed similar theories and thus became the most important contemporary critic of that neglected genre. He asked that tales as well as poems be short enough for a single, uninterrupted reading, and he demonstrated that this brevity produced an intense single effect impossible in the novel. To an age used to leisurely, rambling tales he censured waste and recommended that "in the whole composition, there should be no word written, of which the tendency, direct or indirect, is not to the one pre-established design"(11:108).

Poetry. The Poe canon includes only about fifty poems, but there are many variants of these, for Poe was fond of revising his work, sometimes drastically. On the whole, his poems exemplify his poetic theory, especially in their brevity, concentration on mood, and freedom from didacticism.

3. Poe's best-known critical pieces are "Letter to B——" (1831); his 1842 review of Hawthorne's *Twice-Told Tales;* "The Philosophy of Composition" (1846); and "The Poetic Principle" (delivered as a lecture 1848–1849).

4. Quotations are from *The Complete Works of Edgar Allan Poe,* ed. James A. Harrison, Virginia Ed., 17 vols. (New York: T. Y. Crowell, 1902).

With such later works as "The Bells" (an experiment in onomatopoeia), he proved his mastery of sound effects; yet this very mastery almost drowned out meaning and justified Emerson's calling him "the jingle-man."

"Sonnet—To Science" (1829). A lament that science has victimized the poet, here depicted as Icarian.

"Romance" (1829). A lyric contrasting the author's youthful and mature attitudes toward poetry.

"To Helen" (1831). A lyric celebrating ideal love and beauty (as embodied in antiquity) and portraying their effect on the poet who seeks them. Note the allusions to Ulysses and Helen of Troy, the classical restraint, and the many variations in the four-stress meter.

"Israfel" (1831). Poe's poetic ideals expressed in cosmic imagery and highly melodic stanzas of irregular length.

"The City in the Sea" (1831). A masterpiece of dominant impression; a ghastly vision variously thought to represent a dead city bounded by water (Keefer), an ancient sunken city like Tyre (Pound), a Babylon-like place for dead sinners awaiting the Last Judgment (Campbell), a temporary state of quietude for all dead souls before they sink into the sea of oblivion (Stovall).

"The Sleeper" (a later version of "Irene," first published 1831). A fine example of poetry as movement. The poem slowly narrows its focus from a cosmic landscape to the chamber of the "sleeper," slowly reveals that she is dead, subtly identifies the poet as her lover, and closes on a note of irony.

"Lenore" (1831). In early versions a dramatic monologue; in later versions a balladlike dramatic dialogue between a bereaved lover (Guy De Vere) and those he accuses of Lenore's death.

"Dream-Land" (1844). A surrealistic poem recreating the dream state in weird, topographical imagery and in a repetitive style characteristic of Poe's later works.

"The Raven" (1845). Poe's most famous poem. In "The Philosophy of Composition" he explains its methodical composition, brevity, tone and subject, functional refrain, and novel versification.[5] Not until the closing stanzas did he give the poem suggestiveness by equating the raven with *"Mournful and Never-ending Remembrance"* (14:208).

"Ulalume" (1847). Narrative of a conflict between the poet's soul (Psyche) and his body, which seeks a new love to replace the poet's wife, now dead one year. Spiritual love ultimately seems to prevail over fleshly love (Astarte). Incremental repetition and long *o*'s contribute to the strange, melancholy tone.

Eureka (1848). An ambitious prose poem on the unity of the universe.

"Eldorado" (written 1849). An ambiguous poem variously interpreted as

5. Allen (*American Prosody,* pp. 74–76) notes a tendency toward syncopation caused by feminine rhymes and alliterative pairs. Stovall (*Edgar Poe the Poet,* pp. 226–228) shows that the regularity of the meter (unusual for Poe) is offset by irregularly spaced iterations, rhymes, and caesuras.

a satire of the gold rush, an expression of Poe's idealism, and an ironic narrative of futility.

"Annabel Lee" (1849). A ballad on death caused by envious spirits (a common folklore motif) but transcended by the evocative power of the narrator's dreams. Stanza by stanza, Poe builds increasingly complex sound patterns, including several kinds of rhyme and reiteration.

Tales. The best of Poe's tales include horror stories such as "A Descent into the Maelström" (1841), "The Pit and the Pendulum" (1842), "The Tell-Tale Heart" (1843), and "The Black Cat" (1843); psychological narratives like "The Man of the Crowd" (1840), which contains the "double," or *doppelgänger,* motif; and tales of ratiocination—mystery and detective stories—like "The Gold Bug" (1843) and "The Murders in the Rue Morgue" (1841). In his day Poe was a widely respected fictionist; today his significance looms even larger. Above all, he streamlined the tale, following his own theories of brevity and single effect. He pioneered in science fiction and invented the modern detective story. In his superdetective M. Dupin and Dupin's admiring sidekick (the narrator) are foreshadowed Sherlock Holmes and Dr. Watson.

"Ligeia" (1838). A tale of reincarnation that may be regarded as a traditional terror device meant to be taken literally (Lauber) or as the narrator's hallucination (Basler). Ligeia may represent Poe's muse (West), Poe's mother (Morrison), a gothic heroine (Ramakrishna), or the ideal—achieved, lost, and imagined (Gargano).

"The Fall of the House of Usher" (1839). Poe's most frequently analyzed tale; a gothic masterpiece in which setting and symbols reveal character and conflict, not just atmosphere (Abel). It has been called a study of fear (Spitzer), an expression of theories later used in *Eureka* (Beebe, Smith), a fictional portrait of a real-life family close to Poe's mother (Mabbott), and the symbolic victory of irrationality in Poe's own psyche (Feidelson). The twins, Roderick and Madeline Usher, represent a split personality (symbolized by the crack in the house), and their relationship seems incestuous (D. H. Lawrence). The reasons why Roderick prematurely buries Madeline remain moot. Equally obscure but deliciously gothic is Madeline's return from the vault.

"The Masque of the Red Death" (1842). A gothic allegory on the inevitability of death. The bloody, beshrouded masquer is generally thought to represent death itself, in particular, cholera; but he has also been identified as the father in an oedipal triangle (Bonaparte) and the mere image of death created by those who fear it (Roppolo).

"The Purloined Letter" (preferred version first published in the *Gift,* 1845). One of the world's greatest detective stories. The detective Dupin recovers the letter by exercising imagination as well as reason, thus demonstrating Poe's theory that intuition is a prerequisite for the highest flights of analysis.

"The Cask of Amontillado" (1846). A horror story rich in folklore, irony (Gargano), and puns (Steele, Mabbott). Critics suggest that Montresor immures the ironically named Fortunato out of perversity (Rea), revenge for real or imagined wrongs, and even a Catholic antipathy toward the Freemasons (Harris). But Fortunato falls silent before the last stone is laid, perhaps dying from a cause other than suffocation, the fate Montresor had planned for him.

HERMAN MELVILLE (1819–1891)

Generally ignored in his own time and almost forgotten in the years after his death, Melville has since then emerged as one of the giants of American literature.

Life. Most of the outward drama in Melville's life occurred between his nineteenth and twenty-fifth years. Born into a New York family whose fortunes fell after his father's early death, Melville tried his hand at clerking, farming, and teaching before he found what was to be the subject of his greatest writing—the sea. In 1839 he shipped as a common sailor on a merchant ship to Liverpool (an experience used in *Redburn*). Thereafter he served on three whaling ships that made lengthy voyages to the South Seas, jumped ship in the Marquesas Islands, and lived for a month among cannibals (experiences variously used in *Typee*, 1846; *Omoo*, 1847; and especially *Moby-Dick*, 1851). In Hawaii he shipped aboard a U.S. Navy frigate that returned him to the States (material used in *White-Jacket*, 1850). His only other major voyage was to the Holy Land in 1856. His early popularity, based on *Typee* and *Omoo*, waned with *Mardi* (1849), returned briefly with *Redburn* and *White-Jacket*, but disappeared entirely after *Moby-Dick* and *Pierre* (1852). Following *The Confidence-Man* (1857), also a failure, he gave up fiction for poetry, and lived a life of genteel poverty as a customs inspector in the port of New York. His poetry was generally privately published and unknown in his own time. Forty years after the publication of *Moby-Dick* he died in obscurity. In 1924 the manuscript of his novella *Billy Budd*, the work of his old age and his first fiction after thirty years, was discovered and published. This aided in the revival of interest in his work, which began in the 1920s and has continued to the present. It is now conceded that Melville is one of America's major authors and that *Moby-Dick* is one of the world's great books.

Early Works

Typee (1846). Melville's first novel. The narrator and his friend desert their whaling ship in the Marquesas Islands and spend three months with the Typee cannibals. The narrator admires the easy primitive life of the islanders and is especially fond of the lovely Fayaway. But the peaceful interval ends when he comes to suspect that the Typees will eat him if he tries to leave. By trickery he manages to escape amid a hail of arrows.

Omoo (1847). A sequel to *Typee*. The narrator and most of the rest of the crew desert their whaler because of an eccentric captain and bad living conditions. They are jailed in Tahiti, and later the narrator and his friend Captain Long Ghost (the first of Melville's memorable characters) travel about the islands. The narrator finally ships aboard another whaler, leaving Long Ghost in Tahiti.

To the student of Melville, these two novels reveal a habit of composition Melville was to use in much of his work: They are based on personal experience combined with a good deal of research. Though apprentice work, *Typee* and *Omoo* are readable. True, one could not guess from them that their author would write *Moby-Dick;* yet in retrospect they reveal many of the elements of Melville's later work. The love of the exotic and far-off, the contrast between civilization and primitive life, the clash between orthodoxy and natural religious values—all these motifs recur later.

Mardi (1849). Melville's third novel understandably puzzled readers of the first two books. It begins, as the earlier ones do, as a realistic voyage in the South Seas, recounted by a first-person narrator. Then, abruptly, it turns symbolic and allegorical, and nearly impossible to follow as narrative. Melville had not yet mastered the form of symbolic narrative he was to use with such ease in *Moby-Dick,* nor had he yet learned to make his discursive asides relevant to his story. Into it Melville poured all the questions that were beginning to torment him and would continue to do so for the next forty years: whether the universe is patterned or chaotic, whether any orthodoxy can lay claim to truth, whether the terms "good" and "evil" can be anything more than relative. The narrator rescues a mysterious maiden named Yillah who has come from some strange Eden-like island. She seems to hold the answers to all the narrator's questions, but he rescues her at the cost of murdering one of her kinsmen and thus pursues his quest with bloody hands. Yillah disappears, and the narrator follows her from island to island; in each place he engages in lengthy discussions with a poet and a philosopher as well as the ruler. The talks vary in form from direct Socratic dialogue to Swiftian satire, and in subject matter from slavery in the American South to the Roman church. As the narrative pattern reappears from time to time, it becomes clear that Yillah is a metaphor for truth. Significantly, the narrator never finds her again, and at the end of the book he is heading out into the open sea in his vain pursuit, followed by those who would avenge his earlier crimes.

Transition Works. In *Redburn* and *White-Jacket* Melville returned to the simple adventure voyage that had brought him his early fame. But in the meantime he had advanced as an artist, and both books differ in kind from his first two stories. Beneath the simple narrative surface run currents of symbolic meaning. Melville would never rewrite the incredibly symbolic *Mardi,* but neither would he ever rewrite the innocuous *Typee* and *Omoo.*

Redburn (1849). Another first-person narrative, this novel follows the adventures of young Wellingborough Redburn, a cabin boy on a ship bound from New York to Liverpool. The boy spends some time in Liverpool, appalled by the cruel conditions in the slum areas. He meets Harry Bolton, a profligate young aristocrat who takes him on a wild trip to London, where the boy is shocked at Bolton's excesses. Together they sign on as seamen for the return voyage, a horrible trip on which many of the steerage passengers die of cholera. They part in New York, Bolton to sign aboard a whaler on which he is later killed.

White-Jacket (1850). In this novel, again narrated in the first person, Melville depicts regimented life aboard a U.S. Navy frigate. The narrator wears a white pea jacket, which gives him his shipboard name and the book its title. Although the coat keeps him warm, it nearly kills him by blowing up over his head in a storm and pitching him into the sea. Melville stresses the arrogance of the ship's officers and the brutalized life of the enlisted men. Young White Jacket develops a hero worship for his foretop captain, Jack Chase, who is not only a glamorous figure, greatly admired by all the crew, but a voice of sanity as well. When the men threaten mutiny on being ordered to shave off their beards, Chase joshes them out of it.

Recent critics have frequently seen both *Redburn* and *White-Jacket* as so-called initiation stories in which a young and relatively unsophisticated hero comes into his first contact with the moral and social evils of the world. Young Redburn discovers among his shipmates grays and blacks of moral decisions. There is a man named Jackson whose inexplicable hatred of the hero foreshadows *Billy Budd.* Both Redburn and White Jacket encounter the wrongs that society inflicts upon its citizens: Redburn among the slums and docks of Liverpool, White Jacket in the brutal community of the American navy. But in both books there are pinpoints of goodness, as in the later characters Queequeg and Billy Budd: Harry Bolton (after he reforms) and Jack Chase (*Billy Budd* is dedicated to Jack Chase). In brief, the books are worthy predecessors of Melville's later work, both in theme and technique. They are realistic narratives interlarded with relevant authorial comment and focus symbolically on the tormenting ambiguity of good and evil in a world that refuses to reveal itself clearly as either one or the other.

"Hawthorne and His Mosses" (1850). In this review of Hawthorne's *Mosses from an Old Manse,* Melville repeats the argument of many of his contemporaries, that American literature has "come of age" and need no longer look to England for its literary models. In a burst of literary jingoism, he compares Hawthorne to Shakespeare, praising both as "truth divers" who probe beneath surface reality in an attempt to find ultimate truth. Hawthorne, like Shakespeare, had the "power of blackness," the capacity for seeing and revealing "the blackness of darkness" that lies behind, or beneath, the appearance of this "world of lies."

Chief Works

Moby-Dick (1851). Probably no other American book has attracted the comment and critical interpretation that this one has. It is the *Hamlet* of American literature. As is the case with all very great works of art, no single critical perspective reveals it in its totality. For example, we have a good deal of biographical information relating to the composition of the book. We know that during Melville's writing and revision of it he was reading both Hawthorne (to whom the book is dedicated) and Shakespeare, and that he found in both writers a profound sense of the evil at what Melville called the very axis of reality. Certainly Ahab's Shakespearean rhetoric and his obsession with evil, for him symbolized by the white whale, bear out the importance of this biographical knowledge, but it does not explain the book. It seems clear enough that Melville tried to cast Ahab in the mold of such Shakespearean heroes as Macbeth and Lear, but this does not explain the book either. Other biographical information is equally interesting but does not provide total enlightenment. We know from Melville's letters that he seemed not entirely conscious of all he was doing in the book, and critics have thus been led to the problem of unintentional or unconscious meaning. As Leon Howard has said, the tragic plot of the book seemed "so deeply moving to the author that it apparently colored his unconscious imagination and gave the story an uncalculated emotional and intellectual coherence."[6]

It is this belief in the book's coherence that has led commentators to deal with such subjects as the structure and various techniques Melville used. Like *Mardi,* the book begins as realistic first-person narrative, then turns not only to interrupting discursive chapters but also to such Elizabethan dramatic devices as the aside and the soliloquy. But in *Moby-Dick,* unlike *Mardi,* these deviations from straightforward narrative succeed. The soliloquies anticipate the stream of consciousness technique of later writers such as Joyce and Proust. Melville's gamble pays off: The book seems all of a piece, whether we describe it as a novel using epic and dramatic devices or whether we categorize it in some other way.

Thematically, *Moby-Dick* (like most of Melville's other mature work) is dialectical. It presents arguments, both dramatically and discursively, about great philosophical and religious questions that trouble men's minds. Probably the most basic and useful way of viewing the book is as a debate between Ahab's ideas and actions and Ishmael's reflections on them, with subsidiary comments and actions by other characters. Ahab's world view and its consequent actions are simple and dramatic: There is operative in the universe a positive evil, whether it is principal or agent, and he intends

6. Howard (GB), p. 163.

to destroy it or be destroyed by it in direct confrontation. For him the white whale is the incarnation of this evil. Ishmael cannot accept this simplistic, basically religious outlook. To the end, the whale remains cryptic for him— inscrutable and unknowable as the God who may or may not exist. Thus, interwoven with the intense dramatic action of the whale hunt is the debate between the fanatic believer and the skeptic, and the book leaves open the great question of whether the universe is ruled by chance or by pattern and, if by pattern, whether that pattern is good or evil, or even knowable.

It is easy to see why *Moby-Dick,* and Melville's work in general, is so appealing to our time, for Melville, like contemporary existentialists and absurdists, calls into question all the old seeming certainties and opens up the appalling possibility of the ultimate meaninglessness of man and the world. If meaning may metaphorically be described as color, then the real hue of the world may be as blank and white as that of *Moby-Dick* himself.

Pierre (1852). The possibility of evil, or nothingness, at the world's axis is again dramatized by Melville in *Pierre,* one of the strangest works in all American fiction, a work so bizarre in tone and language that the best edition of it is prefaced by a hundred-page introduction written not by a literary critic but by a practicing psychologist.

The hero of *Pierre* finds, to his distress, that all his consciously good actions seem to be motivated by unconscious evil impulses: Thus his attempt to save the girl who may be his half-sister is revealed as veiled incestuous lust. The only answer suggested in the book, which ends tragically in the deaths of the major characters, is set forth in a pamphlet that the hero finds by accident. It argues that to try to abide by absolute moral standards is inevitably to do evil; one must act according to relative and shifting moral values.

A short summary can give no notion of the book's wild and whirling quality: the grandiloquence of its rhetoric (partly satirical but partly serious), the sense that Melville is wrestling with a theme too large and amorphous for him to handle coherently. There were larger fish than whales, he told Hawthorne after finishing *Moby-Dick;* there were kraken (sea monsters). The modern reader is likely to see Melville struggling toward a working conception of the unconscious mind and its role in human affairs, as Hawthorne does in his darker stories. And with both writers, unwilling inheritors of the Calvinistic sense of man's natural depravity, their explorations of the unconscious give unorthodox witness to that grim belief.

"Bartleby the Scrivener" (1853). Melville's most famous short tale. Bartleby's occupations suggest the theme of the story: He has worked in the dead letter department of the post office and has been a scrivener, a copier of legal documents. It would be hard to find two more telling symbols of the meaninglessness of existence. Furthermore, in his job as scrivener he prefers to gaze out of a window at a perfectly blank wall (the subtitle is "A Story of Wall Street"); and when asked to carry out some meaningful kind of action he simply replies that he "prefers not to." Eventually he is sent to debtors' prison, where he spends his days staring at the prison wall; and it is at the foot of the blank gray wall that he is found dead.

The Encantadas (1854). A series of ten sketches describing the desolate Galapagos Islands in the South Pacific. A few of the sketches contain narratives of historical or legendary visitors to the islands; all stress the infernal aspect of the place. The eighth sketch (the most famous) has a plot that had apparently been haunting Melville for some time. In 1852 he wrote Hawthorne of a story he had heard about a young woman abandoned for years by her husband, a woman who had suffered with incredible patience and dignity. He suggested that Hawthorne might use it, but when Hawthorne did not, Melville told his own version: the story of the Cholo Indian woman of Sketch Eight. She, her husband, and her brother are left at one of the islands by a French whaling captain. They are to stay for four months collecting tortoise oil. Her husband and brother drown; the French captain never returns; and Hunilla is left for years to undergo experiences Melville only hints at, one of them being rape by crewmen from a passing whaler who then leave her again alone to guess at the passing years and to pray. She becomes "a heart of yearning in a frame of steel. A heart of earthly yearning, frozen by the frost which falleth from the sky." When she is finally rescued, she rides an ass into her village, gazing at the beast's harness, which Melville calls an "armorial cross."

Benito Cereno (1855). A novella that depicts as clearly as anything Melville ever wrote his sense of evil lying behind the world's neutral appearance. An American sea captain boards a Spanish slave ship off southern Chile because the ship is drifting toward the rocky coast. He senses something wrong but is reassured by the Spanish captain, Don Benito Cereno. A Negro slave, Babo, hovers over Cereno, apparently solicitous of his every want. As the American is leaving, Cereno leaps into his boat and reveals the whole horrible story behind the appearances. The Negroes have revolted, tortured, and killed many of the Spaniards, and Babo has been Cereno's master, not his slave. The leaders of the rebellion are taken into court, and the whole story is retold in the form of legal depositions.

The Confidence-Man (1857). A novel, Melville's last fiction before *Billy Budd*, that moves on many levels of irony. Abandoning all but the merest appearance of realistic fiction, Melville gives his major character mythic qualities. Within the framework of a steamer voyage down the Mississippi, Melville presents a series of vignettes in which the confidence man, in various identities, swindles, dupes, and ruins a number of characters. The confidence man is a satanic figure of remarkable guile and persuasiveness, but his successes are possible only because of the inherent greed, stupidity, and general wickedness of the passengers.

Billy Budd (written by 1891, published 1924). Melville's last work, the novella *Billy Budd*, has stirred readers' interest for several reasons. It marked a return to fiction after a thirty-year gap, and it was unknown to students of Melville for more than another thirty years. Until recently, scholars and critics were working with an imperfect text, not the version that Melville apparently arrived at just before his death (even that version is perhaps not the final version that he had in mind). The authentic text was not produced until Harrison Hayford and Merton M. Sealts, Jr., examined the original manuscript and found many sections that Melville may have intended to omit and some corrections made in Mrs. Melville's handwriting, presumably after Melville's death. It was not until 1962 that the two scholars reconstructed what is now called the *Genetic Text*. The story, even the version based on the Genetic Text, is tormentingly ambiguous. Various critics have found it to be an old man's final acceptance of the world, the end of Melville's quarrel with God. Others have argued that it repeats in ironic form the ambiguity of good and evil that haunted Melville for more than fifty years.

Billy Budd is a moral innocent tricked into a murder he does not mean to commit and hanged by a ship captain who knows him to be morally innocent. Billy is frequently described as a Christ figure: He blesses the captain before the hanging, and the hanging itself is described in terms that unmistakably echo Christ's crucifixion. But Captain Vere is not a villain, not even a Pilate seeking to avoid responsibility. He loves Billy but acts for what he seems to believe is the common good. Civilization must abide by measured forms; crimes must be punished, and in this world moral intentions are irrelevant. The world's value is not that of Thoreau—the supremacy of the private conscience—but that of the larger social good. The dialectical facts of the story are clear enough, as they always are in Melville's work. The question the critics debate is whether Melville accepted this kind of world as the best of all possible worlds, or the only possible world, or an evil world, perhaps even the worst of all possible worlds. The answer must be sought partly in the body of Melville's work as a whole and partly in the authorial tone of *Billy Budd*.

Melville's Poetry

In recent years Melville's poetry for the first time has begun to receive serious attention. For one who began writing poetry only in mid-life, Melville achieved a surprising degree of technical competence in verse. But the modern reader will likely find his verse old-fashioned, more interesting as a continuation of his thought than for its own sake. There are a few single poems (such as "The Maldive Shark") and parts of other poems in which he attains something like Dickinson's intensity and compression of phrase and image (in "The Portent" he sees the figure of John Brown as "the meteor of the war"). And his facility with certain verse forms is clear enough: for example, the rhyming iambic tetrameter lines in the very long *Clarel* and the blank verse in "The House-Top" describing the suppression in the New York draft riots. But in most of his poems the thought outstrips the form in which it is conveyed. *Clarel* is a case in point. The regular rhyming tetrameter lines grow tiresome, as the poem continues Melville's old "quarrel with God" (Lawrance Thompson) that began with *Mardi* and continued through the other prose works. The story of the poem is weak, but the usual Melville dialectic is not. Various religious and philosophical viewpoints are aired—a shallow form of Christianity, agnosticism, and other shades of doubt and belief. The young hero, seeking truth in the Holy Land, ultimately finds only uncertainty, at best a need to keep a balance between the agnosticism of the head and the hope of the heart.[7]

---

7. J. E. Miller, Jr., *A Reader's Guide to Herman Melville* (New York: Farrar, Straus & Giroux, 1962), p. 216.

12
New England Poets

Longfellow, Whittier, and Lowell all enjoyed immense popularity in their day but have been neglected in ours. Together with Bryant and Holmes, they are known as the household or schoolroom poets, because their works were read to the family around the hearthside and were standard offerings in the schools. Today their writings have survived piecemeal in scores of quotations still in common use. Longfellow gave us "The Wreck of the Hesperus," Lowell "And what is so rare as a day in June?" and Whittier the words of Barbara Frietchie, "Shoot, if you must, this old gray head." Nevertheless, the reputation of these poets has worsened to the danger point. It will probably improve only if more attention is given to those works of theirs that best satisfy modern taste, although such works are but a small fraction of their total output.

HENRY WADSWORTH LONGFELLOW (1807–1882)

Longfellow was among the most widely read and frequently quoted nineteenth-century English and American poets. Of the household poets, he was certainly the most versatile and romantic. Wonder and mystery, mythology and legend, primitivism, medievalism, and sentimentalism all found expression in his works, which, though traditional, were marvelously varied in form. Above all, he helped to universalize American romanticism by broadening the purview of its art to include such hitherto neglected areas as Italy and Scandinavia.

Life. Longfellow spent his early life in Portland, Maine. A classmate of Hawthorne's, he graduated (1825) from Bowdoin College where, after three years of preparation abroad, he taught modern languages (1829–1835). He took his professorial duties seriously, yet still found time to compose the Irving-like prose sketches published as *Outre-Mer* (1835). A second trip to

123

Europe (1835–1836) improved his German and added Dutch, Danish, Swedish, Norwegian, and Finnish to the French, Spanish, and Italian he already knew. Thus equipped, he assumed the chair of modern languages at Harvard (1836), becoming the first American professor-poet of any note. Soon he wrote *Hyperion* (1839), his first novel, and *Voices of the Night* (1839), his first volume of verse. Popularity came quickly, and other books followed, including the narrative poem *Evangeline* (1847) and another novel, *Kavanagh* (1849), so that by 1854 Longfellow was able to resign his professorship in order to labor solely as an author. After this he wrote three of his best works: *The Song of Hiawatha* (1855), *The Courtship of Miles Standish* (1858), and *Tales of a Wayside Inn* (1863, 1872, 1873).

Longfellow was married twice. His first wife, Mary Storer Porter, whom he married in 1831, died in 1835 while she and the poet were visiting northern Europe. In 1843 he married Frances Elizabeth Appleton, who was burned to death in 1861 when her dress caught fire. To recover from this shattering loss of a wife who had borne him six children, Longfellow wrote harder than ever, completing a now-standard translation (1865–1867) of Dante's *Divine Comedy,* composing ambitious works of his own, and earning much acclaim. On his last trip to Europe (1868–1869), he received honorary degrees from both Oxford and Cambridge. He was the first American to have his bust in the Poet's Corner of Westminster Abbey.

Poetry. To facilitate discussion of their types, prosody, rhyme, and tone, we have selected Longfellow's most significant and well-known poems and listed them in alphabetical order:

(1) "The Arsenal at Springfield," (2) "The Beleaguered City," (3) "The Building of the Ship," (4) "Chaucer," (5) "The Children's Hour," (6) *Christus (The Divine Tragedy, The Golden Legend,* and *The New England Tragedies),* (7) *The Courtship of Miles Standish,* (8) "The Cross of Snow," (9) "The Day Is Done," (10–15) "Divina Commedia" (six sonnets), (16) "A Dutch Picture," (17) *Evangeline,* (18) "The Evening Star," (19) "Hawthorne," (20) "Hymn to the Night," (21) "In the Churchyard at Cambridge," (22) "The Jewish Cemetery at Newport," (23) "Jugurtha," (24) "King Witlaf's Drinking Horn," (25) "Mezzo Cammin," (26) *Michael Angelo,* (27) "Milton," (28) "Morituri Salutamus," (29) "My Lost Youth," (30) "Nature," (31) "Nuremberg," (32) "Paul Revere's Ride," (33) "A Psalm of Life," (34) "The Saga of King Olaf," (35) "Seaweed," (36) "Shakespeare," (37) "The Skeleton in Armor," (38) *The Song of Hiawatha,* (39) "The Sound of the Sea," (40) *The Spanish Student,* (41) "The Village Blacksmith," (42) "The Three Silences of Molinos," (43) "The Tide Rises, the Tide Falls," (44) "Venice," (45) "The Wreck of the Hesperus."

The wide range of Longfellow's art may be demonstrated by classifying his poems in different ways. First, we may group them into the various traditional types of poetry: narrative (poems 2, 7, 17, 24, 32, 34, 37, 38, 43, and 45 in the list above); dramatic (poems 6, 26, 40); and lyric (1, 5, 9, 19, 20, 21, 22, 28, 29, 31, 33, 35), including such subcategories of lyric as ode (3) and sonnet (4, 8, 10–15, 18, 25, 27, 30, 36, 39, 42, 44). Longfellow became not only one of America's best sonneteers but probably its greatest narrative poet. His most extensive narrative, *Tales of a Wayside Inn* (1863, 1872, 1873), contains twenty-two story-poems in a setting reminiscent of Chaucer's *Canterbury Tales* and Boccaccio's *Decameron*.

Classified according to their prosodic features, these poems exhibit still more variety. Longfellow could write impressively in falling as well as rising meters; that is, in trochaic (33, 34, 35, 38) and dactylic (7, 17) as well as anapestic (32) and iambic. To suit his purposes he could compose in long, leisurely, sometimes proselike lines (7, 17) or in short, swift, chantlike lines (24, 37, and parts of 34). Of course, he alternated four- and three-stress lines to form ballad stanzas (2, 41, 45); but he also experimented with other combinations, such as five- and three-stress alternating lines (19, 20), and even with an unpatterned variety of line lengths (3). While it is possible to say that he wrote in blank verse (6, 26, 40) or the heroic couplet (28), few of his poems bear the curse of unrelieved regularity. His sonnets, for instance, are basically iambic pentameter; however, not one is without reversed feet, spondees, feminine endings, or other metrical nuances. In fact, some of these sonnets (11, 27) have as many as ten irregular lines. It is often more accurate, therefore, to call his poems two-, four-, or six-stress verse, as the case may be, rather than giving them such labels as trochaic dimeter, iambic tetrameter, or dactylic hexameter. Among his three-stress poems—5, 9, 24, 37, and parts of 34, for example—this would reveal one of the few similarities in lines like "Wĕ mŭst drínk tŏ óne Sàint móre!" (1:278),[1] "Skóal! tŏ thĕ Nórthlănd! skóal!" (1:60), and "Thĕy álmŏst dĕvóur mĕ wĭth kíssĕs" (3:65).

Great variety also appears in the overall structure of Longfellow's poetry. He tended to compose poems of considerable length in verse paragraphs, sometimes unrhymed (7, 17, 38), but most of his works are in rhymed stanzas. These disclose a remarkable inventiveness. One poem, "The Saga of King Olaf," has no less than seventeen different rhyme schemes. Here and elsewhere Longfellow composed stanzas of two, three, four, five, six (21, 35, 41), seven, and eight (37) lines, sometimes extending the length with refrains, a device in which he excelled (23, 29, 43). His four-line stanzas generally rhymed either *a b c b* (5, 9, 24, 45), which is ballad rhyme, or *a b a b* (1, 2, 19, 20, 22, 33), which is elegiac rhyme. Occasionally both these schemes seem out of place, especially when accompanied by monotonous meter or short lines that quicken the rhyming and make it too jingly for the sober subject matter (9, 33). On the other hand, Longfellow was especially

---

1. *The Works of Henry Wadsworth Longfellow*, 14 vols. (Boston: Houghton Mifflin, 1891).

adept at creating interesting patterns with feminine (that is, double) rhymes (1, 23, 33, 35).

All Longfellow's sonnets are Italian in form: They consist of an octave that rhymes *a b b a a b b a* and a sestet that adds new rhymes in various combinations. Analysis of the sonnets listed above reveals such sestet patterns as *c d e c d e* (4, 8, 11, 13, 14, 15, 27, 30, 36, 39, 44), *c d c d c d* (10, 25, 42), *c d c d e e* (18), and *c c d e e d* (12). More important, rhyme and punctuation are synchronized so that main clauses begin and end with the sound patterns themselves, and octaves invariably terminate in the strongest marks of punctuation: periods, exclamation points, or semicolons. However, Longfellow exercises noticeable freedom with traditional minor breaks, for example, in the occasional lack of punctuation at the end of lines four and eleven, the midpoints of quatrain and sestet (4, 10, 14, 30).

In regard to the tone of this poetry, Longfellow tended "to preach when he should only sing";[2] yet some of his works, especially the verse-narratives, were remarkably free of that didacticism so characteristic of the nineteenth century and so irritating to modern ears. At their worst his messages came in every stanza or took up half the poem, thereby spoiling the other half (2, 35). At their best they were merely implied (43). He wrote very few love poems (only "Serenade" and "The Evening Star" come readily to mind), but he frequently expressed his admiration for romantic places and for the authors of world literature. Although nostalgia and various shades of melancholy permeate his work, there is also genuine humor (7, 24, 38), sometimes in its more subtle forms of wit, irony, and mock epic (5, 16, 21, 23).

Representative Works

"A Psalm of Life" (1838). A didactic lyric mixing the *carpe diem* ("seize the day") motif with an activist philosophy stimulated by study of Goethe. This is the poem that brought Longfellow his initial popularity and is still remembered for the phrase "footprints on the sands of time" (1:21). To modern taste, however, "A Psalm of Life" lacks artistry; its imagery seems confused, its rhythm monotonous, and its message too direct.

"Hymn to the Night" (1839). A melancholy lyric (in elegiac rhyme) placed first in the author's first volume of verse, *Voices of the Night*. Four stanzas comprise a personification of night; the final two stanzas, an apostrophe to her. The gloomy setting and escapist message are generally considered romantic.

"The Skeleton in Armor" (1841). One of Longfellow's best ballads; a narrative of abduction and suicide told from the abductor's point of view, without nineteenth-century moralizing. The story utilizes two local ruins: a

2. Edwin P. Whipple, *Essays and Reviews,* 2 vols. (Boston: Houghton, Osgood, 1880), 1: 61.

skeleton found at Fall River and a tower at Newport (see Cooper's *Red Rover*), both supposedly dating back to Viking days.

"The Arsenal at Springfield" (1844). An antiwar poem, appropriately in elegiac stanzas (*a b a b*) with feminine *a* rhymes. Suggested by Longfellow's wife, the basic simile is visual (the stacked guns look like organ pipes), but its development is auditory—a dream of war sounds followed by the "holy melodies of love" (1:197).

"Seaweed" (1845). An eight-stanza allegory that conceives analogies between the movement of seaweed and the development of poems. The modern reader may wince at the strained comparisons but will discover interesting examples of romanticism in the wild, panoramic seascape of the first four stanzas and in the stress on emotion in the last four.

Evangeline: A Tale of Acadie (1847). A verse narrative in two parts, the first an idyll, the second an odyssey. The story begins in Grand-Pré, a French village in Acadie (Nova Scotia), which is described in pastoral terms. When the Acadians are exiled by the British, the two lovers, Evangeline Bellefontaine and Gabriel Lajeunesse, are separated. The rest of the poem tells how Evangeline searches for her betrothed, wandering down the Mississippi to Louisiana (where the Acadians came to be known as Cajuns), out to the western plains, up to the Michigan forests, and finally to Philadelphia, only to find him dying in an almshouse there. Her humble acceptance of God's will indicates that her journey has been a spiritual one, a pilgrimage to the Heavenly City. The expansive settings of this poem demanded many descriptive passages, which Longfellow wrote from seeing John Banvard's moving diorama of the Mississippi when it was in Boston.

The unusual meter of *Evangeline* may be described as unrhymed dactylic hexameter, with plentiful substitutions of trochees and spondees. The opening lines are typical:

Thís ĭs thĕ | fórĕst prī | mévăl. Thĕ | múrmŭrīng | pínes ănd thĕ | hémlŏcks.
Beárdĕd wĭth | móss, ănd ĭn | gármĕnts | gréen, ĭndīs | tínct ĭn thĕ | twílĭght.
(ll. 19)

"The Jewish Cemetery at Newport" (1854). A graveyard meditation in the verse form of Gray's "Elegy." The poem develops associatively in stages marked with various types of contrasts. In the first seven stanzas they are sensory: speech versus silence, motion versus rest, the seen versus the unseen. The next stage is forcefully announced with the oxymoron "Christian hate" as the poet contemplates the "merciless and blind" persecution of Jews (3:35). By stanza 13 he is imagining patriarchal figures parading through time. This brings him to another contrast—man's vain attempt to make past tradition a part of the future. In the final paradox the Jews have sunk with other dead nations into the earth that once gave them life.

"My Lost Youth" (1855). A lyric of nostalgia, in particular for Portland, Maine, but in general for the freedom and far-reaching thoughts of boyhood. To match its subject, the poem is loose in form, but not to the point of wildness. The predominantly irregular meter could easily be called *sprung rhythm,* for it contains noticeable variations in the number of unaccented syllables between accents. Nevertheless it is not free verse: From stanza to stanza the number of accented syllables in corresponding lines remains rather constant. Lines 2, 5, 6, and 7 of each stanza generally contain three stresses; lines 1, 3, 4, and 8, four stresses; line 9 contains five stresses. Longfellow achieved a similar modified freedom by slightly varying his refrain from stanza to stanza. This refrain came from a Lappish song via J. G. von Herder, who translated it as "Knabenwille ist Windeswille, / Jünglings Gedanken lange Gedanken." By changing the second line to "And the thoughts of youth are long, long thoughts" (3:41–44) Longfellow achieved greater emphasis on length through repetition and protraction.

The Song of Hiawatha (1855). An epic, replete with cantos, catalogs, formal speeches, boasts, battles, a journey to the underworld, and other conventional elements. The setting is not merely broad but cosmic, including the moon and the home of the West Wind; it moves from mythic to historic times, beginning with a period before the present order of things—a time of easy communications between gods and men and of few distinctions between men and animals—and ending with the bringing of Christianity to the Indians. The hero, too, is mythic and historic, a composite of Manabozho (an Algonquin god who appears in some tales as an animal and who may be hero, trickster, or dupe) and Hiawatha (an Iroquois statesman). Despite this confusion, attributable not so much to Longfellow as to Henry Rowe Schoolcraft, whose works provided most of the poem's subject matter, Hiawatha qualifies as a traditional epic hero who labors for the good of his people. To depict him thus, Longfellow simplified his original mythical character, ignoring his role as animal and dupe and assigning his role as trickster to Pau-Puk-Keewis. With a rare altruism, Hiawatha slays the spirit of disease and pestilence; marries Minnehaha, a Dacotah, to ensure peace among the tribes; and teaches the arts of healing, picture writing, and planting and harvesting corn. When the Jesuit missionaries come, his job is over and he sails into the sunset.

The poem abounds in folk materials. There are helpful animals; an unpromising hero (Kwasind); magic moccasins (comparable to seven-league boots); narrative forms such as local legends, myths, etiological tales, and tall tales; instances of shapeshifting; and modified versions of totemism and animism (at times expressed as pathetic fallacy). Survivals of ancient fertility rites appear in Hiawatha's wrestling matches with Mondamin, the corn god, and in Minnehaha's naked midnight walk around the fields. However, while this material came from some of the best sources available at the time, not only were these sources sometimes inaccurate, but

Longfellow adapted them selectively (omitting references to scalping, for example), so that his epic is reflective of Indian life and lore to only a limited degree.

The often-parodied rhythm of the poem is both structural and accentual as the following passage indicates:

> Fróm hĭs wándĕrĭngs fár tŏ eástwărd,
> Fróm thĕ régĭons óf thĕ mórnĭng,
> Fróm thĕ shínĭng lánd ŏf Wábŭn,
> Hómewărd nów rĕtúrned Ĭágŏo,
> Thĕ grĕat trávĕllĕr, thĕ grĕat bóastĕr,
> Fúll ŏf néw ănd stránge ădvéntŭres,
> Márvĕls mánў, ănd mánў wóndĕrs.
>
> (2:271)

The structural rhythm consists of the parallelism so obvious in the first three lines; the accentual rhythm consists of the unrhymed trochaic tetrameter that characterizes all the lines but the last, although the fifth line could also be legitimately scanned ⌣ ⁄ ⁄ ⌢ ⌣ ⌣ ⁄ ⌣. Longfellow borrowed this rhythm not from Indian poetry but from Anton Schiefner's German translation of *Kalevala,* the ancient Finnish epic.

"Divina Commedia" (1864, 1866). Six sonnets written to accompany Longfellow's translation of Dante's *Divine Comedy.* Throughout these tributes to Dante the *Divine Comedy* is compared to a medieval cathedral. In Sonnet I Longfellow used this simile to explain the motives that prompted his translation and the reverence with which he approached the task. Sonnet IV, while alluding to Dante's vision of Beatrice in canto xxx of the *Purgatorio,* reminds us of the real-life scene in which Longfellow's dying wife appeared, like Beatrice, in "garments as of flame" (10:10). Sonnet VI acclaims Dante's influence on later ages by comparing him to the morning star and the Holy Ghost, a figure anticipated in line 11 of Sonnet V.

"Milton" (w. 1873). A sonnet extolling Milton as the English Homer and attributing to his verse the mighty power of ocean waves. The cumulative roll of the octave is itself Miltonic.

"Chaucer" (w. 1873). A sonnet-tribute to the medieval poet. Longfellow sets the scene with details from Chaucer's *Book of the Duchess,* creates medieval effects by using "eth" endings and by making "clerk" rhyme with "lark" (3:200), sees in Chaucer the "dawn" of English literature, and praises him for his ability to evoke nature and its sensory impressions.

"Morituri Salutamus: Poem for the Fiftieth Anniversary of the Class of 1825 in Bowdoin College" (w. 1874). One of Longfellow's rare occasional poems. Its ultimate message, that in old age one may yet accomplish something, invites comparison with Tennyson's "Ulysses."

"The Tide Rises, the Tide Falls" (w. 1879). A subtle allegory depicting the end of every man's life as the disappearance of a traveler along the seashore. Lurking pessimism is suggested by the water's effacement of the traveler's footprints (ll. 8–9). Technically the poem is more complex than it seems. The rhyme scheme interlocks, employing only four sounds in all three stanzas; and the meter, while basically iambic tetrameter, is irregular in two-thirds of the lines. Finally, the two-part movement of each line (obvious, for example, in the superb refrain) perfectly suggests the inevitability of the sea and of death.

"The Cross of Snow" (w. 1879). A sonnet in which Longfellow reveals his continuing grief over the loss of his wife eighteen years before. The octave with such words as "halo," "soul," "martyrdom," and "legend" (which in older usage meant the life of a saint) (13:425) expresses his reverence for her. This religious tone is continued in the sestet, where his grief is compared to a snow-cross on a mountainside he had found in a book of scenic views.

JOHN GREENLEAF WHITTIER (1807–1892)

John Greenleaf Whittier was a Quaker author like John Woolman (whose *Journal* he edited), an abolitionist editor like Bryant, a propagandist like Freneau, and a workingman's poet like Whitman. He also stands squarely in the rural tradition that includes Burns, Goldsmith, Timothy Dwight, and Robert Frost. The many indigenous beliefs and tales in his prose and poetry make him of special interest to folklorists and place him among the precursors of the local-color movement.

Life. Whittier was born on a farm near Haverhill, Massachusetts, the same farm that was the setting for "Telling the Bees" and *Snow-Bound*. His ancestors had been Quakers for over a century; that he continued in their ways is evident not only in his letters, which contain many a *thee* and *thou,* but also in such devotional poems as "First-Day Thoughts" and "The Eternal Goodness." Although educated meagerly at a district school and briefly at Haverhill Academy, he tried his hand at verse after encountering the work of Robert Burns and by 1827 had written and had published in local newspapers some eighty poems. From 1829 until the Civil War he edited various reform journals in Hartford, Philadelphia, and Washington. He became one of the country's leading abolitionists, not only as editor and pamphleteer (the publication in 1833 of his *Justice and Expediency* earned him national fame), but also as lobbyist, delegate to the National Anti-slavery Convention (1833), founder of the Liberty Party (1839), and presidential elector (1860, 1864). On several occasions he was victimized by mobs for his abolitionist activities. Meanwhile he began to collect his writings for separate publication. *Legends of New England* (1831) was followed by *Moll Pitcher* (1832), *Ballads and Other Poems* (1884), *The Supernaturalism of New England* (1847), *The Tent on the Beach* (1867), and nearly three dozen other titles. In 1866 with the publication of *Snow-Bound*, which is said to have earned him $10,000 at first printing, he finally became financially secure, and his later years were marked with many honors. Yet, constantly plagued with ill health, he never married, and the deaths of his mother (1858) and younger sister (1864), memorialized in "Telling the Bees" and *Snow-Bound*, affected him deeply.

Representative Works

"Massachusetts to Virginia" (1843). An antislavery lyric condemning Virginians for betraying their forefathers' passion for freedom, citing in contrast the New Englanders' faithfulness to their freedom-loving Puritan forebears, and declaring in conclusion that there will be "No fetters in the Bay State! No slave upon her land!"[3] The thumping seven-stress meter suits this declamatory poem, which was written for a protest meeting. Other ingredients, including the sustained audio and topographical imagery and the many local-color details (landscape, place names, occupations), impart more significance and artistry than usually appear in such occasional verse.

"The Shoemakers" (1845). One of Whittier's "Songs of Labor," a group of six poems that anticipated Whitman in praising the workingman. Whittier lends dignity and importance to the shoemaker's craft (one at which he himself had worked) by putting it in a worldwide and historical context.

"Proem" (w. 1847). Used to introduce *Poems* (1849) and later collections. Whittier apologizes for his shortcomings but offers as compensation a sincere love of freedom. While this poem may interest us as a revelation of Whittier's attitude toward his art, it offers little to the ear. Especially awkward is the elongated fifth line in each stanza, possibly an attempt to imitate the alexandrines of Spenser, who is mentioned in line 3.

Leaves from Margaret Smith's Journal (1849). Whittier's most important prose work; a sort of historical novel embodying the thoughts of an outlander, an English girl who visits Massachusetts in 1678–1679.

"Ichabod" (1850). A dirge for Daniel Webster occasioned by his notorious Seventh of March Speech in support of the Fugitive Slave Law and other aspects of the Compromise of 1850. Disillusioned, Whittier pictured Webster now as a fallen angel from whose "great eyes / The soul has fled" (4:63). The name "Ichabod" means "without glory" (I Samuel iv: 21) and to Whittier's Quaker mind, must have connoted the departure of the Inner Light, a theme he artistically sustained with light-dark images. As a significant example of tempered invective, the poem remains applicable to any deserter of a cause.

"Skipper Ireson's Ride" (1857). A tragicomic ballad of the captain who, having sailed away from his townsmen's sinking ship, was "tarred and

---

3. *The Works of John Greenleaf Whittier*, 7 vols., Standard Library Ed. (Boston: Houghton Mifflin [1892]), 3:85. Subsequent quotations are from this edition.

feathered and carried in a cart" by their widows, "the women of Marblehead" (1:175). Upon his repentance and the mob's realization of the futility of revenge, he was released. Whittier took nearly thirty years to work up this ballad from "a fragment of rhyme" recited by one of his "early schoolmates" (1:174).[4] Within the framework of ballad conventions (including the *in medias res* opening and the development through dialogue and refrain) he tells a moving story that begins in a comic mood compounded of native dialect, classical allusions, and a jerky four-stress rhythm but ends in controlled pathos unmarred by moralizing.

"Telling the Bees" (1858). One of Whittier's finest ballads, though atypical of that form in rhyme and meter. Narrated in the first person, it takes its readers along the route of the poet's visit to his beloved and with muted emotion tells how he slowly becomes aware of her death. The theme is derived from the folk custom of informing the bees of a family death and then draping their hives in black. With great subtlety, Whittier shifts the tone of the narrative from confidence to apprehension to dismay.

"Laus Deo" (1865). A lyric praising God for ending slavery in the nation. Composed in a Quaker meetinghouse, it responds to and even imitates the pealing of bells that celebrated the Thirteenth Amendment. While the poem may seem haphazardly developed with its multiple addressees (God, the bells, the poet, his readers), there is a clearly stated central idea, and the structural looseness has the advantage of reproducing the actual jumble of thoughts during a moment of joy. The meter is clipped iambic dimeter ($\smallsmile\,\smile\,\prime$) and tetrameter ($\prime\,\smile\,\prime\,\smile\,\prime\,\smile\,\prime$), which was a favorite of Whittier's.

"Abraham Davenport" (1866). Narrative sketch of an eighteenth-century Connecticut legislator who continued to work during an eclipse while his colleagues cowered in fear. Note the humor (sometimes satirical and even mock-heroic), the unobtrusive last-line moral, and the well-handled blank verse.

Snow-Bound: A Winter Idyl (1866). Whittier's masterpiece; 759 iambic tetrameter lines mostly in couplets, recounting the experience of a household during a snowstorm. *Snow-Bound* has three main parts, usually separated and sometimes subdivided by philosophical passages. The first (ll. 1–178) describes the storm and the resulting isolation of the Whittier farm; the second (ll. 212–628) sketches various members of the family circle and their two guests as they enjoy a snowbound night that begins with riddles, recitations, and stories and ends with sleep and dreams; the third (ll. 629–714) announces the arrival of the teamsters, the doctor, and the newspaper—all of which betoken an end to "the chill embargo of the snow" (l. 711) (2:158). There is humor in these words, however; for the storm has proved ineffective from the first. Its chill was offset by the hearth fire; its

4. As legend, the tale enjoyed a vigorous circulation on oral and printed levels. As history, it seems inaccurate; the original Skipper Ireson was apparently punished by men (not women) who carried him in a dory for a crime of which he was innocent.

embargo was thwarted by far-ranging thoughts generated in the warmth of companionship and family affection. A review of the second part will reveal dozens of purposeful allusions to remote ages, climes, and seasons (especially summer). The poem achieves breadth not only through these images but also through an expanded cast of characters. True, some of the snow-bound group may be stereotypes; but they tell stories of French Canadian villages and of trappers, Indians, and witches. The two guests supply even more exotic connections. The schoolmaster recounts legends of ancient Greece and Rome, while a woman visitor described as "tropical" (l. 534) (2:152) recalls Malta, Jerusalem, and Lebanon.

Whittier called *Snow-Bound* a collection of "Flemish pictures" (l. 747) (2:159), but this label may mislead us, for although the poem comes close to such genre painting in emphasizing verisimilitude and daily life, it has far more philosophical content. There are passages on slavery (ll. 214–223, 485–500, 738–739); on the future of social reform (ll. 485–509); on the folly of attempting to determine human guilt (ll. 565–589); and above all, on the meaning of death (ll. 210–211, 422–437, 729–759). Whittier almost never superimposes these ideas; he lets them grow out of the imagery. The snowstorm's fantastic alteration of the landscape (ll. 54–65) is a case in point. Although it can be enjoyed simply for its scenic value, it converges with the central image of storm versus hearth fire to reinforce the message that nature's alterations are never permanent. A thaw will end the storm's architecture, and family affection combined with faith will conquer even death, nature's greatest alteration. *Snow-Bound* therefore has significance not just as a picture of Whittier's boyhood, or as a piece of New England local color, or even as a folklife study of rural America. It is all these and much more—a superb work of art with universal meaning.

JAMES RUSSELL LOWELL (1819–1891)

Like Longfellow and Whittier, Lowell qualified as a household poet, but he differed markedly from both of these authors. In technique he stood somewhere between them, lacking Longfellow's narrative talents and prosodic range but surpassing Whittier in rhymes and meters. His aristocratic background kept him from identifying with common people as convincingly as Whittier did; yet he came close in *The Biglow Papers,* which comprise some of the best dialect poems in American literature. By virtue of this work, he also belongs with the Down East humorists and plays a part in the history of regionalism.

Life. Much of Lowell's life was spent in Cambridge, Massachusetts, where he was born and educated, graduating from Harvard College in 1838 and from Harvard Law School in 1840. Strongly influenced by the idealism of Maria White, whom he married in 1843, he collected his early work into *A*

Year's Life and Other Poems (1841) and contributed to the leading anti-slavery periodicals of the day. In 1848 he published not only *The Biglow Papers (First Series), A Fable for Critics,* and the two-volume *Poems* but also *The Vision of Sir Launfal,* the narrative with that well-worn line "And what is so rare as a day in June?"[5] With these he earned a national reputation, but his personal life was darkened by the death of three children in five years and of his wife in 1853. In 1857 he married Frances Dunlap. Meanwhile he had succeeded Longfellow as Smith Professor of Modern Languages at Harvard. From 1857 to 1861 he served capably as the *Atlantic Monthly's* first editor, and from 1863 to 1872 he coedited the already long-lived *North American Review.* A true man of parts, he also distinguished himself in public affairs, not only as a writer of political essays and patriotic odes, but also as a convention delegate, presidential elector, and diplomat. He was minister both to Spain (1877–1880) and to England (1880–1885). His final years were spent in delivering lectures and supervising a collected edition of his works.

Lowell is remembered for his prose as well as his poems. The wide range of this prose, which includes social and political analysis, history, and literary criticism, manifests itself in such essays as "On a Certain Condescension in Foreigners" (1868), "Democracy," "New England Two Centuries Ago" (1865), "Thoreau" (1865), "Emerson the Lecturer," and his review (1865) of *The Marble Faun.* Generally this work reveals Lowell as perceptive, witty, and forthright, but not without tact.

Lowell's reputation rests, however, on his poetry. Much of it is in such romantic forms as the sonnet and the ode, but some continues the neoclassic tradition of satire; and while poems like *A Fable for Critics* may be as digressive as the familiar essay, others exhibit tight construction and firm control.

Representative Works

"To the Dandelion" (1845). A nature lyric demonstrating that even this humble flower has its value. From this paradox, developed chiefly by associating the dandelion's golden color with wealth, the poet learns to respect the value of all men. Note the suggestions of democracy in lines 14–15.

The Biglow Papers, First Series (first published in journals from 1846 to 1848, then in book form in 1848). Humorous Down East dialect poems purportedly by Hosea Biglow, a homespun village bard. This series was directed against the Mexican War, which Lowell believed was part of a design to extend slavery. In Number 1, introduced by his father (Ezekiel Biglow), Hosea rants against recruiting sergeants in particular and war in

5. *The Complete Writings of James Russell Lowell,* 16 vols. (Boston and New York: Houghton Mifflin, 1904), 9:302. Subsequent quotations are from this edition.

general. One of its best-known stanzas may serve to illustrate the prevalence of Bible-based arguments (and, incidentally, trochaic meter) in *The Biglow Papers* as a whole:

> Éz fĕr wár, Í càll ĭt múrdĕr,—
> Thére yŏu hév ĭt pláin ăn' flát;
> Í dŏn't wánt tŏ gó nŏ fúrdĕr
> Thán mў Téstўmént fĕr thát;
> Gód hĕz séd sŏ plúmp ăn' fáirlў,
> Ìt's ĕz lóng ĕz ít ĭs bróad,
> Àn' yŏu've gút tŏ gít ŭp aírlў
> Èf yŏu wánt tŏ táke ĭn Gód.
>
> (10:62)

Number 3, "What Mr. Robinson Thinks," is heavy with irony and contains some caustic satire of manifest destiny and of politicians who serve only themselves. The other seven numbers in this series have been largely forgotten. (See below for the *Second Series*.)

To extend the range of the *Biglow Papers* Lowell created the Rev. Homer Wilbur, Hosea's editor. Given far too much space in the book, the parson tires us with his verbose introductions and stuffy footnotes. More interesting is Birdofredum Sawin, a rustic who joins the army full of high hopes and patriotism but comes back a physical and moral ruin. Introduced as a clown, he ultimately serves a nobler purpose, teaching us that some people learn only through experience, while others, like Hosea, are saved from this bitter necessity through their innate common sense.

A Fable for Critics (1848). A verse-satire of contemporary authors that belongs in the tradition of Pope's *Dunciad,* Byron's *English Bards and Scotch Reviewers,* and Leigh Hunt's *The Feast of the Poets.* As the following lines demonstrate, Lowell utilized anapestic meter, puns, and outrageous rhymes to make this a genuinely funny poem:

> Thère ĭs Brýănt, ăs quíĕt, ăs cóol, ănd ăs dígnĭfíed,
> Às ă smóoth, sìlĕnt ícebĕrg, thăt névĕr ĭs ígnĭfíed,
> Săve whén bў rĕfléctĭon 'tĭs kíndlĕd ŏ' níghts
> Wìth ă sémblănce ŏf fláme bў thĕ chíll Nòrthĕrn Líghts.
> Hè măy ránk (Grìswŏld sáys sŏ) fìrst bárd òf yŏur nátĭon
> (Thère's nŏ doúbt thàt hĕ stánds ìn sŭpréme ìceŏlátĭon)
>
> (12:49)

Even though Lowell later realized that he had treated Bryant somewhat unjustly, there was a good deal of truth behind all the sketches, whether of such minor figures as John Neal and Margaret Fuller or of such major figures as Hawthorne and Emerson. Nor has time reversed many of his opinions. If we see more wit than wisdom in his characterization of Poe as "three fifths . . . genius and two fifths sheer fudge" (12:67), we readily agree that Whittier's grammar and rhymes were "not always correct" (12:52) and that many of Cooper's characters are "clothes upon sticks" (12:58).

"The Washers of the Shroud" (1861). A poem—part narrative, part lyric, and part philosophical—that utilizes a Celtic myth in a dream framework to express apprehension for the Union, then in the throes of the Civil War. Here Lowell modified the pacifism of his earlier works by noting that "the sheathed blade may rust with darker sin" (13:7) (l. 100).

"Emerson the Lecturer" (1861, revised 1868). An impressionistic essay that attributes Emerson's platform success to his "masculine faculty of fecundating other minds" (2:393) and his ability to make even the most carefully prepared phrases appear as if they had "just dropped down . . . from the clouds"—"as unexpected to him as to us!" (2:402–403). Lowell's own prose style as exhibited here is nostalgic, allusive, witty, and humorous.

Biglow Papers, Second Series (published in the *Atlantic Monthly* 1862–1866, in book form 1867). Dialect poems written in support of the North during the Civil War. While the second series was generally inferior to its predecessor, it did produce two gems. The first, "Sunthin' in the Pastoral Line," excels not only as a rare description of a region in the dialect of that region but also as a New World adaptation of the pastoral poetry of Virgil, Spenser, and Milton. Early in the poem, by carefully depicting the peculiar approach of spring as a native phenomenon, Lowell sets the scene and foreshadows the ultimate message: that the problem of slavery in America can be no more successfully attacked with the religious militarism of the past (represented by Hosea's Puritan ancestor) than an American season can be accurately described with the outmoded rhetoric of foreign poets. The second gem of this series, "The Courtin'," also qualifies as a pastoral. Huldy and Zekle, with their awkward manners, are further developments of the simple rustics in Madam Knight's *Journal* and other works.

"Ode Recited at the Harvard Commemoration" (read by the poet July 21, 1865 at the ceremony honoring Harvard's participants in the Civil War). Lowell pictures these men as representative of "a new imperial race" of Americans willing to serve truth through action (13:29) (l. 328); defines the poet as one who keeps "measure with his people" (13:31) (l. 380) by celebrating their actions with his words; and pledges the service of all its citizens to a redeemed and purified nation that is now the envy of Europe. In the sixth strophe he again stresses the indigenous, praising Lincoln as a hero not of European mold but the "new birth of our new soil" (13:25) (l. 208). The "Harvard Ode" is irregular in form, persistently varying its basic iambic meter, its line lengths, and its rhyme schemes.

"Democracy" (delivered October 6, 1884). Lowell's inaugural address as president of an educational society for English workingmen. While admitting that democracy rotted easily in big cities, Lowell pictured it as a generally successful experiment that had sprung from an "acorn . . . ripened on the British oak" (7:12). Tact, wit, and reflection characterize this address.

"Auspex" (1888). A lyric in which Lowell laments the end of his poetry-making days. The urge to write remains (l. 1); but instead of aspiring poems (ll. 5, 9), he now produces less impressive works (ll. 2, 7). Even these will stop when he enters the later stages of his life (connoted by the leaves and snow of ll. 6, 14–18). Closely allied to the basic metaphor, equating the poet's heart with a bird's nest, is the persona—an auspex or Roman diviner, here pictured as tracing the future by observing the actions of birds (orni-thomancy). Each stanza opens with an observation and closes with a predic-tion.

13
Humorists, Wits, and Informal Essayists

American humor had accumulated an impressive history when in the second half of the nineteenth century it peaked in the work of Mark Twain. Every period of American literature, even the Puritan, can be shown to have had some kind of humor, whether in its more obvious forms or in the guise of satire, irony, and wit. The most striking characteristic of humor in America was its variety. In this chapter we will find that it encompasses the understatement of Yankees and the tall talk of frontiersmen, the sophisticated intellectualism of the Autocrat of the Breakfast Table and the uncouth anti-intellectualism of Sut Lovingood, the fantasy of comic situations and the realism of local color.

As it developed, humor infiltrated many genres, including mock epics, plays, picaresque novels, and letters to the editor. Some humorists expressed themselves through the informal essay, adopting the urbane approach and polished style that Americans like Franklin and Irving had found in Englishmen like Addison and Goldsmith. While the informal essay could thrive on its own as a comic genre, it was frequently combined with narrative. The humorous hybrids thus produced included the table talk books of Oliver Wendell Holmes—books with more talk than action—and the short stories of some Southwestern humorists—narratives with long, leisurely descriptive and expository passages that develop the mood and setting, establish the narrator as an Addisonian spectator, and moralize on the characters and their actions.

As we briefly review the early American humorists and analyze their successors, the indigenous aspects of their work will become clear. On the whole, their humor was inevitably American in subject, frequently American in attitude, and sometimes American in expression.

THE EARLY HUMORISTS

The first American humor may be described as genuine but incidental—stray bits from seventeenth-century statesmen and ministers, like William Bradford, Samuel Sewall, and Nathaniel Ward. Of the works analyzed in chapter 2 only Thomas Morton's *New English Canaan* strikes us as consistently and intentionally humorous.

From the beginning, American humor was based on native materials. In the eighteenth and early nineteenth centuries it became more indigenous. True, its techniques were usually derivative. Franklin was indebted to Addison and Swift; the Connecticut Wits borrowed from Samuel Butler; Brackenridge drew upon Cervantes; Freneau, Irving, and Paulding probably modeled their outlanders on Goldsmith's Citizen of the World. Nevertheless, there was a native purpose behind much of this humor: The satire, especially, aimed to expunge Old World vices from the New World, and of course pieces like Trumbull's *M'Fingal* and Hopkinson's "Battle of the Kegs" served as Revolutionary War propaganda. As it became a vehicle for native attitudes, American humor also began to discover native character types. Madam Knight found country bumpkins in the backwoods of New England; William Byrd satirized poor whites on the Virginia-Carolina border; and, most important, Royall Tyler depicted a full-length stage Yankee from Down East. Bearing such names as Doolittle, Homespun, and Nathan, the stage Yankee was destined to become a stock character in American drama, probably reaching his finest moment as Jonathan Ploughboy in Samuel Woodworth's *A Forest Rose* (1825).

DOWN EAST HUMORISTS

In the 1830s the Down East school of American humor emerged, as Seba Smith and others developed another comic character, the epistolary Yankee, a seemingly naive New England rustic who reveals much shrewd-ness and common sense in a series of dialect letters usually addressed to relatives, friends, and editors. Probably the first writer to develop such a character was George W. Arnold (1783–1838), whose Joe Strickland letters began appearing in a New York newspaper in 1825.[1]

Seba Smith (1792–1868). Seba Smith very likely had the Strickland letters in mind when in 1830 he created his epistolary Yankee, Major Jack Downing of Downingville, Maine. Moreover, he was himself an authentic Down East Yankee. Most of his life was spent in his native Maine, first in the back-woods, then in Portland where, after graduating from Bowdoin College (1818), he edited various journals, including the daily *Courier* and the

1. The letters are collected and analyzed in Allen Walker Read, "The World of Joe Strickland," *JAF* 76 (1963): 277–308.

weekly *Downing Gazette*. After 1839 he became a Yankee among Knickerbockers, working in New York City as author and journalist.

Smith deserves to be remembered for more than political satire. Some of the best Jack Downing material, including the title story of Smith's *May-Day in New-York* (1845), is nonpolitical. Often, too, the political letters reveal larger implications and universal values. Finally, we need to see Smith as a pioneer local-colorist, whether in the Downing letters or in the more conventional local-color sketches represented in his '*Way down East* (1854).

Representative Works

The Life and Writings of Major Jack Downing, of Downingville, Away down East in the State of Maine. Written by Himself (Boston, 1833). Comic letters written for the *Portland Courier* under the pseudonyms of "Jack Downing," his "Cousin Nabby," "Uncle Joshua," and other fictitious natives of Downingville, an equally fictitious place. Jack begins as a naive outlander wandering into sessions of the state legislature and getting his first taste of politics. When the representatives refuse to seat one of the new electees, Jack considers it "a needless piece of cruelty, for they want crowded, and there was a number of seats empty" (Jan. 18, 1830).[2] Later he garbles Shakespeare in a fit of pique over the growing number of spurious Major Downings then beginning to appear in the press: "He that steals my munny-pus steals trash, but he that steals my name ought to have his head broke" (June 25, 1833). Counterbalancing these misunderstandings, misquotations, mispronunciations, and misspellings is Jack's native shrewdness. At first there are hints of the Yankee peddler in his character. He comes to Portland to sell ax handles, cheese, and footings; he has already sold a steer that died within a month; and he even perpetrates a hoax that folklorists know as "Paying for Bread with Beer" (motif K233.4 in Stith Thompson's *Motif Index*). Soon the role of peddler is dropped, and the Yankee tricks with it, but the wisdom of a crackerbox philosopher remains. Jack leaves Portland for Washington and becomes President Jackson's confidant. In this way Smith broadened his satire, abandoning local events for national topics, including the spoils system, the Peggy Eaton affair, and the nullification controversy. Even this satire has been diluted with time, but there are still potent passages that mix sympathy with smiles. While we feel for President Jackson as he collapses in the midst of his campaign, we also see the humor in Jack's shaking hands for him.

My Thirty Years out of the Senate (1859). Jack Downing letters from January 18, 1830 to January 21, 1856, including many revisions of letters in the 1833 collection and carrying Smith's satire into the Pierce administration. The letter for July 20, 1852, which ridicules Pierce's nomination, ap-

---

2. *The Life and Writings of Major Jack Downing, of Downingville* (Boston: Lilly, Wait, Colman, & Holden, 1833).

plies as well to modern politics. Its discussion of Pierce's war record is a fine example of anticlimax.

LATER DOWN EAST HUMORISTS

As it developed through the nineteenth century, Down East humor underwent various changes without losing its stress on homespun common sense. The epistolary device of Arnold, Smith, and their many imitators gave way to dialogue, verse, and other forms. Satire became harsher, as can be seen in Charles Augustus Davis's *Letters of J. Downing* (1834) and Lowell's *Biglow Papers*. New comic characters appeared and were enthusiastically received. Around 1835 Thomas Chandler Haliburton (1796–1865) created Sam Slick, an aphoristic itinerant clockmaker who resembled both a Yankee peddler and Poor Richard. Like Major Downing, he was taken up by other writers. Meanwhile, beginning in the 1840s, the female comic figure came to the fore, gaining immense popularity as Widow Bedott in the work of Frances M. Whitcher (1811?–1852) and as Mrs. Partington (an American Mrs. Malaprop) in that of Benjamin P. Shillaber (1814–1890). Finally, let it be noted that not all Down East humor was written by New Englanders. Haliburton hailed from Nova Scotia; Davis and Whitcher, from New York.

HUMORISTS OF THE OLD SOUTHWEST

Substantially different from Down East humor was the humor of the Old Southwest (Georgia, Alabama, Mississippi, Tennessee, Louisiana, Arkansas, and Missouri). Like its Yankee counterpart, it began to flower during the second quarter of the nineteenth century, nourished by roots in the past. William Byrd, Mason Locke Weems (1759–1825), James K. Paulding (1778–1860), Timothy Flint (1780–1840), and Washington Irving should be considered some of its most important ancestors; they prepared its public and provided models for its character types by writing early descriptions of frontiersmen.

Compared to the Down Easters, the Southwestern humorists depicted a wider variety of characters, used more dialect to greater advantage, and committed themselves earlier to the local-colorist's role of carefully recording the society about him. A good part of this society was coarse and subliterate—a motley array of yokels, loafers, squatters, clay eaters, sharpers, and brawlers commonly labeled poor whites. The Southwestern humorist often showed more sympathy than satire toward these people and tended to make them into his most colorful characters. Still, he knew how to keep them at a safe distance by moralizing on their misdeeds and by placing his own graceful literary style next to their rude vernacular. Whatever the degree of this detachment, which varied from author to author, Southwestern humor often appears fascinatingly wild. There are orgiastic camp meetings; fights replete with gouging and biting; and such practical jokes as setting a mule on fire, breaking up a funeral procession, and cutting the face from a corpse to scare a nosy landlady. (This emphasis on the macabre and grotesque prefigures the work of William Faulkner, Truman Capote, Flannery O'Connor, Carson McCullers, and other modern Southern writers.) Southwestern humor could be just as uninhibited in language as in action. Instead of the Down East humorists' Yankee understatements, we have the opposite—lusty tall talk bristling with fantastic metaphors.

Augustus Baldwin Longstreet (1790–1870). The first Southwestern humorist, Augustus Baldwin Longstreet, had so many professions that he could well afford to regard writing as an avocation. After studying at a South Carolina academy, at Yale, and at law school in Litchfield, Connecticut, he practiced law in his native Georgia, was elected to the state legislature (1821), and served as judge of the superior court (1822–1825). Espousing the doctrines of his friend John C. Calhoun, he edited the Augusta, Georgia, *State Rights Sentinel* from 1834 to 1836. The death of one of his children had converted Longstreet from his earlier skepticism, and in 1838 he was admitted into the Methodist ministry. He also served as president of Emory College in Georgia (1839–1848), Centenary College in Louisiana (1849), the University of Mississippi (1849–1856), and the University of South Carolina (1858–1861). After the Civil War, during which his house at Oxford was burned down, Longstreet devoted himself to writing on religious and sectional matters.

Longstreet's finest work is a potpourri of newspaper sketches called *Georgia Scenes* (1835). Although this book includes sentimental, romantic pieces, its best parts have a strong realism compounded of local color and humor. According to its subtitle, *Georgia Scenes* treats of "Characters, Incidents, &c., in the First Half Century of the Republic."[3] These characters include the high and low in comic juxtaposition. The narrator's Addisonian urbanity and learned style are in sharp contrast to the rowdy behavior and homespun speech of the poor whites. Here Longstreet also recorded frontier customs, especially in such detailed sketches as "The Shooting Match," "The Gander Pulling," and "The Turn Out," which have a certain historical value.

Chief Stories in *Georgia Scenes*

"Georgia Theatrics" (1833). Short short tale of a quixotic mock fight. Much of the story is developed through contrasts, including those between the past and present condition of Lincoln County's "Dark Corner," the

3. Quoted from the quaintly illustrated "2d ed.": *Georgia Scenes . . . by a Native Georgian* (New York: Harper, 1840).

sacred serenity of the landscape and the sacrilegious violence of the rehearsal, and the narrator's literary speech and the ploughboy's earthy dialect. With its tall talk, boasting, gory imagery, and dialect this story easily began to migrate into the Davy Crockett literature.

"The Horse Swap" (1833). A short story in which the soft-spoken elderly Peter Ketch outwits the loudmouthed young Blossom by trading him a blind and deaf horse (Kit) for his sore-backed one (Bullet). Both characters specialize in indirections: Peter in verbal irony (saying the opposite of what he means), Blossom in boasting and tall talk. It is through a series of ironies that Blossom is duped: After Peter has proved wrong in calling Kit scary and mean, we expect more irony in his statement that Kit is blind, yet this time it is the plain truth. Other fine points artfully develop this story, which is based on the age-old motif of the trickster tricked: the narrator's Twain-like concern for the minutiae of animal behavior (for example, his description of Bullet's tail); the contrast between the narrator's sympathy and the crowd's levity; clever foreshadowing as in the words "Kit threw up his head rather as if something pricked him under the chin than as if fearing a blow" (p. 28).

"The Fight" (1833). Short story in which two friends come to blows only after their wives and a troublemaker named Ransy Sniffle bring them to it. The brutality of their "fair fight" (p. 64), resulting in the loss of an ear, a cheek, a finger, and a nose, represents the frontier at its worst; and while Longstreet expresses his own apparently sincere disapproval of such barbarity, he spares us no gore. Also intriguingly repulsive is the clay eater Ransy Sniffle, a descendant of the mischief-makers in English plays like *Gammer Gurton's Needle* and also a prototype of the ubiquitous Ugly Man in Southwestern humor.

"The Character of a Native Georgian" (1834). A loose-jointed but hilarious tale of a three-day orgy of practical jokes perpetrated by Ned Brace, a supertrickster.

Thomas Bangs Thorpe (1815–1878). T. B. Thorpe, the author of the most famous yarn of the Old Southwest, "The Big Bear of Arkansas," though not a native of the area, was well qualified to write a frontier sporting tale of this type. As a professional painter of portraits, landscapes, and still lifes, he could observe and describe with remarkable skill. He had studied nature carefully while living in Connecticut, New York, and Louisiana; and in the South he had met frontiersmen.

Thorpe's masterpiece "The Big Bear of Arkansas" was first printed in the *Spirit of the Times* for March 27, 1841. It is a splendid example of a frame story (one that encloses an inner narrative with the circumstances of its telling). Thorpe's tale opens with the frame, a Mississippi steamboat with its passengers described by the narrator, himself a passenger. Jim Doggett, an Arkansas frontiersman, regales those in the bar with his boasting and is easily persuaded to spin his best bear-hunt yarn. Now the frame gives way to the inner narrative as Doggett tells of his repeated attempts to kill a gigantic "creation bar" (p. 44).[4] One chase ends under water, with the wrong bear getting killed and the big "bar" mysteriously escaping, much to the chagrin of the hunter and his superdog, Bowie-knife. Angered by his neighbors' laughter, Doggett vows to kill the big bear at all costs on the next Monday. On Sunday, however, the bear comes to Doggett while the hunter is defecating (euphemistically put) in the woods. Caught with his "unexpressibles" down (p. 43), Doggett shoots once but can't follow up. The bear dies anyway, as Doggett says, only because his time had come (p. 44). The narrative then gives way to the frame and ends with the author describing his departure from the steamboat.

Thorpe's yarn offers genuine comedy of the tall-tale type, yet behind it a primitivistic message emerges. Jim Doggett is truly nature's nobleman; out of the wilderness he becomes a greenhorn, but in it he excels. His thinking is in tune with nature, as when he refuses to condemn Arkansas's giant mosquitoes, for "mosquitoes is natur, and I never find fault with her" (p. 43). Instead, he looks for natural fitness in things. Most of all, he treats the big bear as if nature had predestined it for him—the biggest bear for the best bear hunter—therefore he welcomes it "like a brother" (p. 44). Thorpe seems also to be saying that only a backwoodsman is sensitive to the "mysteries of the backwoods" (the title of his first book); Doggett not only stands in awe of the "unhuntable bar" but finds it "puzzling" that any bear can run at all (p. 44). As the story ends, the passengers observe a "grave silence" (p. 44) but apparently only because Doggett himself appears so awed. They know nothing of nature's mysteries, and perhaps that is why throughout the story he calls them strangers.

George Washington Harris (1814–1869). The lustiest humor of the Old Southwest came, paradoxically, from a strict Presbyterian, George Washington Harris. His *Sut Lovingood's Yarns* is one of those strange, grotesque books filled with violence and sex that fascinate and at the same time repel. Scholars have traced its influence on Twain, Faulkner, and others.

Harris exhibited more craftsmanship than the leading Southwestern humorists, although his formal education possibly totaled less than two years. Born in Pennsylvania, he moved to Tennessee in 1819 and thereafter lived chiefly in Knoxville, where he became a respected metalworker with shorter stints as steamboat captain and postmaster. Work as superintendent of the Ducktown copper mines in southeast Tennessee gave him material for the Sut Lovingood stories. By 1869 he had finished the manuscript of a second book, but he died that year, and the manuscript has never been located for publication.

The short stories that comprise *Sut Lovingood's Yarns* (1867) stand both

4. T. B. T., "The Big Bear of Arkansas," *The Spirit of the Times,* 11 (March 27, 1841): 43–44.

inside and outside the tradition of Old Southwestern humor. Even the conventional ingredients in this work—the local-color details, the dialect, and the trickster-hero—strike us as unusual. Local color here seems subordinate to satire. And if Sut Lovingood is but one of many trickster-heroes in this literature, he is probably the most complex.

The uniqueness of the Lovingood tales stems, in fact, from Sut himself. He insists on being known as a "nat'ral born durn'd fool,"[5] the second greatest fool in the world (the first is his own father). He repeatedly calls himself a coward and denies that he has a soul. Given this premise, we might expect a frame tale narrated in literary language by an author who feels superior to the fool. Harris gives us the frame tale all right but reduces the literary language to a minimum and makes the fool feel superior to the author. "George," says Sut, "yu don't onderstan life yet scarcely at all, got a heap tu larn, a heap" (p. 89). What Sut has to teach is a hedonism surprising for the nineteenth century: "Men wer made a-purpus jis' tu eat, drink, an' fur stayin awake in the yearly part ove the nites: an' wimen wer made tu cook the vittils, mix the sperits, an' help the men du the stayin awake" (p. 88). Nor does Sut confine sex to such philosophical passages; it also abounds in the descriptive and narrative passages. In fact, many of the plots culminate in the loss of someone's clothes, often symbolizing the exposure of hypocrisy. Churchmen, law officers, Yankees, women, and intellectuals appear throughout the book as hypocrites who become the victims of Sut's practical jokes. Unlike him, they refuse to admit their knavery and so are exposed and punished.

At its best, Harris's art offers more complex and thus more interesting characterization than do most trickster stories (whether literary or folk), achieves a comedy of whirlwind motion equal to Faulkner's "Spotted Horses," and serves well to counterbalance romanticism by satirizing some of its conventions.

The *Yarns,* as published in 1867, contained twenty-four of Harris's stories. Most were apparently written for the book, but eight have proven to be careful revisions of sketches already printed in the 1840s and 1850s.

Chief Stories in *Sut Lovingood's Yarns*

"Blown up with Soda" (revised from a sketch published at an undetermined date in the Savannah *Morning News,* then reprinted in the Nashville *Daily Gazette,* July 21, 1857). Sure that he is swallowing a love potion, Sut drinks a concoction of soda powders that Sicily Burns promises will give him "*a new sensashun*" (p. 80). Much to the delight of Sicily, whom he had hoped to seduce, Sut rides off spewing foam and scaring a passing circuit rider. Sut blames this trick on Sicily and the Yankee peddler who sold her the powders, but he is actually the victim of his own imagina-

5. This phrase appears even in the subtitle of the first edition—*Sut Lovingood* (New York: Dick & Fitzgerald, 1867)—the source of quotations throughout this section.

tion. His sensual description of Sicily's breasts, probably mocking a literary cliché, did not appear in the earlier version of this yarn.

"Sicily Burns's Wedding" (April 15, 1858). Angry with Sicily Burns for the above-mentioned soda incident and for not inviting him to her wedding, Sut causes Ole Sock, the Burnses' bull, to go on a rampage, upsetting house and guests. Preliminary to this superbly depicted mayhem are passages satirizing the Church (Parson Bullen is accused of poisoning his congregation with moonshine of his own brewing) and summarizing the roles of Sut, his Daddy, and his Mam. The main episode is concluded in "Old Burns's Bull-Ride."

"Mrs. Yardley's Quilting" (no previous publication). Sut ruins a quilting party by spooking a dandy's horse. His description of this rural gathering should be compared to depictions of husking bees by Barlow, the local colorists, and genre painters. While they admit a few innocent kisses, Sut depicts the quilting as a near orgy good "fer poperlatin a country fast" (p. 139). Further, by having Mrs. Yardley die when one of her quilts is ruined, Harris was undoubtedly laughing at a stock motif of romanticism—death from a broken heart.

OTHER SOUTHWESTERN HUMORISTS

Although aspects of Southwestern humor can be found in such later writers as Twain and Faulkner, it reached its heights in the quarter century between the publication of *Georgia Scenes* and the start of the Civil War. Scores of pseudonymous authors wrote for the *Spirit of the Times* (a New York sporting magazine) and various Southern periodicals. The most popular stories were collected in anthologies like *The Big Bear of Arkansas and Other Sketches* (1845), edited by William T. Porter (1809–1858), but some authors had their own books, usually with titles denoting setting, persona, or main character—for example, *Major Jones's Courtship* (1843) by William Tappan Thompson (1812–1882), *Some Adventures of Captain Simon Suggs* (1845) by Johnson Jones Hooper (1815–1862), *Odd Leaves from the Life of a Louisiana Swamp Doctor* (1850) by Henry Clay Lewis (1825–1850), and *Flush Times in Alabama and Mississippi* (1853) by Joseph Glover Baldwin (1815–1864). In work ranging from gory medical crudities in Lewis to legal sophistication in Baldwin, these humorists as a group succeeded remarkably well in their goal of eliciting laughter.

OLIVER WENDELL HOLMES (1809–1894)

Of all the authors discussed in this chapter, Oliver Wendell Holmes is the most difficult to classify. He belonged to neither the Down East nor the Southwest schools of humor, and he differed substantially from Lowell,

Whittier, and the other household poets with whom he is usually grouped. Nevertheless, since he not only specialized but excelled in humorous prose and verse, he will be treated here.

Some of the best informal essays of this period came from his pen. Yet while indulging in the freedom of thought and form so characteristic of romanticism, he could hardly be called a romantic. He never joined such groups as the transcendentalists and abolitionists, and he tempered the sentimentality of romanticism with frequent applications of humor and satire. In this, and in the resemblance of his work to that of Addison, Steele, and Boswell, he might be considered an eighteenth-century writer out of his time.

Life. Holmes was born in Cambridge, Massachusetts, the eldest son of a Calvinist minister and descended on his mother's side from Anne Bradstreet. Except for studying medicine in Paris (1833–1835), he attended only New England schools: Phillips Academy at Andover (1824–1825), Harvard (1825–1829), law school at Cambridge (1829–1830), and medical school at Boston (1830–1833). In 1836 he received an M.D. from Harvard. Holmes distinguished himself in medicine, not only as the author of important treatises on puerperal fever and other diseases, but even more significantly as a dynamic professor in the Harvard Medical School (1847–1882). His literary career proved equally distinguished. The patriotic poem "Old Ironsides" won him early fame, and there were collected editions of his verse in 1836 and 1849. During the 1850s he gave lyceum lectures on literary topics. Not until he began contributing "The Autocrat Papers" to the newly founded *Atlantic Monthly*, however, did he truly commit himself to literature. When published in book form (1858), these essays reportedly sold an amazing 10,000 copies in three days. Holmes was no longer just a medical man who composed on occasion and engaged in lively talk with local intelligentsia in meetings of the Saturday Club. He was now an author of wide reputation who wrote steadily, had a regular publisher, and received fan mail from both sides of the Atlantic.

Besides his most famous book, *The Autocrat of the Breakfast Table,* Holmes wrote three other conversation books: *The Professor at the Breakfast Table* (1860), *The Poet at the Breakfast Table* (1872), and *Over the Tea Cups* (1891). Of lesser importance are his biographies, *John Lothrop Motley* (1879) and *Ralph Waldo Emerson* (1885), and his so-called medicated novels—*Elsie Venner* (1861), which opens with an essay on "The Brahmin Caste of New England," *The Guardian Angel* (1867), and *A Mortal Antipathy* (1885).

The poems dated 1858 below were published in Chapters IV, VII, and XI of *The Autocrat* and should ideally be read in that context.

Representative Works

"The Ballad of the Oysterman" (1830). Mock-heroic ballad that recounts the clandestine affair between an oysterman and a fisherman's daughter as a reenactment of the Hero and Leander story and includes several passages satirizing nineteenth-century romanticism.

"Old Ironsides" (1830). A lyric in ballad form protesting the scrapping of the frigate *Constitution*, which had defeated the *Guerrière* in the War of 1812.

"The Last Leaf" (1831). Seriocomic lyric on old age, which is represented by a Boston eccentric, Herman Melville's grandfather Thomas Melville. The poet sympathizes with his loneliness but smiles at his strange appearance. As Holmes explained in his full headnote to the poem, line 45 reads "spring" rather than "winter" to provide a sharper contrast between old age and youth. Less subtle contrasts appear in stanzas 5 and 6. Instead of attaining the measured dignity appropriate to a more sentimental approach, the poem has a playful lilt. The lines are unusually short; the rhymes are rapid-fire.

"My Aunt" (1831). A lyric in ballad form gently satirizing finishing schools, overprotective fathers, and unhappy spinsters. The mock-epic humor of lines 33–44 is tempered by lines 45–48, which are characteristically sympathetic.

The Autocrat of the Breakfast Table (originally twelve installments in the *Atlantic Monthly*, November 1857–October 1858; published in book form 1858). Imaginary conversations at a Boston boardinghouse. The landlady, her son, her daughter, the old gentleman opposite, the schoolmistress, the divinity student, and other boarders participate; but the table talk is dominated by the Autocrat (Holmes himself), who narrates it in the first person, sometimes also quoting his alter egos the Professor and the Poet. The exact genre of these pieces is difficult to determine. They have elements of biography, novel, and drama, especially in passages depicting the boarders' reactions to Holmes's words; yet they qualify best as personal or informal essays, not only revealing much of their author's character, but doing so in an artfully casual manner. Nothing was more casual than their plot. Of slight importance anyway, it was apparently open to revisions suggested by readers whose letters Holmes received while writing his monthly installments. Thus not until the ninth installment did Holmes foreshadow (or even foresee?) the Autocrat's proposal to the schoolmistress in the eleventh installment and their marriage in the twelfth. Equally true to the informal essay is the way in which Holmes slips easily from one topic to another. In Chapter I, for example, there are fifteen sections, all of unequal length and each devoted to a different topic. The first section opens casually with "I was just going to say, when I was interrupted" (1:1)[6]—a classic understatement referring to a hiatus of no less than twenty-five years between the present series and two earlier "Autocrat" essays published in the *New-England Magazine* for 1831–1832 (but never collected). The other sections of

6. *The Works of Oliver Wendell Holmes*, 13 vols. (Boston: Houghton Mifflin, 1892).

Chapter I, like those throughout the book, begin with a dash; and one therefore need only look for this punctuation to discover transitions between topics. These transitions appear as colloquial and spontaneous as conversation itself; yet they must have been carefully planned. In some of the most impressive, Holmes repeats the questions of his listeners ("—If a logical mind ever found out anything with its logic?"), makes sweeping statements ("—all generous minds have a horror of what is commonly called 'facts' "), or begins a new analogy ("—We are the Romans of the modern world,—the great assimilating people") (1:14, 5, 19). The informality and verisimilitude of the essays are further enhanced with the numerous explanatory asides Holmes encloses with brackets.

In tone *The Autocrat* mixes contradictory elements. Holmes is nostalgic, rhapsodic, personal, and sentimental, as when describing his courtship of the schoolmistress; yet he seldom fails also to be humorous. His snobbishness, relieved by good humor, finds expression in apologies for mutual admiration societies and men of genius and in such proclamations as "I allow no 'facts' at this table" (1:5).

The ideas developed in *The Autocrat* are widely varied and often startling or unusual. For example, Holmes maintained that Heaven will be more lenient with poor drunkards than with rich drunkards; that the attractions of vice should be admitted, not ignored or hidden; that sermons could be improved if clergymen would learn to box; that we should not be ashamed of repeating ourselves in conversation; that intellectuals need not read much; that conceit has its good effects; and that in a dialogue between, say, John and Thomas, at least six personalities take part. Some of these ideas are concise enough to be called aphorisms: "The race that shortens its weapons lengthens its boundaries" (1:19); "Stupidity oftens saves a man from going mad" (1:42). More are memorable analogies: "Sin has many tools, but a lie is the handle which fits them all" (1:124).

"The Chambered Nautilus" (1858). Probably the most famous of Holmes's serious poems. It advocates spiritual striving in imitation of the nautilus, which each year moves into the new chamber it has added to its spiral shell. In form this lyric is unusual if not unique, combining pentameter, trimeter, and hexameter ($a^5a^3b^3b^5b^5c^3c^6$). Moreover, Holmes frequently varied its basic iambic pattern with spondees and reversed initial feet, as in this line: "Whère ĭts dím dréamĭng lífe wăs wónt tŏ dwéll" (1:98).

"The Living Temple" (1858). Also known as "The Anatomist's Hymn"; a lyric glorifying the human body in terms of classical architecture and associated images. Its reverential attitude, in contrast to the Puritan view that the body is corrupt, has been compared to Whitman's *Leaves of Grass* and Giles Fletcher's "The Purple Island" (1633).

"The Deacon's Masterpiece or, The Wonderful 'One-Hoss Shay': A Logical Story" (1858). A narrative satire on systems based on supposedly irrefutable logic. Many scholars regard the story as a clever spoof of New

England Calvinism and Jonathan Edwards, whose *Freedom of the Will* (1754) was grounded on principles repugnant to Holmes. The abundant descriptive details, the well-handled dialect, and the anapest-enlivened meter all combine to make the story eminently readable, whatever the meaning of its allegory.

"Contentment" (1858). A lyric example of verbal irony.

"Dorothy Q." (1871). Sentimental lyric ruminating on a portrait of Dorothy Quincy, an ancestor of both the poet and his wife (see l. 39). Note the autocratic pride in family, speculative tone, audio imagery, and occasionally dramatic passages.

14
Writers in the Civil War

This chapter discusses four of the many American writers who were profoundly affected by the Civil War. The first, Abraham Lincoln, developed during the war not only as a man but also as a prose stylist. As he felt more and more aware of his country's—and his own—dependence upon God's mysterious purposes, his prose took on a new emotional and imaginative richness. The other three writers were professional poets from the South. Two of them, Henry Timrod and Paul Hamilton Hayne, served the South so faithfully that they became known as its poet laureates. Sidney Lanier, slightly younger than Timrod and Hayne, was destined to be remembered, like Poe, as the creator of an ethereal art that knows no region; yet his ties with the South were strong. He began his career with a Civil War novel; later he composed poetry that dealt with the Southern landscape and even with the Southern economy. A few of these poems were in the dialect of Georgia Crackers.

ABRAHAM LINCOLN (1809–1865)

By today's standards Abraham Lincoln wrote highly artistic prose, but his contemporaries, brought up on more ornate products, usually failed to appreciate it. Not even in the famous tributes to his genius written by Bryant, Lowell, and Whitman do we find any mention of his masterful prose style.

This style, which reveals much of Lincoln's personality, is (1) simple, yet controlled and sophisticated; (2) clear, logical, orderly, well constructed; (3) precise, accurate; (4) rhythmical; and (5) flexible, that is, adjustable to the occasion. The result of Lincoln's uncanny empathic powers, which enabled him to analyze the thinking and anticipate the reaction of his audience, this last quality made his prose both restrained and emotional, detached and sympathetic, colloquial and mystically solemn, poetic and free of pretentious figures of speech.

Lincoln's artistry can be traced to his lifelong habits and interests as well as to the environment in which fate placed him. His reading, limited generally to a comparatively few masterpieces, provided him with ideas and techniques. His favorites were first the Bible and Shakespeare, then (in no special order) Bunyan, Defoe, Parson Weems, Henry Clay, Sir William Blackstone, Petroleum V. Nasby (David Ross Locke), Hawthorne, Jefferson, Edward Gibbon, Burns, Poe, and Aesop. Lincoln did more than read these authors; he studied them. He read everything aloud, so as to hear as well as see; he searched out the precise definitions of words, entered interesting passages in a copybook or committed them to memory, reflected upon his reading in private, and discussed it with friends. Moreover he continued these habits throughout his life. Of no less importance to the development of his artistry was his fixation with style or the expression of ideas. He would spend half a day, one of his friends reported, just deciding on the best of three ways to put a single sentence. His style undoubtedly benefited, too, from his painstaking study of logic and grammar. Of course, no amount of preparation could have made a master writer of Lincoln if he had nothing to say. As it was, however, he was the chief actor in a very dramatic period—a statesman who, like Jefferson and Franklin, contributed to both the history and literature of America.

Representative Works

"Cooper Union Address" (delivered Feb. 27, 1860). An excellent example of Lincoln's controlled, unemotional style, as devastating in its relentless logic as anything by Jonathan Edwards. The refrainlike quotations from Stephen A. Douglas, whom Lincoln was refuting, accumulate ironical force by repetition.

"Farewell Address at Springfield, Illinois" (delivered Feb. 11, 1861). Emotional, yet curiously detached; meditative; mystical; rhythmical.

"Open Letter to Horace Greeley" (Aug. 22, 1862). Candid, rhythmical, full of reiteration.

"The Gettysburg Address" (delivered Nov. 19, 1863). One of the world's greatest speeches. More complex than its brevity and simple diction indicate, it moves simultaneously through three major progressions: (1) past-present-future; (2) continent-nation-battlefield-nation-earth (first Lincoln narrows the focus, then widens it); and (3) birth-death-rebirth. Everywhere we find such poetic devices as rhythm ("The world will little note nor long remember") and reiteration ("of the people, by the people, for the people"—a phrase probably adapted from an antislavery speech by Theodore Parker).[1] In all, Lincoln combined logic, emotion, and poetry to

1. *Complete Works of Abraham Lincoln,* ed. John G. Nicolay and John Hay, 12 vols. (New York: Francis D. Tandy Company, 1905), 9:210.

explain the meaning of the war, which he saw as testing the concepts of Jefferson's Declaration of Independence and as achieving a rebirth of freedom through the kind of sacrificial death portrayed in the Bible.

"Second Inaugural Address" (delivered March 4, 1865). Remembered chiefly for the phrase "with malice toward none; with charity for all" (11:46)—one of several fine examples of parallelism. The last three paragraphs reveal Lincoln's ever-growing conviction that the Civil War was a working-out of God's mysterious will.

HENRY TIMROD (1828–1867)

In spite of a short life and a small output, Henry Timrod is today regarded as the South's most important poet between Poe and Lanier.

Timrod was educated in his native Charleston. (Paul Hamilton Hayne, who became his closest literary friend and his biographer, was one of his schoolmates.) In 1845 Timrod entered the University of Georgia but left sometime in 1846 without earning a degree. Later he served as a tutor on several plantations, jobs that afforded him leisure to continue the writing he had done for Southern journals as early as 1846. During the Civil War he enlisted in the Confederate army but was forced by ill health to drop out; nor was he able to last long as war correspondent for the Charleston *Mercury*. It was through his verse that he best served the South and his own reputation. The *Poems* of 1859 (erroneously dated 1860), his only book not published posthumously, had revealed him as a genuine and competent poet, but one without a cause. With the war his work became more interesting, as he used it to sing of Southern problems and attitudes. Still, he lived from hand to mouth, editing and contributing to various Southern journals that could seldom pay for his work. With the end of the war his health and finances worsened even more, and he died soon afterward.

At his best Timrod achieved an unusual blend of emotion, control, and classical simplicity. As Hayne remarked, beneath the "dignity and calmness" of Timrod's work lay "unsounded depths of ardor and enthusiasm" (p. 36).[2]

Representative Works

"Ethnogenesis: Written during the Meeting of the First Southern Congress, at Montgomery, February, 1861." An ode of five strophes celebrating the start of the Confederacy (the title means "the birth of a nation"). The first four strophes are devoted to delineating sides: the South with its

2. Hayne was speaking only of "Ethnogenesis" here, but he would have readily agreed to a wider application of his remarks. Quoted from *The Poems of Henry Timrod: Edited, with a Sketch of the Poet's Life by Paul H. Hayne* (New York: E. J. Hale & Son, 1873).

allies, God and nature, against the North with its ally, the Devil. (Especially effective are the military metaphors used in the first strophe to describe nature's kindness to the South.) The final strophe defines the South's mission as essentially humanitarian (ll. 95–101) and, in predicting the spread of Southern influence around the world, artfully employs the metaphor of the Gulf Stream.

"The Cotton Boll" (1861). An ode celebrating the South's most important product and praying for victory over the North. Timrod's vision of cotton as the symbol of Southern commerce, which he predicted would eventually bring peace and unity to the world (ll. 108–131), is anticipated as early as lines 8–10. Throughout the poem this theme of unity is echoed in images appropriately involving weaving (see ll. 13–16, 70–71, 116, 140–141). Other striking figures compare the cotton boll to an ocean shell (ll. 20–28), the poet to Cornish miners (ll. 132–145), and the Northern soldiers to Goths (l. 162)— a particularly adroit metaphor, by implication equating the Southerners with Romans. Also well done is the image of the persona himself, who as he lies beneath his "immemorial pine" (p. 6),[3] gazing into the cotton boll in his hand, becomes a symbol of the prophetic bard.

"Charleston" (1862). A lyric that describes Charleston in the winter of 1862 and, while wondering whether the city will still be safe come spring, stoically resigns its destiny to "the temple of the Fates" (p. 148). The poem gains in complexity and interest from subtle tensions between its calm surface tone and the underlying apprehension.

"Ode" (sung June 16, 1866, at a grave-decorating ceremony honoring the Confederate dead in Magnolia Cemetery, Charleston). Sometimes cited as Timrod's best poem. Although written for a specific occasion, it has very few topical references and seems appropriate to all "martyrs of a fallen cause" (p. 164). Timrod composed a second version, which differs significantly in strophe 3. Both versions have proved popular with modern anthologists.

PAUL HAMILTON HAYNE (1830–1886)

Paul Hamilton Hayne wrote well over 400 poems. More important, he depended upon them for his income and was in that sense a truly professional (although not truly successful) poet.

Hayne studied law for a short time after graduating from Charleston College (1850), but he soon devoted himself exclusively to poetry and journalism. From the beginning his career stood on perilous ground. The Civil War nearly ended it. The bombardment of Charleston destroyed his ancestral home; Southern magazines could ill afford to pay for his contribu-

3. All quotations are from *Poems of Henry Timrod* (Boston: Houghton Mifflin, 1899).

tions; and for a time during the postwar years certain Northern magazines rejected his work out of pure sectionalism. Reduced to real poverty, Hayne moved to the pine barrens of Groveton, Georgia, where he lived with his family in a cottage furnished with little more than packing cases and decorated with pictures clipped from magazines. Yet he continued to write his poems, to encourage Southern authors, and to maintain friendly relations with such Northerners as Longfellow, Whittier, Holmes, Bryant, Edwin Percy Whipple, and Moses Coit Tyler.

Hayne clearly belongs to the romantic tradition of English and American literature. Critics have linked him not only with Shelley, Keats, and Poe but also with such Victorian romantics as Tennyson and William Morris. While he became best known for his sonnets, he also worked with other romantic forms such as the ballad and the nature lyric.

Even though he wrote too much and revised too little, even though his verse today seems thought-starved, cliché-ridden, and overly delicate, Hayne could delight the senses. He had a fine ear and a Keatsian gift for synesthesia.

Representative Works

"Aspects of the Pines" (1875). A nature lyric that sensuously depicts a gentle progression of landscape moods (sadness in the morning, peace at noon, and joy at sunset). The poet effects a religious feeling by using such words as "mystical," "solemn," and "vesper" (pp. 191–192),[4] yet there is no moralizing. The subtle variety of the scene is reflected in the meter, which, while basically iambic pentameter, contains so many spondees, reversed feet, and trisyllabic feet that 80 percent of its lines are irregular.

"The Mocking-Bird" (1882). Another nature lyric. In various letters and poems Hayne showed himself fascinated with this bird, the Southern counterpart of the English nightingale. Here he compresses all into a dramatic moment in which he, the typical solitary persona of the romantic poets, is "Heart-trilled to ecstasy" (p. 239). The poem recalls Keats in its use of synesthesia, Poe in its abundant alliteration and assonance. Because at least three-quarters of its lines contain spondees, pyrrhics, or other irregularities, it has the surface appearance of free verse, but underneath we find a fairly consistent, though unusual, pattern of alternating iambic trimeter and pentameter.

SIDNEY LANIER (1842–1881)

In prose as well as poetry Sidney Lanier made significant contributions to American literature. His *Science of English Verse* went much farther than

4. All quotations are from *Poems of Paul Hamilton Hayne* (Boston: D. Lothrop and Company, 1882).

anything written on prosody by Bryant or Poe. He nearly surpassed Poe also in the creation of ultramusical poetry and Timrod in the poetic treatment of economic problems. His dialect verses were pioneer documents in the local-color movement.

Life. Born in Macon, Georgia, and graduated from Oglethorpe University (1860), Lanier served in the Confederate army from 1861 to 1865, spending the last four months in a Union prison. As early as 1860 he had begun work on the autobiographical novel that was published in 1867 as *Tiger-Lilies,* but his greatest interest lay in music. Competent on several instruments, he played first flute with the Peabody Symphony Orchestra in Baltimore. From about 1874 on, however, he began to spend more time on writing than on music. Suffering acutely from tuberculosis and financially insecure for much of his life, he took to hack work, writing a guidebook to Florida (1875) and expurgating various classics to make them suitable for children (for example, *The Boy's King Arthur,* 1880). Fortunately for his reputation, he also composed a good deal of verse, lectured locally, and wrote a textbook, *The Science of English Verse* (1880), which was published shortly before his death. His lecture notes were issued posthumously as *The English Novel* (1883) and *Shakspere and His Forerunners* (1902).

Central Ideas. Although Lanier died too early to develop a complete philosophy, his published ideas do identify him as part-romantic, part-realist. According to his concept of "etherealization," the physical world— man and nature—becomes more and more spiritualized as it develops, gradually moving into states of beauty, gentleness, domestication, and love. (See his poem "The Symphony," l. 169 ff.) Art, too, had etherealized, Lanier believed; and he therefore preferred Shakespeare to *Beowulf,* Tennyson to Milton. Etherealization does not imply art-for-art's-sake or romantic escapism, however. The artist, in Lanier's view, was obligated by a social function: to represent love to a world plagued with industrialism and mercantilism, both of which he compressed into a single contemptuous word—trade. Lanier also urged American poets to mix the past with the present in order to create a culture "of higher mould."[5] In his own work he tried to solve current economic problems with an updated concept of chivalry.

Prosodic Theory and Practice. Lanier's handbook of prosody, *The Science of English Verse* (1880), is an impressive and useful work. True, it slights such topics as blank verse and onomatopoeia, holds to the now discountenanced notion that poetry and music are governed by identical laws, and insists that rhymes be exact in both sound and meaning—a rule that neither Emerson nor Emily Dickinson, nor for that matter Lanier himself, could have followed. Lanier also hints that the poem which "melt[s its

5. "Corn," p. 56 of *Poems of Sidney Lanier Edited by His Wife* (New York: Charles Scribner's Sons, 1910), from which all verse-quotations are taken.

words] flowingly into each other" is superior to the poem "which saws the ear with sharp notches of sound" (p. 306)[6]—a preference that reveals little understanding of the metaphysicals and other poets who deliberately roughened their verse. Nevertheless, Lanier made his book as scientific and as complete as possible, even to the point of citing technical treatises, transposing verse into musical annotations, and quoting frequently from Anglo-Saxon poems. Of special value to students is his concern with function. He showed, for instance, that alliteration can make a poem more interesting by adding its irregular repetitions to the regular repetitions of the meter. Lanier's professed goal was to educate the ear "to the highest possible plane of culture."

Lanier's own ear had been improving all along. His early poetry might be called stilted, but "Corn" (1874) revealed a new melodiousness and greater metrical freedom. After that he kept experimenting, not with such uncommon devices as free verse, but with traditional techniques like rhyme, alliteration, compound epithets, and phonetic junction (juxtaposing words that may be easily yoked in pronunciation, for example, *lal lal lal lal lal* as opposed to *bag bag bag bag bag*). The result was some of the most musical poetry ever produced by an American.

Although arranged chronologically here, Lanier's poems can also be divided into two distinct stylistic groups: (1) those in the lush musical style noted above and (2) those in a plainer style. The latter group includes "Thar's More in the Man than Thar Is in the Land," "Evening Song," "The Revenge of Hamish," "The Stirrup-Cup," and "A Ballad of Trees and the Master."

Representative Works

"Thar's More in the Man than Thar Is in the Land" (1871). A satirical narrative in the dialect of the Georgia Cracker. Jones grows nothing but cotton; Brown grows corn and wheat, thus exemplifying the theory of crop diversification Lanier recommended for the South.

"Corn" (w. 1874). A Cowleyan or irregular ode that envisions better days brought about by diversifying the South's economy. The poem's chief fault is its abrupt shift from a reverential to a satirical tone (ll. 122–130). Its merits include sensuous imagery, sustained metaphors, and powerful indigenous symbols created from unromantic objects (corn and the "old deserted Georgian hill" of l. 125). Occasional references to the persona remind us of his abiding presence, and throughout most sections there runs a thread of imagery dealing with mixing, blending, and the reconciliation of opposites.

"The Symphony" (1875; revised 1877, 1884). An ambitious attempt to give words the power of music. There are several persistent themes: (1) trade is evil—the cause of poverty and the ruin of chivalry; (2) the problems

6. *The Science of English Verse* (New York: Scribner, 1901).

trade creates and compounds can be solved only with love, not mere thought; (3) art speaks for nature, which asks for man's love. To express these themes Lanier personified the violins, flute, clarionet, horn, and hautboy, letting each take a turn at speaking to his audience just as if these instruments were performing their part in a symphony. Musical effects are achieved by initial, medial, and final iteration; refrain; other repetitions of words, phrases, and lines; rhymes of various kinds and clusters; and sudden shifts to shorter lines (this device quickens the rhyming and therefore provides an interesting change of pace).

"Evening Song" (w. 1876). A love lyric that takes its chief figures from nature and a Cleopatra legend.

"Song of the Chattahoochee" (w. 1877). A well-known example of personification and onomatopoeia. Its music is so overwhelming that readers may miss the moral (obedience to the call of duty). A mixture of iambic trimeter and tetrameter with frequently interspersed anapests, the lines move swiftly, as befitting the subject. Parallelism, initial iteration, end rhyme, internal rhyme, half-line refrains, and other repetitions contribute to the overall music, which shows the influence of Poe and invites comparison with Tennyson's "The Brook."

"The Stirrup-Cup" (1877). A lyric based on the folk custom of offering guests a parting drink as they mount to leave. The poet, by "right smilingly" (l. 12) accepting the cup that Time (his host) offers him, avows his willingness to accept death. (When Lanier wrote this poem, he had been warned that his own death was near.)

"The Revenge of Hamish" (1878). A ballad that closely follows William Black's *Macleod of Dare* in its exciting plot but is experimental in its use of dactyls.

"The Marshes of Glynn" (1878). Probably Lanier's best-known poem; memorable for its music though puzzling in its message. As can be seen in assorted lines, Lanier achieved an orchestral effect by widely varying the line lengths and the basically anapestic meter. Like Poe, Lanier ran the gamut of audio devices, including assonance, alliteration, and phonetic junction. Still, the poem is less overpowering in its music than "The Song of the Chattahoochee," and its obscurity stems just as much from its ambiguous allegory as from its heavy emphasis on sound. Lanier possibly meant to equate the woods with nature, the marshes with death, and the sea with the afterlife (an interesting reversal of the Darwinism of his day, which taught that animal life had evolved from the sea). If so, the allegory could be interpreted something like this: At first, although the poet benefited from contact with nature (l. 20), he feared death (l. 33). Gradually, however, communion with nature (l. 25) makes him desirous of facing death and the prospect of eternity (ll. 25–26). He grows older, comes closer to death, learns still more from nature (ll. 65–70), finds time running out (l. 89), and enters upon eternity (ll. 97–98) with curiosity (l. 104) but no fear.

"A Ballad of Trees and the Master" (1880). A sixteen-line narrative that shows the healing power of nature by telling of Christ in the Garden of Olives (Matt. 26: 36–46). The poem has been justly praised for its simplicity of diction and haunting repetitions.

15
Walt Whitman

A truly great poet, Walt Whitman (1819–1892) has much to offer literary historians and general readers alike. Historians see him as continuing (sometimes climaxing) the old and proclaiming the new. He embodies the art of the Psalmists, the mysticism and humanitarianism of the Quakers, the nationalism of the Connecticut Wits, the poetic vision of Freneau and Bryant, and the transcendentalism of his immediate predecessors. Yet in the very act of enriching the literature of his day he helped to achieve its passage into the modern age, with its interest in psychology, sex, science, evolution, urbanism, realism, organic structure, and experimentation. Moreover, his influence clearly appears in such twentieth-century writers as Carl Sandburg and Allen Ginsberg. Even outside this historical perspective Whitman proves exciting. He gives his readers a cosmic awareness and a sense of human worth; he simultaneously stirs the senses and the inner man; and he offers an art no longer new yet still impressive in its complex form and supreme sonority.

Life. In Whitman's life as in his writings the rural and the urban were both important. He was born on a Long Island farm, but in 1823 the family moved to Brooklyn, where he got his early schooling, worked as an office boy, and entered the printing trade. Although from 1836 to 1841 he tried his hand at teaching in village schools on Long Island, he became increasingly involved in journalism, editing such papers as the Brooklyn *Daily Eagle* and the New York City *Aurora*. Then in a single year, 1848, he went to New Orleans, worked on the *Crescent,* possibly had a brief love affair (see his "Once I Pass'd through a Populous City"), and returned northward by way of the Mississippi and Great Lakes. Later, as his father (a carpenter) declined in health, Walt supported the family by speculating in real estate.

Meanwhile he read creatively, kept notebooks, studied astronomy, history, and other subjects, absorbed the nationalism of the time, haunted the opera and the theater, and cultivated friendships with artists as well as workingmen. Out of these and many more experiences came *Leaves of Grass*, first issued in 1855. Its preface and twelve untitled poems shocked many readers, and almost no one recognized this small book as a masterpiece. However, it did receive some encouraging reviews, and Emerson called it "the most extraordinary piece of wit and wisdom that America has yet contributed," writing further: "I greet you at the beginning of a great career."[1] Whitman enlarged the book into a second and a third edition (1856, 1860–1861). Too old to enlist in the Civil War, he settled in Washington to nurse in army hospitals, while at the same time working part-time as a copyist in the army paymaster's office. When dismissed from that position because his poems were considered immoral, he was immediately hired by the attorney general's office.

In 1873 Whitman suffered a paralytic stroke. For the rest of his life he lived in Camden, New Jersey. Summers on a nearby farm helped him to recover some of his health, and he was even able to take two long trips, to Colorado (1879) and Canada (1880). Almost until his death he continued to publish new collections of his work, for although his contemporaries had neglected him, he was confident of eventually gaining a high place among American authors.[2]

Language and Technique. Whitman believed that poems should unfold naturally; he disliked ornamentation, and he insisted that thought always came first with him, sound second. Yet from edition to edition his poems reveal an increasing concern with the conventional poetic devices and with sound. Several of the best poems have even been compared with symphonies, operas, and oratorios.

1. Language. He chose words carefully, sometimes from manuscript lists he compiled; and he ranged freely for his sources. Slang *(so long, well hung)* and Americanisms *(worm fence, Kanuck)* decrease in the later poems. Contrariwise, archaisms *(anon, nay)* increase. He was notorious for borrowing and adapting foreign words, a practice that invites both mockery (see Randall Jarrell on Whitman's use of *habitan*) and admiration (note the multiple meanings evoked by the word *Eleves* in "Song of Myself," section 38). He was fond of creating neologisms through suffixes *(deliveress, presidentiad)* and of indulging in functional shift, for example, changing *habit* to a verb, *soothe* to a noun.

2. Catalogs. See, for example "Song of Myself," section 15. This enumerative technique, often used in epics, provides breadth and

1. Whitman quoted and answered Emerson's letter in the 1856 edition of *Leaves of Grass*. As Whitman later admitted, Emerson had played a considerable part in the gestation of *Leaves* by helping Whitman to " 'find himself' ": " 'I was simmering, simmering, simmering; Emerson brought me to a boil.' " Quoted in John Townsend Trowbridge, *My Own Story* (Boston and New York: Houghton Mifflin, 1903), p. 367.

2. Unless noted otherwise, quotations are taken from the ninth or "deathbed edition": *Leaves of Grass* (Philadelphia: McKay, 1891–1892).

concreteness, serves as a kind of name-magic (evoking things simply by naming them), and because it subordinates none of the listed items, expresses the egalitarianism that the poet as mystic and democrat stands for. Yet it can tire the reader, and Whitman abandoned it in his later work.

3. Versification. Whitman wrote in free verse, a form he pioneered in fully using. While iambs and other feet are easy enough to identify in his work, they are not grouped into standard metrical patterns, and scholars have found it more rewarding to look for larger effects, such as peaks or climaxes in a single line or group of lines. Whitman himself likened his verse to the irregular breaking of waves on the shore. He achieved further naturalness by avoiding enjambment, rhyme, and stanza. Instead he generally wrote lines that contained complete clauses or phrases and thus might be extremely long. Among the few works he composed in rhyme and/or stanza are "For You O Democracy," "Pioneers! O Pioneers!" "Beat! Beat! Drums!" and "O Captain! My Captain!"

4. Parallelism and reiteration. Whitman made up for neglecting two kinds of repetition (rhyme and meter) by relying heavily on other kinds, including alliteration, assonance, parallelism, and reiteration.[3] One good example is the line "I celebrate myself, and sing myself" (p. 29), where the words *celebrate* and *sing* are similar if not identical in meaning and are linked through alliteration as well as parallel position. Another illustration appears in an envelope structure that Whitman occasionally used:

> Smile O voluptuous cool-breath'd earth!
> Earth of the slumbering and liquid trees!
> . . . .
> Earth of shine and dark mottling the tide of the river!
> Earth of the limpid gray of clouds brighter and clearer for my sake!
> Far-swooping elbow'd earth—rich apple-blossom'd earth!
> Smile, for your lover comes.
>
> (p. 46)

Here the parallel appositives, with their initial reiteration (epanaphora) are placed between the parallel commands, with their initial reiteration. (For an excellent example of parallelism and reiteration used for contrast see "Give Me the Splendid Silent Sun.")

Chief Poems. *Leaves of Grass,* which Whitman eventually thought of as one long poem, comprises all the poems he wanted preserved. These in turn are arranged in groups or clusters such as "Calamus," "Sea-Drift," "Drum-Taps," "Memories of President Lincoln," and the "Children of Adam" section (devoted to men-women relationships).

"Song of Myself" (first printed in 1855 without title or section numbers; later revised, commas replacing dots to mark caesuras). Whitman's most

---

3. The most likely source of the parallelism and reiteration was the Bible.

important poem. While it celebrates a personal self (and thus opens the poet to the charge of egotism), it also celebrates a representative and cosmic self. Critics once considered the poem formless but have since discovered evidence of structure. According to James E. Miller, for example, "Song of Myself" is a dramatic adaptation of traditional mystical experiences. In sections 1–5 Whitman enters the mystical state; in sections 6–16 he becomes conscious of other forms of being and of the grand design that gives them meaning; in sections 17–32 he purifies himself by accepting base things and by reconciling opposites; in sections 33–37 he finds mystical illumination but also gropes for a time in despair. Then he arrives at the height of mystical experience, a supreme union that allows him to identify with Christ as sufferer and healer, to accept the religions of all ages, and to perceive the meaning of death and immortality (sections 38–49). In sections 50–52 the poet takes leave of his readers. Interpretations of this poem vary considerably but often agree on its large movements and most memorable scenes. Easily recognized, for example, is the journey of the ego. The opening section pictures the poet in a reclining position, but the ego soon migrates and at the end disappears into the air and ground. Another movement involves the poet's progression through conjecture to certitude (sections 6 and 33). He also moves from observation to participation to identification— a progression not easily detected by eyes dazzled with Whitman's kaleidoscopic technique (as in section 15). Important and memorable sections are 5, erotic imagery used to express the union of body and soul that produces intuitive knowledge and a sense of brotherhood with all creation; 6, the symbolic meaning of grass; 11, a sexual interpretation of loneliness; 33, the beginning of time travel; 35–36, a naval battle during the Revolutionary War.

"There Was a Child Went Forth" (1855). A catalog of impressions retained by a sensitive child whose experiences are portrayed as a journey. Scholars regard the poem as semiautobiographical.

"Crossing Brooklyn Ferry" (1856). A virtuoso performance in which Whitman gives mystic meaning to everyday experience. Few scenes could have been more familiar to him than Brooklyn Ferry, which he crossed almost daily from 1850 to 1860, and in his poem he happily succeeds in compressing these sensations into a magnificent kaleidoscope. Motion dominates the poem—not simply the motion of the boats and the river, but also the motion of the poet's imagination, which transcends time and space, projects itself into the future, looks back to the past, and then returns to the present. Motion appears also in the form of changing emphases. In section 3, for example, the ratio of light and shade is reversed as night approaches. Another shift occurs between section 6, where Whitman stresses the evil he shares with all humanity, and section 9, where he stresses their common divinity. The most important motion is that which leads to the union of the poet and his future readers, a climax appropriately described in liquid, sexual imagery (see l. 97). Section 9 continues these erotic suggestions with a series of parallel commands that pulsate in an ecstatic grammatical rhythm.

"Out of the Cradle Endlessly Rocking" (1859). A poetic account of how Whitman became a poet. Undergoing a kind of ritual, a rite of passage, he immerses himself in nature to watch and wait patiently for a special message. From a pair of mockingbirds he learns the meaning of love and the meaning of pain; from the sea (the ancient mother rocking the cradle) he learns the meaning of death and its relation to life. The opening section (ll.1–22), though puzzling at first encounter, has important functions: It achieves suspense and dignity through its inverted syntax, power through its parallelism, depth through its shifting point of view, and foreshadowing through such allusions as "cradle," "brother," and "word stronger and more delicious than any," which later prove to be the sea, the male bird, and the word *death* (pp. 196, 197). The poem is written in an elliptical style with few predicates and many fragments. This adds to the ecstatic tone of the work and helps to convey a sense of multiplicity, as if hundreds of discrete hints were flooding in upon the poet to be interpreted and connected by him.

The "Calamus" group (1860). Deals with "manly love," "comradeship," and "adhesiveness," terms that imply everything from a sense of democratic brotherhood to homosexuality (the latter denied by Whitman). Best remembered of the group is "I Saw in Louisiana a Live-Oak Growing."

"When I Heard the Learn'd Astronomer" (1865). Not a repudiation of science but a transcendental reminder that charts and lectures are for the mystic's "idle times" (as Emerson would call them), when nature cannot be read directly. Note the emphasis on solitude, a hallmark of romanticism.

Drum-Taps (1865). Whitman's Civil War poems. Though mostly conventional, they are not without interest. "Beat! Beat! Drums!" has great audio potential and can be read onomatopoeically in marching rhythm, while "Cavalry Crossing a Ford," "Bivouac on a Mountain Side," and "By the Bivouac's Fitful Flame" resemble the panoramic paintings of the day. Throughout the book appear the new grim realities of war (see, for example, "The Wound-Dresser"). Yet there is the old idealism, too, as when the poet calls the enemy "a man divine as myself" ("Reconciliation"), sees Christ in the face of a dead soldier ("A Sight in Camp in the Daybreak Gray and Dim"), or envisions an end to the conflict and a reappearance of "the sisters Death and Night" to "softly wash . . . this soil'd world" ("Reconciliation").

"When Lilacs Last in the Dooryard Bloom'd" (w. 1865). A pastoral elegy; Whitman's greatest tribute to Abraham Lincoln,[4] although the poem rises above a specific death to the death of all men everywhere. As usual

4. Whitman often saw Lincoln but never knew him personally. There were affinities between the two, especially a dedication to democracy and a desire to treat the beaten South without rancor. After Lincoln died, Whitman wrote several poems and prose pieces to his memory. One, "O Captain! My Captain!" (1865), has been listed among the ten best-known poems in English.

with this genre, the death of an individual is portrayed without naming him; nature participates in the mourning; and the poet's mood changes from despair to acceptance and joy. The poem progresses toward this reconciliation by taking up three major symbols separately and successively, returning to them several times, and finally fusing them. These symbols—the lilac, the evening star, and the song of a swamp-hidden bird (probably the hermit thrush)—seem eminently appropriate to the poem's subjects and themes, in particular the themes of love and rebirth. When the murdered Lincoln's body was carried on a funeral train from Washington to Springfield, the lilacs were in bloom, Venus was the evening star, and the hermit thrush was warbling its mating call. In short, the time was spring, the season traditionally employed in elegies to point up the ironic contrast between nature's renewal and human death and to promise new life to the soul. Whitman also uses spring to represent recurring grief (see l. 3). The lilac, with its heart-shaped leaves and its perfume, symbolizes the poet's love and is given further meaning when he puts a sprig of it on Lincoln's coffin, thus repeating an ancient ritual gesture associated with fertility worship. The evening star in turn represents Lincoln or all the dead. As it goes down, we have a reenactment of the assassination (or the death of everyman). As in earlier poems, Whitman gains knowledge through mystical experience. He hears the voice of nature (the bird's song), echoes it in his heart (l. 163), envisions the soldiers killed in the Civil War, and sees that they are at rest while their mourners suffer.

"A Noiseless Patient Spider" (1868). A poem in which the second stage (or stanza) draws an analogy from the first. An earlier version, which limits the spider motif to one line, has the soul yearning clearly for love of the "Calamus" type (that is, comradeship). Later, Whitman expanded the spider passage and deliberately obscured the object of the soul's longing, thereby increasing the poem's appeal.

"Passage to India" (1871). A cross between an ode and a dramatic monologue (the poet speaking to his soul as they embark, through death, upon the spiritual stage of existence). Whitman begins by celebrating the Atlantic cable, the Suez Canal, and the transcontinental railway—recent marvels that had helped to span the world. But his imagination soon moves him into the past and the future. He envisions the early explorers and traders, lingers a bit on Columbus, sees them all as furthering the divine intention of fusing the continents, predicts the coming of the poet who will complete this work by "absolutely" fusing nature and man (l. 116), and then, beginning in section 7, ecstatically launches his soul on their spiritual voyage (the most daring exploration of all)—"Passage to more than India!"—passage "to primal thought" and union with God "the Comrade perfect" (ll. 234, 166, 201). Here we see a somewhat different Whitman from in the other major poems, a man not content with deciphering death but anxious to experience it.

"To a Locomotive in Winter" (1876). Whitman pictures the locomotive as modern, powerful, and unusual, a lawless, "Fierce-throated beauty!" (p. 359). Perhaps, as George Arms suggests, the poet was slyly describing his own verse here. (Compare Dickinson's "I Like to See It Lap the Miles.")

Chief Prose Works. Although he could write in a clear, journalistic style, as evidenced in *Specimen Days,* much of Whitman's prose was poetic— tiresome and confusing at worst, lyrical and moving at best.

Preface to *Leaves of Grass* (1855 edition). A program for American poetry and at the same time a description of Whitman's own work and intentions. As Crèvecoeur had seen this new land producing a new breed of men, Whitman saw it producing a new breed of poets. Like Emerson, he considered America itself to be embryonic poetry awaiting writers worthy enough to deliver it to the world. He itemized particular topics pressing for the poet's attention, and he offered a lyrical catalog of the personality traits of common people. The new poet, said Whitman, will welcome science, exude optimism, and avoid morbid moralizing. In his art he will strive for freedom and simplicity, letting the form of his poems grow naturally from within (here Whitman paralleled the functionalism then being applied to architecture by Horatio Greenough). Finally, the poet will work toward the day when poets will become the new priests of a new religion, founded in America but affecting the entire globe.

Democratic Vistas (1870). An exploration of American culture. Vague, disjointed, and frequently obscure, the book nevertheless presents a sometimes forgotten critical side of Whitman, showing him quite willing to enumerate and condemn America's faults. He admits the difficulty of reconciling democracy with individualism.[5] Declaring that only the "rare, cosmical, artist-mind" can truly appreciate collective man in all his offensiveness,[6] he calls for a new class of native writers to provide moral leadership.

Specimen Days and Collect (1882). Prose miscellanies, including juvenilia, prefaces, and essays. "Specimen Days," the first section, constitutes an informal autobiography and is especially valuable as an inside record of the Civil War. It includes passages on seashore rambles, ferryboat crossings, nakedness, workingmen, and Lincoln, as well as interesting evaluations of Emerson and other poets.

"A Backward Glance o'er Travel'd Roads" (Preface to *November Boughs,* 1888). Whitman's own valuable analysis of his intent and achievements during some thirty years as poet.

---

5. Of course, this was the kind of bifocalism he attempted in his own verse. See "One's-Self I Sing."

6. Whitman's *Complete Prose Works* (Philadelphia: McKay, 1892), p. 215.

16
Compiling and Updating
Your Own Bibliography

To supplement the various bibliographies in this book you should consult the sources listed below. For dictionaries, indexes, and other reference tools see our General Bibliography.

SECONDARY BIBLIOGRAPHIES

The bibliographies in this section are designed to help you discover writings *on* American authors and their works. Although a few of these compilations come from other fields or take an interdisciplinary approach, most deal primarily with American literature. Those with the widest scope, i.e., those that treat *all* American authors, genres, and literary periods, have been starred (*); and four of the most useful have been double starred (**). Note, however, that under certain circumstances the unstarred sources may prove equally valuable. For example, if you are looking merely for explications of a poem and have no present need for biographical or cultural background studies, you would profit most from consulting, not the starred items, but Kuntz and *The Explicator*.

Starting Points

**LHUS (commonly known as Spiller): the third volume (ed. Thomas H. Johnson) of Spiller, Robert E.; Thorp, Willard; Johnson, Thomas H.; and Canby, Henry S., eds. *Literary History of the United States*. (See General Bibliography for vols. 1–2.) An indispensable bibliography in paragraph form with some annotations. Published in 1948, it covers material through 1946. The first half treats of periods, types, arts and language, folk materials, popular literature, regionalism, and so on. The second half contains bibliographies of individual authors. Should not be used alone but with

****Ludwig, Richard M., ed. *Literary History of the United States: Bibliography Supplement*. New York: Macmillan, 1959. Covers through 1957. Sometimes bound with the 1948 bibliography (above) and sometimes with the 1972 supplement (below); in such cases a single index may serve the several volumes. At any rate, the user should be sure to consult

**Spiller, Robert E.; Thorp, Willard; Johnson, Thomas H.; Canby, Henry S.; and Ludwig, Richard M., eds. *Literary History of the United States: Bibliography Supplement II.* New York: Macmillan, 1972. Covers 1958–1970.

*Leary, Lewis. *Articles on American Literature.* 2 vols. Durham, N.C.: Duke University Press. Vol. 1 (1954) lists articles published from 1900 to 1950; vol. 2 (1970), from 1950 to 1967. Has sections on individual authors (including many lesser-known figures) and on subjects like biography, humor, Negroes, and science.

Gohdes, Clarence. *Bibliographical Guide to the Study of the Literature of the United States.* 3d ed., rev. and enl. Durham, N.C.: Duke University Press, 1970. Annotated. No author bibliographies but a good variety of subjects.

Update the Above Bibliographies With

*"Articles on American Literature Appearing in Current Periodicals," a quarterly bibliography in *American Literature* since November 1929. Anyone interested in completeness should check each issue at least as far back as the latest edition of Leary, which is the only cumulation of this bibliography. Authors are grouped alphabetically within periods: (a) 1607–1800, (b) 1800–1870, (c) 1870–1920, (d) 1920–. There is also a "General" section.

***MLA International Bibliography.* Reprint. New York: Kraus, 1964–. An annual compilation issued through 1968 as part of *PMLA* but since 1969 in separate format. Annual coverage begins with 1921. Has an American section divided into periods. Unlike the *American Literature* bibliography (above) it lists books, festschriften, and dissertation abstracts as well as articles.

*erican *MLA Abstracts of Articles in Scholarly Journals.* New York: Modern Language Association of America, 1972–. Articles abstracted in this annual are marked with an asterisk in the *MLA International Bibliography.* Coverage begins with 1970.

American Literary Scholarship: An Annual. Durham, N.C.: Duke University Press, 1965–. Bibliographical essays by various authorities reviewing the year's work on American literature. Coverage starts with 1963.

American Literature Abstracts, a semiannual publication begun in 1967. Author-prepared abstracts of current articles on American literature. Also contains a "Book Review Consensus" section.

Annual Bibliography of English Language and Literature* (1921–); commonly known as *MHRA Bibliography.* London: Modern Humanities Research Association. Coverage begins with 1920. Arranged by period. British and American authors are alphabetized together.

For Explications of Poems, Short Stories, Novels, Plays

Kuntz, Joseph M. *Poetry Explication: A Checklist of Interpretation since 1925 of British and American Poems Past and Present.* Rev. ed. Chicago: Swallow, 1962. Covers 1925–1959.

Walker, Warren S. *Twentieth-Century Short Story Explication: Interpretations, 1900–1966, of Short Fiction since 1800.* 2d ed. Hamden, Conn.: Shoe String, 1967. Supplements published in 1970, 1973.

Thurston, Jarvis; Emerson, O. B.; Hartman, Carl; and Wright, Elizabeth V. *Short Fiction Criticism: A Checklist of Interpretations since 1925 of Stories and Novelettes (American, British, Continental) 1800–1958.* Chicago: Swallow, 1960.

Gerstenberger, Donna, and Hendrick, George. *The American Novel, 1789–1959: A Checklist of Twentieth-Century Criticism.* Chicago: Swallow, 1961. A supplementary volume is *A Checklist of Criticism on Novels Written since 1789, Volume II: Criticism Written 1960–1968.* Chicago: Swallow, 1970.

Palmer, Helen H., and Dyson, Jane A. *American Drama Criticism: Interpretations, 1890–1965 Inclusive, of American Drama since the First Play Produced in America.* Hamden, Conn.: Shoe String, 1967. *Supplement I.* Hamden, Conn.: Shoe String, 1970.

Ryan, Pat M. *American Drama Bibliography: A Checklist of Publications in English.* Fort Wayne, Ind.: Fort Wayne Public Library, 1969.

Update These Genre Bibliographies With

"A Check List of Explication," an annual bibliography in *The Explicator* since 1944. Mostly concerned with poetry.

"Bibliography [of Short Fiction Criticism]," in the Summer issues of *Studies in Short Fiction.* Annual March through March coverage except for the first bibliography (Summer 1964), which covers 1960 through March 1964.

For an Interdisciplinary, American Studies Approach

"Articles in American Studies," annual bibliography in the summer issues of the *American Quarterly* since 1955 (for 1954). Only articles of an interdisciplinary nature are listed. They are grouped in sections denoting their primary field (e.g., literature, geography, folklore, mass culture, psychiatry) but are also given initials denoting their secondary fields. Thus an article on Calvinism in *Moby-Dick* receives a full listing in the literature section but bears the initials *P* and *R* to indicate its pertinence to philosophy and religion. Annotated.

Harvard Guide to American History. Edited by Frank Freidel, with the assistance of Richard K. Showman. 2 vols. Rev. ed. Cambridge, Mass.: Harvard University Press, Belknap Press, 1974. Contains sections on travel books, serials, biographies, language, popular literature, and the arts. The original edition of the *Harvard Guide to American History,* edited by Oscar Handlin and others (Cambridge, Mass.: Harvard University Press, 1954) is also useful, with sections on historical fiction and poems.

Library of Congress. *A Guide to the Study of the United States of America.* Washington, D.C.: Library of Congress, 1960. 6,487 entries under such headings as literature, language, literary history and criticism, periodicals and journalism, the American Indian, travel, entertainment, books and libraries, science, and law. Paragraph-size annotations.

America: History and Life: A Guide to Periodical Literature (1964–). Santa Barbara, Calif.: Clio. Abstracts and bibliography.

Other Bibliographies of Secondary Sources

Clark, Harry H. *American Literature: Poe through Garland.* Goldentree Bibliographies in Language and Literature. Northbrook, Ill.: AHM Publishing Co., 1971.

Cline, Gloria Stark, and Baker, Jeffrey A. *An Index to Criticisms of British and American Poetry.* Metuchen, N.J.: Scarecrow, 1973.

Davis, Richard Beale. *American Literature through Bryant.* Goldentree Bibliographies in Language and Literature. New York: Appleton, 1969.

Eichelberger, Clayton L. *A Guide to Critical Reviews of United States Fiction, 1870–1910.* 2 vols. Metuchen, N.J.: Scarecrow, 1971, 1974.

Gohdes, Clarence. *Literature and Theater of the States and Regions of the U. S. A.: An Historical Bibliography.* Durham, N.C.: Duke University Press, 1967. Geographical arrangement.

Porter, Dorothy B. *The Negro in the United States: A Selected Bibliography.* Washington, D.C.: Library of Congress, 1970. Includes sections on literature, folklore, and art.

Rubin, Louis D., Jr., ed. *A Bibliographical Guide to the Study of Southern Literature.* Baton Rouge: Louisiana State University Press, 1969. Supplemented by "Bibliography: A Checklist of Scholarship on Southern Literature," published annually since 1969 in *Mississippi Quarterly.*

Turner, Darwin T. *Afro-American Writers.* Goldentree Bibliographies in Language and Literature. Northbrook, Ill.: AHM Publishing Co., 1970.

Woodress, James. *Dissertations in American Literature, 1891–1966.* Durham, N.C.: Duke University Press, 1968. Lists Ph.D. dissertations (completed and in progress) on individual authors and on subjects like criticism, nonfictional prose, Puritanism, and travel. Supplemented by "Research in Progress," published quarterly in *American Literature* magazine. A list of current Ph.D. dissertations and other scholarly projects.

Extensive bibliographies also appear in the following books listed in the General Bibliography: Blair (1937, 1960), *CHAL* (1917–1921), Hubbell (1954), Quinn et al. (1951), Taylor (1936), *Eight American Authors* (1971), *Fifteen American Authors before 1900* (1971).

PRIMARY BIBLIOGRAPHIES

To gather bibliography of works *by* an American author you should consult the following sources:

LHUS, vol. 3 and supplements. The bibliographies of separate works under individual authors will usually prove adequate unless you need to know the name of the publisher, the number of pages, and the like. In such cases go to

BAL, Jacob Blanck's multivolume *Bibliography of American Literature* (New Haven: Yale University Press, 1955–), which contains technical, detailed information.

Wright, Lyle H. *American Fiction: 1774–1850.* 2d rev. ed. San Marino, Calif.: Huntington Library, 1969. *American Fiction: 1851–1875.* San Marino, Calif.: Huntington Library, 1957.

MISCELLANEOUS TOOLS

Altick, Richard D., and Wright, Andrew. *Selective Bibliography for the Study of English and American Literature*. 5th ed. New York: Macmillan, 1975.
Dictionary of American Biography. Edited by Allen Johnson and Dumas Malone. 20 vols. and index. New York: Scribner's, 1928–1937.
Nilon, Charles H. *Bibliography of Bibliographies in American Literature*. New York: Bowker, 1970.

General Bibliography

Although this general bibliography (GB) offers the reader a chance to browse, it is designed primarily as a list of books cited in short form in two or more of the chapter bibliographies. Arrangement is alphabetical by author or editor. For individual authors and for such topics as Puritanism, romanticism, transcendentalism, and humor, the chapter bibliographies should be consulted.

Aarne, Antti, and Thompson, Stith. *The Types of the Folktale*. 2d revision. Folklore Fellows Communications, no. 184. Helsinki: Suomalainen Tiedeakatemia, Academia Scientiarum Fennica, 1961.

Aaron, Daniel. *The Unwritten War: American Writers and the Civil War*. New York: Knopf, 1973.

Abel, Darrel, ed. *Critical Theory in the American Renaissance*. Hartford, Conn.: Transcendental Books, 1969.

Allen, Gay Wilson. *American Prosody*. New York: American Book, 1935.

Altick, Richard D., and Wright, Andrew. See chapter 16.

Anderson, Charles R., ed. *American Literary Masters*. 2 vols. New York: Holt, Rinehart & Winston, 1965.

Arms, George. *The Fields Were Green: A New View of Bryant, Whittier, Holmes, Lowell and Longfellow, with a Selection of Their Poems*. Stanford, Calif.: Stanford University Press, 1953.

Austin, James C., and Koch, Donald A., eds. *Popular Literature in America: A Symposium in Honor of Lyon N. Richardson*. Bowling Green, Oh.: Bowling Green University Popular Press, 1972.

Baritz, Loren. *City on a Hill*. New York: Wiley, 1964.

———. "The Idea of the West." *American Historical Review* 66 (1961): 618–640.

Basler, Roy P. *Sex, Symbolism and Psychology in Literature*. New Brunswick, N.J.: Rutgers University Press, 1948.

Baym, Max I. *A History of Literary Aesthetics in America*. New York: Ungar, 1973.

Berbrich, Joan D. *Three Voices from Paumanok: The Influence of Long Island on James Fenimore Cooper, William Cullen Bryant, Walt Whitman*. Port Washington, N.Y.: Kennikat, Friedman, 1969.

Bewley, Marius. *The Complex Fate: Hawthorne, Henry James and Some Other American Writers*. London: Chatto & Windus, 1952.

———. *Eccentric Design: Form in the Classic American Novel*. New York: Columbia University Press, 1959.

———. *Masks & Mirrors*. New York: Atheneum, 1970.

Bier, Jesse. *The Rise and Fall of American Humor*. New York: Holt, Rinehart & Winston, 1968.

Bigelow, Gordon E. *Rhetoric and American Poetry of the Early National Period*. Gainesville: University of Florida Press, 1960.

Blair, Walter. *Horse Sense in American Humor*. 1942. Reprint. New York: Atheneum, Russell & Russell, 1962.

———. *Native American Humor (1800–1900)*. New York: American Book, 1937.

———. *Native American Humor*. San Francisco: Chandler, 1960. Lacks the individual author bibliographies of the 1937 edition, but the general bibliography and introduction are updated.

Bone, Robert A. *The Negro Novel in America*. New Haven: Yale University Press, 1958.

Botkin, B. A., ed. *A Treasury of American Folklore*. New York: Crown, 1944.

Bowen, James K., and Van Der Beets, Richard, eds. *American Short Fiction: Readings and Criticism*. Indianapolis: Bobbs-Merrill, 1970.

Bridgman, Richard. *The Colloquial Style in America*. New York: Oxford University Press, 1966.

Brigance, William Norwood, ed. *A History and Criticism of American Public Address*. 2 vols. 1943. Reprint. New York: Atheneum, Russell & Russell, 1960.

Brooks, Van Wyck. *The Flowering of New England, 1815–1865*. New York: Dutton, 1936.

———. *The Times of Melville and Whitman*. New York: Dutton, 1947.

———. *The World of Washington Irving*. New York: Dutton, 1944.

———, and Bettmann, Otto L. *Our Literary Heritage: A Pictorial History of the Writer in America*. New York: Dutton, 1956.

Brown, Clarence A., ed. *The Achievement of American Criticism*. New York: Ronald, 1954.

Brown, Herbert Ross. *The Sentimental Novel in America, 1789–1860*. 1940. Reprint. New York: Pageant, 1959.

Brown, Sterling. *The Negro in American Fiction* [and] *Negro Poetry and Drama*. New York: Arno, 1969.

Browne, Ray B., and Light, Martin, eds. *Critical Approaches to American Literature*. 2 vols. New York: T. Y. Crowell, 1965.

Brownell, William C. *American Prose Masters*. Edited by Howard Mumford Jones. 1909. Reprint. Cambridge, Mass.: Harvard University Press, 1963.

Bruccoli, Matthew J., ed. *The Chief Glory of Every People: Essays on Classic American Writers*. Carbondale: Southern Illinois University Press, 1973.

Brumm, Ursula. *American Thought and Religious Typology*. New Brunswick, N.J.: Rutgers University Press, 1970.

Burke, John G., ed. *Regional Perspectives: An Examination of America's Literary Heritage*. Chicago: American Library Association, 1973.

Burr, Nelson R. *A Critical Bibliography of Religion in America*. Vol. 4, pts. 1 and 2 of *Religion in American Life*. Edited by James Ward Smith and A. Leland Jamison. Princeton: Princeton University Press, 1961.

Cady, Edwin H. *The Gentleman in America*. Syracuse, N.Y.: Syracuse University Press, 1949.

Callow, James T. *Kindred Spirits: Knickerbocker Writers and American Artists, 1807–1855*. Chapel Hill: University of North Carolina Press, 1967.

Canby, Henry Seidel. *Classic Americans: A Study of Eminent American Writers from Irving to Whitman*. New York: Harcourt, 1931.

Cargill, Oscar. *Intellectual America*. New York: Macmillan, 1941.

Carpenter, Frederic I. *American Literature and the Dream*. New York: Philosophical Library, 1955.

Cawelti, John G. *Apostles of the Self-Made Man*. Chicago: University of Chicago Press, 1965.

Charvat, William. *The Profession of Authorship in America, 1800–1870: The Papers of William Charvat*. Edited by Matthew J. Bruccoli. Columbus: Ohio State University Press, 1968.

Chase, Richard [Volney]. *The American Novel and Its Tradition*. Garden City, N.Y.: Doubleday, 1957.

Clark, Harry Hayden, ed. *Major American Poets*. New York: American Book, 1936.

————, ed. *Transitions in American Literary History*. Durham, N.C.: Duke University Press, 1953.

Clark, J. Scott. *A Study of English Prose Writers: A Laboratory Method*. New York: Scribner, 1900.

Cline, Gloria S., and Baker, J. A. See chapter 16.

Cohen, Hennig, ed. *Landmarks of American Writing*. New York: Basic Books, 1969.

Conner, Frederick W. *Cosmic Optimism: A Study of the Interpretation of Evolution by American Poets from Emerson to Robinson*. Gainesville: University of Florida Press, 1949.

Cowie, Alexander. *The Rise of the American Novel*. New York: American Book, 1948.

Cowley, Malcolm. *A Many-Windowed House: Collected Essays on American Writers and American Writing*. Edited by Henry D. Piper. Carbondale: Southern Illinois University Press, 1970.

Cunliffe, Marcus, ed. *American Literature to 1900*. Vol. 8 of *History of Literature in the English Language*. London: Barrie & Jenkins, 1973.

Curtis, Richard. *The Genial Idiots: The American Saga as Seen by Our Humorists*. New York: Crowell-Collier, 1968.

Davidson, Philip. *Propaganda and the American Revolution, 1763–1783*. Chapel Hill: University of North Carolina Press, 1941.

Davis, David B. *Homicide in American Fiction, 1798–1860*. Ithaca, N.Y.: Cornell University Press, 1957.

Davis, Richard Beale. *Literature and Society in Early Virginia, 1608–1840*. Baton Rouge: Louisiana State University Press, 1973.

Deakin, Motley, and Lisca, Peter, eds. *From Irving to Steinbeck: Studies of American Literature in Honor of Harry R. Warfel*. Gainesville: University of Florida Press, 1972.

DeMille, George E. *Literary Criticism in America*. New York: L. Mac Veagh, 1931.

Dorson, Richard, ed. *America Begins*. New York: Pantheon, 1950.

————. *American Folklore*. Chicago: University of Chicago Press, 1959.

Downs, Robert B. *Books that Changed America*. New York: Macmillan, 1970.

Dunlap, George Arthur. *The City in the American Novel, 1789–1900*. 1934. Reprint. New York: Atheneum, Russell & Russell, 1965.

Ehrenpreis, Irvin, ed. *American Poetry*. Stratford-upon-Avon Studies, no. 7. London: Edward Arnold, 1965.

Eichelberger, Clayton L. See chapter 16.

Emerson, Everett, ed. *Major Writers of Early American Literature*. Madison: University of Wisconsin Press, 1972.

Feidelson, Charles, Jr. *Symbolism and American Literature*. Chicago: University of Chicago Press, 1953.

——, and Brodtkorb, Paul, Jr., eds. *Interpretations of American Literature*. New York: Oxford University Press, 1959.

Fiedler, Leslie A. *An End to Innocence*. Boston: Beacon, 1955.

——. *Love and Death in the American Novel*. New York: Criterion, 1960.

Foerster, Norman. *American Criticism: A Study in Literary Theory from Poe to the Present*. Boston: Houghton Mifflin, 1928.

——. *Nature in American Literature*. New York: Macmillan, 1923.

——. *The Reinterpretation of American Literature*. New York: Harcourt, 1928.

Folsom, James K. *The American Western Novel*. New Haven: College and University Press, 1966.

Franklin, H. Bruce. *Future Perfect: American Science Fiction of the Nineteenth Century*. New York: Oxford University Press, 1966.

Frederick, John T. *The Darkened Sky: Nineteenth Century American Novelists and Religion*. Notre Dame, Ind.: University of Notre Dame Press, 1969.

Freidel, Frank. See chapter 16.

Fussell, Edwin. *Frontier: American Literature and the American West*. Princeton: Princeton University Press, 1965.

——. *Lucifer in Harness: American Meter, Metaphor, and Diction*. Princeton: Princeton University Press, 1973.

Gaines, Francis P. *The Southern Plantation*. New York: Columbia University Press, 1925.

Gallagher, Kent G. *The Foreigner in Early American Drama*. The Hague: Mouton, 1966. Covers up to 1830.

Gardiner, Harold C., S. J., ed. *American Classics Reconsidered: A Christian Appraisal*. New York: Scribner, 1958.

Gay, Peter. *A Loss of Mastery*. Berkeley: University of California Press, 1966.

Gerstenberger, Donna, and Hendrick, George. See chapter 16.

Gohdes, Clarence, ed. *Essays on American Literature in Honor of Jay B. Hubbell*. Durham, N.C.: Duke University Press, 1967.

Granger, Bruce I. *Political Satire in the American Revolution, 1763–1783*. Ithaca, N.Y.: Cornell University Press, 1960.

Grimsted, David. *Melodrama Unveiled: American Theater and Culture 1800–1850*. Chicago: University of Chicago Press, 1968.

Gross, Seymour L., and Hardy, John Edward, eds. *Images of the Negro in American Literature*. Chicago: University of Chicago Press, 1966.

Gross, Theodore L. *The Heroic Ideal in American Literature*. New York: Free Press, 1971.

Hall, Wade W. *Reflections of the Civil War in Southern Humor*. Monographs, Humanities. Gainesville: University of Florida, 1962.

Hart, James D. *Oxford Companion to American Literature*. 4th ed., rev. & enl. New York: Oxford University Press, 1965.

Hauck, Richard B. *A Cheerful Nihilism: Confidence and "The Absurd" in American Humorous Fiction*. Bloomington: Indiana University Press, 1971.

Hazard, Lucy L. *The Frontier in American Literature*. New York: Barnes & Noble, 1941.

Herron, Ima H. *The Small Town in American Drama*. Dallas: Southern Methodist University Press, 1969.

————. *The Small Town in American Literature*. Durham, N.C.: Duke University Press, 1939.

Herzberg, Max J., and the staff of the T. Y. Crowell Company. *Reader's Encyclopedia of American Literature*. London: Methuen, 1963.

Hicks, Granville. *The Great Tradition*. New York: Macmillan, 1933.

Hintz, Howard W. *The Quaker Influence in American Literature*. 1940. Reprint. Port Washington, N.Y.: Kennikat, 1965.

Hirsch, David H. *Reality and Idea in the Early American Novel*. The Hague: Mouton, 1971.

Hoffman, Daniel. *Form and Fable in American Fiction*. New York: Oxford University Press, 1961.

Horton, Rod W., and Edwards, Herbert W. *Backgrounds of American Literary Thought*. 2d ed. New York: Appleton, 1967.

Howard, Leon. *Literature and the American Tradition*. New York: Doubleday, 1960.

Hubbell, Jay B. *The South in American Literature: 1607–1900*. Durham, N.C.: Duke University Press, 1954.

————. *Who Are the Major American Writers? A Study of the Changing Literary Canon*. Durham, N.C.: Duke University Press, 1972.

Hughes, Glenn. *A History of the American Theatre, 1700–1950*. New York: French, [1951].

Ives, Sumner. "A Theory of Literary Dialect." *TSE* 2 (1950): 137–182.

Jantz, Harold. *The First Century of New England Verse*. 1944. Reprint. New York: Atheneum, Russell & Russell, 1962.

Jones, Howard Mumford. *Belief and Disbelief in American Literature*. Chicago: University of Chicago Press, 1967.

————. *O Strange New World: American Culture: The Formative Years*. New York: Viking, 1964.

————. *The Theory of American Literature*. Ithaca, N.Y.: Cornell University Press, 1965.

Kaplan, Harold. *Democratic Humanism and American Literature*. Chicago: University of Chicago Press, 1972.

Kerr, Howard. *Mediums, and Spirit-Rappers, and Roaring Radicals: Spiritualism in American Literature, 1850–1900*. Urbana: University of Illinois Press, 1972.

Kolodny, Annette. *The Lay of the Land: Metaphor as Experience and History in American Life and Letters*. Chapel Hill: University of North Carolina Press, 1975.

Kramer, Aaron. *The Prophetic Tradition in American Poetry, 1835-1900*. Rutherford, N.J.: Fairleigh Dickinson University Press, 1968.

Krapp, George Philip. *The English Language in America*. 2 vols. 1925. Reprint. New York: Ungar, 1960.

Kreymborg, Alfred. *Our Singing Strength: An Outline of American Poetry (1620–

1930). New York: Coward-McCann, 1929.

Kuhlmann, Susan. *Knave, Fool, and Genius: The Confidence Man as He Appears in Nineteenth-Century American Fiction.* Chapel Hill: University of North Carolina Press, 1973.

Kuntz, Joseph M. See chapter 16.

Lawrence, D. H. *Studies in Classic American Literature.* 1923. Reprint. New York: Viking, 1964.

Leary, Lewis. See chapter 16.

Leisy, Ernest E. *The American Historical Novel.* Norman: University of Oklahoma Press, 1950.

Lemay, J. A. Leo. *Men of Letters in Colonial Maryland.* Knoxville: University of Tennessee Press, 1972.

Lerner, Arthur. *Psychoanalytically Oriented Criticism of Three American Poets: Poe, Whitman, and Aiken.* Rutherford, N.J.: Fairleigh Dickinson University Press, 1970.

Lewis, R. W. B. *The American Adam: Innocence, Tragedy and Tradition in the Nineteenth Century.* 1955. Reprint. Chicago: University of Chicago Press, 1958.

Lieber, Todd M. *Endless Experiments: Essays on the Heroic Experience in American Romanticism.* Columbus: Ohio State University Press, 1973.

Liptzin, Sol. *The Jew in American Literature.* New York: Bloch [1966].

Loggins, Vernon. *The Negro Author: His Development in America to 1900.* 1931. Reprint. Port Washington, N.Y.: Kennikat, 1964.

Loshe, Lillie Deming. *The Early American Novel, 1789–1830.* 1907. Reprint. New York: Ungar, 1958.

Lovell, John, Jr. *Digests of Great American Plays.* New York: T. Y. Crowell, 1961.

Lynen, John F. *The Design of the Present: Essays on Time and Form in American Literature.* New Haven: Yale University Press, 1969.

McGiffert, Michael, ed. *Puritanism and the American Experience.* Reading, Mass.: Addison-Wesley, 1969.

McIlwaine, Shields. *The Southern Poor-White from Lubberland to Tobacco Road.* Norman: University of Oklahoma Press, 1939.

McKerrow, Ronald B. *An Introduction to Bibliography for Literary Students.* Oxford: Clarendon, 1927.

McNeir, Waldo, and Levy, Leo B., eds. *Studies in American Literature.* Baton Rouge: Louisiana State University Press, 1960.

Madison, Charles A. *Irving to Irving: Author-Publisher Relations 1800–1974.* New York: Bowker, 1974.

Marble, Annie Russell. *Heralds of American Literature: A Group of Patriot Writers of the Revolutionary and National Periods.* Chicago: University of Chicago Press, 1907.

Marckwardt, Albert H. *American English.* New York: Oxford University Press, 1958.

Marx, Leo. *The Machine in the Garden: Technology and the Pastoral Ideal in America.* New York: Oxford University Press, 1964.

Mathews, Mitford M., ed. *A Dictionary of Americanisms on Historical Principles.* 2 vols. Chicago: University of Chicago Press, 1951.

Matthiessen, F. O. *American Renaissance: Art and Expression in the Age of Emerson and Whitman.* New York: Oxford University Press, 1941.

May, John R. *Toward a New Earth: Apocalypse in the American Novel.* Notre Dame,

Ind.: University of Notre Dame Press, 1972.

Mencken, Henry L. *The American Language*. 4th ed., cor., enl., and rewritten. New York: Knopf, 1936. With supplements in 1945, 1948.

Merrill, Dana K. *American Biography*. New York: Bowker, 1957.

Miller, Perry. *The New England Mind: The Seventeenth Century*. New York: Macmillan, 1939.

————, and Johnson, Thomas H., eds. *The Puritans*. 1938. 2 vols. Rev. ed. New York: Harper & Row, 1963. Bibliographies revised by George McCandlish.

Mills, Nicolaus. *American and English Fiction in the Nineteenth Century: An Antigenre Critique and Comparison*. Bloomington: Indiana University Press, 1973.

Milne, Gordon. *The American Political Novel*. Norman: University of Oklahoma Press, 1966.

Minter, David L. *The Interpreted Design as a Structural Principle in American Prose*. New Haven: Yale University Press, 1969.

Mitchell, Loften. *Black Drama: The Story of the American Negro in the Theatre*. New York: Hawthorn, 1967.

Mizener, Arthur. *Twelve Great American Novels*. Cleveland: World Publishing, 1969.

Morison, Samuel Eliot. *Builders of the Bay Colony*. 2d ed., rev. & enl. Boston: Houghton Mifflin [1958].

Moses, Montrose J. *The American Dramatist*. 1925. Reprint. New York: Blom, 1964.

Mott, Frank Luther. *Golden Multitudes: The Story of Best Sellers in the United States*. New York: Macmillan, 1947.

————. *A History of American Magazines*. 5 vols. Cambridge, Mass.: Harvard University Press, 1957–1968.

Murdock, Kenneth B. *Literature & Theology in Colonial New England*. 1949. Reprint. New York: Harper & Row, 1963.

Narasimhaiah, C. D., ed. *Asian Response to American Literature*. New York: Barnes & Noble, 1972.

Nilon, Charles H. See chapter 16.

Noble, David W. *The Eternal Adam and the New World Garden: The Central Myth in the American Novel since 1830*. New York: Braziller, 1968.

Nye, Russell B., and Grabo, Norman S., eds. *American Thought and Writing*. 2 vols. Boston: Houghton Mifflin, 1965.

O'Neill, Edward H. *A History of American Biography 1800–1935*. 1935. Reprint. New York: Atheneum, Russell & Russell, 1968.

Orians, G. Harrison. *A Short History of American Literature Analyzed by Decades*. New York: Crofts, 1940.

Palmer, Helen H., and Dyson, Jane A. See chapter 16.

Parks, Edd W. *Ante-Bellum Southern Critics*. Athens: University of Georgia Press, 1962.

Parrington, Vernon L. *The Colonial Mind, 1620–1800* (1927) and *The Romantic Revolution in America* (1927). Reprinted as vols. 1 and 2 of his *Main Currents in American Thought*. New York: Harcourt, 1930.

Pattee, Fred Lewis. *The Development of the American Short Story*. 1923. Reprint. New York: Biblo & Tannen, 1966.

————. *The First Century of American Literature, 1770–1870*. New York: Appleton, 1935.

Pearce, Roy Harvey. *The Continuity of American Poetry.* Princeton: Princeton University Press, 1961.

Peltola, Niilo. *The Compound Epithet and Its Use in American Poetry, from Bradstreet through Whitman.* Helsinki: Academiae Scientiarum Fennicae, 1956.

Piercy, Josephine K. *Studies in Literary Types in Seventeenth Century America (1607–1710).* 2d ed. Hamden, Conn.: Archon, 1969.

Pochmann, Henry A. *German Culture in America: Philosophical and Literary Influences, 1600–1900.* Madison: University of Wisconsin Press, 1957.

Porte, Joel. *The Romance in America: Studies in Cooper, Poe, Hawthorne, Melville, and James.* Middletown, Conn.: Wesleyan University Press, 1969.

Pritchard, John Paul. *Return to the Fountains: Some Classical Sources of American Criticism.* Durham, N.C.: Duke University Press, 1942.

———. *Criticism in America.* Norman: University of Oklahoma Press, 1956.

Quinn, Arthur Hobson. *American Fiction: An Historical and Critical Survey.* New York: Appleton, 1936.

———. *A History of the American Drama from the Beginning to the Civil War.* 1923. 2d ed. New York: Appleton, 1943.

———; Murdock, Kenneth B.; Gohdes, Clarence; and Whicher, George F. *The Literature of the American People.* New York: Appleton, 1951.

Rayapati, J. P. Rao. *Early American Interest in Vedanta: Pre-Emersonian Interest in Vedic Literature and Vedantic Philosophy.* New York: Asia Publishing House, 1973.

Redding, Saunders. *To Make a Poet Black.* Chapel Hill: University of North Carolina Press, 1939.

Reed, Perley Isaac. *The Realistic Presentation of American Characters in Native Plays prior to Eighteen Seventy.* Contributions in Language and Literature, no. 1. Columbus: Ohio State University Press, 1918.

Rees, Robert A., and Harbert, Earl N. *Fifteen American Authors before 1900: Bibliographic Essays on Research and Criticism.* Madison: University of Wisconsin Press, 1971.

Richardson, Lyon N. *A History of Early American Magazines, 1741–1789.* New York: T. Nelson, 1931.

Rideout, Walter B. *The Radical Novel in the United States, 1900–1954.* Cambridge, Mass.: Harvard University Press, 1964.

Ringe, Donald A. *The Pictorial Mode: Space & Time in the Art of Bryant, Irving, & Cooper.* Lexington: University Press of Kentucky, 1971.

Robinson, Cecil. *With the Ears of Strangers: The Mexican in American Literature.* Tucson: University of Arizona Press, 1963.

Rourke, Constance. *American Humor.* 1931. Reprint. New York: Doubleday, 1953.

Rubin, Louis D., Jr., ed. *The Comic Imagination in American Literature.* New Brunswick, N.J.: Rutgers University Press, 1973.

———, ed. 1969. See chapter 16.

Ruland, Richard, ed. *The Native Muse: Theories of American Literature.* Vol. 1. New York: Dutton, 1972.

Sanford, Charles. *The Quest for Paradise.* Urbana: University of Illinois Press, 1961.

Shapiro, Charles, ed. *Twelve Original Essays on Great American Novels.* Detroit: Wayne State University Press, 1958.

Shapiro, Karl; Miller, James E.; and Slote, Bernice. *Start with the Sun: Studies in Cosmic Poetry.* Lincoln: University of Nebraska Press, 1960.

Shea, Daniel B., Jr. *Spiritual Autobiography in Early America*. Princeton: Princeton University Press, 1968.

Silverman, Kenneth, ed. *Colonial American Poetry*. New York: Hafner, 1968.

Simon, Myron, and Parsons, Thornton H., eds. *Transcendentalism and Its Legacy*. Ann Arbor: University of Michigan Press, 1966.

Simonini, R. C., Jr. *Southern Writers: Appraisals in Our Time*. Charlottesville: University Press of Virginia, 1964.

Simpson, Lewis P. *The Man of Letters in New England and the South: Essays on the History of the Literary Vocation in America*. Baton Rouge: Louisiana State University Press, 1973.

Skard, Sigmund, ed. *USA in Focus*. Oslo: Universitetsforlaget, 1966.

Slotkin, Richard. *Regeneration through Violence: The Mythology of the American Frontier, 1600–1860*. Middletown, Conn.: Wesleyan University Press, 1973.

Smith, Henry Nash. *Virgin Land: The American West as Symbol and Myth*. Cambridge, Mass.: Harvard University Press, 1950.

Smithline, Arnold. *Natural Religion in American Literature*. New Haven: College and University Press, 1966.

Snell, George. *The Shapers of American Fiction, 1789–1947*. 1947. Reprint. New York: Cooper Square, 1961.

Spiller, Robert E.; Thorp, Willard; Johnson, Thomas H.; and Canby, Henry Seidel, eds. *Literary History of the United States*. Rev. ed. in one vol. New York: Macmillan, 1953. A comprehensive history by fifty-five scholars. When first published in 1948, this history formed vols. 1 and 2 of a three-volume set; for vol. 3 and supplements see chapter 16.

Spiller, Robert E. *The Cycle of American Literature*. New York: Free Press, 1955.

Starke, Catherine J. *Black Portraiture in American Fiction: Stock Characters, Archetypes, and Individuals*. New York: Basic Books, 1971.

Stedman, Edmund Clarence. *Poets of America*. Boston: Houghton Mifflin, 1898.

Stegner, Wallace E., ed. *The American Novel from James Fenimore Cooper to William Faulkner*. New York: Basic Books [1965].

Stewart, Randall. *American Literature and Christian Doctrine*. Baton Rouge: Louisiana State University Press, 1958.

Stovall, Floyd, ed. *The Development of American Literary Criticism*. Chapel Hill: University of North Carolina Press, 1955.

Sullivan, Wilson. *New England Men of Letters*. New York: Macmillan, 1972.

Tandy, Jennette. *Crackerbox Philosophers in American Humor and Satire*. 1925. Reprint. Port Washington, N.Y.: Kennikat, 1964.

Tanner, Tony. *The Reign of Wonder: Naivety and Reality in American Literature*. [Cambridge]: University Press, 1965.

Taylor, Walter Fuller. *A History of American Letters, with Bibliographies by Harry Hartwick*. New York: American Book, 1936.

———. *The Story of American Letters*. Chicago: Regnery, 1956.

Tebbel, John. *A History of Book Publishing in the United States*. Vol. 1: *The Creation of an Industry*. New York: Bowker, 1972. Covers 1630–1865.

Thompson, Stith. *Motif-Index of Folk-Literature*. 6 vols. Rev. & enl. ed. Bloomington: Indiana University Press, 1955–1958.

Thrall, William Flint; Hibbard, Addison; and Holman, C. Hugh. *A Handbook to Literature*. Rev. & enl. ed. New York: Odyssey, 1960.

Thurston, Jarvis; Emerson, O. B.; Hartman, Carl; and Wright, Elizabeth V. See chapter 16.

Trent, William P.; Erskine, John; Sherman, Stuart P.; and Van Doren, Carl, eds. *Cambridge History of American Literature*. 4 vols. New York: Putnam, 1917–1921.

Tyler, Moses C. *A History of American Literature: 1607–1765*. 1878. Reprint. Ithaca, N.Y.: Cornell University Press, 1949.

———. *The Literary History of the American Revolution*. 2 vols. 1897. Reprint. New York: Ungar, 1957.

Van Doren, Carl C. *The American Novel, 1789–1939*. New York: Macmillan, 1940.

Van Doren, Mark. *Introduction to Poetry*. New York: Holt, Rinehart & Winston, Dryden Press, 1951.

Van Nostrand, A. D. *Everyman His Own Poet: Romantic Gospels in American Literature*. New York: McGraw-Hill, 1968.

———. *Literary Criticism in America*. New York: Liberal Arts Press, 1957.

Vogel, Dan. *The Three Masks of American Tragedy*. Baton Rouge: Louisiana State University Press, 1974.

Voss, Arthur. *The American Short Story: A Critical Survey*. Norman: University of Oklahoma Press, 1973.

Wagenknecht, Edward. *Cavalcade of the American Novel*. New York: Holt, 1952.

Wager, Willis. *American Literature: A World View*. New York: New York University Press, 1968.

Waggoner, Hyatt H. *American Poets from the Puritans to the Present*. Boston: Houghton Mifflin, 1968.

Walcutt, Charles C., and Whitesell, J. Edwin. *The Explicator Cyclopedia*. 3 vols. New York: Quadrangle, 1966–1968.

Walker, Warren S. See chapter 16.

Warren, Austin. *The New England Conscience*. Ann Arbor: University of Michigan Press, 1966.

Welsch, Erwin K. *The Negro in the United States: A Research Guide*. Bloomington: Indiana University Press, 1965.

Whitlow, Roger. *Black American Literature: A Critical History*. Chicago: Nelson-Hall, 1973.

Williams, Stanley. *The Spanish Background of American Literature*. 2 vols. New Haven: Yale University Press, 1955.

Wilson, Edmund. *Patriotic Gore: Studies in the Literature of the American Civil War*. London: Andre Deutsch, 1962.

Wilson, Garff B. *Three Hundred Years of American Drama and Theatre: From Ye Bear and Ye Cubb to Hair*. Englewood Cliffs, N.J.: Prentice-Hall, 1973.

Woodress, James, ed. *Eight American Authors: A Review of Research and Criticism*. Rev. ed. New York: Norton, 1971.

———, ed., with the assistance of Townsend Ludington and Joseph Arpad. *Essays Mostly on Periodical Publishing in America: A Collection in Honor of Clarence Gohdes*. Durham, N.C.: Duke University Press, 1973.

Wright, Louis B. *The First Gentlemen of Virginia*. San Marino, Calif.: Huntington Library, 1940.

Wright, Nathalia. *American Novelists in Italy: The Discoverers: Allston to James*. Philadelphia: University of Pennsylvania Press, 1965.

Yellin, Jean F. *The Intricate Knot: Black Figures in American Literature 1776–1863*. New York: New York University Press, 1972.

Young, Philip. *Three Bags Full: Essays in American Fiction*. New York: Harcourt Brace Jovanovich [1972].

Young, Thomas D., and Fine, Ronald E., eds. *American Literature: A Critical Survey*. 2 vols. New York: American Book, 1968.

Chapter-by-Chapter Bibliographies

These bibliographies are designed to supplement and document the discussions in the text of this guide. To gather further bibliography the reader should consult chapter 16.

See pp. vii–x for list of abbreviations used.

1: EARLIEST AMERICAN WRITING

TEXTS. Dorson (GB:1950); *Narratives of Early Virginia, 1606–1625,* ed. L. G. Tyler (Original Narratives of Early American History, 1907; reprint ed., New York: Barnes & Noble, 1959); *The Elizabethan's America: A Collection of Early Reports by Englishmen on the New World,* ed. Louis B. Wright (Stratford-upon-Avon Library; Leeds, England: E. J. Arnold, 1965).

STUDIES. Howard Mumford Jones, *The Literature of Virginia in the Seventeenth Century* (1946; 2d ed., Charlottesville: University Press of Virginia, 1968); Roy Harvey Pearce, "The Significance of the Captivity Narrative," *AL* 19 (1947): 1–20; Lemay (GB), for George Alsop.

Captain John Smith

TEXTS. *Travels and Works of Captain John Smith,* ed. Edward Arber, with Biographical and Critical Introduction by A. C. Bradley, 2 vols. (Edinburgh: John Grant, 1910), standard; *Captain John Smith's America,* edited with introduction by John Lankford (New York: Harper & Row, 1967), selections from *The Generall Historie* and *Advertisements for the Unexperienced Planters of New-England, or Any Where.*

BIOGRAPHY. Smith's veracity was attacked by Henry Adams and Lewis L. Kropf in the nineteenth century, but since then Smith's most thorough biographers have convincingly defended him. See Bradford Smith, *Captain John Smith, His Life & Legend* (Philadelphia: Lippincott, 1953), a complete life and penetrating psychological study; Laura P. Striker and Bradford Smith, "The Rehabilitation of Captain John Smith," *JSH* 28 (1962): 474–481; Philip Barbour, *The Three*

Worlds of Captain John Smith (Boston: Houghton Mifflin, 1964), an exhaustive biography, with pictures, maps, and genealogical charts.

CRITICISM. There are fewer studies of Smith as a writer than as a man of action. Everett H. Emerson treats the subject fully in *Captain John Smith* (TUSAS: 1971) and briefly in "Captain John Smith as Editor: *The Generall Historie*," *VMHB* 75 (1967): 143–156 and "Captain John Smith, Autobiographer," *EALN* 2 (1967): 18–23. Edwin C. Rozwenc, in his "Captain John Smith's Image of America," *WMQ*, 3d ser. 16 (1959): 27–36, relates Smith's works to the tradition of the chivalric romance; but H. M. Jones (GB:1964), pp. 238–239, suggests the *Aeneid* as another possible influence. Also see Jones, *The Literature of Virginia* (above), pp. 35–57; Tyler (GB:1878), 2:16–38.

BIBLIOGRAPHY. Emerson (above, 1971).

2: PURITANS AND NON-PURITANS

TEXTS. *Seventeenth-Century American Poetry*, ed. Harrison T. Meserole (New York: New York University Press, 1968); Silverman (GB); Miller and Johnson (GB); Nye and Grabo (GB); *The Bay Psalm Book* (Chicago: University of Chicago Press [1956]), facsimile of the 1640 edition.

STUDIES. Piercy (GB); Murdock (GB), an important study; Tyler (GB:1878), a pioneer work; Gay (GB), on the historians of the period; Jantz (GB); Norman S. Grabo, "How Bad Is the *Bay Psalm Book?*" *PMASAL* 46 (1961): 605–615; Zoltán Haraszti, *The Enigma of the Bay Psalm Book* (Chicago: University of Chicago Press, 1956); Thomas G. Wright, *Literary Culture in Early New England, 1620–1730* (New Haven: Yale University Press, 1920).

BIBLIOGRAPHY. Miller and Johnson (GB); R. B. Davis (GB); "Literature to 1800" in *ALS*, an annual review.

William Bradford

TEXTS. *History of Plymouth Plantation, 1620–1647*, ed. Worthington Chauncey Ford, 2 vols. (Boston: Houghton Mifflin, 1912), is standard and thoroughly annotated. However, *Of Plymouth Plantation, 1620–1647*, ed. Samuel Eliot Morison (New York: Knopf, 1952), another complete and well-annotated text, is easier to read, for it modernizes Bradford's spelling. On pp. xl–xlii Morison evaluates previous editions, including *Bradford's History of Plymouth Plantation, 1606–1646*, ed. William T. Davis (Original Narratives of American History, 1908; reprint ed., New York: Barnes & Noble, 1959), useful for its footnotes and introduction. *Of Plymouth Plantation*, ed. Harvey Wish (New York: Putnam, Capricorn Books, 1962), abridges the text by half, retains the original spelling, and has a twenty-two-page introduction in lieu of footnotes. Reprints of Bradford's miscellaneous writings are mentioned in *LHUS*, 3:412–413. *Mourt's Relation* (1622), a day-by-day account of the first year of the Pilgrims' settlement in America, is perhaps the work of Bradford in collaboration with Edward Winslow. Thus it supplements *Of Plymouth Plantation*. In 1865 Henry M. Dexter edited *Mourt's Relation* with copious notes (reprint ed., Richmond, Va.: Garrett, 1969). *A Journal of the Pilgrims at Plymouth: Mourt's Relation*, ed. Dwight B. Heath (Corinth, 1963) offers modernized text, an introduction, notes, and helpful illustrations.

BIOGRAPHY. One of Bradford's descendants, Bradford Smith, has written the best life: *Bradford of Plymouth* (Philadelphia: Lippincott, 1951). Still one of the chief sources of information on Bradford's early years is Cotton Mather's often-re-printed sketch of him in *Magnalia Christi Americana* (1702).

STUDIES. E. F. Bradford, "Conscious Art in Bradford's *History of Plymouth Plantation,*" *NEQ* 1 (1928): 133–157; Tyler (GB:1878), 1:116–126; David Levin in Emerson (GB), pp. 11–31; Jesper Rosenmeier in Sacvan Bercovitch, *Typology and Early American Literature* (Amherst: University of Massachusetts Press, 1972), pp. 69–105; Alan B. Howard, "Art and History in Bradford's *Of Plymouth Plantation,*" *WMQ* 28 (1971): 237–266; Norman Grabo in Cohen (GB), pp. 3–19; John Griffith, "*Of Plymouth Plantation* as a Mercantile Epic," *Arizona Quarterly* 28 (1972): 231–242.

Samuel Sewall

TEXTS. *The Diary of Samuel Sewall: 1674–1729,* ed. Thomas M. Halsey, 2 vols. (New York: Farrar, Straus & Giroux, 1973); *Diary of Samuel Sewall, 1674–1729,* vols. 5–7 (1878–1882) of the Coll. Mass. Hist. Soc., 5th ser., both editions with annotations and index; *The Selling of Joseph,* ed. Sidney Kaplan (Amherst: University of Massachusetts Press, 1969). For Sewall's other writings see *LHUS.*

Biographies include Ola Elizabeth Winslow, *Samuel Sewall of Boston* (New York: Macmillan [1964]) especially valuable for its examination of Sewall's business activities; T. B. Strandness, *Samuel Sewall: A Puritan Portrait* (East Lansing: Michigan State University Press, 1967); and the entry on Sewall in *DAB.*

Anne Bradstreet

TEXTS. *The Works of Anne Bradstreet,* ed. Jeannine Hensley, foreword by Adrienne Rich (Cambridge, Mass.: Harvard University Press, 1967), with notes, introduction, and index; *Poems of Anne Bradstreet,* ed. Robert Hutchinson (New York: Dover, 1969).

STUDIES. Josephine K. Piercy, *Anne Bradstreet* (TUSAS: 1965), a full analysis of Bradstreet's spiritual and poetical maturation; Elizabeth W. White, *Anne Bradstreet: "The Tenth Muse"* (New York: Oxford University Press, 1971); Tyler (GB:1878), 1:277–292; Lyon N. Richardson in *DAB;* Morison (GB), pp. 320–336; Ann Stanford, "Anne Bradstreet as a Meditative Writer," *California English Journal* 2 (1966): 24–31, useful for "Contemplations"; Robert D. Richardson, Jr., "The Puritan Poetry of Anne Bradstreet," *TSLL* 9 (1967): 317–331; Rosemary M. Laughlin, "Anne Bradstreet: Poet in Search of Form," *AL* 42 (1970): 1–17, on changes in versification, imagery, themes, and structure; A. H. Rosenfeld, "Anne Bradstreet's 'Contemplations,' " *NEQ* 43 (1970): 79–96; Kenneth A. Requa, "Anne Bradstreet's Poetic Voices," *EAL* 9 (1974): 3–18; Ann Stanford in Emerson (GB), pp. 33–58.

BIBLIOGRAPHY. Ann Stanford, "Anne Bradstreet: An Annotated Checklist," *EAL* 3 (1968–1969):217–228, including primary and secondary materials.

Michael Wigglesworth

TEXTS. *The Day of Doom* has been edited by J. W. Dean and W. H. Burr (New York: American News, 1867) and Kenneth B. Murdock (1929; reprint ed., New York:

Atheneum, Russell & Russell, 1966). His diary, a frank, detailed spiritual record, covers only 1653–1657: *The Diary of Michael Wigglesworth,* ed. Edmund S. Morgan (1951; reprint ed., New York: Harper & Row, 1965).

STUDIES. Richard Crowder's *No Featherbed to Heaven: A Biography of Michael Wigglesworth, 1631–1705* (East Lansing: Michigan State University Press, 1962) is a full-length modern portrait stressing Wigglesworth's religious orthodoxy and strong sexual drives. Also see F. O. Matthiessen, "Michael Wigglesworth: A Puritan Artist," *NEQ* 1 (1928): 491–504; Robert H. Woodward, "Moore's St. Nick: Model and Motif," *NYFQ* 15 (1959): 251–254, which demonstrates parallels between *The Day of Doom* and *A Visit from St. Nicholas;* Tyler (GB:1878), 2:23–35; Mott (GB:1947), pp. 12–14; Gerhard T. Alexis, "Wigglesworth's 'Easiest Room,' " *NEQ* 42 (1969): 573–583, on stanza 181.

Edward Taylor

TEXTS. *The Poems of Edward Taylor,* ed. Donald E. Stanford (New Haven: Yale University Press, 1960), the largest collection, also available in an abridged paperback edition (1963); *The Poetical Works of Edward Taylor,* ed. Thomas H. Johnson (1939; reprint ed., Princeton: Princeton University Press, 1966); *Edward Taylor's Christographia,* ed. Norman Grabo (New Haven: Yale University Press, 1962), fourteen of Taylor's Sacrament Day sermons and their corresponding poems; *The Diary of Edward Taylor,* ed. Francis Murphy (1880; reprint ed., Springfield, Mass.: Conn. Valley Historical Museum, 1964).

A Concordance to the Poems of Edward Taylor, compiled by Gene Russell (Washington, D.C.: Microcard Editions, 1973), is essential to a close reading of Taylor.

STUDIES. Norman S. Grabo, *Edward Taylor* (TUSAS: 1961), an important treatment of the life, thought, and techniques; William J. Scheick, *The Will and the Word: The Poetry of Edward Taylor* (Athens: University of Georgia Press, 1974); Karl Keller, *The Example of Edward Taylor* (Amherst: University of Massachusetts Press, 1975), a critical biography; Wallace Cable Brown, "Edward Taylor: An American 'Metaphysical,' " *AL* 16 (1944): 186–197, connecting Taylor's intellectuality, wit, syntax and metrics with the Metaphysical poets of England; Thomas H. Johnson, "Edward Taylor: A Puritan 'Sacred Poet,' " *NEQ* 10 (1937): 290–322; Peltola (GB), pp. 44–47, 194–196; Donald E. Stanford, *Edward Taylor* (UMPAW: 1965), a pamphlet; Gene Russell, "Dialectal and Phonetic Features of Edward Taylor's Rhymes: A Brief Study Based upon a Computer Concordance of His Poems," *AL* 43 (1971): 165–180; Donald E. Stanford, "Edward Taylor," in Emerson (GB), pp. 59–91, authoritative.

STUDIES OF INDIVIDUAL POEMS. William K. Bottorff, "Edward Taylor, an Explication: 'Another Meditation at the Same Time,' " *EAL* 3 (1968): 17–21, on Meditation Six (First Series); Gerhard T. Alexis, "Taylor's 'Meditation Eight,' " *Expl* 24 (1966), item 77; John Clendenning, "Piety and Imagery in Edward Taylor's 'The Reflexion,' " *AQ* 16 (1964): 203–210; Norman Grabo, "Edward Taylor's Spiritual Huswifery," *PMLA* 79 (1964): 554–560, an indispensable study of "Huswifery"; Francis A. Simonetti, "Prosody as a Unifying Element in 'Huswifery,' " *Ball State University Forum* 14 (1973): 30–31; Judson B. Allen, "Edward Taylor's Catholic Wasp: Exegetical Convention in 'Upon a Spider Catching a

Fly,' " *ELN* 7 (1970): 257–260; Raymond J. Jordan, "Taylor's 'The Ebb and Flow,' " *Expl* 20 (1962), item 67.

GOD'S DETERMINATIONS. Nathalia Wright, "The Morality Tradition in the Poetry of Edward Taylor," *AL* 18 (1946): 1–17; Stephen Fender, "Edward Taylor and 'The Application of Redemption,' " *MLR* 59 (1964): 331–334; Dale Doepke, "A Suggestion for Reading Edward Taylor's 'The Preface,' " *EAL* 5 (1971): 80–82.

STUDIES OF GROUPS AND SERIES. James T. Callow, "Edward Taylor Obeys Saint Paul," *EAL* 4 (1969–1970): 89–96, on Meditations 19–22 (First Series); Robert Reiter, "Poetry and Typology: Edward Taylor's *Preparatory Meditations,* Second Series, Numbers 1–30," *EAL* 5 (1970): 111–123.

BIBLIOGRAPHY. Norman S. Grabo, "Edward Taylor," in *Fifteen American Authors before 1900* (GB), pp. 333–356, an essay-review of the scholarship; Constance J. Gefvert, *Edward Taylor: An Annotated Bibliography, 1668–1970* (Kent, Oh.: Kent State University Press, 1971).

Roger Williams

TEXTS. *Complete Writings of Roger Williams,* 6 vols. (1866–1874; reprinted with a 7th volume, New York: Atheneum, Russell & Russell, 1963), containing a twenty-one-page "Essay in Interpretation" by Perry Miller; *A Key into the Language of America,* ed. John J. Teunissen and Evelyn J. Hinz (Detroit: Wayne State University Press, 1973).

STUDIES. Ola Winslow's *Master Roger Williams* (New York: Macmillan, 1957) provides literary and historical analysis as well as trustworthy biography. Samuel H. Brockunier, *The Irrepressible Democrat, Roger Williams* (New York: Ronald, 1940); James E. Ernst, *The Political Thought of Roger Williams* (Seattle: University of Washington Press, 1929); and Parrington, *Colonial Mind* (GB), pp. 61–75, treat Williams as a democratic pioneer; but their conclusions are considerably modified by later studies, which emphasize the religious foundation of Williams' political theories: Mauro Calamandrei, "Neglected Aspects of Roger Williams' Thought," *Church History* 21 (1952): 239–258; Alan Simpson, "How Democratic Was Roger Williams?" *WMQ,* 3d ser. 13 (1956): 53–67; Perry Miller, *Roger Williams: His Contribution to the American Tradition* (Indianapolis: Bobbs-Merrill, 1953), a combination anthology and critical interpretation. Also see Edmund Morgan, *Roger Williams: The Church and the State* (New York: Harcourt, 1967).

Thomas Morton

TEXT. *The New English Canaan,* ed. Charles Francis Adams, Jr. (Boston: Prince Society, 1883) is copiously annotated, with a long introduction.

STUDIES. In *Thomas Morton* (TUSAS: 1969) Donald Francis Connors shows the value of Morton's book as promotional, pastoral, and satirical literature. Also see Minor Wallace Major, "William Bradford versus Thomas Morton," *EAL* 5 (1970): 1–13, which suggests that Morton brought on his deportation, contrary to Bradford's charge, by encouraging sexual intercourse between the Indian girls and his men; Robert D. Arner, "Mythology and the Maypole of Merrymount: Some Notes on Thomas Morton's 'Rise Oedipus,' " *EAL* 6 (1971): 156–164; William J. Scheick, "Morton's *New English Canaan,*" *Expl* 31 (1973), item 47.

BIBLIOGRAPHY. Connors (above).

3: LATER PURITANS

For the decay of Puritanism see Horton and Edwards (GB), pp. 41–44; Clarence H. Faust, "The Decline of Puritanism," in H. H. Clark, ed. (GB:1953), pp. 3–47.

Cotton Mather

TEXTS. There is no collected edition of the 468 items listed in Thomas J. Holmes's *A Bibliography of His Works*, 3 vols. (Cambridge, Mass.: Harvard University Press, 1940); but some of the most important books have been reprinted. The best complete text of *Wonders of the Invisible World* was edited by S. G. Drake as vol. 1 (Woodward's Historical Series, no. 5) of *The Witchcraft Delusion in New England* (1866; reprint ed., New York: Franklin, 1970). Vols. 2 and 3 (nos. 6 and 7 of this series) reprint Robert Calef's *More Wonders of the Invisible World* (1700), a bitter attack on Mather and others involved in the witchcraft trials. The index to all three of these well-annotated volumes is in vol. 3. For large selections from Mather's *Wonders* and other writings on witchcraft see George L. Burr, ed., *Narratives of the Witchcraft Cases, 1648–1706* (Original Narratives of American History, 1914; reprint ed., New York: Barnes & Noble, 1950), with introduction, notes, index, and excellent bibliographical information. *Magnalia Christi Americana* has been edited by Thomas Robbins, 2 vols. Hartford, Conn.: (Silas Andrus, 1853–1855) and (Books I and II only) by Kenneth B. Murdock (Cambridge, Mass.: Harvard University Press, 1975). Also see *Bonifacius*, ed. David Levin (Cambridge, Mass.: Harvard University Press, 1966); *Days of Humiliation*, with introduction by George H. Orians (Gainesville, Fla.: Scholars' Facsimiles & Reprints, 1970); *The Christian Philosopher*, with introduction by Josephine K. Piercy (Gainesville, Fla.: Scholars' Facsimiles & Reprints, 1968); *Selections from Cotton Mather*, ed. Kenneth B. Murdock (1926; reprint ed., Darien, Conn.: Hafner [1960]).

BIOGRAPHY AND DIARIES. *Diary of Cotton Mather*, ed. W. C. Ford (1911–1912; reprint ed., 2 vols., New York: Ungar, 1957); *The Diary of Cotton Mather . . . for the Year 1712*, ed. William R. Manierre II (Charlottesville: University Press of Virginia, 1964); Barrett Wendell, *Cotton Mather, the Puritan Priest* (New York: Dodd, Mead, 1891); Robert Middlekauff, *The Mathers: Three Generations of Puritan Intellectuals, 1596–1728* (New York: Oxford University Press, 1971).

STUDIES. In addition to the introductions mentioned above see Sacvan Bercovitch in Emerson (GB), pp. 93–149; Eugene E. White, "Cotton Mather's *Manuductio ad Ministerium*," *QJS* 49 (1963): 308–319; Kennerly M. Woody, "Cotton Mather's *Manuductio ad Theologiam*: The 'More Quiet and Hopeful Way,' " *EAL* 4 (1969): 3–48, another treatment of the *Manuductio ad Ministerium;* Warren (GB), pp. 76–87, useful for Mather's diary. For *Wonders of the Invisible World* see Marion L. Starkey, *The Devil in Massachusetts* (1950; reprint ed., New York: Time-Life, 1963), pp. 253–257, and the witchcraft studies mentioned in *LHUS*, 3:643.

The *Magnalia* has been analyzed in Sacvan Bercovitch, "New England Epic: Cotton Mather's *Magnalia Christi Americana*," *ELH* 33 (1966): 337–350; Gay (GB), pp. 53–87, 146–152; Reginald E. Watters, "Biographical Technique in Cotton Mather's *Magnalia*," *WMQ*, 3d ser. 2 (1945): 154–163; William R. Manierre II, "Cotton Mather and the Biographical Parallel," *AQ* 13 (1961): 153–160; Peter

H. Smith's "Politics and Sainthood: Biography by Cotton Mather," *WMQ*, 3d ser. 20 (1963): 186–206; Austin Warren, "Grandfather Mather and His Wonder Book," *SR* 72 (1964), 96–116; William R. Manierre, "Verbal Patterns in Cotton Mather's *Magnalia*," *QJS* 47 (1961): 402–413, an important analysis of Mather's style; William R. Manierre, "Some Characteristic Mather Redactions,"*NEQ* 31 (1958): 496–505; Thomas J. Steele, S.J., "The Biblical Meaning of Mather's Bradford," *Bull. of the Rocky Mountain MLA* 24 (1970): 147–154, on the Pauline parallels in this frequently anthologized section.

Jonathan Edwards

TEXTS. *The Works of Jonathan Edwards*, Perry Miller, general editor (New Haven: Yale University Press, 1957–), is designed to be definitive. *Jonathan Edwards: Representative Selections, with Introduction, Bibliography, and Notes by Clarence H. Faust and Thomas H. Johnson*, rev. ed. (New York: Hill & Wang, 1962) is an excellent one-volume anthology.

BIOGRAPHIES. Ola Winslow's *Jonathan Edwards* (New York: Macmillan, 1940) is standard.

COLLECTIONS OF SECONDARY MATERIALS. *Jonathan Edwards: A Profile*, ed. David Levin (New York: Hill & Wang, 1969); *Jonathan Edwards and the Enlightenment*, ed. John Opie (Lexington, Mass.: Heath, 1969).

STUDIES. William S. Morris, "The Reappraisal of Edwards," *NEQ* 30 (1957): 515–525; Baritz (GB: 1964), pp. 47–89, a convenient introduction to Edwards's thought; "Jonathan Edwards as a Thinker," pp. xiv–xcviii of the "Introduction" to Faust and Johnson (above); Perry Miller, *Jonathan Edwards* (New York: Sloane, 1949); Alfred Owen Aldridge, *Jonathan Edwards* (Great American Thinkers Series; New York: Simon & Schuster, Washington Square Press, 1964); Edward H. Davidson, *Jonathan Edwards: The Narrative of a Puritan Mind* (Riverside Studies in Literature; Boston: Houghton Mifflin, 1966); Douglas J. Elwood, *The Philosophical Theology of Jonathan Edwards* (New York: Columbia University Press, 1960); Conrad Cherry, *The Theology of Jonathan Edwards: A Reappraisal* (New York: Doubleday, 1966); Roland A. Delattre, *Beauty and Sensibility in the Thought of Jonathan Edwards* (New Haven: Yale University Press, 1968); Edward M. Griffin, *Jonathan Edwards* (UMPAW: 1971); Daniel B. Shea, Jr., in Emerson (GB), pp. 179–204, a general treatment.

STUDIES OF THE INDIVIDUAL WRITINGS. In "The Artistry of Jonathan Edwards," *NEQ* 22 (1949): 61–72, Edwin H. Cady shows that the most successful imagery of *Sinners in the Hands of an Angry God* is not only familiar, homely, and kinesthetic but also organically related to Edwards's message. "Sarah Pierrepont" is analyzed by Davidson (above), pp. 23–26. The *Personal Narrative*, the *Diary*, the "Resolutions," and *The Nature of True Virtue* are all discussed in Warren (GB), pp. 88–101. Other interpretations include Daniel B. Shea, Jr., "The Art and Instruction of Jonathan Edwards's *Personal Narrative*," *AL* 37 (1965): 17–32; Norman S. Grabo, "Jonathan Edwards's *Personal Narrative*: Dynamic Stasis," *Literatur in Wissenschaft und Unterricht* 2 (1969): 141–148. Also worth consulting are the full introductions to such volumes as *Freedom of the Will* (1957) in *The Works of Jonathan Edwards* (above).

For Edwards's style and artistry see Faust and Johnson (above), pp. cix–cxv; John Griffith, "Jonathan Edwards as a Literary Artist," *Criticism* 15 (1973): 156–

173; Ron Loewinsohn, "Jonathan Edwards' Opticks: Images and Metaphors of Light in Some of His Major Works," *EAL* 8 (1973): 21–32; Paul R. Baumgartner, "Jonathan Edwards: The Theory behind His Use of Figurative Language," *PMLA* 78 (1963): 321–325; and Miller (above), pp. 48–51. Miller's analysis in itself is a work of art.

BIBLIOGRAPHY. Everett H. Emerson in *Fifteen American Authors before 1900* (GB), pp. 169–184, an essay-review of the scholarship; Faust and Johnson (above), updated by Stephen S. Webb.

4: DIARISTS

A useful annotated bibliography is William Matthews, *American Diaries* (Boston: Canner, 1959). On p. ix Matthews explains the difference between diaries and journals.

Sarah Kemble Knight

TEXTS AND BIOGRAPHY. *The Journal of Madam Knight* (Boston: David R. Godine, 1972) is a handsome edition with a brief but well-informed introduction by Malcolm Freiberg. Some earlier editions are *The Journals of Madam Knight, and Rev. Mr. Buckingham,* ed. Theodore Dwight (New-York: Wilder & Campbell, 1825), the first edition; "The Private Journal Kept by Madam Knight," *Littell's Living Age* 57 (1858): 967–980, with an introduction by W. R. Deane (pp. 963–967); *The Private Journal . . . Kept by Madam Knight* (Albany, N.Y.: Little, 1865), with an introduction, notes, and index; and *The Journal of Madam Knight* (1920; reprint ed., New York: Peter Smith, 1935), with a useful map and an "Introductory Note" by George P. Winship. All three reprints contain Dwight's introduction to the 1825 edition. But all the introductions of these early editions are to be read with caution; Alan Margolies corrects many of their errors in "The Editing and Publication of 'The Journal of Madam Knight,' " *PBSA* 58 (1964):25–32. Also see the *DAB* for biography and some bibliography.

STUDIES. Robert O. Stephens, "The Odyssey of Sarah Kemble Knight," *CLAJour* 7 (1964):247–255, a pioneering study that discovers the mock-epic ingredients in her work and assigns a mythic meaning to them; Peter Thorpe, "Sarah Kemble Knight and the Picaresque Tradition," *CLAJour* 10 (1966): 114–121.

William Byrd

TEXTS. *The Secret Diary of William Byrd of Westover, 1709–1712,* ed. Louis B. Wright and Marion Tinling (Richmond, Va.: Dietz, 1941); *Another Secret Diary of William Byrd of Westover, 1739–1741, with Letters & Literary Exercises, 1696–1726,* ed. Maude H. Woodfin (Richmond, Va.: Dietz, 1942); *The London Diary (1717–1721) and Other Writings,* ed. Louis B. Wright and Marion Tinling (New York: Oxford University Press, 1958); *The Prose Works of William Byrd of Westover,* ed. Louis B. Wright (Cambridge, Mass.: Harvard University Press, 1966); *William Byrd's Histories of the Dividing Line betwixt Virginia and North Carolina,* ed. William K. Boyd (1929; reprinted with important additions, New

York: Dover, 1967), with a parallel arrangement of texts making it easy to contrast *The Secret History* with the *History*.

STUDIES. Pierre Marambaud, *William Byrd of Westover, 1674–1744* (Charlottesville: University Press of Virginia, 1971), covering the life, letters, and times; Richard C. Beatty, *William Byrd of Westover* (Boston: Houghton Mifflin, 1932), a biography; Richard Beale Davis in Emerson (GB), pp. 151–177; L. B. Wright (GB), pp. 312–347; Marshall Fishwick, "The Pepys of the Old Dominion," *AH* 11 (1959): 5–7, 117–119, illustrated; Hubbell (GB), pp. 40–51; James R. Masterson, "William Byrd in Lubberland," *AL* 9 (1937): 153–170, showing that the charges Byrd made against North Carolinian frontiersmen were not new; McIlwaine (GB), contending that Byrd satirized "poor whites" to raise his own position; Kenneth Lynn, "The Style of a Gentleman," *Mark Twain and Southwestern Humor* (Boston: Little, Brown, 1959), pp. 3–22, demonstrating that Byrd achieved an aristocratic style to accompany his aristocratic image.

BIBLIOGRAPHY. Hubbell (GB), pp. 919–921.

John Woolman

The Journal of John Woolman, with an Introduction by John G. Whittier (Boston: Osgood, 1871), probably the most influential edition; *The Journal and Major Essays of John Woolman,* ed. Phillips P. Moulton (New York: Oxford University Press, 1971), definitive.

STUDIES. Janet Whitney, *John Woolman, American Quaker* (Boston: Little, Brown, 1942) is a full-length biography. For a shorter but reliable life of Woolman, try the biographical sketch in Gummere's edition of the journal.

Edwin H. Cady, *John Woolman* (Great American Thinkers Series; New York: Simon & Schuster, Washington Square Press, 1965) with a wide range of topics, including Woolman's life, thought, style, and influence; W. Forrest Altman, "John Woolman's Reading of the Mystics," *Bulletin of Friends Historical Association* 48 (1959): 103–115; Reginald Reynolds, *The Wisdom of John Woolman* (London: Allen & Unwin, 1948), a combined anthology and analysis, with long prefaces to selections on divine inspiration, charity, poverty and wealth, slavery, and peace; Paul Rosenblatt, *John Woolman* (TUSAS: 1969); Shea (GB), on the *Journal;* Phillips P. Moulton, "The Influence of the Writings of John Woolman," *Quaker History* 60 (1971): 3–13.

BIBLIOGRAPHY. Cady (above), annotated; Rosenblatt (above), annotated.

5: ESSAYISTS, STATESMEN, AND PROPAGANDISTS

Benjamin Franklin

TEXTS. *The Writings of Benjamin Franklin,* ed. Albert H. Smyth, 10 vols. (New York: Macmillan, 1905–1907) is being superseded as the standard edition by *The Papers of Benjamin Franklin,* ed. Leonard W. Labaree (New Haven: Yale University Press, 1959–), a monumental project. *Benjamin Franklin: Representative Selections, with Introduction, Bibliography, and Notes* by Chester E. Jorgenson and Frank Luther Mott (rev. ed., New York: Hill & Wang, 1962) is an excellent one-volume anthology. *The Autobiography of Benjamin Franklin,* ed. Leonard W.

Labaree, Ralph L. Ketcham, Helen C. Boatfield, and Helene H. Fineman (New Haven: Yale University Press, 1964), the standard text, is equipped with biographical notes and a very useful index. For comparative purposes, consult *Benjamin Franklin's Memoirs: Parallel Text Edition,* ed. Max Farrand (Berkeley: University of California Press, 1949). The bagatelles have been edited by Richard E. Amacher as *Franklin's Wit & Folly* (New Brunswick, N.J.: Rutgers University Press, 1953) and by Claude-Anne Lopez as *The Bagatelles from Passy* (New York: Eakins, 1968). Also see *"The Sayings of Poor Richard": The Prefaces, Proverbs, and Poems of Benjamin Franklin Originally Printed in Poor Richard's Almanacs for 1733–1758,* ed. P. L. Ford (Privately printed, 1890).

BIOGRAPHICAL, CRITICAL, AND SPECIAL STUDIES: *Benjamin Franklin as a Man of Letters* by John Bach McMaster (Boston: Houghton, 1887); *The Many-Sided Franklin* by Paul L. Ford (New York: Century, 1899); *Franklin and His French Contemporaries* by Alfred O. Aldridge (New York: New York University Press, 1957); "The American Image of Benjamin Franklin" by Richard D. Miles, *AQ* 9 (1957): 117–143; *Benjamin Franklin* by Richard E. Amacher (TUSAS: 1962); *Benjamin Franklin* by Theodore Hornberger (UMPAW: 1962); *Benjamin Franklin, an American Man of Letters* by Bruce I. Granger (Ithaca, N.Y.: Cornell University Press, 1964); *Benjamin Franklin, Philosopher & Man* by Alfred O. Aldridge (Philadelphia: Lippincott, 1965); *Poor Richard's Politicks* by Paul W. Conner (New York: Oxford University Press, 1965); *A Sweet Instruction: Franklin's Journalism as a Literary Apprenticeship* by James A. Sappenfield (Carbondale: Southern Illinois University Press, 1973). Also see Blair (GB:1942), pp. 1–23; J. A. Leo Lemay in Emerson (GB), pp. 205–243.

Frances M. Barbour has compiled *A Concordance to the Sayings in Franklin's Poor Richard* (Detroit: Gale, 1974). The fullest study of *Poor Richard's Almanack*—Robert H. Newcomb's "The Sources of Benjamin Franklin's Sayings of Poor Richard" (Ph.D. dissertation, University of Maryland, 1957)—is summarized in *DA* 17 (1957): 2584–2585. Some of this material is also discussed in Newcomb's "Franklin and Richardson," *JEGP* 57 (1958): 27–35 and "Poor Richard and the English Epigram," *PQ* 40 (1961): 270–280. Charles W. Meister's "Franklin as a Proverb Stylist," *AL* 24 (1952): 157–166 shows how Franklin used proverbs in all his writings. For Poor Richard as a persona, see John F. Ross's "The Character of Poor Richard: Its Source and Alteration," *PMLA* 55 (1940): 785–794. Harold A. Larrabee's "Poor Richard in an Age of Plenty," *Harper's* 212 (1956): 64–68 distinguishes this persona from the real Franklin. In "Franklin's *Way to Wealth:* A Florilegium of Proverbs and Wise Sayings," *JEGP* 48 (1949): 229–251, Stuart A. Gallacher discusses the sources and revisions of 105 proverbs and aphorisms. Archer Taylor's *The Proverb and An Index to the Proverb* (Hatboro, Pa.: Folklore Associates, 1962) is a good introduction to this genre.

For the satires, see Paul Baender's "The Basis of Franklin's Duplicative Satires," *AL* 32 (1960): 267–279, useful for "An Edict by the King of Prussia"; George Simson's "Legal Sources for Franklin's 'Edict [by the King of Prussia],' " *AL* 32 (1960): 152–157, which cites various parliamentary acts; Max Hall's *Benjamin Franklin & Polly Baker: The History of a Literary Deception* (Chapel Hill: University of North Carolina Press, 1960); and Bruce I. Granger's *Political Satire in the American Revolution, 1763–1783* (Ithaca, N.Y.: Cornell University Press, 1960).

There are chapters on the bagatelles in both Amacher's and Granger's *Benjamin Franklin,* and in Aldridge's *Franklin and His French Contemporaries.* For background, see Claude-Anne Lopez, *Mon Cher Papa: Franklin and the Ladies of Paris* (New Haven: Yale University Press, 1966). Also consult Gilbert Chinard's "Random Notes on Two 'Bagatelles,' " *PAPS* 103 (1959): 727–760 for a thorough study of the "Letter to Madame Helvetius" and "The Ephemera," and A. O. Aldridge's "The Sources of Franklin's 'The Ephemera,' " *NEQ* 27 (1954): 388–391.

A good place to begin research on the *Autobiography* is the Yale edition previously cited. Its introduction discusses the *Autobiography*'s artistic and native qualities, composition, publication, and influence. Granger (*Benjamin Franklin,* pp. 209–238) analyzes its structure, diction, and genre, placing it in the Plutarchian tradition. Among the studies which show that the Franklin of the *Autobiography* was a distortion of the real Franklin are David Levin's "*The Autobiography of Benjamin Franklin:* The Puritan Experimenter in Life and Art," *YR* 53 (1964): 258–275; John William Ward's "Who Was Benjamin Franklin?" *ASch* 32 (1963): 541–543; and Robert F. Sayre's *The Examined Self* (Princeton: Princeton University Press, 1964). Levin attributes this image making to Franklin's humorous understatements; Ward, to his frequent manipulation of appearance and reality; Sayre, to his assumption of three roles—the "retired country gentleman" in part 1, the "simple Quaker philosopher" in part 2, and the "busy Philadelphian" in part 3.

BIBLIOGRAPHY. Bruce Granger in *Fifteen American Authors before 1900* (GB), pp. 185–206, an essay-review of primary and secondary materials.

Thomas Paine

TEXTS AND STUDIES. *The Writings of Thomas Paine,* ed. Moncure D. Conway, 4 vols. (1894–1896; reprint ed., New York: AMS Press, 1967); *Thomas Paine: Representative Selections, with Introduction, Bibliography, and Notes* by Harry Hayden Clark (rev. ed.; New York: Hill & Wang, 1961); Alfred Owen Aldridge, *Man of Reason: The Life of Thomas Paine* (Philadelphia: Lippincott, 1959); David Freeman Hawke, *Paine* (New York: Harper & Row, 1974). Research on individual works of Paine might well begin with these two biographies and the long notes in Clark.

For *Common Sense* and *The Crisis* see Granger (GB), pp. 125–128, 219, 244–245; Tyler (GB:1957), 1:58–74, and 2:37–41; Davidson (GB), pp. 13–14, 131–133, 212, 215, 349–350, 407.

The *Rights of Man* is covered in *The Burke-Paine Controversy: Texts and Criticism,* ed. Ray B. Browne (New York: Harcourt, 1963), a casebook. *The Age of Reason* is the chief source for Ira M. Thompson, Jr., in *The Religious Beliefs of Thomas Paine* (New York: Vantage, 1965), and for the chapter on Paine in Smithline (GB).

For Paine's style see Clark (above), pp. cviii–cxviii; James T. Boulton, "Tom Paine and the Vulgar Style," *Essays in Criticism* (New York: Oxford Book) 12 (1962): 18–33.

BIBLIOGRAPHY. Jerome D. Wilson, "Thomas Paine in America: An Annotated Bibliography: 1900–1973," *BB* 31 (1974): 133–151; Clark (above), annotated.

Thomas Jefferson

TEXTS. *The Writings of Thomas Jefferson,* ed. Paul L. Ford, 10 vols. (New York: Putnam, 1892–1899) and *The Writings of Thomas Jefferson,* ed. Andrew A. Lipscomb and Albert L. Bergh, 20 vols. (Washington, D.C.: Jefferson Memorial Assoc., 1903), being superseded by *The Papers of Thomas Jefferson,* ed. Julian Boyd (Princeton: Princeton University Press, 1950–); *Notes on the State of Virginia,* ed. William Peden (Chapel Hill: University of North Carolina Press, 1955); *Adams-Jefferson Letters: The Complete Correspondence between Thomas Jefferson and Abigail and John Adams,* ed. Lester J. Cappon, 2 vols. (Chapel Hill: University of North Carolina Press, 1959).

STUDIES. See Gilbert Chinard's *Thomas Jefferson: The Apostle of Americanism* (2d ed., rev.; Boston: Little, 1939) and Dumas Malone's multivolume *Jefferson and His Time* (Boston: Little, 1948–).

Adrienne Koch's *The Philosophy of Thomas Jefferson* (New York: Columbia University Press, 1943) is standard. Jefferson's liberalism is discussed in Parrington's *Colonial Mind,* pp. 342–356; his theory of natural aristocracy in Cawelti (GB), pp. 24–29, and his deism in Smithline (GB), pp. 56–64.

Thomas Jefferson among the Arts (New York: Philosophical Library, 1947) by Eleanor Davidson Berman analyzes Jefferson's interest in aesthetics, rhetoric, literature, criticism, music, and the visual arts. Edd Winfield Parks, in "Jefferson as a Man of Letters," *Georgia Review* 6 (1952): 450–459, sketches Jefferson's views on poets, prosody, rhyme, and the uses of literature.

For *Notes on the State of Virginia,* see the introduction to Peden's edition, pp. xi–xxv; Chinard, pp. 118–136; Dwight Boehm and Edward Schwartz, "Jefferson and the Theory of Degeneracy," *AQ* 9 (1957): 448–453. The *First Inaugural Address* is analyzed in bk. 1, chap. 7 of Henry Adams's *History of the United States during the Administration of Thomas Jefferson and James Madison* (1889–1891). The Adams-Jefferson letters have prompted a sixty-page casebook—*Adams and Jefferson: "Posterity Must Judge,"* ed. Adrienne Koch (Skokie, Ill.: Rand McNally, 1963)—and a 349-page narrative reconstruction, John Murray Allison's *Adams and Jefferson: The Story of a Friendship* (Norman: University of Oklahoma Press, 1966).

THE DECLARATION OF INDEPENDENCE. Carl Becker, *The Declaration of Independence* (New York: Knopf, 1945); Edwin Gittleman, "Jefferson's 'Slave Narrative': The Declaration of Independence as a Literary Text," *EAL* 8 (1974): 239–256; Julian P. Boyd, *The Declaration of Independence: The Evolution of the Text* (Washington, D.C.: Library of Congress, 1943); Malone, 1: 219–231; Chinard, bk. 2, chap. 1; and Tyler (GB:1957), chap. 23; William R. Smith, "The Rhetoric of the Declaration of Independence," *CE* 26 (1965): 306–309; Wilbur Samuel Howell, "The Declaration of Independence and Eighteenth-Century Logic," *WMQ,* 3d ser. 18 (1961): 463–484.

The Federalist

The Federalist, ed. Jacob E. Cooke (Middletown, Ct.: Wesleyan University Press, 1961) is a standard text. Other editions might be cited for their critical material: *The Federalist,* ed. Benjamin F. Wright (Cambridge, Mass.: Harvard University Press, 1961), with an especially full index; *The Enduring Federalist,* ed. Charles A. Beard (New York: Doubleday, 1948).

There are chapters on *The Federalist* in Irving Brant, *James Madison, Father of the Constitution, 1787–1800* (Indianapolis: Bobbs-Merrill, 1950), pp. 172–184, and Broadus Mitchell, *Alexander Hamilton: Youth to Maturity, 1755–1788* (New York: Macmillan, 1957), pp. 414–425. Also see Clinton Rossiter, *Alexander Hamilton and the Constitution* (New York: Harcourt, 1964), pp. 51–60; Melvin K. Whiteleather in Cohen (GB), pp. 46–55; Louis C. Schaedler, "James Madison, Literary Craftsman," *WMQ* 3d ser. 3 (1946): 515–533; Alpheus T. Mason, "The Federalist—A Split Personality," *American Historical Review* 57 (1952): 625–643, on differences in the thinking of Hamilton and Madison; Maynard Smith, "Reason, Passion and Political Freedom in *The Federalist*," *Journal of Politics* 22 (1960): 525–544; James P. Scanlon, "*The Federalist* and Human Nature," *Review of Politics* 21 (1959): 657–677.

Number 10 of *The Federalist* has received special attention in Ralph L. Ketcham, "Notes on James Madison's Sources for the Tenth Federalist Paper," *Midwest Journal of Political Science* (1957): 20–25, and in two articles by Douglass Adair: " 'That Politics May Be Reduced to a Science': David Hume, James Madison, and the Tenth *Federalist*," *HLQ* 20 (1957): 343–360, and "The Tenth *Federalist* Revisited," *WMQ* 3d ser. 8 (1951): 48–67.

6: NEOCLASSIC POETS

The Connecticut Wits, ed. Vernon Louis Parrington (Hamden, Conn.: Archon, 1963) offers an introduction and generous selections. Leon Howard's *The Connecticut Wits* (Chicago: University of Chicago Press, 1943) contains important analyses and bibliographies of works by both major and minor figures.

John Trumbull

Trumbull himself supervised the preparation of *The Poetical Works of John Trumbull*, 2 vols. (Hartford, Conn.: Goodrich, 1820). There are several twentieth-century reprints. *The Satiric Poems of John Trumbull*, ed. Edwin T. Bowden (Austin: University of Texas Press, 1962) contains the complete texts of *M'Fingal* and *The Progress of Dulness*, including Trumbull's rarely printed prose introductions to the three parts. *M'Fingal: An Epic Poem by John Trumbull*, ed. Benson J. Lossing (New York: Am. Bk. Exchange, 1881) has copious historical notes.

STUDIES. Alexander Cowie, *John Trumbull: Connecticut Wit* (Chapel Hill: University of North Carolina Press, 1936); Alexander Cowie, "John Trumbull as a Critic of Poetry," *NEQ* 11 (1938): 773–793; Bruce I. Granger, "John Trumbull and Religion," *AL* 23 (1951): 57–79; Granger (GB), pp. 6–7, 13, 15–16, 300–301, on the Hudibrastic elements in *M'Fingal;* Victor E. Grimmestad, *John Trumbull* (TUSAS: 1974), with annotated bibliography.

Timothy Dwight

TEXTS. *The Major Poems of Timothy Dwight*, ed. William J. McTaggart and William K. Bottorff (Gainesville, Fla.: Scholars' Facsimiles and Reprints, 1969); *Travels in New England and New York*, ed. Barbara M. Solomon and Patricia M. King, 4 vols. (Cambridge, Mass.: Harvard University Press, Belknap, 1969).

STUDIES. Charles E. Cunningham, *Timothy Dwight* (New York: Macmillan, 1942); Leon Howard, *The Connecticut Wits*, pp. 71–111, 342–401; Kenneth Silverman, *Timothy Dwight* (TUSAS: 1969); Percy H. Boynton, "Timothy Dwight and His

Connecticut," *MP* 38 (1940): 193–203, based on Dwight's *Travels;* Kathryn Whitford, "Excursions into Romanticism: Timothy Dwight's *Travels,*" *PLL* 2 (1966): 225–233; Lewis E. Buchanan, "A Conservative View of the Frontier," *RS* 25 (1957): 49–56, proof that Dwight anticipated Frederick Jackson Turner in seeing the frontier as a safety valve.

Joel Barlow

TEXTS. *The Works of Joel Barlow,* 2 vols. (Gainesville, Fla.: Scholars' Facsimiles and Reprints, 1970), with an introduction by William K. Bottorff and Arthur L. Ford.

STUDIES. James Woodress, *A Yankee's Odyssey: The Life of Joel Barlow* (Philadelphia: Lippincott, 1958); Charles Burr Todd, *Life and Letters of Joel Barlow* (New York: Putnam, 1886); Theodore A. Zunder, *The Early Days of Joel Barlow* (New Haven: Yale University Press, 1934), with chapters on *The Anarchiad* and *Vision of Columbus;* L. Howard, *The Connecticut Wits,* pp. 133–165.

Individual works are treated in Robert D. Arner, "Joel Barlow's Poetics: 'Advice to a Raven in Russia,' " *Connecticut Review* 5 (1972): 38–43; Theodore Grieder, "Joel Barlow's *The Hasty Pudding:* A Study in American Neoclassicism," *British Association for American Studies Bulletin,* n.s., no. 11 (1965): 35–42; Don Yoder, "Pennsylvanians Called It Mush," *Pennsylvania Folklife* 13 (1962–1963): 27–49, useful for background and illustrations; Robert D. Arner, "The Smooth and Emblematic Song: Joel Barlow's *The Hasty Pudding,*" *EAL* 7 (1972): 76–91.

BIBLIOGRAPHY. L. Howard, *The Connecticut Wits,* pp. 271–341; Arthur L. Ford, *Joel Barlow* (TUSAS: 1971), pp. 137–141.

Phillis Wheatley

The Poems of Phillis Wheatley, ed. Julian D. Mason, Jr. (Chapel Hill: University of North Carolina Press, 1966), based on the collection issued in 1773, contains an introduction by the editor. Kenneth Silverman prints "Four New Letters by Phillis Wheatley" in *EAL* 8 (1974): 257–271, while Robert C. Kuncio offers "Some Unpublished Poems of Phillis Wheatley" in *NEQ* 43 (1970): 287–297. Studies include William H. Robinson, "Phillis Wheatley: Colonial Quandary," *CLA Jour* 9 (1965): 25–38; M. A. Richmond, *Bid the Vassal Soar: Interpretive Essays on the Life and Poetry of Phillis Wheatley (ca. 1753–1784) and George Moses Horton (ca. 1797–1883)* (Washington, D.C.: Howard University Press, 1974).

7: PREROMANTICS

For romanticism and related concepts see Edwin R. A. Seligman and Alvin Johnson, eds., *Encyclopaedia of the Social Sciences,* 15 vols. (New York: Macmillan, 1930–1935) and Thrall, Hibbard, and Holman (GB) under the words *romanticism, primitivism,* and pertinent cross-references.

St. John de Crèvecoeur

TEXTS. *Letters from an American Farmer* has been reprinted with introduction by Ludwig Lewisohn (New York: Fox, Duffield, 1904); with introduction by Warren Barton Blake, plus helpful notes and index (New York: Dutton, 1957); and with foreword by Albert E. Stone, Jr. (New York: New American Library, 1963). Other writings by Crèvecoeur include *Sketches of Eighteenth Century America,* ed. Henri L. Bourdin, Ralph H. Gabriel, and Stanley T. Williams (New Haven: Yale University Press, 1925); *Journey into Northern Pennsylvania and the State of New York* (Ann Arbor: University of Michigan Press, 1964), a translation by Clarissa Spencer Bostelmann of Crèvecoeur's *Voyage dans la Haute Pensylvanie et dans l'Etat de New-York* (1801); and *Crèvecoeur's Eighteenth-Century Travels in Pennsylvania & New York,* trans. and ed. with full introduction by Percy G. Adams (Lexington: University Press of Kentucky, 1961), selections from the *Voyage.*

STUDIES. Two early biographies—Robert de Crèvecoeur's *Saint John de Crèvecoeur* (Paris: Librairie des Bibliophiles, 1883), written in French, and Julia Post Mitchell's *St. Jean de Crèvecoeur* (New York: Columbia University Press, 1916)—are still worth consulting. An excellent general work is Thomas Philbrick, *St. John de Crèvecoeur* (TUSAS: 1970). In "Some Notes . . . on The American Farmer's *Letters,"* *Colophon,* pt. 18 (1934), 7 unnumbered pp., Howard C. Rice presents findings otherwise available only in chap. 2 of his *Le Cultivateur Américain: Etude sur l'oeuvre de Saint John de Crèvecoeur* (Paris: Champion, 1933). Studies of the *Letters* include Marius Bewley, "The Cage and the Prairie: Two Notes on Symbolism," *HudR* 10 (1957): 403–414; James R. Masterson, "The Tale of the Living Fang," *AL* 11 (1939): 66–73; Albert E. Stone, Jr., "Crèvecoeur's *Letters* and the Beginnings of an American Literature," *EUQ* 18 (1962): 197–213; and Russel B. Nye in Cohen (GB), pp. 32–45. For the historical context of two important ideas in "What Is an American?" see Cecil D. Eby, "America as 'Asylum': A Dual Image," *AQ* 14 (1962): 483–489 and Philip Gleason, "The Melting Pot: Symbol of Fusion or Confusion?" *AQ* 16 (1964): 20–46.

BIBLIOGRAPHY. Rice (above, 1933 and 1934) for primary sources; Philbrick (above) for secondary sources (annotated).

Philip Freneau

TEXTS (ALL WITH FULL INTRODUCTIONS AND NOTES). *The Poems of Philip Freneau,* ed. Fred Lewis Pattee, 3 vols. (Princeton: [Princeton] University Library, 1902–1907); *Poems of Freneau,* ed. Harry Hayden Clark (1929; reprint ed., Darien, Ct.: Hafner, 1960); *A Freneau Sampler,* ed. Philip M. Marsh (Metuchen, N.J.: Scarecrow, 1963), containing prose as well as poetry, plus the most trustworthy brief life (pp. 9–18).

STUDIES. Biographies include Jacob Axelrad's *Philip Freneau: Champion of Democracy* (Austin: University of Texas Press, 1967) and Philip M. Marsh's *Philip Freneau, Poet and Journalist* (Minneapolis: Dillon, 1967). The standard critical biography—Lewis Leary's *That Rascal Freneau: A Study in Literary Failure* (1941; reprint ed., New York: Octagon, 1964)—has useful comments on individual poems, although the index sometimes lists them only under their original titles. In *Philip Freneau and the Cosmic Enigma: The Religious and Philosophical Speculations of an American Poet* (New York: New York University Press, 1949) Nelson F. Adkins locates four often contradictory strains in Freneau's thought: orthodoxy, nature, deism, and classicism. Also see Philip M. Marsh, *The Works of Philip Freneau, a Critical Study* (Metuchen, N.J.:

Scarecrow, 1968). Laurence B. Holland's survey "Philip Freneau: Poet in the New Nation" appears in *The Literary Heritage of New Jersey*, Vol. 20, New Jersey Historical Series (New York: D. Van Nostrand, 1964), pp. 3–41. In "The Literary Influences of Philip Freneau," *SP* 22 (1926): 1–33 Harry Hayden Clark discusses Freneau's reading and traces his use of such authors as Collins and Addison. Also see Lewis Leary in Emerson (GB), pp. 245–271; Harry H. Clark, "What Made Freneau the Father of American Poetry?" *SP* 26 (1929): 1–22; Philip M. Marsh, "Philip Freneau's Fame," *PNJHS* 80 (1962): 75–93, 197–212, a detailed history of the scholarship; Smithline (GB), pp. 65–73; Allen (GB), pp. 1–26, a prosodic analysis.

STUDIES OF INDIVIDUAL WORKS. G. I. E. and Olybrius, "Freneau's 'On a Honey Bee Drinking &c.,' " *Expl* 5 (1946–1947), query 1 and item 57; G. Ferris Cronkhite, "Freneau's 'The House of Night,' " *Cornell Library Journal* 8 (1969): 3–19; Robert D. Arner, "Neoclassicism and Romanticism: A Reading of Freneau's 'The Wild Honey Suckle,' " *EAL* 9 (1974): 53–61; The Editors, "Freneau's 'The Indian Burying Ground,' " *Expl* 2 (1944), item 55; Harry Modean Campbell, "A Note on Freneau's 'The Indian Burying Ground,' " *MLN* 68 (1953): 551–552; George R. Wasserman, "Freneau's 'The Indian Burying Ground,' " *Expl* 20 (1962), item 43.

BIBLIOGRAPHY. See Leary (above), pp. 418–480; Philip Marsh, *Freneau's Published Prose: A Bibliography* (Metuchen, N.J.: Scarecrow, 1970) for primary materials; Owen P. Thomas, "Philip Freneau: A Bibliography," *PNJHS* 75 (1957): 197–205 for secondary sources.

8: EARLY FICTION AND DRAMA

Edmund S. Morgan, "Puritan Hostility to the Theatre," *PAPS* 110 (1966): 340–347; Hugh F. Rankin, *The Theater in Colonial America* (Chapel Hill: University of North Carolina Press, 1965), covering the years 1716–1774; G. Harrison Orians, "Censure of Fiction in American Romances and Magazines, 1789–1810," *PMLA* 52 (1937): 195–214; Terence Martin, "Social Institutions in the Early American Novel," *AQ* 9 (1957): 72–84, especially concerned with nation and family; Terence Martin, *The Instructed Vision: Scottish Common Sense Philosophy and the Origins of American Fiction* (Bloomington: Indiana University Press, 1961); Henri Petter, *The Early American Novel* (Columbus: Ohio State University Press, 1971); Robert B. Winans, "The Growth of a Novel-Reading Public in Late Eighteenth-Century America," *EAL* 9 (1975): 267–275.

Hugh Henry Brackenridge

TEXTS. *Modern Chivalry*, ed. Claude Newlin (1937; reprint ed., Darien, Ct.: Hafner, 1962), the complete edition; *Modern Chivalry*, ed. Lewis Leary (New Haven: College & University Press, 1965); *A Hugh Henry Brackenridge Reader, 1770–1815*, ed. Daniel Marder (Pittsburgh: University of Pittsburgh Press, 1970).

STUDIES. Claude M. Newlin, *The Life and Writings of Hugh Henry Brackenridge* (Princeton: Princeton University Press, 1932), a biography; Daniel Marder, *Hugh Henry Brackenridge* (TUSAS; 1967), a critical work.

MODERN CHIVALRY. William L. Nance, "Satiric Elements in Brackenridge's *Modern Chivalry,*" *TSLL* 9 (1967): 381–389; William Bruce Craddock, "A Structural Examination of Hugh Henry Brackenridge's *Modern Chivalry,*" *DA* 27 (1967): 3040A; Mary S. Mattfield, "*Modern Chivalry:* The Form," *WPHM* 50 (1967): 305–326; 51 (1968): 17–29, an analysis of the book as a Menippean satire; Joseph H. Harkey, "The *Don Quixote* of the Frontier: Brackenridge's *Modern Chivalry,*" *EAL* 8 (1973): 193–203; Cawelti (GB), pp. 32–35, on vertical mobility.

BIBLIOGRAPHY. Marder (above), pp. 151–157 (annotated).

Charles Brockden Brown

TEXTS. *Charles Brockden Brown's Novels,* 6 vols. (1887; reprint ed., Port Washington, N.Y.: Kennikat, 1963); *Wieland, or the Transformation, together with Memoirs of Carwin the Biloquist, a Fragment,* ed. Fred Lewis Pattee (1926; reprint ed., Darien, Ct.: Hafner, 1958); *Edgar Huntly,* ed. David Stineback (New Haven: College & University Press, 1928); *Ormond,* ed. Ernest Marchand (1937; reprint ed., Darien, Ct.: Hafner, 1962); *Arthur Mervyn,* ed. Warner Berthoff (New York: Holt, 1962); and "Essays und Rezensionen von Charles Brockden Brown," ed. Alfred Weber, *JA* 6 (1961): 168–330, a collection of Brown's essays and reviews—only the introduction and footnotes are in German.

Studies include Donald A. Ringe in Emerson (GB), pp. 273–294; Harry R. Warfel, *Charles Brockden Brown, American Gothic Novelist* (Gainesville: University of Florida Press, 1949); and David Lee Clark, *Charles Brockden Brown, Pioneer Voice of America* (Durham, N.C.: Duke University Press, 1952), which mixes literary analysis with biography. In *Charles Brockden Brown* (TUSAS: 1966), Donald A. Ringe devotes a chapter apiece to the four main novels, treating *Wieland* as a criticism of eighteenth-century psychology. Lulu Rumsey Wiley, *The Sources and Influence of the Novels of Charles Brockden Brown* (New York: Vantage, 1950) is laden with quotations and plot summaries. Also see Arthur Kimball, *Rational Fictions: A Study of Charles Brockden Brown* (McMinnville, Or.: Linfield Research Institute, 1968); Scott Garrow, "Character Transformation in *Wieland,*" *SoQ* 4 (1966): 308–318; William M. Manly, "The Importance of Point of View in Brockden Brown's *Wieland,*" *AL* 35 (1963): 311–321; Joseph Katz, "Analytical Bibliography and Literary History: The Writing and Printing of *Wieland,*" *Proof* 1 (1971): 8–34; Dieter Schulz, "*Edgar Huntly* as Quest Romance," *AL* 43 (1971): 323–335.

BIBLIOGRAPHY. Paul Witherington, "Charles Brockden Brown: A Bibliographical Essay," *EAL* 9 (1974): 164–187.

Royall Tyler

TEXTS. *The Contrast,* ed. James B. Wilbur (Boston: Houghton Mifflin, 1920); *The Verse of Royall Tyler,* ed. Marius B. Péladeau (Charlottesville: University Press of Virginia, 1968); *The Prose of Royall Tyler,* ed. Marius B. Péladeau (Rutland, Vt.: Tuttle, 1972); *The Algerine Captive,* introduction by Jack B. Moore (Gainesville, Fla.: Scholars' Facsimiles & Reprints, 1967).

STUDIES. G. Thomas Tanselle, *Royall Tyler* (Cambridge, Mass.: Harvard University Press, 1967), a fully documented treatment of Tyler's life, writings, and reputation; John Lauber, "*The Contrast:* A Study in the Concept of Innocence," *ELN*

1 (1963): 33–37; Roger B. Stein, "Royall Tyler and the Question of Our Speech," *NEQ* 38 (1965): 454–474, showing that while the types of speech enrich the play as character masks, each is satirized by Tyler. Also see Gallagher (GB), pp. 60–66.

9: THE KNICKERBOCKERS

Kendall B. Taft's *Minor Knickerbockers: Representative Selections, with Introduction, Bibliography, and Notes* (New York: American Book, 1947) is an aid to understanding the period. For the contributions of Irving, Paulding, Clement Clarke Moore and other Gothamites to the evolution of Santa Claus in American culture see Charles W. Jones, "Knickerbocker Santa Claus," *New-York Historical Society Quarterly* 38 (1954): 357–383.

Washington Irving

TEXTS. *The Complete Works of Washington Irving,* ed. Henry A. Pochmann, Herbert L. Kleinfield, and Edwin T. Bowden (Madison: University of Wisconsin Press, 1969–), is a multivolume set designed to supersede such standard collections as *The Works of Washington Irving,* 21 vols., Author's Uniform Rev. Ed. (New York: Putnam, 1860–1861) and *The Journals of Washington Irving,* ed. William P. Trent and George S. Hellman, 3 vols. (Boston: Bibliophile Soc., 1919), covering 1815–1842 (subsequent editions of various notebooks and journals are listed in *LHUS* 3:580). Editions of single works include *Diedrich Knickerbocker's A History of New York,* edited with introduction by Stanley Williams and Tremaine McDowell, American Authors Series (New York: Harcourt, 1927), text of the 1809 ed.; *A History of New York,* edited with introduction by Edwin T. Bowden (New Haven: College & University Press, 1964), text of the 1812 ed.; *A Tour on the Prairies,* ed. John F. McDermott (Norman: University of Oklahoma Press, 1956); *Astoria,* with introduction by William H. Goetzmann (Philadelphia: Lippincott, 1961) and ed. Edgeley W. Todd (Norman: University of Oklahoma Press, 1964); *Adventures of Captain Bonneville,* ed. Edgeley W. Todd (Norman: University of Oklahoma Press, 1961). *Washington Irving: Representative Selections,* AWS (New York: American Book, 1934) has a long introduction, annotated bibliography, and notes by Henry A. Pochmann.

BIOGRAPHY. The indispensable standard biography is Stanley T. Williams, *The Life of Washington Irving,* 2 vols. (New York: Oxford University Press, 1935). Also see Claude G. Bowers, *The Spanish Adventures of Washington Irving* (Boston: Houghton Mifflin, 1940); George S. Hellman, *Washington Irving, Esquire: Ambassador at Large from the New World to the Old* (New York: Knopf, 1925); Pierre M. Irving, *The Life and Letters of Washington Irving,* 4 vols. (1862–1864; reprint ed., Detroit: Gale, 1967), the authorized biography, still valuable; Ben Harris McClary, *Washington Irving and the House of Murray* (Knoxville: University of Tennessee Press, 1969), on Irving's relationship with his British publisher; Andrew B. Myers, *The Worlds of Washington Irving, 1783–1859* (Tarrytown, N.Y.: Sleepy Hollow Restorations, 1974); Edward Wagenknecht, *Washington Irving: Moderation Displayed* (New York: Oxford University Press, 1962).

IRVING AND THE FINE ARTS. See Callow (GB) and Ringe (GB) for extensive coverage. A portfolio of illustrations and paintings inspired by Irving's work is in *AH* 13 (1961): 41–55.

CRITICISM. The biography by Williams (above) is indispensable in this category, too. Also see *Washington Irving Reconsidered: A Symposium,* ed. Ralph M. Aderman (Hartford, Ct.: Transcendental Books, 1969), 12 essays; John Clendenning, "Irving and the Gothic Tradition," *BuR* 12 (1964): 90–98; *Irvingiana: A Memorial to Washington Irving,* ed. Evert A. Duyckinck (New York: Charles B. Richardson, 1860), by Irving's contemporaries; William L. Hedges, *Washington Irving: An American Study, 1802–1832* (Baltimore: Johns Hopkins Press, 1965); Wayne R. Kime, "Washington Irving and Frontier Speech," *AS* 42 (1967): 5–18; Lewis Leary, *Washington Irving* (UMPAW: 1963), a pamphlet; Terence Martin, "Rip, Ichabod, and the American Imagination," *AL* 31 (1959): 137–149; Henry A. Pochmann, "Irving's German Tour and Its Influence on His Tales," *PMLA* 45 (1930): 1150–1187; idem, "Washington Irving: Amateur or Professional?" in Gohdes (GB), pp. 63–76; Walter A. Reichart, *Washington Irving and Germany* (Ann Arbor: University of Michigan Press, 1957); Donald A. Ringe, "New York and New England: Irving's Criticism of American Society," *AL* 38 (1967): 455–467; Sara P. Rodes, "Washington Irving's Use of Traditional Folklore," *SFQ* 20 (1956): 143–153; Williams (GB), 2:3–45; N. Wright (GB), pp. 45–50.

Knickerbocker's History. Edwin A. Greenlaw, "Washington Irving's Comedy of Politics," *Texas Review* 1 (1916): 291–306; Clarence M. Webster, "Irving's Expurgation of the 1809 *History of New York,*" *AL* 4 (1932): 293–295; Charlton G. Laird, "Tragedy and Irony in *Knickerbocker's History,*" *AL* 7 (1940): 157–172; Harry M. Lydenberg, "Irving's Knickerbocker and Some of Its Sources," *BNYPL* 56 (1952): 544–553, 596–619, suggesting that Samuel L. Mitchill's *Picture of New-York* (1807) may not have been the book the Irvings began to parody; Wayne R. Kime, "The Satiric Use of Names in Irving's History of New York," *Names* 16 (1968): 380–389; Michael L. Black, "*A History of New York:* Significant Revision in 1848," in Aderman (above), pp. 40–47; David Durand, "Aeolism in *Knickerbocker's A History of New York,*" *AL* 41 (1970): 493–506; Donald R. Noble, Jr., "Washington Irving's 'Peter' Pun," *AN&Q* 8 (1970): 103–104. Also see the prefaces to editions of the *History* listed under "Texts" above.

The Sketch Book. Henry A. Pochmann, "Irving's German Sources in *The Sketch Book,*" *SP* 27 (1930): 477–507; W. B. Gates, "Shakespearean Elements in Irving's *Sketch Book,*" *AL* 30 (1959): 450–458; William L. Hedges in Cohen (GB), pp. 56–65.

"RIP VAN WINKLE." Interpretations by Louis Le Fevre, Marcel Heiman, Terence Martin, and Philip Young are abstracted in Bowen and Van Der Beets (GB), pp. 18–23. Also see Robert H. Woodward, "Dating the Action of 'Rip Van Winkle,' " *NYFQ* 15 (1959): 70; Marvin E. Mengeling, "Characterization in 'Rip Van Winkle,' " *EJ* 53 (1964): 643–646; Helen Lee, "Clue Patterns in 'Rip Van Winkle,' " *EJ* 55 (1966): 192–194, 200, on foreshadowing; Marvin E. Mengeling, "Structure and Tone in 'Rip Van Winkle': The Irony of Silence," *Discourse* 9 (1966): 457–463. Pochmann in *SP* 27 (1930): 477–498 discusses the German sources, putting the texts of "Rip" and "Peter Klaus" in parallel columns; also see Reichart, *Washington Irving and Germany,* pp. 22–30.

"THE LEGEND OF SLEEPY HOLLOW." Martin (above, under "Criticism"); Hoffman (GB), pp. 83–95; Robert A. Bone, "Irving's Headless Hessian: Prosperity and the Inner Life," *AQ* 15 (1963): 167–175; Marjorie W. Bruner, "The 'Legend of Sleepy Hollow': A Mythological Parody," *CE* 25 (1964): 278–283. Oral S. Coad in *JEGP* 24 (1925): 83–84 suggests Burns's "Tam O'Shanter" as a source of this tale, which Coad classifies as "sportive Gothic." A German parallel is noted by Pochmann in *SP* 27 (1930): 498–504 and Reichart in *Washington Irving and Germany*, pp. 30–32, 169–170.

OTHER INDIVIDUAL WORKS. Nathalia Wright, "Irving's Use of His Italian Experiences in *Tales of a Traveller:* The Beginning of an American Tradition," *AL* 31 (1959): 191–196; Louisa M. Hoffman, "Irving's Use of Spanish Sources in *The Conquest of Granada,*" *Hispania* 28 (1945): 483–498; Wayne Kime, "The Completeness of Washington Irving's *A Tour on the Prairies,*" *WAL* 8 (1973): 55–65; Kathryn Whitford, "Romantic Metamorphosis in Irving's Western Tour," in Aderman (above), pp. 31–36, on *A Tour on the Prairies;* Charles Zug III, "The Construction of 'The Devil and Tom Walker': A Study of Irving's Later Use of Folklore," *NYFQ* 24 (1968): 243–260.

BIBLIOGRAPHY. Henry A. Pochmann, "Washington Irving" in *Fifteen American Authors before 1900* (GB), pp. 245–261, a bibliographical essay.

James Fenimore Cooper

TEXTS. *Cooper's Novels,* illus. F. O. C. Darley, 32 vols. (Chicago: Townsend, 1859–1861); *J. Fenimore Cooper's Works,* 32 vols. (Household Ed., New York and Boston: Hurd & Houghton, 1876–1884) (15 of the novels contain prefaces by Cooper's daughter Susan); *The Correspondence of James Fenimore Cooper,* ed. James Fenimore Cooper [the novelist's grandson], 2 vols. (New Haven: Yale University Press, 1929), still useful for its letters to Cooper; *The Letters and Journals of James Fenimore Cooper,* ed. James F. Beard, 6 vols. (Cambridge, Mass.: Harvard University Press, 1960–1968), carefully edited with valuable introductions and notes; *The American Democrat,* introduction by H. L. Mencken (New York: Knopf, Vintage, 1956); *The Bravo,* ed. Donald A. Ringe (New Haven: College & University Press, 1963); *The Crater,* ed. Thomas Philbrick (Cambridge, Mass.: Harvard University Press, 1962); *The Deerslayer,* introduction by James Grossman (New York: Simon & Schuster, Washington Square Press, 1961); *Early Critical Essays, 1820–1822,* introduction by James F. Beard (Gainesville, Fla.: Scholars' Facsimiles & Reprints, 1955); *Gleanings in Europe,* ed. Robert E. Spiller, 2 vols. (New York: Oxford University Press, 1928, 1930), on France and England; *Home as Found,* introduction by Lewis Leary (New York: Putnam, Capricorn, 1961); *The Last of the Mohicans,* introduction by William Charvat (Riverside Ed., Boston: Houghton Mifflin, 1958); *Notions of the Americans,* introduction by Robert E. Spiller, 2 vols. (New York: Ungar, 1963); *The Pathfinder,* introduction by Robert E. Spiller (Lunenburg, Vt.: Limited Editions Club, 1965); *The Pioneers,* introduction by Leon Howard (Rinehart Ed.; New York: Holt, Rinehart & Winston, 1959); *The Prairie,* introduction by Henry Nash Smith (Rinehart Ed.; Holt, Rinehart & Winston, 1960); *The Red Rover,* introduction by Warren S. Walker (Lincoln: University of Nebraska Press, 1963); *Satanstoe,* introduction by Robert L. Hough (Lincoln: University of Nebraska Press, 1962); *The Sea Lions,* introduction by Warren S. Walker (Lincoln: University of Nebraska Press, 1965); *The Spy,* introduction by Tremaine

McDowell (New York: Scribner, 1931); *Tales for Fifteen,* introduction by James F. Beard (Gainesville, Fla.: Scholars' Facsimiles & Reprints, 1959).

BIOGRAPHIES. All contain criticism as well. Most trustworthy for biographical details are James Grossman, *James Fenimore Cooper* (1949; reprint ed., Stanford, Calif.: Stanford University Press, 1967) and James F. Beard's introductions to the various sections of Cooper's *Letters and Journals.* Also important are Henry W. Boynton, *James Fenimore Cooper* (New York: Century, 1931); Thomas R. Lounsbury, *James Fenimore Cooper* (American Men of Letters; Boston: Houghton Mifflin, 1882); Robert E. Spiller, *Fenimore Cooper: Critic of His Times* (New York: Minton, Balch, 1931).

STUDIES. Berbrich (GB), pp. 5–58; Bewley (GB:1959), chaps. 3, 4; Charles A. Brady in Gardiner (GB), pp. 59–97; Cady (GB), chaps. 6, 7; Marcel Clavel, *Fenimore Cooper and His Critics* (Aix-en-Provence: Imprimerie Universitaire de Provence, 1938); George Dekker, *James Fenimore Cooper: The American Scott* (New York: Barnes & Noble, 1967); Fiedler (GB:1960), chap. 6; W. B. Gates, "Cooper's Indebtedness to Shakespeare," *PMLA* 67 (1952): 716–731; D. H. Lawrence (GB), chaps. 4, 5; John P. McWilliams, Jr., *Political Justice in a Republic: James Fenimore Cooper's America* (Berkeley: University of California Press, 1972); Thomas Philbrick, *James Fenimore Cooper and the Development of American Sea Fiction* (Cambridge, Mass.: Harvard University Press, 1961); Donald A. Ringe, *James Fenimore Cooper* (TUSAS: 1962); John F. Ross, *The Social Criticism of Fenimore Cooper* (Berkeley: University of California Press, 1933); Arvid Shulenberger, *Cooper's Theory of Fiction: His Prefaces and Their Relation to His Novels* (Lawrence: University of Kansas Publications, 1955); Robert E. Spiller, *James Fenimore Cooper* (UMPAW: 1965), a pamphlet incorporating parts of Spiller's introduction to *James Fenimore Cooper: Representative Selections* (AWS; New York: American Book, 1936); James W. Tuttleton, *The Novel of Manners in America* (Chapel Hill: University of North Carolina Press, 1972), pp. 28–47; Warren S. Walker, *James Fenimore Cooper: An Introduction and Interpretation* (AACS; New York: Barnes & Noble, 1962); N. Wright (GB), chap. 3.

COLLECTIONS OF CRITICISM. *James Fenimore Cooper: A Re-Appraisal* (Cooperstown: New York State Historical Association, 1954); *Fenimore Cooper: The Critical Heritage,* ed. George Dekker and John P. McWilliams (London: Routledge & Kegan Paul, 1973).

COOPER AND THE FINE ARTS. Callow (GB) traces Cooper's friendship with Samuel Morse and other artists, his use of landscape, and his advocacy of functionalism in architecture. Ringe (GB) shows how the painterly techniques in Cooper's novels serve to communicate a moral vision.

INDIANS AND OTHER CHARACTERS. Kay Seymour House, *Cooper's Americans* (Columbus: Ohio State University Press, 1965), with chapters on women, Indians, Negroes, Dutchmen, gentry, Yankees, and seamen; Barrie Hayne, "*Ossian,* Scott and Cooper's Indians," *JAmS* 3 (1969): 73–87; James W. Tuttleton, "The New England Character in Cooper's Social Novels," *BNYPL* 70 (1966): 305–317; also see Leatherstocking (below).

LEATHERSTOCKING AND THE LEATHERSTOCKING TALES. Warren S. Walker has collected thirty of the chief evaluations, from Cooper's day to our own, in *Leatherstocking and the Critics* (Glenview, Ill.: Scott, Foresman, 1965). Also see Charles Boewe, "Cooper's Doctrine of Gifts," *TSL* 7 (1962): 27–35; Lewis (GB), pp. 98–105; David W. Noble, "Cooper, Leatherstocking and the Death of the American Adam," *AQ* 16 (1964): 419–431, which takes issue with R. W. B. Lewis (above); Warren S. Walker, "Buckskin West: Leatherstocking at High Noon," *NYFQ* 24 (1968): 88–102, part of a symposium, followed by discussion on pp. 144–159; Robert H. Zoellner, "Conceptual Ambivalence in Cooper's Leatherstocking," *AL* 31 (1960): 397–420, one of the most convincing interpretations.

Deerslayer. Mizener (GB), pp. 1–8; David Brion Davis, "The Deerslayer, a Democratic Knight of the Wilderness: Cooper, 1841," in Shapiro (GB:1958).

Mohicans. Thomas Philbrick, "*The Last of the Mohicans* and the Sounds of Discord," *AL* 43 (1971): 25–41; Donald Darnell, "Uncas as Hero: The *Ubi Sunt* Formula in *The Last of the Mohicans*," *AL* 37 (1965): 259–266.

Pathfinder. Sargent Bush, Jr., "Charles Cap of *The Pathfinder*: A Foil to Cooper's Views on the American Character in the 1840's," *NCF* 20 (1965): 267–273; Lura N. and Duilio T. Pedrini, "Similes and Metaphors in Cooper's *The Pathfinder*," *NYFQ* 23 (1967): 99–108.

Pioneers. Kay Seymour House in Stegner (GB), pp. 1–12; Thomas Philbrick, "Cooper's *The Pioneers*: Origins and Structure," *PMLA* 79 (1964): 579–593, which demonstrates the close connection between setting and plot.

Prairie. Arm Øverland, *The Making and Meaning of an American Classic: James Fenimore Cooper's The Prairie* (Oslo: Universitesforlaget, 1973); William H. Goetzmann in Cohen (GB), pp. 66–78; William Wasserstrom, "Cooper, Freud, and the Origins of Culture," *AI* 17 (1960): 423–437.

THE LITTLEPAGE TRILOGY. Donald A. Ringe, "Cooper's Littlepage Novels: Change and Stability in American Society," *AL* 32 (1960): 280–290; Jesse Bier, "The Bisection of Cooper: *Satanstoe* as Prime Example," *TSLL* 9 (1968): 511–521.

OTHER INDIVIDUAL WORKS. John P. McWilliams, Jr., "Cooper and the Conservative Democrat," *AQ* 22 (1970): 665–677, on *The American Democrat;* Charles O'Donnell, "The Moral Basis of Civilization: Cooper's Home Novels," *NCF* 17 (1962): 265–273; James H. Pickering, ed., "Enoch Crosby, Secret Agent of the Neutral Ground: His Own Story," *NYH* 47 (1966): 61–73, useful for *The Spy;* Tremaine McDowell, "James Fenimore Cooper as Self-Critic," *SP* 27 (1930): 508–516, proof that Cooper did revise *The Spy* with great care; James H. Pickering, "New York in the Revolution: Cooper's *Wyandotté*," *NYH* 49 (1968): 121–141; Donald A. Ringe, "Cooper's Last Novels, 1847–1850," *PMLA* 75 (1960): 583–590. Also see the introductions and bibliographies in the editions cited under "Texts."

BIBLIOGRAPHY. James Franklin Beard, in *Fifteen American Authors before 1900* (GB), pp. 63–96, an essay on the scholarship, including previous bibliographies.

William Cullen Bryant

TEXTS. *The Poetical Works of William Cullen Bryant,* 2 vols. (New York: Appleton, 1883) and *Prose Writings of William Cullen Bryant,* 2 vols. (New York: Appleton, 1884), both sets edited by Parke Godwin; *The Embargo,* introduction by Thomas O. Mabbott (Gainesville, Fla.: Scholars' Facsimiles & Reprints, 1955); *William Cullen Bryant: Representative Selections* (AWS; New York: American Book, 1935), with long introduction and notes by Tremaine McDowell; *The Let-*

ters of William Cullen Bryant, ed. William Cullen Bryant II and Thomas G. Voss (Bronx, N.Y.: Fordham University Press, 1975–), fully annotated.

BIOGRAPHY. Charles H. Brown, *William Cullen Bryant* (New York: Scribner, 1971); Parke Godwin (Bryant's son-in-law), *A Biography of William Cullen Bryant,* 2 vols. (New York: Appleton, 1883); John Bigelow, *William Cullen Bryant* (Boston: Houghton Mifflin, 1893); William Cullen Bryant II, *Bryant: The Middle Years: A Study in Cultural Fellowship* (Ph.D. dissertation, Columbia University, 1954; Ann Arbor, Mich.: University Microfilms, 1954), covering the years 1825–1850.

BRYANT AND THE FINE ARTS. Callow (GB) discusses Bryant's services to artists and their organizations and his contributions to the development of landscape and genre art as well as city planning; for the activities of the Sketch Club see pp. 12–29. The minutes of this society are being edited by J. T. Callow. Also see William Cullen Bryant II, "Poetry and Painting: A Love Affair of Long Ago," *AQ* 22 (1970): 859–882, an authoritative study of Bryant's affinities with American artists; and Ringe (GB), who thoroughly analyzes Bryant's use of pictorialism.

BRYANT AS CRITIC. H. H. Clark (GB:1936), p. 797, a summary of Bryant's theories; William Charvat, *The Origins of American Critical Thought: 1810–1835* (1936; reprint ed., Cranbury, N.J.: A. S. Barnes, 1961), *passim;* John Paul Pritchard, *Literary Wise Men of Gotham: Criticism in New York, 1815–1860* (Baton Rouge: Louisiana State University Press, 1963), *passim;* William J. Free, "William Cullen Bryant on Nationalism, Imitation, and Originality in Poetry," *SP* 66 (1969): 672–687.

BRYANT AS JOURNALIST. Allan Nevins, *The Evening Post: A Century of Journalism* (New York: Boni and Liveright, 1922); Curtiss S. Johnson, *Politics and a Bellyfull: The Journalistic Career of William Cullen Bryant* (New York: Vantage, 1962).

CRITICISM. An indispensable analysis of Bryant's thought and writing is McDowell's fifty-six-page introduction to *William Cullen Bryant: Representative Selections* (above). The fullest treatment of the poetry is *William Cullen Bryant* (TUSAS: 1964), by Albert McLean, Jr. Also see Stedman (GB), pp. 62–94; William A. Bradley, *William Cullen Bryant* (New York: Macmillan, 1905); N. Foerster, *Nature in American Literature,* pp. 1–19; Allen (GB), pp. 27–53, a valuable study of Bryant's prosodic theories and techniques; Tremaine McDowell, "Bryant's Practice in Composition and Revision," *PMLA* 52 (1937): 474–502; Arms (GB), pp. 9–19; Donald A. Ringe, "William Cullen Bryant and the Science of Geology," *AL* 26 (1955): 507–514; Evans Harrington, "Sensuousness in the Poetry of William Cullen Bryant," *UMSE* 7 (1966): 25–42; Berbrich (GB), pp. 61–107; Richard E. Peck, "Two Lost Bryant Poems: Evidence of Thomson's Influence," *AL* 39 (1967): 88–94, proof that Thomson's *Seasons* influenced Bryant at least three years before he read Wordsworth's *Lyrical Ballads;* Alan B. Donovan, "William Cullen Bryant: 'Father of American Song,' " *NEQ* 41 (1968): 505–520.

"THANATOPSIS." Pp. 65–81 of McLean (above) are a full analysis. In "The Genesis of 'Thanatopsis,' " *NEQ* 21 (1948): 163–184, William Cullen Bryant II argues convincingly that this work was composed in 1815 and that since 1813 Bryant had been writing lesser poems on the same subject. Because of these findings Carl Van Doren's "The Growth of 'Thanatopsis,' " *Nation,* Oct. 7, 1915, pp. 432–433 must be used with caution; but it is still worth consulting on the influence of Henry Kirke White and on the later revisions.

"TO A WATERFOWL." In "The Waterfowl in Retrospect," *NEQ* 30 (1957): 181–189 William Cullen Bryant II corrects Godwin's dating of this poem, shows that it was born of Bryant's early fear of public speaking, and traces its unusual stanzaic form to Southey's "The Ebb Tide." Also see Arms (GB), pp. 17–18; Donald Davie, "Bryant: 'To a Waterfowl,' " in *Interpretations,* ed. John Wain (London: Routledge & Kegan Paul, 1955), pp. 129–137.

"THE PRAIRIES." Ralph N. Miller, "Nationalism in Bryant's 'The Prairies,' " *AL* 21 (1949): 227–232; Curtis Dahl, "Mound-Builders, Mormons, and William Cullen Bryant," *NEQ* 34 (1961): 178–190.

BIBLIOGRAPHY. James E. Rocks in *Fifteen American Authors before 1900* (GB), pp. 37–62, an essay-review of the scholarship; McDowell, *William Cullen Bryant: Representative Selections,* pp. lxxiii–lxxxii, 359–362, listing primary and secondary materials; Judith Turner Phair, *A Bibliography of William Cullen Bryant and His Critics, 1808–1972* (Troy, N.Y.: Whitson, 1975), annotated.

10: THE TRANSCENDENTALISTS

TEXTS. *The American Transcendentalists: Their Prose and Poetry,* ed. Perry Miller (New York: Doubleday, 1957); *Selected Writings of the American Transcendentalists,* ed. George Hochfield (New York: New American Library, 1966).

BOOKS ON TRANSCENDENTALISM. Octavius B. Frothingham, *Transcendentalism in New England: A History* (1876; reprint ed., New York: Harper & Row, 1959); Clarence Gohdes, *The Periodicals of American Transcendentalism* (Durham, N.C.: Duke University Press, 1931); Simon and Parsons (GB); Lawrence Buell, *Literary Transcendentalism: Style and Vision in the American Renaissance* (Ithaca, N.Y.: Cornell University Press, 1973); *American Transcendentalism: An Anthology of Criticism,* ed. Brian M. Barbour (Notre Dame, Ind.: University of Notre Dame Press, 1973).

SHORTER STUDIES OF TRANSCENDENTALISM. Articles by O. B. Frothingham in *The New Schaff-Herzog Encyclopedia of Religious Knowledge,* Walter Harding in *Americana,* and J. J. McAleer in *The Catholic Encyclopedia;* Alexander Kern, "The Rise of Transcendentalism, 1815–1860," in H. H. Clark (GB:1953), pp. 245–314; Pochmann (GB), pp. 79–255.

Bibliographies of New England transcendentalism are in *LHUS;* Lud; and Burr (GB), pp. 237–255, an important bibliographical essay.

Ralph Waldo Emerson

TEXTS. *The Collected Works of Ralph Waldo Emerson,* eds. Alfred R. Ferguson, William H. Gilman, Robert E. Spiller, Carl F. Strauch, and others (Cambridge, Mass.: Harvard University Press, 1971–) and *The Journals and Miscellaneous Notebooks of Ralph Waldo Emerson,* ed. William H. Gilman, Alfred R. Ferguson, and others (Cambridge, Mass.: Harvard University Press, 1960–) are designed to supersede *The Complete Works of Ralph Waldo Emerson,* ed. Edward Waldo Emerson, 12 vols. (Centenary Ed.; Boston: Houghton Mifflin,

1903–1904) and *The Journals of Ralph Waldo Emerson,* ed. Edward Waldo Emerson and Waldo Emerson Forbes, 10 vols. (Boston: Houghton Mifflin, 1909–1914). Other collections and editions are *The Letters of Ralph Waldo Emerson,* ed. Ralph L. Rusk, 6 vols. (New York: Columbia University Press, 1939); *The Correspondence of Emerson and Carlyle,* ed. Joseph Slater (New York: Columbia University Press, 1964); *The Early Lectures of Ralph Waldo Emerson,* ed. Stephen E. Whicher, Robert E. Spiller, and Wallace E. Williams (Cambridge, Mass.: Harvard University Press, 1959–1972); *Nature (1836) by Ralph Waldo Emerson,* edited with introduction, index-concordance, and bibliographical appendixes by Kenneth W. Cameron (Gainesville, Fla.: Scholars' Facsimiles & Reprints, 1940); *English Traits,* ed. Howard Mumford Jones (Cambridge, Mass.: Harvard University Press, 1966); *Ralph Waldo Emerson: Representative Selections, with Introduction, Bibliography, and Notes by Frederick I. Carpenter* (New York: American Book, 1934).

Emerson Handbook (New York: Hendricks, 1953), by Frederick I. Carpenter, contains sections on Emerson's biography, prose and poetry, ideas, and connections with world literature.

BIOGRAPHY. Ralph L. Rusk, *The Life of Ralph Waldo Emerson* (1949; reprint ed., New York: Columbia University Press, 1957), full, scholarly, standard; *Ralph Waldo Emerson: A Profile,* ed. Carl Bode (American Profiles; New York: Hill & Wang, 1969); James E. Cabot, *A Memoir of Ralph Waldo Emerson,* 2 vols. (Boston: Houghton Mifflin, 1887), the authorized biography, still valuable; Henry F. Pommer, *Emerson's First Marriage* (Carbondale: Southern Illinois University Press, 1967); Edward Wagenknecht, *Ralph Waldo Emerson: Portrait of a Balanced Soul* (New York: Oxford University Press, 1974).

COLLECTIONS OF CRITICISM. *Emerson: A Collection of Critical Essays,* ed. Milton Konvitz and Stephen Whicher (TCV; Englewood Cliffs, N.J.: Prentice-Hall, 1962); *Critics on Emerson,* ed. Thomas J. Rountree (Coral Gables, Fla.: University of Miami Press, 1973); *The Recognition of Ralph Waldo Emerson: Selected Criticism since 1837,* ed. Milton R. Konvitz (Ann Arbor: University of Michigan Press, 1972).

STUDIES. John Q. Anderson, *The Liberating Gods: Emerson on Poets and Poetry* (Coral Gables, Fla.: University of Miami Press, 1971); Edmund C. Berry, *Emerson's Plutarch* (Cambridge, Mass.: Harvard University Press, 1961); Jonathan Bishop, *Emerson on the Soul* (Cambridge, Mass.: Harvard University Press, 1964); Kenneth W. Cameron, *Emerson the Essayist* (Hartford, Ct.: Transcendental Books, 1945); Frederick I. Carpenter, *Emerson and Asia* (1930; reprint ed., New York: Haskell, 1968); Michael H. Cowan, *City of the West: Emerson, America, and Urban Metaphor* (New Haven: Yale University Press, 1967); Jeffrey L. Duncan, *The Power and Form of Emerson's Thought* (Charlottesville: University Press of Virginia, 1973); Oscar W. Firkins, *Ralph Waldo Emerson* (Boston: Houghton Mifflin, 1915); Elamanamadathil V. Francis, *Emerson and Hindu Scriptures* (Cochin: Academic Publishers, 1972); Leyle Goren, *Elements of Brahmanism in the Transcendentalism of Emerson* (1959), reprinted in *ESQ* 34 supp. (1964); Henry D. Gray, *Emerson: A Statement of New England Transcendentalism as Expressed in the Philosophy of Its Chief Exponent* (1917; reprint ed., New York: Ungar, 1958); John S. Harrison, *The Teachers of Emerson* (1910; reprint ed., New York: Haskell, 1966), on

Emerson's Platonism; Vivian C. Hopkins, *Spires of Form: A Study of Emerson's Aesthetic Theory* (Cambridge, Mass.: Harvard University Press, 1951); Matthiessen (GB), bk. 1; Charles R. Metzger, *Emerson and Greenough: Transcendental Pioneers of an American Esthetic* (Berkeley: University of California Press, 1954), on two champions of organic form; Josephine Miles, *Ralph Waldo Emerson* (UMPAW: 1964), a pamphlet; Sherman Paul, *Emerson's Angle of Vision* (Cambridge, Mass.: Harvard University Press, 1952); Bliss Perry, *Emerson Today* (Princeton: Princeton University Press, 1931); Joel Porte, *Emerson and Thoreau: Transcendentalists in Conflict* (Middletown, Ct.: Wesleyan University Press, 1966); William J. Sowder, *Emerson's Reviewers and Commentators: A Biographical and Bibliographical Analysis of Nineteenth-Century Periodical Criticism—with a Detailed Index* (Hartford, Ct.: Transcendental Books, 1968); William J. Sowder, *Emerson's Impact on the British Isles and Canada* (Charlottesville: University Press of Virginia, 1966), with chapter on Emerson and Carlyle; Warren Staebler, *Ralph Waldo Emerson* (New York: Twayne, 1973); Stephen E. Whicher, *Freedom and Fate: An Inner Life of Ralph Waldo Emerson* (Philadelphia: University of Pennsylvania Press, 1953); George E. Woodberry, *Ralph Waldo Emerson* (1907; reprint ed., New York: Macmillan, 1926); William M. Wynkoop, *Three Children of the Universe: Emerson's View of Shakespeare, Bacon, and Milton* (The Hague: Mouton, 1966); Charles L. Young, *Emerson's Montaigne* (New York: Macmillan, 1941).

STUDIES OF THE PROSE. J. S. Clark (GB), pp. 768–799, illustrations of such traits as terseness, illogical structure, suggestiveness, and irony; "Emerson's Strategies of Rhetoric: A Symposium on *Essays: First Series*," *ESQ* 69 (1972): 199–297; David F. Finnigan, "The Man Himself: Emerson's Prose Style," *ESQ* 39 (1965): 13–15; William T. Harris, "The Dialectic Unity of Emerson's Prose," *Journal of Speculative Philosophy* 18 (1884): 195–202; Paul Lauter, "Emerson's Revisions of *Essays* (First Series)," *AL* 33 (1961): 143–158; Donald Ross, Jr., "Emerson and Thoreau: A Comparison of Prose Styles," *Language and Style* 6 (1973): 185–195.

Nature. The 1836 text, passages from the letters, journals, and lectures from which it evolved, and critical estimates through 1967 are contained in *Emerson's "Nature"—Origin, Growth, Meaning*, ed. Merton M. Sealts, Jr., and Alfred R. Ferguson (New York: Dodd, Mead, 1969). Also see Kenneth W. Cameron, *Emerson the Essayist* (above), which offers indexes, notes, and source studies; Richard Tuerk, "Emerson's *Nature*—Miniature Universe," *ATQ* 1 (1969): 110–113.

Other individual prose writings: *"The American Scholar" Today: Emerson's Essay and Some Critical Views*, ed. David C. Mead (New York: Dodd, Mead, 1970); Merton M. Sealts, Jr., "Emerson on the Scholar, 1833–1837," *PMLA* 85 (1970): 185–195 (for "The American Scholar"); Roland F. Lee, "Emerson's 'Compensation' as Argument and as Art," *NEQ* 37 (1964): 291–305; Philip L. Nicoloff, *Emerson on Race and History: An Examination of "English Traits"* (New York: Columbia University Press, 1961); John Lydenberg, "Emerson and the Dark Tradition," *CritQ* 4 (1962): 352–358, on "Experience"; George Sebouhian, "Emerson's 'Experience': An Approach to Content and Method," *ESQ* 47 (1967): 75–78, with an outline; Enno Klammer, "The Spiral Staircase in 'Self-Reliance,' " *ESQ* 47 (1967): 81–83, on the structure.

STUDIES OF THE POETRY. G. W. Allen, *American Prosody*, pp. 91–121; Richard L.

Francis, "Archangel in the Pleached Garden: Emerson's Poetry," *ELH* 33
(1966): 461–472; Seymour L. Gross, "Emerson and Poetry," *SAQ* 54 (1955): 82–
94; Kathryn A. McEuen, "Emerson's Rhymes," *AL* 20 (1948): 31–42; Carl F.
Strauch, "The Year of Emerson's Poetic Maturity: 1834," *PQ* 34 (1955): 353–
377; Carl F. Strauch, "The Mind's Voice: Emerson's Poetic Styles," *ESQ* 60
(1970): 43–59; F. T. Thompson, "Emerson's Theory and Practice of Poetry,"
PMLA 43 (1928): 1170–1184; Waggoner (GB), who sees Emerson as the central
figure among American poets.

INDIVIDUAL POEMS. Bernard J. Paris, "Emerson's 'Bacchus,' " *MLQ* 23 (1962): 150–
159; M. Van Doren (GB), pp. 90–93, for "Brahma"; Andrew M. McLean,
"Emerson's *Brahma* as an Expression of Brahman," *NEQ* 42 (1969): 115–122;
Richard Van Der Beets, "Compensatory Imagery in Emerson's Poem 'Compensation,' " *ESQ* 63 (1971): 12–13; George Arms, "Concord Hymn," *Expl Cyc*
2:136; F. I. Carpenter, *Emerson and Asia*, pp. 186–188, on the Persian elements
in "Days"; George Arms, Joseph Jones, and Edward G. Fletcher in *Expl Cyc*
2:136–138 (for "Days"); Egbert S. Oliver, "Emerson's 'Days,' " *NEQ* 19 (1946):
518–524; Epifanio San Juan, Jr., "Explication of Emerson's 'Each and All,' "
ESQ 43 (1966): 106–109; Norman Miller, "Emerson's 'Each and All' Concept: A
Reexamination," *NEQ* 41 (1968): 381–392; Michael H. Cowan, "Emerson's
'Give All to Love,' " *Expl* 18 (1960), item 49, an important analysis of the
imagery; A. Christy (above), pp. 170–176 (for "Hamatreya"); F. I. Carpenter
(above), pp. 122–127 (for "Hamatreya"); N. F. Adkins, *PMLA* 63 (1948): 662–
671 (for "Merlin"); Kenneth W. Cameron, "The Potent Song in Emerson's
Merlin Poems," *PQ* 32 (1953): 22–28; Carl F. Strauch, "The Background and
Meaning of the 'Ode Inscribed to W. H. Channing,' " *ESQ* 42 supp. (1966): 4–14;
Kenneth W. Cameron, "Early Background for Emerson's 'The Problem,' "
ESQ 27 (1962): 37–46; Carl F. Strauch, *ESQ* 55 (1969): 21–22 (for "The Problem"); Matthiessen (GB), pp. 49–50 (for "The Rhodora"); Strauch, *PQ* 34
(1955): 361–365 (for "The Rhodora"); Matthiessen (GB), pp. 138–140 (for "The
Snow-Storm"); Sister Paula Reiten, "Emerson's 'The Snow-Storm,' " *Expl* 22
(1964), item 39; Thomas R. Whitaker, "The Riddle of Emerson's 'Sphinx,' " *AL*
27 (1955): 179–195; H. D. Thoreau, *Journal* (Boston: Houghton Mifflin, 1906),
1:229–237 (for "The Sphinx"); Melvin G. Storm, Jr., "The Riddle of 'The
Sphinx': Another Approach," *ESQ* 62 (1971): 44–48; August H. Mason,
"Emerson's 'Terminus,' " *Expl* 4 (1946), item 37; E. T. Helmick, "Emerson's
'Uriel' as Poetic Theory," *ATQ* 1 (1969): 35–38; Hugh H. Whitemeyer, " 'Line'
and 'Round' in Emerson's 'Uriel,' " *PMLA* 82 (1967): 98–103.

CONCORDANCES. George S. Hubbell, *A Concordance to the Poems of Ralph Waldo
Emerson* (Bronx, N.Y.: Wilson, 1932); Kenneth W. Cameron, *Index-Concor-
dance to Emerson's Sermons with Homiletical Papers*, 2 vols. (Hartford, Ct.:
Transcendental Books, 1963).

BIBLIOGRAPHIES. Carpenter, *Emerson Handbook* (above), fully annotated; Jackson
R. Bryer and Robert A. Rees, *A Checklist of Emerson Criticism, 1951–1961, with
a Detailed Index* (Hartford, Ct.: Transcendental Books, 1964), annotated periodically and supplemented in *ESQ*; Floyd Stovall, "Emerson," in *Eight
American Authors*, pp. 37–83, a bibliographical essay. *ESQ* carries a continuing
bibliography.

Henry David Thoreau

TEXTS. *The Writings of Henry D. Thoreau,* a multivolume collection ed. Walter Harding and others (Princeton: Princeton University Press, 1971–) is designed to supersede *The Writings of Henry David Thoreau,* 20 vols. (Manuscript and Walden editions, Boston: Houghton Mifflin, 1906), 14 vols. of which contain Thoreau's journals, ed. Bradford Torrey. Also see *Consciousness in Concord: The Text of Thoreau's Hitherto "Lost Journal" (1840–1841),* ed. Perry Miller (Boston: Houghton Mifflin, 1958); *The Correspondence of Henry David Thoreau,* ed. Walter Harding and Carl Bode (New York: New York University Press, 1958); *Collected Poems of Henry Thoreau,* ed. Carl Bode (enl. ed.; Baltimore: Johns Hopkins Press, 1964); *Henry David Thoreau: Representative Selections* (AWS, New York: American Book, 1934), with a full introduction, bibliography, and notes by Bartholow V. Crawford.

BIOGRAPHY. *Thoreau: Man of Concord,* ed. Walter Harding (New York: Holt, Rinehart & Winston, 1960), a collection of estimates by Thoreau's contemporaries; William Ellery Channing, *Thoreau, the Poet-Naturalist* (1873; enl. and rev. ed., edited by F. B. Sanborn, Boston: Charles E. Goodspeed, 1902), by a close friend; Henry S. Salt, *Life of Henry David Thoreau* (1890; rev. ed., London: Walter Scott, Ltd., 1896), still highly regarded; F. B. Sanborn, *The Life of Henry David Thoreau* (1917; reprint ed., Detroit: Gale, 1968); Henry S. Canby, *Thoreau* (1939; reprint ed., Gloucester, Mass.: Peter Smith, 1965); Joseph Wood Krutch, *Henry David Thoreau* (New York: Sloane, 1948); *A Thoreau Profile,* eds. Milton Meltzer and Walter Harding (New York: T. Y. Crowell, 1962), a pictorial biography; Walter Harding, *The Days of Henry Thoreau* (New York: Knopf, 1967).

STUDIES. John A. Christie, *Thoreau as World Traveler* (New York: Columbia University Press, 1965), on the sources and uses of Thoreau's many geographical allusions; Reginald L. Cook, *Passage to Walden* (1949; 2d ed., New York: Atheneum, Russell & Russell, 1966); Leon Edel, *Henry D. Thoreau* (UMPAW: 1970); Walter Harding, *A Thoreau Handbook* (1959; paperback ed., New York: New York University Press, 1961), an important guide to the scholarship on Thoreau's life, works, sources, ideas, and fame; James McIntosh, *Thoreau as Romantic Naturalist* (Ithaca, N.Y.: Cornell University Press, 1974); Matthiessen (GB), bk. 1; Charles R. Metzger, *Thoreau and Whitman: A Study of Their Esthetics* (Seattle: University of Washington Press, 1961); James G. Murray, *Henry David Thoreau* (New York: Simon & Schuster, Washington Square Press, 1968); Sherman Paul, *The Shores of America: Thoreau's Inward Exploration* (Urbana: University of Illinois Press, 1958), on the development of Thoreau's thought; Ethel Seybold, *Thoreau: The Quest and the Classics* (1951; reprint ed., Hamden, Conn.: Shoe String, 1969), on Thoreau's use of classical writings; Leo Stoller, *After Walden: Thoreau's Changing Views on Economic Man* (Stanford, Calif.: Stanford University Press, 1957); Robert F. Stowell, *A Thoreau Gazetteer,* ed. William L. Howarth (Princeton: Princeton University Press, 1970); J. Golden Taylor, *Neighbor Thoreau's Critical Humor* (Logan: Utah State University Press, 1958), proof that Thoreau used humor for serious purposes and was not misanthropic.

COLLECTIONS OF CRITICISM. *Thoreau: A Collection of Critical Essays,* ed. Sherman Paul (Englewood Cliffs, N.J.: Prentice-Hall, 1962); *New Approaches to Thoreau:*

A Symposium, ed. William B. Stein (Hartford, Ct.: Transcendental Books, 1969); *Henry David Thoreau: Studies and Commentaries,* ed. Walter Harding, George Brenner, and Paul A. Doyle (Cranbury, N.J.: Fairleigh Dickinson University Press, 1972); *The Western Thoreau Centenary: Selected Papers,* ed. J. Golden Taylor (Logan: Utah State University Press, 1963); *The Recognition of Henry David Thoreau: Selected Criticism since 1848,* ed. Wendell Glick (Ann Arbor: University of Michigan Press, 1969); *Thoreau in Our Season,* ed. John H. Hicks (Amherst: University of Massachusetts Press, 1966). Walter Harding has edited *Thoreau: A Century of Criticism* (Dallas: Southern Methodist University Press, 1954) and *The Thoreau Centennial* (Albany: State University of New York Press, 1964). Additional collections are listed below, under studies of individual works.

STUDIES OF THE POETRY. Henry W. Wells, "An Evaluation of Thoreau's Poetry," *AL* 16 (1944): 99–109; Paul O. Williams, "The Concept of Inspiration in Thoreau's Poetry," *PMLA* 79 (1964): 466–472; Matthiessen (GB), pp. 165–166 (for "Smoke"); Delmer Rodabaugh, "Thoreau's 'Smoke,' " *Expl* 17 (1959), item 47.

Walden. Many of the most important analyses have been collected in *Twentieth-Century Interpretations of "Walden,"* ed. Richard Ruland (Englewood Cliffs, N.J.: Prentice-Hall, 1968); *Approaches to "Walden,"* ed. Lauriat Lane, Jr. (San Francisco, Calif.: Wadsworth, 1961); *"Walden" and "Civil Disobedience": Authoritative Texts, Background, Reviews and Essays in Criticism,* ed. Owen Thomas (New York: Norton, 1966); *The Merrill Studies in Walden,* ed. Joseph J. Moldenhauer (Columbus, Ohio: Merrill, 1971). Also see *The Variorum Walden,* edited with notes and an illuminating introduction by Walter Harding (1962; paperback ed., New York: Simon & Schuster, Washington Square Press, 1963); *The Annotated "Walden" . . . together with "Civil Disobedience" . . .* [and] *a Detailed Chronology . . . ,* ed. Philip Van Doren Stern (New York: Potter, 1970); Stanley Cavell, *The Senses of Walden* (New York: Viking, 1972); Charles R. Anderson, *The Magic Circle of Walden* (New York: Holt, Rinehart & Winston, 1968), an exhaustive literary analysis; J. Lyndon Shanley, *The Making of "Walden": with the Text of the First Version* (Chicago: University of Chicago Press, 1957), a genetic study; *Walden: A Writer's Edition,* with commentaries and notes by Larzer Ziff (New York: Holt, Rinehart & Winston, 1961), useful for its "Considerations" (pp. 277–332) of each chapter's expository techniques and structural function; J. Stephen Sherwin and Richard C. Reynolds, *A Word Index to "Walden," with Textual Notes* (corrected ed.; Hartford, Ct.: Transcendental Books, 1969); David M. Greene, *The Frail Duration: A Key to Symbolic Structure in "Walden"* (San Diego: San Diego State University Press, 1966), a pamphlet; George F. Whicher, *Walden Revisited* (Chicago: Packard, 1945); Henry B. Kane, *Thoreau's Walden: A Photographic Register* (New York: Knopf, 1946).

"CIVIL DISOBEDIENCE." C. Carroll Hollis, "Thoreau and the State," *Commonweal* 50 (1949): 530–533, a balanced appraisal; John C. Broderick, "Thoreau, Alcott, and the Poll Tax," *SP* 53 (1956): 612–626; George Hendrick, "The Influence of Thoreau's 'Civil Disobedience' on Gandhi's *Satyagraha,*" *NEQ* 29 (1956): 462–471; Don W. Kleine, "Civil Disobedience: The Way to Walden," *MLN* 75 (1960): 297–304; *The Variorum Civil Disobedience,* annotated and with an introduction by Walter Harding (New York: Twayne, 1967), with a few short excerpts from critics and enthusiasts; Edward H. Madden, *Civil Disobedience and Moral Law in Nineteenth-Century American Philosophy* (Seattle: University of Washington Press, 1968), for background; George Anastaplo, "On Civil Disobedience: Thoreau and Socrates," *SWR* 54 (1969): 203–214. Also see *The Annotated "Walden"* . . . [and] *"Civil Disobedience"* (above).

STUDIES OF OTHER INDIVIDUAL WORKS. J. J. Boies, "Circular Imagery in Thoreau's *Week*," *CE* 26 (1965): 350–355; Carl F. Hovde, "Nature into Art: Thoreau's Use of His Journals in *A Week*," *AL* 30 (1958): 165–184; Carl F. Hovde, "Literary Materials in Thoreau's *A Week*," *PMLA* 80 (1965): 76–83; Joyce M. Holland, "Pattern and Meaning in Thoreau's *A Week*," *ESQ* 50 supp. (1968): 48–55; Martin L. Pops, "An Analysis of Thoreau's *Cape Cod*," *BNYPL* 67 (1963): 419–428.

BIBLIOGRAPHY. Walter Harding, *Thoreau Handbook*, for material up to about 1957; *A Bibliography of the Thoreau Society Bulletin Bibliographies, 1941–1969: A Cumulation and Index* [of authors, not subjects], cumulated by Jean C. Advena, ed. Walter Harding (Troy, N.Y.: Whitson, 1971); "Additions to the Thoreau Bibliography," appearing usually in every issue of the *Thoreau Society Bulletin* (not annotated); *Thoreau Abroad: Twelve Bibliographical Essays*, ed. Eugene F. Timpe (Hamden, Conn.: Archon, 1971); Lewis Leary, "Henry David Thoreau," in *Eight American Authors* (GB), pp. 129–171, an essay-review of the scholarship.

11: HAWTHORNE, POE, AND MELVILLE

The literary battles of the period are traced in Perry Miller, *The Raven and the Whale* (New York: Harcourt, 1956). Harry Levin's *The Power of Blackness* (New York: Knopf, Vintage, 1958) is an intensive study of Hawthorne, Poe, and Melville as writers whose vision was the dark antithesis of Emerson's.

Nathaniel Hawthorne

BIBLIOGRAPHY. Buford Jones, *A Checklist of Hawthorne Criticism, 1951–1966* (Hartford, Ct.: Transcendental Books, 1967) gives descriptive summaries for nearly all of its 906 items. This convenient tool and its companion volume, Kenneth Walter Cameron's *Hawthorne Index to Themes, Motifs, Topics, Archetypes, Sources and Key Words Dealt with in Recent Criticism* (Hartford, Ct.: Transcendental Books, 1968), facilitate preliminary research. Also see Walter Blair's bibliographical essay in *Eight American Authors* (GB); the annual chapter on Hawthorne in *ALS*; Maurice Beebe and Jack Hardie, "Criticism of Nathaniel Hawthorne: A Selected Checklist," *Studies in the Novel* 2 (1970): 519–587; C. E. Frazer Clark, Jr., *Checklist of Nathaniel Hawthorne* (Columbus, Ohio: Merrill, 1970); Theodore L. Gross and Stanley Wertheim, *Hawthorne, Melville, Stephen Crane: A Critical Bibliography* (New York: Free Press, 1971).

TEXTS. *The Centenary Edition of the Works of Nathaniel Hawthorne*, ed. Roy Harvey Pearce and others (Columbus: Ohio State University Press, 1962–) supersedes previous multivolume collections.

BIOGRAPHY. Randall Stewart's *Nathaniel Hawthorne* (New Haven: Yale University Press, 1948), the standard biography, has replaced works that presented Hawthorne as a solitary figure. Blair (above), pp. 88–93, analyzes the trends in Hawthorne biography.

COLLECTIONS OF CRITICISM. *Hawthorne among His Contemporaries,* comp. Kenneth W. Cameron (Hartford, Ct.: Transcendental Books, 1968); *The Recognition of Nathaniel Hawthorne: Selected Criticism since 1828,* ed., Bernard B. Cohen (Ann Arbor: University of Michigan Press, 1969); *Hawthorne: The Critical Heritage,* ed. J. Donald Crowley (New York: Barnes & Noble, 1970); *Nathaniel Hawthorne: A Collection of Criticism,* ed. J. Donald Crowley (New York: McGraw-Hill, 1975); *A Casebook on the Hawthorne Question,* ed. Agnes M. Donohue (New York: T. Y. Crowell, 1962); *Hawthorne: A Collection of Critical Essays,* ed. A. N. Kaul (Englewood Cliffs, N.J.: Prentice-Hall, 1966); *Hawthorne Centenary Essays,* ed. Roy Harvey Pearce (Columbus: Ohio State University Press, 1964); *Critics on Hawthorne,* ed. Thomas J. Rountree (Coral Gables, Fla.: University of Miami Press, 1972).

STUDIES. John E. Becker, *Hawthorne's Historical Allegory: An Examination of the American Conscience* (Port Washington, N.Y.: Kennikat, 1971); Millicent Bell, *Hawthorne's View of the Artist* (Albany: State University of New York Press, 1962); Walter Blair, "Color, Light and Shadow in Hawthorne's Fiction," *NEQ* 15 (1942): 74–94; J. Donald Crowley, *Nathaniel Hawthorne* (London: Routledge & Kegan Paul, 1971); Neal F. Doubleday, *Hawthorne's Early Tales: A Critical Study* (Durham, N.C.: Duke University Press, 1972); Richard H. Fogle, *Hawthorne's Fiction: The Light and the Dark* (1952; rev., Norman: University of Oklahoma Press, 1964); Richard H. Fogle, *Hawthorne's Imagery: The "Proper Light and Shadow" in the Major Romances* (Norman: University of Oklahoma Press, 1969); Hubert H. Hoeltje, *Inward Sky* (Durham, N.C.: Duke University Press, 1962); Hugo McPherson, *Hawthorne as Myth-Maker* (Toronto: University of Toronto Press, 1969); Terence Martin, *Nathaniel Hawthorne* (TUSAS: 1965); Jean Normand, *Nathaniel Hawthorne: An Approach to an Analysis of Artistic Creation* (Cleveland: Press of Case Western Reserve University, 1970); Mary Rohrberger, *Hawthorne and the Modern Short Story: A Study in Genre* (The Hague: Mouton, 1966); Arlin Turner, *Nathaniel Hawthorne: An Introduction and Interpretation* (AACS, New York: Barnes & Noble, 1961); Hyatt H. Waggoner, *Nathaniel Hawthorne* (UMPAW: 1962), a pamphlet; Hyatt H. Waggoner, *Hawthorne: A Critical Study* (rev.; Cambridge, Mass.: Harvard University Press, 1963).

"MY KINSMAN, MAJOR MOLINEUX." Seymour L. Gross, "Hawthorne's 'My Kinsman, Major Molineux': History as Moral Adventure," *NCF* 12 (1957): 97–109; Hoffman (GB), chap. 6; Arthur T. Broes, "Journey into Moral Darkness: 'My Kinsman, Major Molineux' as Allegory," *NCF* 19 (1964): 171–184; John Russell, "Allegory and 'My Kinsman, Major Molineux,' " *NEQ* 40 (1967): 432–440; Alexander W. Allison, "The Literary Contexts of 'My Kinsman, Major Molineux,' " *NCF* 23 (1968): 304–311.

"YOUNG GOODMAN BROWN." *Nathaniel Hawthorne: Young Goodman Brown* (Columbus, Ohio: Merrill, 1968), a casebook ed. Thomas E. Connolly, with interpretations by Richard H. Fogle, David Levin, E. Arthur Robinson, James W. Mathews, Paul J. Hurley, and others; Hoffman (GB), chap. 8; Taylor Stoehr,

" 'Young Goodman Brown' and Hawthorne's Theory of Mimesis," *NCF* 23 (1969): 393–412.

"THE MINISTER'S BLACK VEIL." Thomas F. Walsh, Jr., "Mr. Hooper's 'Affable Weakness,' " *MLN* 74 (1959): 404–406; Robert W. Cochran, "Hawthorne's Choice: The Veil or the Jaundiced Eye," *CE* 23 (1962): 342–346; E. Earle Stibitz, "Ironic Unity in Hawthorne's 'The Minister's Black Veil,' " *AL* 34 (1962): 182–190; H. Alan Wycherley, "Hawthorne's 'The Minister's Black Veil,' " *Expl* 23 (1964), item 11; M. L. Allen, "The Black Veil: Three Versions of a Symbol," *ES* 67 (1966): 286–289; Nicholas Canaday, Jr., "Hawthorne's Minister and the Veiling Deceptions of Self," *SSF* 4 (1967): 135–142; Victor Strandberg, "The Artist's Black Veil," *NEQ* 41 (1968): 567–574; Frederick W. Turner III, "Hawthorne's Black Veil," *SSF* 5 (1968): 186–187.

"THE MAYPOLE OF MERRY MOUNT." Hoffman (GB), chap. 7; G. Harrison Orians, "Hawthorne and 'The Maypole of Merry Mount,' " *MLN* 53 (1938): 159–167; Sheldon W. Liebman, "Hawthorne's *Comus:* A Miltonic Source for 'The Maypole of Merrymount,' " *NCF* 27 (1972): 345–351.

"THE CELESTIAL RAILROAD." Clifford A. Wood, "Teaching Hawthorne's 'The Celestial Railroad,' " *EJ* 54 (1965): 601–605; Joseph C. Pattison, " 'The Celestial Railroad' as Dream-Tale," *AQ* 20 (1968): 224–236.

"THE ARTIST OF THE BEAUTIFUL." Henry M. Delaune, "The Beautiful of 'The Artist of the Beautiful,' " *XUS* 1 (1961): 94–99; Robert H. Woodward, "Automata in Hawthorne's 'Artist of the Beautiful' and Taylor's 'Meditation 56,' " *ESQ* 31 (1963): 63–66; Hugh L. Moore, Jr., "Hawthorne's Ideal Artist as Presumptuous Intellectual," *SSF* 2 (1965): 278–283; R. A. Yoder, "Hawthorne and His Artist," *SIR* 7 (1968): 193–206; J. T. McCullen, Jr., "Influences on Hawthorne's 'The Artist of the Beautiful,' " *ESQ* 50 (1968): 43–46.

"RAPPACCINI'S DAUGHTER." Roy R. Male, "The Dual Aspects of Evil in 'Rappaccini's Daughter,' " *PMLA* 69 (1954): 99–109; Charles Boewe, "Rappaccini's Garden," *AL* 30 (1958): 37–49; Bernard McCabe, "Narrative Technique in 'Rappaccini's Daughter,' " *MLN* 74 (1959): 213–217; William Rossky, "Rappaccini's Garden or the Murder of Innocence," *ESQ* 19 (1960): 98–100; Edward H. Rosenberry, "Hawthorne's Allegory of Science: 'Rappaccini's Daughter,' " *AL* 32 (1960): 39–46; Richard B. Hovey, "Love and Hate in 'Rappaccini's Daughter,' " *UKCR* 29 (1962): 137–145; Frederick C. Crews, "Giovanni's Garden," *AQ* 16 (1964): 402–418; Oliver Evans, "Allegory and Incest in 'Rappaccini's Daughter,' " *NCF* 19 (1964): 185–195; Robert Gale, "Rappaccini's Baglioni," *SA* 9 (1964): 83–87; Robert J. Daly, "Fideism and the Allusive Mode in 'Rappaccini's Daughter,' " *NCF* 28 (1973): 25–37.

"ETHAN BRAND." B. A. Sokoloff, "Ethan Brand's Twin," *MLN* 73 (1958): 413–414; Brother Joseph, "Art and Event in 'Ethan Brand,' " *NCF* 15 (1960): 249–257; Alfred J. Levy, " 'Ethan Brand' and the Unpardonable Sin," *Boston Univ. Studies in English* 5 (1961): 185–190, which sees the story as denying the possibility of an Unpardonable Sin per se; Jerry A. Herndon and Sidney P. Moss, "The Identity and Significance of the German Jewish Showman in Hawthorne's 'Ethan Brand,' " *CE* 23 (1962): 362–363; Kermit Vanderbilt, "The Unity of Hawthorne's 'Ethan Brand,' " *CE* 24 (1963): 453–456; Ely Stock, "The Biblical Context of 'Ethan Brand,' " *AL* 37 (1965): 115–134; Richard Allan Davison, "The Villagers and Ethan Brand," *SSF* 4 (1967): 260–262; William M. White,

"Hawthorne's Eighteen-Year Cycle: Ethan Brand and Reuben Bourne," *SSF* 6 (1969): 215–218; John McElroy, "The Brand Metaphor in 'Ethan Brand,' " *AL* 43 (1972): 633–637.

THE ROMANCES. Explications of individual romances are summarized in Jones, listed in Gerstenberger and Hendrick. Also see Robert S. Phillips, Jack Kligerman, Robert Long, and Robert Hastings, "Nathaniel Hawthorne: Criticism of the Four Major Romances: A Selected Bibliography," *Thoth* 3 (1962): 39–50.

The Scarlet Letter. Many of the critics cited in our text are represented in one or more of the following anthologies: *A Scarlet Letter Handbook,* ed. Seymour Gross (Belmont, Calif.: Wadsworth, 1960), which conveniently groups its excerpts into sections on theme, characters, symbolism, and structure and contains an annotated bibliography (pp. 152–161); *The Scarlet Letter: Text, Sources, Criticism,* ed. Kenneth S. Lynn (New York: Harcourt, 1961); *The Scarlet Letter: An Annotated Text, Backgrounds and Sources, Essays in Criticism,* ed. Sculley Bradley, Richmond Croom Beatty, and E. Hudson Long (New York: Norton, 1961, 1962); *Twentieth Century Interpretations of The Scarlet Letter,* ed. John C. Gerber (Englewood Cliffs, N.J.: Prentice-Hall, 1968), with sections on background, form, techniques, and interpretations. Other authors cited are William H. Nolte, "Hawthorne's Dimmesdale: A Small Man Gone Wrong," *NEQ* 38 (1965): 168–186; Adrian Parcher, "Hawthorne's The Scarlet Letter," *Expl* 21 (1963): item 48; Allen Austin, "Hester Prynne's Plan of Escape," *UKCR* 28 (1962): 317–318; Ernest W. Baughman, "Public Confession and *The Scarlet Letter,*" *NEQ* 40 (1967): 532–550; Dan Vogel, "Roger Chillingworth: The Satanic Paradox in 'The Scarlet Letter,' " *Criticism* 5 (1963): 272–280. Representative of the search for sources is Hena Maes-Helinek, "Roger Chillingworth: An Example of the Creative Process in *The Scarlet Letter,*" *ES* 49 (1968): 341–348, which shows parallels between Chillingworth and Francis Cheynell, an Old World Puritan. Studies of "The Custom House" by Ziff, Baskett, Austin, MacShane, Moses, Wagner, and McCall may be found in Jones's *Checklist.* Robert S. Phillips, "*The Scarlet Letter:* A Selected Checklist of Criticism, 1850–1962," *BB* 23 (1962): 213–216, is not annotated.

The House of the Seven Gables. The House of the Seven Gables: An Authoritative Text, Backgrounds and Sources, Essays in Criticism, ed. Seymour L. Gross (New York: Norton, 1967) and *The Merrill Studies in "The House of the Seven Gables,"* ed. Roger Asselineau (Columbus, Ohio: Merrill, 1970) contain all the critics cited in our text.

The Blithedale Romance. Maurice A. Crane, "*The Blithedale Romance* as Theatre," *N&Q* 5 (1958), 84–86; William L. Hedges, "Hawthorne's *Blithedale:* The Function of the Narrator," *NCF* 14 (1960): 303–316; Robert Stanton, "The Trial of Nature: An Analysis of *The Blithedale Romance,*" *PMLA* 76 (1961): 528–538; James F. Ragan, "The Irony in Hawthorne's Blithedale," *NEQ* 35 (1962): 239–246; Robert C. Elliott in Pearce, ed., *Hawthorne Centenary Essays,* pp. 103–117; Allan and Barbara Lefcowitz, "Some Rents in the Veil: New Light on Priscilla and Zenobia in *The Blithedale Romance,*" *NCF* 21 (1966): 263–275; Kelley Griffith, Jr., "Form in *The Blithedale Romance,*" *AL* 40 (1968): 15–26; Nina Baym, "*The Blithedale Romance:* A Radical Reading," *JEGP* 67 (1968): 545–569; Julian Smith, "Why Does Zenobia Kill Herself?" *ELN* 6 (1968): 37–39; Marilyn Gaddis Rose, "Miles Coverdale as Hawthorne's Persona," *ATQ* 1

(1969): 90–91; James H. Justus, "Hawthorne's Character and Art in The Blithedale Romance," *AL* 47 (1975): 21–36.

The Marble Faun. See *The Merrill Studies in "The Marble Faun,"* ed. David B. Kesterson (Columbus, Ohio: Merrill, 1971); *The Marble Faun,* edited with introduction and annotation by Richard H. Rupp (Indianapolis: Bobbs-Merrill, 1971); John A. Huzzard, "Hawthorne's 'The Marble Faun,' " *Italica* 35 (1958): 119–124; John C. Guilds, "Miriam of *The Marble Faun:* Hawthorne's Subtle Sinner," *CairoSE* (1960), pp. 61–68; Joseph Schwartz, "Myth and Ritual in *The Marble Faun,*" *ESQ* 25 (1961): 26–29; John T. Flanagan, "Point of View in *The Marble Faun,*" *NS* 11 (1962): 218–224; Waggoner (GB), pp. 209–225; Harry Levin, "Statues from Italy: *The Marble Faun,*" in Pearce, ed., *Hawthorne Centenary Essays,* pp. 119–140; Sacvan Bercovitch, "Hilda's 'Seven-Branched Allegory': An Echo from Cotton Mather in *The Marble Faun,*" *EALN* 1 (1966): 5–6; Peter G. Beidler, "Theme of the Fortunate Fall in *The Marble Faun,*" *ESQ* 47 (1967): 56–62; Sidney P. Moss, "The Symbolism of the Italian Background in *The Marble Faun,*" *NCF* 23 (1968): 332–336; Clare R. Goldfarb, "*The Marble Faun* and Emersonian Self-Reliance," *ATQ* 1 (1969): 19–23; Daniel J. Schneider, "The Allegory and Symbolism of Hawthorne's *The Marble Faun,*" *Studies in the Novel* 1 (1969): 38–50.

For Hawthorne's books for children, which include *Grandfather's Chair* (1841), *A Wonder Book* (1852), and *Tanglewood Tales* (1853), see Richard D. Hathaway, "Hawthorne and the Paradise of Children," *WHR* 15 (1961): 161–172; Mary S. Mattfield, "Hawthorne's Juvenile Classics," *Discourse* 12 (1969): 346–364.

Plots and Characters in the Fiction and Sketches of Nathaniel Hawthorne (Hamden, Conn.: Archon, 1969) contains useful summaries by Robert L. Gale.

The Nathaniel Hawthorne Journal, an annual, began in 1971 under the editorship of C. E. Frazer Clark, Jr.

Edgar Allan Poe

TEXTS. *The Complete Works of Edgar Allan Poe,* ed. James A. Harrison, 17 vols. (1902; reprint ed., New York: AMS Press, 1965), standard; *Introduction to Poe: A Thematic Reader,* the poetry and prose edited with introduction, bibliography, and interpretive notes by Eric W. Carlson (Glenview, Ill.: Scott, Foresman, 1967); *The Poems of Edgar Allan Poe,* edited with full, helpful notes by Killis Campbell (1917; reprint ed., New York: Atheneum, Russell & Russell, 1962); *The Poems of Edgar Allan Poe,* edited with introduction by Floyd Stovall (Charlottesville: University Press of Virginia, 1965), authoritative text with variant readings; *Poems,* ed. Thomas Ollive Mabbott (Cambridge, Mass.: Harvard University Press, 1969; vol. 1 of the *Collected Works of Edgar Allan Poe*), another authoritative text with variant readings, plus sources and criticism; *Representative Selections, with Introduction, Bibliography, and Notes by Margaret Alterton and Hardin Craig* (AWS, 1935; rev. ed., New York: Hill & Wang, 1962); *Eureka: A Prose Poem: New Edition with Line Numbers, Exploratory Essay, and Bibliographical Guide by Richard P. Benton* (Hartford, Ct.: Transcendental Books, 1973); *Literary Criticism of Edgar Allan Poe,* edited with introduction by Robert L. Hough (Regents Critics Series, Lincoln: University of

Nebraska Press, 1965); *The Letters of Edgar Allan Poe,* ed. John W. Ostrom, 2 vols. (rev. ed., Staten Island, N.Y.: Gordian, 1966).

BIOGRAPHY. George E. Woodberry, *Life of Edgar Allan Poe,* 2 vols. (rev. ed., 1909; reprint ed., New York: Biblo & Tannen, 1965); Hervey Allen, *Israfel: The Life and Times of Edgar Allan Poe,* 2 vols., 2d ed. (New York: George H. Doran, 1926); Arthur H. Quinn, *Edgar Allan Poe: A Critical Biography* (New York: Appleton, 1941); Edward C. Wagenknecht, *Edgar Allan Poe, the Man behind the Legend* (New York: Oxford University Press, 1963); John S. Hill, "The Diabetic Mr. Poe?" *PN* 1 (1968): 31.

COLLECTIONS OF CRITICISM. *The Recognition of Edgar Allan Poe: Selected Criticism since 1829,* ed. Eric W. Carlson (Ann Arbor: University of Michigan Press, 1966); *Poe: A Collection of Critical Essays,* ed. Robert Regan (TCV; Englewood Cliffs, N.J.: Prentice-Hall, 1967); *Critics on Poe,* ed. David B. Kesterson (Coral Gables, Fla.: University of Miami Press, 1973).

STUDIES. Michael Allen, *Poe and the British Magazine Tradition* (New York: Oxford University Press, 1969); Roger Asselineau, *Edgar Allan Poe* (UMPAW: 1970); Haldeen Braddy, *Glorious Incense: The Fulfillment of Edgar Allan Poe* (1953; 2d ed., Port Washington, N.Y.: Kennikat, 1968); Haldeen Braddy, *Three Dimensional Poe* (El Paso: Texas Western Press, University of Texas, 1973); Louis Broussard, *The Measure of Poe* (Norman: University of Oklahoma Press, 1969); Vincent Buranelli, *Edgar Allan Poe* (TUSAS: 1961); Killis Campbell, *The Mind of Poe, and Other Studies* (1933; reprint ed., New York: Atheneum, Russell & Russell, 1962); Edward H. Davidson, *Poe: A Critical Study* (Cambridge, Mass.: Harvard University Press, 1957); N. Bryllion Fagin, *The Histrionic Mr. Poe* (Baltimore: Johns Hopkins Press, 1949); Richard M. Fletcher, *The Stylistic Development of Edgar Allan Poe* (The Hague: Mouton, 1973); David Halliburton, *Edgar Allan Poe: A Phenomenological View* (Princeton: Princeton University Press, 1973); Daniel Hoffman, *Poe Poe Poe Poe Poe Poe Poe* (New York: Doubleday, 1972); Joseph Wood Krutch, *Edgar Allan Poe: A Study in Genius* (1926; reprint ed., New York: Atheneum, Russell & Russell, 1965); Sidney P. Moss, *Poe's Major Crisis: His Libel Suit and New York's Literary World* (Durham, N.C.: Duke University Press, 1970); Burton R. Pollin, *Discoveries in Poe* (Notre Dame, Ind.: University of Notre Dame Press, 1970); Geoffrey Rans, *Edgar Allan Poe* (Edinburgh: Oliver & Boyd, 1965); C. Alphonso Smith, *Edgar Allan Poe: How to Know Him* (Indianapolis: Bobbs-Merrill, 1921).

POE'S CRITICISM. See Margaret Alterton, *Origins of Poe's Critical Theory* (1925; reprint ed., New York: Atheneum, Russell & Russell, 1965); Sidney P. Moss, *Poe's Literary Battles* (Durham, N.C.: Duke University Press, 1963); Edd Winfield Parks, *Edgar Allan Poe as Literary Critic* (Athens: University of Georgia Press, 1964); Robert D. Jacobs, *Poe: Journalist & Critic* (Baton Rouge: Louisiana State University Press, 1969). J. Lasley Dameron and Louis C. Stagg have compiled *An Index to Poe's Critical Vocabulary* (Hartford, Ct.: Transcendental Books, 1966).

THE POETRY. Floyd Stovall's *Edgar Poe the Poet* (Charlottesville: University Press of Virginia, 1969) is indispensable. Also important are G. W. Allen's *American Prosody,* pp. 56–85; James L. Allen, Jr., "Stanza Patterns in the Poetry of Poe," *TSL* 12 (1967): 111–120; *A Concordance of the Poetical Works of Edgar Allan Poe,* comp. Bradford A. Booth and Claude E. Jones (Baltimore: Johns Hopkins

Press, 1941); and the notes in Campbell's edition of *The Poems* (above). Studies of individual poems include Arthur Schwartz, "The Transport: A Matter of Time and Space," *CEA* 31 (1968): 14–15, on "To Helen"; Thomas O. Mabbott, "Poe's 'Israfel,' " *Expl* 2 (1944), item 57; Louise Pound, "On Poe's 'The City in the Sea,' " *AL* 6 (1934): 22–27; Louise Pound, "Poe's 'The City in the Sea' Again," *AL* 8 (1936): 70–71; T. Frederick Keefer, " 'The City in the Sea': A Re-examination," *CE* 25 (1964): 436–439; William O. Clough, "Poe's 'The City in the Sea' Revisited," in Gohdes (GB), pp. 77–89; John C. Broderick, "Poe's Revisions of 'Lenore,' " *AL* 35 (1964): 504–510; Donald R. Swanson, "Poe's 'The Conqueror Worm,' " *Expl* 19 (1961), item 52; Howard M. Jones, "Poe's 'The Raven,' and the Anonymous Young Man," *WHR* 9 (1955): 132–138; J. O. Bailey, "The Geography of Poe's 'Dream-Land' and 'Ulalume,' " *SP* 45 (1948): 512–523; James E. Miller, Jr., " 'Ulalume' Resurrected," *PQ* 34 (1955): 197–205; Eric W. Carlson, "Symbol and Sense in Poe's 'Ulalume,' " *AL* 35 (1963): 22–37; James E. Mulqueen, "The Meaning of Poe's 'Ulalume,' " *ATQ* 1 (1969): 27–30; Eric W. Carlson, "Poe's 'Eldorado,' " *MLN* 76 (1961): 232–233; Paul O. Williams, "A Reading of Poe's 'The Bells,' " *PN* 1 (1968): 24–25.

THE TALES. General studies include *Twentieth Century Interpretations of Poe's Tales,* ed. William L. Howarth (Englewood Cliffs, N.J.: Prentice-Hall, 1971); Howard Haycraft, *Murder for Pleasure* (New York: Appleton, 1941), pp. 1–27, 387–391 for Poe's detective stories; H. B. Franklin (GB), pp. 93–137 for Poe's science fiction; Stuart Levine, *Edgar Poe: Seer and Craftsman* (DeLand, Fla.: Everett/Edwards, 1972); G. R. Thompson, *Poe's Fiction: Romantic Irony in the Gothic Tales* (Madison: University of Wisconsin Press, 1973). Among the many studies of individual tales are John Walsh, *Poe the Detective: The Curious Circumstances Behind "The Mystery of Marie Roget"* (New Brunswick, N.J.: Rutgers University Press, 1967); Basler, in Regan (above), pp. 51–63, for "Ligeia"; Roy P. Basler and James Schroeter, "Poe's 'Ligeia,' " *PMLA* 77 (1962): 675; John Lauber, " 'Ligeia' and Its Critics: A Plea for Literalism," *SSF* 4 (1966): 28–32; Muriel West, "Poe's 'Ligeia,' " *Expl* 22 (1963), item 15; Claudia C. Morrison, "Poe's 'Ligeia': An Analysis," *SSF* 4 (1967): 234–244; D. Ramakrishna, "Poe's 'Ligeia,' " *Expl* 25 (1966), item 19; James W. Gargano, "Poe's 'Ligeia' Dream and Destruction," *CE* 23 (1962): 337–342; Joseph P. Roppolo, "Meaning and 'The Masque of the Red Death,' " *TSE* 13 (1963): 59–69, which summarizes earlier interpretations; Kermit Vanderbilt, "Art and Nature in 'The Masque of the Red Death,' " *NCF* (1968): 379–389; S. L. Varnado, "The Case of the Sublime Purloin; or, Burke's *Inquiry* as the Source of an Anecdote in 'The Purloined Letter,' " *PN* 1 (1968): 27; Charles W. Steele, "Poe's 'The Cask of Amontillado,' " *Expl* 18 (1960), item 43; T. O. Mabbott, "Poe's 'The Cask of Amontillado,' " *Expl* 25 (1966), item 30; James W. Gargano, " 'The Cask of Amontillado': A Masquerade of Motive and Identity," *SSF* 4 (1967): 119–126; J. Rea, "Poe's 'The Cask of Amontillado,' " *SSF* 4 (1966): 57–69; Kathryn M. Harris, "Ironic Revenge in Poe's 'The Cask of Amontillado,' " *SSF* 6 (1969): 333–335; Herbert Reuter, "Edgar Allan Poe's 'The Man of the Crowd,' " *NS,* n.f. 11 (1962): 497–508; John E. Reilly, "The Lesser Death-Watch and 'The Tell-Tale Heart,' " *ATQ* 2 (1969): 3–9.

"THE FALL OF THE HOUSE OF USHER." Robert L. Marrs has compiled " 'The Fall of the House of Usher': A Checklist of Criticism since 1960," *Poe Studies* 5 (1972):

23–24. Several of the studies by authors cited in our text are among those collected in *Twentieth Century Interpretations of The Fall of the House of Usher,* ed. Thomas Woodson (Englewood Cliffs, N.J.: Prentice-Hall, 1969) and *Edgar Allan Poe: "The Fall of the House of Usher,"* ed. Eric W. Carlson (Columbus, Ohio: Merrill, 1971). Also see Maurice Beebe, "The Universe of Roderick Usher," *Personalist* 37 (1956): 147–160; Herbert F. Smith, "Usher's Madness and Poe's Organicism: A Source," *AL* 39 (1967): 379–389; Thomas Ollive Mabbott, "Poe's 'The Fall of the House of Usher,' " *Expl* 15 (1956), item 7; J. O. Bailey, "What Happens in 'The Fall of the House of Usher'?" *AL* 35 (1964): 445–466.

STUDIES OF POE'S INFLUENCE AND IMAGE. T. S. Eliot, "From Poe to Valéry," *HudR* 2 (1949): 327–342, which denies Poe intellectual maturity but admits his influence on French poets; Celestin P. Cambiare, *The Influence of Edgar Allan Poe in France* (New York: G. E. Stechert, 1927); Patrick F. Quinn, *The French Face of Edgar Poe* (Carbondale: Southern Illinois University Press, 1957); Jean Alexander, *Affidavits of Genius: Edgar Allan Poe and the French Critics, 1847– 1924* (Port Washington, N.Y.: Kennikat, 1971); John E. Englekirk, *Edgar Allan Poe in Hispanic Literature* (New York: Instituto de las Españas, 1934); Joan D. Grossman, *Edgar Allan Poe in Russia* (Colloquium Slavicum 3; Würzburg: Jal-Verlag, 1973); Carl L. Anderson, *Poe in Northlight: The Scandinavian Response to His Life and Work* (Durham, N.C.: Duke University Press, 1973).

BIBLIOGRAPHIES. Jay B. Hubbell in *Eight American Authors* (GB), pp. 3–36, an essay covering biography, editions, bibliography, and criticism; J. Lasley Dameron and Irby B. Cauthen, Jr., *Edgar Allan Poe: A Bibliography of Criticism, 1827– 1967* (Charlottesville: University Press of Virginia, 1974).

Supplements are published periodically in *Poe Studies*. Also see the bibliographies in Broussard, *The Measure of Poe* (above), Braddy, *Three-Dimensional Poe* (above), and J. Albert Robbins, *Checklist of Edgar Allan Poe* (Columbus, Ohio: Merrill, 1969).

OTHER TOOLS. Burton R. Pollin has compiled a *Dictionary of Names and Titles in Poe's Collected Works* (New York: Da Capo, 1968) and a list of Poe's neologisms: *Poe, Creator of Words* (Baltimore: Edgar Allan Poe Society, 1974). *Plots and Characters in the Fiction and Poetry of Edgar Allan Poe* (Hamden, Conn.: Archon, 1970), by Robert L. Gale, provides helpful summaries.

Herman Melville

TEXTS. There are three editions of Melville's work, the most nearly complete being *The Works of Herman Melville,* 16 vols. (New York: Atheneum, Russell & Russell, 1963). Two useful editions of *Moby-Dick* are edited by Charles Feidelson (Indianapolis: Bobbs-Merrill, 1964) and Hayford and Parker (New York: Norton, 1967). The preferred text of *Billy Budd* is the genetic text edited from manuscript by Hayford and M. Sealts (Chicago: University of Chicago Press, 1962). M. R. Davis and W. H. Gilman have edited *The Letters of Herman Melville* (New Haven: Yale University Press, 1960).

BIOGRAPHY. Two books that complement each other are Jay Leyda, *The Melville Log* (New York: Harcourt, 1951), which is purely factual, and Leon Howard, *Herman Melville* (Berkeley: University of California Press, 1951), which is interpretive. Other biographical studies include Newton Arvin, *Herman Melville* (New York: Viking, 1950); Raymond Weaver, *Herman Melville: Mariner and Mystic* (1921; reprint ed., New York: Pageant, 1961); Lewis Mumford, *Herman Melville: A Study of His Life and Vision* (New York: Harcourt, 1929); Eleanor Melville Metcalf, *Herman Melville: Cycle and Epicycle* (Cambridge, Mass.: Harvard University Press, 1953); C. R. Anderson, *Melville in the South Seas* (New York: Columbia University Press, 1939, 1966); W. H. Gilman, *Melville's Early Life and Redburn* (New York: New York University Press, 1951); and M. M. Sealts, *Melville as Lecturer* (Folcroft, Pa.: Folcroft, 1970).

STUDIES. Useful introductions are Leon Howard, *Herman Melville* (UMPAW: 1962) and Tyrus Hillway, *Herman Melville* (TUSAS: 1963). Criticism of Melville's work is enormous. Deserving special mention are F. O. Matthiessen's treatment in *American Renaissance* (GB); Richard Chase, *Herman Melville: A Critical Study* (New York: Macmillan, 1949); Lawrance Thompson, *Melville's Quarrel with God* (Princeton: Princeton University Press, 1952); M. R. Stern, *The Fine Hammered Steel of Herman Melville* (Urbana: University of Illinois Press, 1959); and James E. Miller, *A Reader's Guide to Herman Melville* (New York: Farrar, Straus, 1962). Other full-length studies of varying critical emphasis include G. W. Allen, *Melville and his World* (New York: Viking, 1971); James Baird, *Ishmael* (Baltimore: Johns Hopkins Press, 1956); Warner Berthoff, *The Example of Melville* (New York: Norton, 1962); Merlin Bowen, *The Long Encounter: Self and Experience in the Writings of Herman Melville* (Chicago: University of Chicago Press, 1960); William Braswell, *Melville's Religious Thought* (New York: Pageant, 1959); A. C. Bredahl, *Melville's Angles of Vision* (Gainesville: University of Florida Press, 1972); Paul Brodtkorb, *Ishmael's White World* (New Haven: Yale University Press, 1965); R. B. Browne, *Melville's Drive to Humanism* (West Lafayette, Ind.: Purdue University Studies, 1971); Nicholas Canaday, *Melville and Authority* (Gainesville: University of Florida Press, 1968); M. R. Davis, *Melville's Mardi: A Chartless Voyage* (New Haven: Yale University Press, 1952); Wm. B. Dillingham, *An Artist in the Rigging: The Early Work of Herman Melville* (Athens: University of Georgia Press, 1972); Dorothea Finkelstein, *Melville's Orienda* (New Haven: Yale University Press, 1961); H. B. Franklin, *The Wake of the Gods* (Stanford, Calif.: Stanford University Press, 1963); Stanley Geist, *Herman Melville: The Tragic Vision and the Heroic Ideal* (New York: Octagon, 1966); W. S. Gleim, *The Meaning of Moby-Dick* (New York: Atheneum, Russell & Russell, 1962); H. W. Hetherington, *Melville's Reviewers, British and American, 1846–1891* (Chapel Hill: University of North Carolina Press, 1961); C. L. R. James, *Mariners, Renegades and Castaways* (New York: James, 1953); Vincent S. Kenny, *Herman Melville's Clarel: A Spiritual Autobiography* (Hamden, Conn.: Archon, 1973); J. G. Knapp, *Tortured Synthesis: The Meaning of Melville's Clarel* (New York: Philosophical Library, 1971); Aaron Kramer, *Melville's Poetry: Toward the Enlarged Heart* (Cranbury, N.J.: Fairleigh Dickinson University Press, 1972); Kuhlman (GB); H. B. Kulkarni, *Moby-Dick, A Hindu Avatar: A Study of Hindu Myth and Thought in Moby-Dick* (Logan: Utah State University Press, 1970); Alan Lebowitz, *Progress into Silence: A Study of Melville's Heroes* (Bloomington: Indiana University Press, 1970); Ronald Mason, *The Spirit Above the Dust* (Mamaroneck, N.Y.: Appel, 1972); Rollo May, *Power and Innocence: A*

Search for the Sources of Violence (New York: Norton, 1972); Mills (GB);
Charles Olson, *Call Me Ishmael* (New York: Grove, 1947); M. O. Percival, *A
Reading of Moby-Dick* (New York: Octagon, 1967); M. L. Pops, *The Melville
Archetype* (Kent, Ohio: Kent State University Press, 1970); E. H. Rosenberry,
Melville and the Comic Spirit (New York: Octagon, 1969); W. E. Sedgwick,
Herman Melville: The Tragedy of Mind (New York: Atheneum, Russell &
Russell, 1972); John Seelye, *Melville: The Ironic Diagram* (Evanston, Ill.:
Northwestern University Press, 1970); L. F. Seltzer, *The Vision of Melville and
Conrad: A Comparative Study* (Athens: Ohio University Press, 1970); Wm. H.
Shurr, *The Mystery of Iniquity: Melville as Poet, 1857–1891* (Lexington:
University Press of Kentucky, 1972); Wm. B. Stein, *The Poetry of Melville's
Later Years* (Albany: State University of New York Press, 1970); H. P. Vincent,
The Trying-Out of Moby-Dick (Carbondale: Southern Illinois University Press,
1965) and *The Tailoring of Melville's White-Jacket* (Evanston, Ill.: Northwestern
University Press, 1970); Kingsley Widmer, *The Ways of Nihilism: A Study of
Herman Melville's Short Novels* (Pasadena, Calif.: Ward Ritchie, 1970); Na-
thalia Wright, *Melville's Use of the Bible* (Durham, N.C.: Duke University
Press, 1949); and Robert Zoellner, *The Salt-Sea Mastodon: A Reading of Moby-
Dick* (Berkeley: University of California Press, 1973).

COLLECTIONS OF SHORT CRITICISM. General collections are *Melville,* ed. R. Chase
(TCV, Englewood Cliffs, N.J.: Prentice-Hall, 1962) and *The Recognition of
Herman Melville,* ed. H. Parker (Ann Arbor: University of Michigan Press,
1967). Specialized collections dealing with individual works include *Moby-Dick
Centennial Essays,* eds. T. Hillway and L. S. Mansfield (Dallas: Southern
Methodist University Press, 1953); *Discussions of Moby-Dick,* ed. M. R. Stern
(Lexington, Mass.: Heath, 1960); *The Merrill Studies in Moby-Dick,* ed. H. P.
Vincent (Columbus, Ohio: Merrill, 1969); *Moby-Dick as Doubloon: Essays and
Abstracts, 1851–1970,* eds. H. Parker and H. Hayford (New York: Norton,
1970); *The Merrill Studies in Pierre,* ed. Ralph Willett (Columbus, Ohio: Merrill,
1971); *A Benito Cereno Handbook,* ed. S. L. Gross (Belmont, Calif.:
Wadsworth, 1965); *Melville's Benito Cereno, A Text for Guided Research,* ed. J.
P. Runden (Lexington, Mass.: Heath, 1965); *Melville Annual 1965, A Sympo-
sium: Bartleby the Scrivener,* ed. H. P. Vincent (Kent, Ohio: Kent State
University Press, 1966); *Bartleby the Scrivener: A Casebook,* ed. Stanley Schatt
(Dubuque, Iowa: Kendall/Hunt, 1972); *Billy Budd and the Critics,* comp. Wm. T.
Stafford (Belmont, Calif.: Wadsworth, 1968); *The Merrill Studies in Billy Budd,*
comp. H. S. Springer (Columbus, Ohio: Merrill, 1970); and *Twentieth Century
Views of Billy Budd,* ed. H. P. Vincent (Englewood Cliffs, N.J.: Prentice-Hall,
1971).

BIBLIOGRAPHY. Nathalia Wright in *Eight American Authors* (GB), pp. 173–224, a bib-
liographical essay on the scholarship through 1969; Theodore L. Gross and
Stanley Wertheim, *Hawthorne, Melville, Stephen Crane: A Critical Bibliography*
(New York: Free Press, 1971); J. K. Bowen and R. Van Der Beets, *A Critical
Guide to Herman Melville: Abstracts of Forty Years of Criticism* (Glenview, Ill.:
Scott, Foresman, 1971); H. P. Vincent, *The Merrill Checklist of Herman Melville*
(Columbus, Ohio: Merrill, 1969).

Robert L. Gale's *Plots and Characters in the Fiction and Narrative Poetry of
Herman Melville* (Hamden, Conn.: Archon, 1969) offers useful summaries.

12: NEW ENGLAND POETS

Henry Wadsworth Longfellow

TEXTS. *The Works of Henry Wadsworth Longfellow*, 14 vols. (Standard Lib. Ed., Boston: Houghton Mifflin, 1891), one of several sets issued by Houghton Mifflin; *The Complete Poetical Works*, ed. Horace E. Scudder (Cambridge Ed., Boston: Houghton Mifflin, 1893); *Henry Wadsworth Longfellow: Representative Selections, with Introduction, Bibliography, and Notes by Odell Shepard* (AWS, New York: American Book, 1934).

BIOGRAPHIES AND LETTERS. Samuel Longfellow, *The Life of Henry Wadsworth Longfellow*, 2 vols. (Boston: Ticknor, 1886), plus a third volume, *Final Memorials* (Boston: Ticknor, 1887); *Letters of Henry Wadsworth Longfellow*, ed. Andrew Hilen (Cambridge, Mass.: Harvard University Press, 1966–), a definitive multivolume collection; Edward Wagenknecht, *Longfellow: A Full-Length Portrait* (New York: Longmans, Green, 1955), shortened into *Henry Wadsworth Longfellow: Portrait of an American Humanist* (New York: Oxford University Press, 1966).

STUDIES. Newton Arvin, *Longfellow: His Life and Work* (Boston: Little, Brown, 1963), authoritative; Edward Hirsh, *Henry Wadsworth Longfellow* (UMPAW: 1964), listing the essentials of Longfellow's poems on pp. 19–33; Howard Nemerov, *Poetry and Fiction: Essays* (New Brunswick, N.J.: Rutgers University Press, 1963), pp. 143–158; Arms (GB), pp. 204–222; Cecil B. Williams, *Henry Wadsworth Longfellow* (TUSAS: 1964); Richard Ruland, "Longfellow and the Modern Reader," *EJ* 55 (1966): 661–668; Robert S. Ward, "Longfellow's Roots in Yankee Soil," *NEQ* 40 (1968): 180–192.

The Song of Hiawatha studies have tended to concentrate on its sources. Its departures from authentic Indian lore are analyzed in Stith Thompson, "The Indian Legend of Hiawatha," *PMLA* 37 (1922): 128–140, Christabel F. Fiske, "Mercerized Folklore," *Poet-Lore* 31 (1920): 538–575, and Rose M. Davis, "How Indian Is Hiawatha?" *Midwest Folklore* 7 (1957): 5–25. *"Hiawatha" with Its Original Indian Legends*, ed. Chase S. and Stellanova Osborn (Tempe, Ariz.: R. R. Bowker, Jaques Cattell, 1944) allows page-by-page comparison of Longfellow's complete text with the ethnographic material that inspired it. This is a shortened version of the Osborns' *Schoolcraft-Longfellow-Hiawatha* (Tempe, Ariz.: R. R. Bowker, Jaques Cattell, 1942). In *Hiawatha and Kalevala* (Folklore Fellows Communications no. 192; Helsinki: Suomalainen Tiedeakatemia, 1963), Ernest Moyne shows that Longfellow imitated the meter, parallelism, alliteration, characterization, and episodes of the Finnish epic without plagiarizing. Also see Arvin (above), pp. 154–173 for an excellent general discussion; Ernest J. Moyne, "Parodies of Longfellow's *Song of Hiawatha*," *Delaware Notes* 30 (1957): 93–108; and Cecilia Tichi, "Longfellow's Motives for the Structure of 'Hiawatha,' " *AL* 42 (1971): 548–553.

Studies of other individual poems include G. Thomas Tanselle, "Longfellow's 'Serenade' (*The Spanish Student*, I, iii, 8–31)," *Expl* 23 (1965), item 48; Charles A. Huguenin, "The Truth about the Schooner Hesperus," *NYFQ* 16 (1960): 48–53; Robert A. Durr, "Longfellow's 'The Cross of Snow,' " *Expl* 13 (1955), item 32; James M. Cox, "Longfellow and His Cross of Snow," *PMLA* 75 (1960), 97–100; The Editors, "Longfellow's 'Divina Commedia, Sonnet I,' " *Expl* 2 (1943), item 7; R. E. Amacher, "Longfellow's 'Jugurtha,' " *Expl* 6 (1948), item 29; The Editors, "Longfellow's 'Hymn to the Night,' " *Expl* 1 (1942), item 7; Nancy L. Tenfelde, "Longfellow's 'Chaucer,' " *Expl* 22 (1964), item 55; Ely Stock, "Longfellow's 'The Jewish Cemetery at Newport,' " *Rhode Island History* 20 (1961): 81–87; Irving Fitzig, "Longfellow and the Jewish Cemetery at Newport," *AH* 13 (1962): 60–63, useful for its pictures; James Taft Hatfield, "Longfellow's Lapland Song ['My Lost Youth']," *PMLA* 45 (1930): 1188–1192; George Arms, "The Revision of 'My Lost Youth,' " *MLN* 61 (1946): 389–392; M. G. Hill, "Some of Longfellow's Sources for the Second Part of *Evangeline*," *PMLA* 31 (1916): 161–180; Manning Hawthorne and Henry Wadsworth Longfellow Dana, "The Origin of Longfellow's *Evangeline*," *PBSA* 41 (1947): 165–203. *Evangeline* and "The Skeleton in Armor" are covered in Andrew R. Hilen's *Longfellow and Scandinavia* (New Haven: Yale University Press, 1947), *passim*; "A Psalm of Life" and "Hymn to the Night" in Lawrance Thompson's *Young Longfellow* (New York: Macmillan, 1938), *passim*. In his *Practical Criticism* (New York: Harcourt, 1929), pp. 156–170, I. A. Richards evaluates student opinions of "In the Churchyard at Cambridge."

Further explications are in Arvin, Arms, and Williams (above). For expert analysis of metrical features, see Allen (GB), pp. 154–192.

BIBLIOGRAPHY. Richard Dilworth Rust in *Fifteen American Authors before 1900* (GB), pp. 263–283, an essay on the scholarship; Williams (above), pp. 211–214.

John Greenleaf Whittier

TEXTS. *The Writings of John Greenleaf Whittier*, 7 vols. (Riverside Ed., Boston: Houghton Mifflin, 1888–1889) and *Complete Poetical Works*, ed. H. E. Scudder (Cambridge Ed., Boston: Houghton Mifflin, 1894) contain Whittier's own headnotes and subject groupings (e.g., "Narrative and Legendary Poems"). Also see *John Greenleaf Whittier: Representative Selections* (AWS, New York: American Book, 1935), with a long introduction, notes, and an annotated bibliography by Harry H. Clark; *Legends of New England*, introduction by John B. Pickard (Gainesville, Fla.: Scholars' Facsimiles & Reprints, 1965); *Whittier on Writers and Writing*, ed. Edwin H. Cady and H. H. Clark (Syracuse, N.Y.: Syracuse University Press, 1950); *The Supernaturalism of New England* (Norman: University of Oklahoma Press, 1969), *The Letters of John Greenleaf Whittier*, ed. John B. Pickard, 3 vols. (Cambridge, Mass.: Harvard University Press, Belknap Press, 1975).

Life and Letters of John Greenleaf Whittier, 2 vols. (Boston: Houghton Mifflin, 1894), by Samuel T. Pickard, is the authorized biography, indispensable as a primary source. Also valuable is Edward Wagenknecht, *John Greenleaf Whittier: A Portrait in Paradox* (New York: Oxford University Press, 1967), which finds in Whittier such polarities as mysticism and realism, piety and passion.

For the folkloristic in Whittier see Richard M. Dorson, *Jonathan Draws the Long Bow* (Cambridge, Mass.: Harvard University Press, 1946), pp. 204–214; Harry Oster, "Whittier's Use of the *Sage* [i.e., a folk-narrative of an extraordinary event believed to have happened] in His Ballads," a chapter in McNeir and Levy (GB), pp. 58–77; and George C. Carey, "Whittier's Roots in a Folk Culture," *EIHC* 104 (1968): 3–18.

LITERARY STUDIES. A comprehensive treatment of Whittier's writings is John B. Pickard, *John Greenleaf Whittier* (AACS, New York: Barnes & Noble, 1961), with chapters on the prose, the ballads, genre poems, and religious lyrics. Pickard also wrote "Whittier's Ballads: The Maturing of an Artist," *EIHC* 96 (1960): 56–72. Other modern evaluations are in Lewis Leary, *John Greenleaf Whittier* (TUSAS: 1961); Arms (GB), pp. 33–47; Robert Penn Warren, *John Greenleaf Whittier's Poetry: An Appraisal and a Selection* (Minneapolis: University of Minnesota Press, 1971), pp. 3–61; Allen (GB), pp. 127–150; James Stacy Stevens, *Whittier's Use of the Bible* (Orono: University of Maine Press, 1930); Kathryn A. McEuen, "Whittier's Rhymes," *AS* 20 (1945): 51–57. Studies by various authors also appear in *ESQ* 50 (1968): 1–167, a special Whittier issue.

ANALYSES OF INDIVIDUAL POEMS. Jules Zanger, "A Note on Skipper Ireson's Ride," *NEQ* 29 (1956): 236–238; Ives (GB), pp. 155–156 (for "Skipper Ireson's Ride"); W. R. Kime, "Whittier's 'Ichabod,' " *Expl* 28 (1970), item 59; Notley S. Maddox, "Whittier's 'Ichabod,' " *Expl* 18 (1960), item 38.

Snow-Bound is explicated at length in Leary (above), pp. 157–165; Waggoner (GB), pp. 76–83; Arms (GB), pp. 44–47; Pickard (1961), pp. 90–99; John B. Pickard, "Imagistic and Structural Unity in 'Snow-Bound,' " *CE* 21 (1960): 338–343; Winfield T. Scott, *Exiles and Fabrications* (New York: Doubleday, 1961), pp. 25–39; Sidney Poger, " 'Snow-Bound' and Social Responsibility," *ATQ* 1 (1969): 85–87; Donald A. Ringe, "Sound Imagery in Whittier's *Snow-Bound*," *PLL* 5 (1969): 139–144.

BIBLIOGRAPHY. Karl Keller in *Fifteen American Authors before 1900* (GB), pp. 357–386, an essay on the scholarship, Thomas F. Currier, *Bibliography of John Greenleaf Whittier* (Cambridge, Mass.: Harvard University Press, 1937); Wagenknecht (above), pp. 241–249; Pickard (1961), pp. 135–137; Leary (above), pp. 180–184. The *Whittier Newsletter* contains a continuing bibliography.

James Russell Lowell

TEXTS. *The Writings of James Russell Lowell*, 12 vols. (Riverside Ed., Boston: Houghton Mifflin, 1890–1892); *Letters of James Russell Lowell*, ed. Charles Eliot Norton, 2 vols. (New York: Harper, 1894) 3 vols. (Boston: Houghton Mifflin, 1904); *The Complete Poetical Works of James Russell Lowell*, ed. Horace E. Scudder (Cambridge Ed., Boston: Houghton Mifflin, 1897); *James Russell Lowell: Representative Selections, with Introduction, Bibliography, and Notes* by Harry Hayden Clark and Norman Foerster (AWS, New York: American Book, 1947); *The Scholar-Friends: Letters of Francis James Child and James Russell Lowell*, ed. M. A. DeWolfe Howe and G. W. Cottrell, Jr. (Cambridge, Mass.: Harvard University Press, 1952); *Browning to His American Friends: Letters between the Brownings, the Storys and James Russell Lowell, 1841–1890*, ed. Gertrude R. Hudson (New York: Barnes & Noble [1965]); *Literary Criticism of James Russell Lowell*, ed. Herbert F. Smith (Lincoln: University of Nebraska Press, 1969).

BIOGRAPHY. Horace E. Scudder, *James Russell Lowell: A Biography*, 2 vols. (Boston: Houghton Mifflin, 1901); Ferris Greenslet, *James Russell Lowell: His Life and Work* (Boston: Houghton Mifflin, 1905); Martin Duberman, *James Russell Lowell* (Boston: Houghton Mifflin, 1966); Edward Wagenknecht, *James*

Russell Lowell: Portrait of a Many-Sided Man (New York: Oxford University Press, 1971).

Studies of Lowell as a writer include Arms (GB), pp. 123–143 and Leon Howard, *Victorian Knight-Errant: A Study of the Early Literary Career of James Russell Lowell* (Berkeley: University of California Press, 1952).

LOWELL'S SOCIAL AND LITERARY CRITICISM. Brownell (GB), pp. 271–335; Joseph J. Reilly, *James Russell Lowell as a Critic* (New York: Putnam, 1915); Foerster, *American Criticism*, pp. 111–156; DeMille (GB), pp. 49–85; Pritchard (GB: 1956), pp. 126–140.

A Fable for Critics. Howard, pp. 260–268, a genetic treatment, tracing the poem's origin to Lowell's dissatisfaction with Margaret Fuller, should be supplemented with E. J. Nichols, "Identification of Characters in Lowell's *A Fable for Critics,*" *AL* 4 (1932): 191–194, and Heyward Ehrlich, "Charles Frederick Briggs and Lowell's *Fable for Critics,*" *MLQ* 28 (1967): 329–341.

LOWELL'S THEORIES AND USE OF THE LANGUAGE. Russell Nye, "Lowell and American Speech," *PQ* 17 (1939): 249–256; Jayne Crane Harder, "James Russell Lowell: Linguistic Patriot," *AS* 29 (1954): 181–186; Kathryn Anderson McEuen's survey of "Lowell's Puns," *AS* 22 (1947): 24–33. Also see *The Biglow Papers* (below).

The Biglow Papers. In *DA* 19 (1958): 1373–1374 James Walker Downer compares "Features of New England Rustic Pronunciation in James Russell Lowell's *Biglow Papers*" with today's rustic speech and concludes that Lowell was generally accurate. Cf. Krapp (GB), 1:230–236. Other studies include Blair (GB: 1942), pp. 77–101; Tandy (GB), pp. 43–64; Arthur Voss, "Backgrounds of Lowell's Satire in 'The Biglow Papers,' " *NEQ* 23 (1950): 47–64; Arthur W. M. Voss, "The Evolution of Lowell's 'The Courtin',' " *AL* 15 (1943): 42–50; John C. Broderick, "Lowell's 'Sunthin' in the Pastoral Line,' " *AL* 31 (1959): 163–172, proof of unity in a poem that has been considered loosely structured.

HARVARD COMMEMORATION ODE. Sydney Mendel, "A Note on Lowell's 'Ode Recited at the Harvard Commemoration,' " *NEQ* 35 (1962): 102–103; Clark and Foerster (above), pp. 484–485; Arms (GB), pp. 138–140; H. V. Bail, "James Russell Lowell's (Commemoration) Ode," *PBSA* 37 (1943): 169–202.

OTHER POEMS. Richard E. Amacher, "Lowell's 'Auspex,' " *Expl* 9 (1951), item 37; John Q. Anderson, "Lowell's 'The Washers of the Shroud' and the Celtic Legend of the Washer of the Ford," *AL* 35 (1963): 361–363.

BIBLIOGRAPHY. Robert A. Rees in *Fifteen American Authors before 1900* (GB), pp. 285–305, an essay on the scholarship; Clark and Foerster (above), pp. cxliii–clxvi; George W. Cooke, *Bibliography of James Russell Lowell* (Boston: Houghton Mifflin, 1906).

13: HUMORISTS, WITS, AND INFORMAL ESSAYISTS
Down East Humor

TEXTS. Blair (GB:1937, 1960).

STUDIES. See Richard Dorson's *Jonathan Draws the Long Bow* (Cambridge, Mass.: Harvard University Press, 1946) and the following items from the General Bibliography: Blair (1937), pp. 38–62; Tandy, chaps. 1 and 2.

BIBLIOGRAPHY. Blair (GB:1937), pp. 175–196.

Humor of the Old Southwest

TEXTS. *With the Bark On: Popular Humor of the Old South,* ed. John Q. Anderson (Nashville, Tenn.: Vanderbilt University Press, 1967); *Ring-Tailed Roarers: Tall Tales of the American Frontier, 1830–60,* ed. V. L. O. Chittick (Caldwell, Idaho: Caxton, 1946); *Humor of the Old Southwest,* eds. Hennig Cohen and William B. Dillingham (Boston: Houghton Mifflin, 1964); *Humor of the Old Deep South,* ed. Arthur P. Hudson (New York: Macmillan, 1936); *Tall Tales of the Southwest,* ed. Franklin J. Meine (New York: Knopf, 1930).

STUDIES. John Q. Anderson, "Scholarship in Southwestern Humor—Past and Present," *MissQ* 17 (1964): 67–86; James Atkins Shackford, *David Crockett: The Man and the Legend* (Chapel Hill: University of North Carolina Press, 1956), on a frontiersman often grouped with the Southwestern humorists; Norris W. Yates, *William T. Porter and the "Spirit of the Times"* (Baton Rouge: Louisiana State University Press, 1957), on the humorists' favorite magazine and editor; James H. Penrod, "Two Types of Incongruity in Old Southwestern Humor," *KFR* 4 (1958): 163–173. Also see the introductions to the anthologies above and these items from the General Bibliography: Bier, chap. 2; Blair (1937), pp. 62–101; Blair (1962), chaps. 2 ("Davy Crockett") and 5 ("Horse Sense, Southern Style"); McIlwaine, chap. 2; Rubin (1973), pp. 105–116; Tandy, chap. 4.

BIBLIOGRAPHY. Cohen and Dillingham (under "Texts"), pp. 411–420; Hubbell (GB); Rubin, ed. (GB:1969); Blair (GB:1937), pp. 175–196.

Miscellaneous Humor

STUDIES. Bier, chap. 1 ("Early American Humor"); Blair (1937), pp. 3–16 ("The Requisites for 'American Humor' "), pp. 17–37 ("Beginnings"); Dorson (1959), chap. 2 ("The Rise of Native Folk Humor"); D. Hoffman, chap. 3 ("The American Hero: His Masquerade"); Ives; Parrington, *The Romantic Revolution,* bk. 1, pt. 3 ("The Frontier in Letters"); Rourke, chaps. 1 and 2; Harold W. Thompson in *LHUS,* chap. 44 ("Humor"); Rubin (1973).

BIBLIOGRAPHY. Blair (GB:1937), pp. 175–196, for individual authors; Blair (GB:1960), pp. 183–196, for almanacs, periods, schools, and other topics.

Seba Smith

STUDIES. Mary Alice Wyman, *Two American Pioneers: Seba Smith and Elizabeth Oakes Smith* (New York: Columbia University Press, 1927) is a full-length treatment of Smith and his wife. Two detailed chapters deal with the Downing letters, original and spurious. Chap. 3 of Blair (GB:1962) concludes that Smith lost as an artist but gained as a satirist by imitating his own imitator, Charles Augustus Davis. Smith and Davis are said to have started the tradition of journalistic needling in Henry L. Smith's "The Two Major Downings: Rivalry in Political Satire," *JQ* 41 (1964): 74–78, 127. Also see Alan R. Miller, "America's First Political Satirist: Seba Smith of Maine," *JQ* 47 (1970): 488–492. Smith's ballad of the flimsily dressed girl frozen to death while en route to a ball has entered the stream of oral tradition under the names "Young Charlotte" and "Fair Charlotte." See G. Malcolm Laws, Jr., *Native American Balladry,* Publ. of the Amer. Folklore Soc., Bibliographical and Special Ser. 1 rev., 1964, p. 221.

BIBLIOGRAPHY. Wyman, pp. 233–242, and Blair (GB:1937), p. 93.

Augustus Baldwin Longstreet

Georgia Scenes has been reprinted with an introduction by B. R. McElderry, Jr. (1957; reprinted ed., Gloucester, Mass.: Peter Smith, 1970).

STUDIES. The standard biography is John Donald Wade, *Augustus Baldwin Longstreet* (1924; newly edited by M. Thomas Inge, Athens: University of Georgia Press, 1969). It contains two important chapters on *Georgia Scenes* plus a list of the first printed appearance of each sketch. Also see Kenneth Silverman, "Longstreet's 'The Gander Pulling,' " *AQ* 18 (1966): 548–549; Thomas W. Ford, "Ned Brace of *Georgia Scenes,*" *SFQ* 29 (1965): 220–227.

BIBLIOGRAPHY. Hubbell (GB:1954), pp. 947–948; Blair (GB:1937), pp. 187–188; Rubin (GB:1969), pp. 241–242.

Thomas Bangs Thorpe

STUDIES. Milton Rickels, *Thomas Bangs Thorpe* (Baton Rouge: Louisiana State University Press, 1962), indispensable; Walter Blair, "The Technique of 'The Big Bear of Arkansas,' " *SWR* 28 (1943): 426–435; Katherine G. Simoneaux, "Symbolism in Thorpe's 'The Big Bear of Arkansas,' " *Arkansas Historical Quarterly* 25 (1966): 240–247, which links the killing of the bear with the destruction of the frontier by advancing civilization; J. A. Leo Lemay, "The Text, Tradition, and Themes of 'The Big Bear of Arkansas,' " *AL* (1975):321–342.

Bibliography, compiled by Rickels, is in Rubin (GB:1969), pp. 308–309.

George Washington Harris

TEXTS. *Sut Lovingood's Yarns* has been edited (with an excellent introduction, a glossary, and twenty-two pieces not in the 1867 edition) by M. Thomas Inge (New Haven: College & University Press, 1966). Inge also edited Harris's *High Times and Hard Times* (Nashville, Tenn.: Vanderbilt University Press, 1967), which makes available, in a corrected text, all of Harris's known writings not included in the 1867 collection.

The Lovingood Papers (1962–1965), an annual edited by Ben Harris McClary for The Sut Society, contains important work by and about Harris. McClary's note "On Quilts" (1965, pp. 61–62) provides background for "Mrs. Yardley's Quilting."

OTHER STUDIES. Donald Day's "The Life of George Washington Harris," *Tennessee Historical Quarterly* 6 (1947): 3–38 remains the fullest biography. An outstanding critical treatment is Milton Rickels, *George Washington Harris* (TUSAS: 1965), which analyzes Sut Lovingood as fool, the yarns as myth, and Harris as a seeker after vicarious freedom from authority. Also see James H. Penrod, "Folk Humor in *Sut Lovingood's Yarns,*" *Tennessee Folklore Society Bulletin* 16 (1950): 76–84; Elmo Howell, "Timon in Tennessee: The Moral Fervor of George Washington Harris," *GaR* 24 (1970): 311–319.

Annotated bibliographies are in Rickels, pp. 145–151, and Ben Harris McClary, "George and Sut: A Working Bibliography," *Lovingood Papers* (1962), pp. 5–9. From Rickels, pp. 145–147, one may learn the original publication date of each yarn.

Oliver Wendell Holmes

TEXTS. *The Works of Oliver Wendell Holmes,* 13 vols. (Standard Library Ed., Boston: Houghton Mifflin, 1892). The fullest collection of the poetry—*The Complete Poetical Works of Oliver Wendell Holmes* (Cambridge Ed., Boston: Houghton Mifflin, 1895)—contains helpful notes, many with Holmes's own comments. Other important one-volume anthologies are *Oliver Wendell Holmes: Representative Selections, with Introduction, Bibliography, and Notes by S. I. Hayakawa and Howard Mumford Jones* (AWS, New York: American Book, 1939) and *The Autocrat's Miscellanies,* ed. Albert Mordell (New York: Twayne, 1959), previously uncollected articles by Holmes.

The *Autocrat of the Breakfast Table* has been frequently reprinted. Some editions have an index, which serves to demonstrate the great scope of these essays. G. K. Chesterton wrote the introduction and E. H. Blakeney the notes for the Red Letter Library edition (London: Blackie, 1904). Franklin T. Baker edited *The Autocrat* for the Modern Readers' Series (New York: Macmillan, 1928). The Everyman's Library edition (London: Dent, 1960) includes an index and an introduction by Van Wyck Brooks.

BIOGRAPHIES. John T. Morse, Jr., *Life and Letters of Oliver Wendell Holmes,* 2 vols. (Boston: Houghton Mifflin, 1896) and Eleanor M. Tilton, *Amiable Autocrat* (New York: Schuman, 1947) are indispensable.

Holmes as humorist is discussed by Lewis Leary in Rubin (GB:1973), pp. 117–130.

THE POETRY. In his analysis of "The 'Lesson' in 'The Chambered Nautilus,' " *ESQ* 27 (2d Quarter, 1962): 48–50, Cecil Eby, Jr., finds ambiguities and scientific inaccuracies that must inevitably temper the more sympathetic and equally important evaluations of the poem in Arms (GB), pp. 108–110, and Waggoner (GB), pp. 53–55. Allen, pp. 207–209, suggests the possibility of symbolism in its rhythm. According to J. Stanley Mattson's "Oliver Wendell Holmes and 'The Deacon's Masterpiece': A Logical Story?" *NEQ* 41 (1968): 104–114, we must distinguish between the deacon and the parson, who symbolize respectively practicality and otherworldliness. "Contentment," another poem from *The Autocrat,* is shown by Harold H. Scudder in "The 'Contentment' of Dr. Holmes," *AL* 20 (1949): 443–446, to have derived from Matthew Green's *The Spleen.*

THE PROSE. For the novels, see *The Psychiatric Novels of Oliver Wendell Holmes: Abridgment, Introduction, and Psychiatric Annotations by Clarence P. Oberndorf* (2d ed., rev and enl.; New York: Columbia University Press, 1943); Gerstenberger and Hendrick (GB). J. S. Clark (GB), pp. 837–863, discovers in Holmes's essay style such traits as "familiarity," "whimsical paradox," and "localism"; each trait is carefully documented.

In their very enlightening section on Holmes as essayist, Hayakawa and Jones (pp. c–cxiii) stress not only the uniqueness of form in the breakfast-table books but also its suitability to Holmes's personality. For an Englishman's evaluation of Holmes's essays, see Leslie Stephen, *Studies of a Biographer* (New York: Knickerbocker, 1907), 2:149–182. Tilton, pp. 233–246, demonstrates how material in *The Autocrat* was frequently based on Holmes's lectures and on recent events in his life. Also see Miriam Rossiter Small, *Oliver Wendell Holmes* (TUSAS: 1963), pp. 89–100 and Morse (above), 1:203–224.

BIBLIOGRAPHY. Thomas Franklin Currier, *A Bibliography of Oliver Wendell Holmes,* ed. Eleanor M. Tilton (New York: New York University Press, 1953), comprehensive; Hayakawa and Jones (above), pp. cxvii-cxxix, with brief annotations; Barry Menikoff in *Fifteen American Authors before 1900* (GB), pp. 207–228, a review-essay of the scholarship.

14: WRITERS IN THE CIVIL WAR

Studies listed in the General Bibliography: Aaron, Hall, Parks, E. Wilson.

Abraham Lincoln

TEXTS. *The Collected Works of Abraham Lincoln,* eds. Roy P. Basler, Marion Dolores Pratt, Lloyd A. Dunlap, 9 vols. (New Brunswick, N.J.: Rutgers University Press, 1953) has superseded the *Complete Works of Abraham Lincoln,* ed. John G. Nicolay and John Hay, 12 vols. (New & enl. ed.; New York: Tandy, 1905).

STUDIES. In their *Lincoln the Writer* (Orono: University of Maine Studies, 2d ser., no. 76; 1962)—an indispensable full-length treatment—Herbert J. Edwards and John E. Hankins trace the development of the logical and the poetic in Lincoln's style. Also see David D. Anderson, *Abraham Lincoln* (TUSAS: 1970); Jacques Barzun, *Lincoln the Literary Genius* (Evanston, Ill.: Schori, 1960), a brief study with especially interesting comments on the "Springfield Farewell Address" (pp. 45–47); Roy P. Basler, "Abraham Lincoln's Rhetoric," *AL* 11 (1939): 167–182, a perceptive analysis of repetition, parallelism, antithesis, and figures of speech in Lincoln's work; Mildred Freburg Berry, "Abraham Lincoln: His Development in the Skills of the Platform," in Brigance (GB), pp. 828–858, well-documented; Daniel Kilham Dodge, *Abraham Lincoln, Master of Words* (New York: Appleton, 1924), concerned largely with the reactions of Lincoln's contemporaries; Wilson (GB), pp. 99–130; William W. Betts, *Lincoln and the Poets: An Anthology with a Commentary* (Pittsburgh: University of Pittsburgh Press, 1965).

BIBLIOGRAPHY. *LHUS* and supplements; Anderson (above), pp. 196–199.

Henry Timrod

TEXTS. *The Collected Poems of Henry Timrod: A Variorum Edition,* ed. Edd Winfield Parks and Aileen Wells Parks (Athens: University of Georgia Press, 1965), with an introduction and valuable notes; *Poems of Henry Timrod* (Memorial Ed., Boston: Houghton Mifflin, 1899); *The Uncollected Poems of Henry Timrod,* ed. Guy A. Cardwell, Jr. (Athens: University of Georgia Press, 1942); *The Poems of Henry Timrod: Edited, with a Sketch of the Poet's Life, by Paul H. Hayne* (New York: E. J. Hale, 1873), which went through a "New Revised Edition" also dated 1873 but containing twenty additional poems; *The Last Years of Henry Timrod, 1864–1867,* ed. Jay B. Hubbell (Durham, N.C.: Duke University Press, 1941), with letters of and about Timrod, plus uncollected poems and prose pieces; *The Essays of Henry Timrod,* ed. Edd Winfield Parks (Athens: University of Georgia Press, 1942), with an "Editor's Introduction: Timrod as Critic" (pp. 3–60).

STUDIES. Indispensable for its biography, chronology, and criticism is Edd Winfield Parks, *Henry Timrod* (TUSAS: 1964), with chapters on Timrod as an ethical critic and as a poet of love, nature, and war. See also Hubbell (GB:1954), pp. 466–474; Allen (GB), p. 303; Parks (GB), pp. 193–226; Louis D. Rubin, Jr., "Henry Timrod and the Dying of the Light," *Miss. Q.* 11 (1958): 101–111, on "Charleston."

BIBLIOGRAPHY. Parks, *Henry Timrod,* pp. 146–149; Hubbell (GB:1954), pp. 965–966.

Paul Hamilton Hayne

TEXTS. *Poems of Paul Hamilton Hayne* ("Complete Edition," New York: Lothrop, 1882), by no means complete; *A Collection of Hayne Letters,* ed. Daniel M. McKeithan (Austin: University of Texas Press, 1944).

STUDIES. Rayburn S. Moore, *Paul Hamilton Hayne* (TUSAS: 1972), the best treatment; Kate Harbes Becker, *Paul Hamilton Hayne: Life and Letters* (Belmont, N.C.: The Outline Co., 1951), adulatory and poorly documented; Hubbell (GB:1954), pp. 743–757; Allen (GB), pp. 303–304; Parks (GB), pp. 227–259; L. Moody Simms, Jr., "Paul Hamilton Hayne's Methods of Poetic Composition," *MissQ* 24 (1971): 57–62.

BIBLIOGRAPHY. Hubbell (GB:1954), pp. 935–937; Moore (above); Rubin (GB), pp. 215–217.

Sidney Lanier

TEXTS. *The Centennial Edition of the Works of Sidney Lanier,* general ed. Charles R. Anderson, 10 vols. (Baltimore: Johns Hopkins Press, 1945), with helpful introductions and notes, plus an index that includes such subject entries as logaoedic dactyl, etherealization, opposition, phonetic syzygy; *Tiger-Lilies: A Novel,* introduction by Richard Harwell (Chapel Hill: University of North Carolina Press, 1969).

Philip Graham and Joseph Jones have compiled *A Concordance to the Poems of Sidney Lanier* (Austin: University of Texas Press, 1939).

STUDIES (BIOGRAPHICAL AND CRITICAL). Aubrey Harrison Starke's *Sidney Lanier* (1933; reprint ed., New York: Atheneum, Russell & Russell, 1964), the standard critical biography, should be consulted for individual poems. In his *Sidney Lanier: The Man, the Poet, the Critic* (Athens: University of Georgia Press, 1968), a good introduction, Edd Winfield Parks portrays Lanier as a remarkably active consumptive whose poetic practice did more than his critical theories "to loosen up the technique of English versification" (p. 103). Also see Jack De Bellis, *Sidney Lanier* (TUSAS: 1972); Philip Graham, "Sidney Lanier and the Pattern of Contrast," *AQ* 11 (1959): 503–508; Harry R. Warfel, "Mystic Vision in 'The Marshes of Glynn,' " *MissQ* 19 (1965–1966): 34–40; Robert H. Ross, " 'The Marshes of Glynn': A Study in Symbolic Obscurity," *AL* 32 (1961): 403–416; Owen J. Reamer, "Lanier's 'The Marshes of Glynn' Revisited," *MissQ* 23 (1970): 57–63; and (from the General Bibliography) Foerster (1923), pp. 221–237; Hubbell (1954), pp. 758–777; H. H. Clark (1936), pp. 907–913 (notes); E. Wilson, pp. 450–466; Allen, pp. 277–301 (for Lanier's prosodic theory and practice).

BIBLIOGRAPHY. C. H. Edwards, Jr., "Bibliography of Sidney Lanier: 1942–1973," *BB* 31 (1974): 29–31; Starke (above), pp. 455–473.

15: WALT WHITMAN

TEXTS. *The Collected Writings of Walt Whitman,* ed. Gay W. Allen and Sculley Bradley (New York: New York University Press, 1961–), a multivolume set of the prose, poetry, and correspondence, is definitive. One of its volumes—*Leaves of Grass: Comprehensive Reader's Edition,* edited with useful notes by Harold W. Blodgett and Sculley Bradley (1965; reprint ed., New York: Norton, 1968)— contains the various prefaces and all but the earliest poetry. *Walt Whitman's Poems* (1955; reprint ed., New York: Grove, 1959) is an anthology with a fifty-one-page introduction and excellent "Critical Aids" by Gay W. Allen and Charles T. Davis. Also see *Walt Whitman's Blue Book,* with textual analysis by Arthur Golden, 2 vols. (New York: New York Public Library, 1968), which reproduces Whitman's manuscript revisions in multicolor.

BIOGRAPHIES. Gay W. Allen, *The Solitary Singer: A Critical Biography of Walt Whitman* (New York: Macmillan, 1955), the standard life, indispensable as background for the poetry; Roger Asselineau, *The Evolution of Walt Whitman: The Creation of a Personality* (Cambridge, Mass.: Harvard University Press, 1960); Henry S. Canby, *Walt Whitman, an American: A Study in Biography* (Boston: Houghton Mifflin, 1943); Emory Holloway, *Whitman: An Interpretation in Narrative* (1926; new ed., New York: Biblo & Tannen, 1969); Bliss Perry, *Walt Whitman: His Life and Work* (Boston: Houghton Mifflin, 1906); Joseph Jay Rubin, *The Historic Whitman* (University Park: Pennsylvania State University Press, 1973), on Whitman's career in journalism up to 1855.

STUDIES (BOOKS). Gay W. Allen, *Walt Whitman Handbook* (Chicago: Packard, 1946), invaluable for Whitman's thought, technique, and place in world literature; Gay W. Allen, *Walt Whitman as Man, Poet, and Legend* (Carbondale: Southern Illinois University Press, 1961); Gay W. Allen, *Walt Whitman* (rev., Detroit: Wayne State University Press, 1969); Gay W. Allen, *A Reader's Guide to Walt Whitman* (New York: Farrar, Straus & Giroux, 1970); Gay W. Allen, *New Walt Whitman Handbook* (New York: New York University Press, 1976); Roger Asselineau, *The Evolution of Walt Whitman: The Creation of a Book* (Cambridge, Mass.: Harvard University Press, 1962), indispensable for the growth of Whitman's thought and art, with chapters on themes, style, language, and prosody; Newton Arvin, *Whitman* (1938; reprint ed., New York: Atheneum, Russell & Russell, 1969); Joseph Beaver, *Walt Whitman, Poet of Science* (New York: King's Crown, 1951); Berbrich (GB), pp. 111–196; Harold Blodgett, *Walt Whitman in England* (Ithaca, N.Y.: Cornell University Press, 1934), on Whitman's reputation; Thomas L. Brasher, *Whitman as Editor of the "Brooklyn Daily Eagle"* (Detroit: Wayne State University Press, 1970); E. Fred Carlisle, *The Uncertain Self: Whitman's Drama of Identity* (East Lansing: Michigan State University Press, 1973); V. K. Chari, *Walt Whitman in the Light of Vedantic Mysticism* (Lincoln: University of Nebraska Press, 1964); Richard V. Chase, *Walt Whitman Reconsidered* (London: Gollancz, 1955); Thomas E. Crawley, *The Structure of "Leaves of Grass"* (Austin: University of Texas Press, 1970); Geoffrey Dutton, *Whitman* (New York: Grove, 1961); Robert D. Faner, *Whitman & Opera* (Philadelphia: University of Pennsylvania Press, 1951); Maurice O. Johnson, *Walt Whitman as a Critic of Literature* (Studies in Language, Literature, and Criticism 16, Lincoln: University of Nebraska Press,

1938), 73 pp.; Barbara Marinacci, *O Wondrous Singer! An Introduction to Walt Whitman* (New York: Dodd, Mead, 1970); Charles R. Metzger, *Thoreau and Whitman: A Study of Their Esthetics* (Seattle: University of Washington Press, 1961); Edwin H. Miller, *Walt Whitman's Poetry: A Psychological Journey* (New York: New York University Press, 1969), containing many explications; James E. Miller, Jr., *A Critical Guide to Leaves of Grass* (Chicago: University of Chicago Press, 1957), a valuable interpretation; James E. Miller, Jr., *Walt Whitman* (TUSAS: 1962); James E. Miller, Jr., Karl Shapiro, and Bernice Slote, *Start with the Sun: Studies in Cosmic Poetry* (Lincoln: University of Nebraska Press, 1960), on the Whitman tradition among twentieth-century writers; S. Musgrove, *T. S. Eliot and Walt Whitman* (Wellington: New Zealand University Press, 1952); T. R. Rajasekharaiah, *The Roots of Whitman's Grass* (Cranbury, N.J.: Fairleigh Dickinson University Press, 1970); Frederik Schyberg, *Walt Whitman*, trans. from the Danish by Evie A. Allen (New York: Columbia University Press, 1951), valuable for its edition-by-edition analysis of *Leaves*; Jan Christian Smuts, *Walt Whitman: A Study in the Evolution of Personality*, ed. Alan L. McLeod (Detroit: Wayne State University Press, 1973); Floyd Stovall, *The Foreground of "Leaves of Grass"* (Charlottesville: University Press of Virginia, 1974); Howard J. Waskow, *Whitman: Explorations in Form* (Chicago: University of Chicago Press, 1966); Charles B. Willard, *Whitman's American Fame: The Growth of His Reputation in America after 1892* (Providence, R.I.: Brown University Press, 1950).

SHORTER STUDIES. Sculley Bradley, "The Fundamental Metrical Principle in Whitman's Poetry," *AL* 10 (1939): 437–459; E. F. Carlisle, "Walt Whitman: The Drama of Identity," *Criticism* 10 (1968): 259–276; Richard Chase, *Walt Whitman* (UMPAW: 1961); E. H. Eby, "Walt Whitman's 'Indirections,' " *WWR* 12 (1966): 5–16; C. Carroll Hollis, "Whitman and the American Idiom," *QJS* 43 (1957): 408–420; idem, "Names in *Leaves of Grass*," *Names* 5 (1957): 129–156; Edward Hungerford, "Walt Whitman and His Chart of Bumps," *AL* 2 (1931): 350–384, on his use of phrenology; Randall Jarrell, "Some Lines from Whitman," *Poetry and the Age* (New York: Knopf, 1953), pp. 112–132; James McNally, "Varieties of Alliteration in Whitman," *WWR* 13 (1967): 28–32; Alfred H. Marks, "Whitman's Triadic Imagery," *AL* 23 (1951): 99–126; Matthiessen, (GB), chap. 13; Roger Mitchell, "A Prosody for Whitman?" *PMLA* 84 (1969): 1606–1612; Peltola (GB), pp. 140–160; Georgiana Pollak, "The Relationship of Music to 'Leaves of Grass,' " *CE* 15 (1954): 384–394; Lawrence Templin, "The Quaker Influence on Walt Whitman," *AL* 42 (1970): 165–180; Lois Ware, "Poetic Conventions in *Leaves of Grass*," *SP* 26 (1929): 47–57.

COLLECTIONS OF CRITICISM. John C. Broderick has edited *Whitman the Poet* (Belmont, Calif.: Wadsworth, 1962), a very useful anthology of primary and secondary sources arranged under such topics as persona, prosody, style, and language. Also see *Walt Whitman Abroad*, ed. Gay W. Allen (Syracuse, N.Y.: Syracuse University Press, 1955); *Leaves of Grass*, eds. Sculley Bradley and W. Harold Blodgett (New York: Norton, 1973); *The Poet and the President: Whitman's Lincoln Poems*, ed. William Coyle (New York: Odyssey, 1962); *Leaves of Grass One Hundred Years After*, ed. Milton Hindus (Stanford, Calif.: Stanford University Press, 1955); *The Presence of Walt Whitman: Selected Papers from the English Institute*, ed. R. W. B. Lewis (New York: Columbia University Press, 1962); *A Century of Whitman Criticism*, ed. Edwin H. Miller

(Bloomington: Indiana University Press, 1969); *Whitman: A Collection of Critical Essays,* ed. Roy H. Pearce (Englewood Cliffs, N.J.: Prentice-Hall, 1962).

"SONG OF MYSELF." James E. Miller, Jr., has edited Whitman's *"Song of Myself"— Origin, Growth, Meaning* (New York: Dodd, Mead, 1964), which contains an early notebook version of the poem, the 1855 and 1892 texts placed on facing pages, his own study of " 'Song of Myself' as Inverted Mystical Experience," and other studies by Carl F. Strauch, Randall Jarrell, Richard Chase, Roy Harvey Pearce, and Malcolm Cowley. Also see explications by Eric W. Carlson and T. O. Mabbott in *Expl Cyc* 2:353–355; Sydney J. Krause, "Whitman's Yawping Bird as Comic Defense," *BNYPL* 68 (1964): 347–360; Roger Seamon, "Sinners in the Hands of a Happy God: Hierarchical Values in 'Song of Myself,' " *Canadian Association for American Studies Bulletin* 2 (1967): 3–18; Michael Orth, "Walt Whitman, Metaphysical Teapot: The Structure of 'Song of Myself,' " *WWR* 14 (1968): 16–24; Robin Magowan, "The Horse of the Gods: Possession in 'Song of Myself,' " *WWR* 15 (1969): 67–76; V. Sachithanandan, "Whitman and the Serpent Power," *WWR* 16 (1970): 50–55, on Section 5; D. M. McKeithan, *Whitman's "Song of Myself" 34 and Its Background* (Essays and Studies on American Language and Literature 18, Uppsala: Lundequistska, 1969).

"OUT OF THE CRADLE." Explications by S. E. Whicher, C. W. M. Johnson, and Roy P. Basler in *Expl Cyc* 2:350–352; Leo Spitzer, *"Explications de Texte* Applied to Walt Whitman's Poem 'Out of the Cradle Endlessly Rocking,' " *ELH* 16 (1949): 229–249, a full analysis; essays by Paul Fussell, Jr., R. W. B. Lewis, and Stephen Whicher in *The Presence of Walt Whitman,* ed. R. W. B. Lewis, pp. 1–71.

"WHEN LILACS LAST IN THE DOORYARD BLOOM'D." *The Poet and the President,* ed. W. Coyle (above), a full collection of background and criticism.

EXPLICATIONS OF OTHER POEMS. Dale Doepke, "Whitman's Theme in 'Cavalry Crossing a Ford,' " *WWR* 18 (1972): 132–136; Stanley K. Coffman, Jr., " 'Crossing Brooklyn Ferry' A Note on the Catalogue Technique in Whitman's Poetry," *MP* 51 (1954): 225–232; James W. Gargano, "Technique in 'Crossing Brooklyn Ferry': The Everlasting Moment," *JEGP* 62 (1963): 262–269; M. Van Doren (GB), pp. 42–45 (for "A Noiseless Patient Spider"); Wilton Eckley, "Whitman's 'A Noiseless Patient Spider," *Expl* 22 (1963), item 20; Stanley K. Coffman, Jr., "Form and Meaning in Whitman's 'Passage to India,' " *PMLA* 70 (1955): 337–349; J. E. Miller, *Critical Guide,* pp. 120–129 (for the structure of "Passage to India"); William A. Wortman, "Spiritual Progression in 'A Sight in Camp,' " *WWR* 14 (1968): 24–26; R. W. Vance, "A Reading of 'The Sleepers,' " *WWR* 18 (1972): 17–28; Michael S. Reynolds, "Whitman's Early Prose and 'The Sleepers,' " *AL* 41 (1969): 406–414; Sister Eva Mary, "Shades of Darkness in 'The Sleepers,' " *WWR* 15 (1969): 187–190; E. H. Miller (above), pp. 24–40 (for "There Was a Child Went Forth"); Harold Aspiz, "Educating the Kosmos: 'There Was a Child Went Forth,' " *AQ* 18 (1966): 655–666; G[eorge]. W. A[rms]., "Whitman's 'To a Locomotive in Winter,' " *Expl* 5 (1946), item 14; Ronald Christ, "Walt Whitman: Image and Credo," *AQ* 17 (1965): 92–102, on "To a Locomotive in Winter."

BIBLIOGRAPHIES. James T. F. Tanner, "Walt Whitman Bibliographies, 1902–1964," *BB* 25 (1968): 131–132; Evie A. Allen, "A Check List of Whitman Publications: 1945–1960," in G. W. Allen, *Walt Whitman as Man, Poet, and Legend,* pp. 177–

244; *CHAL* 2:551–581; G. W. Allen, *Twenty-Five Years of Walt Whitman Bibliography, 1918–1942* (Bulletin of Bibliography Pamphlets 38, 1943); Gay W. Allen, *Walt Whitman Handbook* (1946), annotated bibliographies at the ends of chapters; *Whitman the Poet,* ed. J. C. Broderick, pp. 171–186, fully annotated; James T. F. Tanner, *Walt Whitman: A Supplementary Bibliography, 1961–1967* (Kent, Ohio: Kent State University Press, 1968); Roger Asselineau [and Willard Thorp], "Walt Whitman," in *Eight American Authors* (GB), pp. 225–272, an excellent bibliographical essay; William White, *Walt Whitman's Journalism: A Bibliography* (Detroit: Wayne State University Press, 1969); Carolyn Wells and A. F. Goldsmith, *A Concise Bibliography of the Works of Walt Whitman* (1922; reprint ed., New York: Franklin, 1965). Important annotated bibliographies appear annually in *ALS* and quarterly in *WWR*.

A Concordance of Walt Whitman's "Leaves of Grass" and Selected Prose Writings (Seattle: University of Washington Press, 1949–1955) has been compiled by Edwin H. Eby.

Index

"Abraham Davenport," 132
Account . . . of Inoculating the Small-Pox, 24
Adams, John, 49, 50, 55
Adventures of Captain Bonneville, U. S. A., The, 77
"Adventures of the German Student, The," 79
"Advice to a Raven in Russia," 60
Advice to the Privileged Orders, 59
Afloat and Ashore, 85
"After the Death of John Brown," 100
Age of Reason, The, 48
Alcott, Amos Bronson, 92, 94, 102
Algerine Captive, The, 68, 73
Alhambra, The, 76
Allegory, 114, 116, 129–130, 150, 158; in Hawthorne, 107, 109
Allen, Ethan, 42
Alliteration, 9, 47, 90, 155, 157; function of, 38, 98
Alsop, George, 4, 183
Alsop, Richard, 54
American Democrat, The, 81–82
"American Scholar, The," 95–96
Anarchiad, The, 54, 58
"Anatomist's Hymn, The," 149
André, 72
"Annabel Lee," 114
Anticlimax, 44, 78, 141
Antiquarianism, 61, 123

"Apology, The," 96, 97
Apostrophe, 12, 59, 60, 126
Arnold, George W., 139
"Arsenal at Springfield, The," 124–126, 127
Arthur Mervyn, 71
"Artist of the Beautiful, The," 107
"Aspects of the Pines," 155
Astoria, 77
"Auspex," 137
"Author to Her Book, The," 13
"Author's Account of Himself, The," 78
Autobiography, 30, 38–40, 100, 166
Autobiography (Franklin), 45–46
Autocrat of the Breakfast Table, The, 148–149

"Bacchus," 97
"Bacons Epitaph, Made by His Man," 4
"Backward Glance o'er Travel'd Roads, A," 166
Bagatelles, 43, 45
Baldwin, Joseph Glover, 146
Ballad, 125, 126–127, 147–148; Poe, 113, 114; Whittier, 131–132
Ballads and Other Poems, 130
"Ballad of the Oysterman, The," 147–148
"Ballad of Trees and the Master, A," 159
Barker, James Nelson, 72

Barlow, Joel, 58–60, 146, 196
"Bartleby the Scrivener," 119–120
Bartram, John, 62
Bartram, William, 62
"Battle-Field, The," 90
"Battle of the Kegs, The," 54, 139
Bay Psalm Book, 11–12
"Beat Beat Drums!" 162, 164
"Beleaguered City, The," 124–126
"Bells, The," 113
Benito Cereno, 120
Bible: in the Puritan period before the
    nineteenth century, 7–21 passim, 41–
    42, 48; later use of, 131, 135, 159, 162
*Big Bear of Arkansas and Other
    Sketches, The,* 146
"Big Bear of Arkansas, The," 143–144
Biglow Papers, The, 134–135, 136
Billy Budd, 115, 117, 120–121
Biography, Mather and, 25–26
Bird, Robert Montgomery, 80
"Bivouac on a Mountain Side," 164
"Black Cat, The," 114
Blank verse, 58, 97–99, 103, 122, 125,
    132; Bryant's, 88–90
Blithedale Romance, The, 110–111
Blockade, The, 72
Bloody Tenent Yet More Bloody, The, 19
Bloudy Tenent of Persecution, The, 19
"Blown up with Soda," 145–146
Boker, George Henry, 72
Bonifacius, 26
Boy's King Arthur, The, 156
Bracebridge Hall, 76
Brackenridge, Hugh Henry, 68–69, 72,
    198–199
Bradford, William, 7–9, 20, 26, 27, 184–
    185
Bradstreet, Anne, 12–13, 185
"Brahma," 99
"Brahmin Caste of New England, The,"
    147
Bravo, The, 82
Bread and Cheese Club, 81
Briefe and True Report, A, 2
British Prison-Ship, The, 64
Brook Farm, 93, 105, 110–111
Brown, Charles Brockden, 69–71, 199
Brown, William Hill, 67, 68
Brownson, Orestes A., 92, 93
Bryant, William Cullen, 85–90, 135, 155,
    204–206
"Building of the Ship, The," 124–126

Bunyan, John, 107, 152
Burgoyne, John, 72
Burke, Edmund, 48, 59, 107
Burns, Robert, 65, 66, 130, 152
Byrd, William II, 35–38, 41, 141, 190–191
"By the Bivouac's Fitful Flame," 164

Caesura, 89, 113 n.5
"Calamus," 162, 164, 165
Carlyle, Thomas, 92, 94, 95 n.2
"Cask of Amontillado, The," 115
Cavalier writers, 20
"Cavalry Crossing a Ford," 164
"Celestial Railroad, The," 107
Cervantes, Miguel de. *See* Quixotism
Chainbearer, The, 82
"Chambered Nautilus, The," 149
Channing, William Ellery, 92
"Character of a Native Georgian, The,"
    143
*Character of the Province of MaryLand,
    A,* 4
"Charleston," 154
Charlotte Temple, 68
"Chaucer," 124–126, 129
Chesterfield, Lord, 54, 73
Chiaroscuro, 81, 105
Chiasmus, 14, 16, 44, 88
"Children of Adam," 162
"Children's Hour, The," 124–126
Christus, 124
Churches' Quarrel Espoused, The, 42
"Circles," 98
"City in the Sea, The," 113
"Civil Disobedience," 102–103
Clarel, 121–122
Clari, or the Maid of Milan, 72
Clarke, James Freeman, 92
Clarke, M'Donald, 75
Clipped meter, 65, 66, 132
Coleridge, Samuel Taylor, 87, 92, 95 n.2,
    112
"Colon & Spondee," 73
"Columbia, Columbia, to Glory Arise,"
    57
Columbiad, The, 58
Common Sense, 46–47
"Concord Hymn," 97–98
Conduct of Life, The, 95
Confidence-Man, The, 120
Connecticut Wits, 54–60
Conquest of Canaan, 57
Conquest of Granada, 76

Conspiracy of Kings, The, 58
"Contemplations," 12–13
"Contentment," 150
Contrast, The, 73–74
Cook, Ebenezer, 54
Cooper, James Fenimore, 80–85, 136, 202–204
Cooper, Judge William, 80
"Cooper Union Address," 152
Coquette, The, 68
"Corn," 157
Cotton, John, 24
Cotton, John (of Queen's Creek, Virginia), 4
"Cotton Boll, The," 154
Couplets, 53
"Courtin', The," 136
Courtship of Miles Standish, The, 124–126
Cranch, Christopher Pearse, 92
Crater, The, 82
Crèvecoeur, St. John de, 62–64, 196–197
Crisis, The, 47–48
Crockett, Davy, 143
"Cross of Snow, The," 124–126, 130
"Crossing Brooklyn Ferry," 163–164

Dactylic meter, 127, 158
Davis, Charles Augustus, 141
"Day Is Done, The," 124–126
Day of Doom, The, 13–14
"Days," 99
"Deacon's Masterpiece, The," 149–150
"Death of Lincoln, The," 90
Debate, 13, 19, 118–119
Declaration of Independence, The, 43, 47, 48–49, 153, 194
Deerslayer, The, 84–85
Deism, 42, 48, 50, 57, 92
Democracy, 19, 69, 81–82, 161–166
"Democracy," 134, 136–137
Democratic Vistas, 166
Dennie, Joseph, 62, 73
"Descent into the Maelström, A," 114
Description of New England, A, 3
Detective story, 114
Dial, The, 92, 94, 99, 103
Dialect, 35, 141–146, 156, 157; Down East, 134–136, 139–141, 150
"Dialogue between Franklin and the Gout," 43
Dickinson, Emily, 12, 97, 166
Dickinson, John, 47

Diction, 15, 97; poetic, 13, 53, 59, 60
"Divina Commedia," 124–126, 129
Divine and Supernatural Light, A, 29–30
Divinity School Address, 94, 98
"Dogood Papers," 26
"Dorothy Q.," 150
Drake, Joseph Rodman, 75
Drama, early, 72–74
Dramatic monologue, 113, 165
"Dream-Land," 113
"Drum-Taps," 162, 164
Dunlap, William, 72, 81
"Dutch Picture, A," 124–126
Dwight, Timothy, 57–58, 195–196

"Each and All," 97
"Earth," 87
Edgar Huntly, 71
Edict by the King of Prussia, An, 45
Edwards, Jonathan, 28–32, 40, 41, 57, 149–150, 189–190
"Eldorado," 113–114
Elegy, 164–165
Eliot, John, 11, 26, 27
Elsie Venner, 147
Embargo, The, 86
Emerson, Ralph Waldo, 91–93 passim, 93–99, 113, 161, 166, 206–209
"Emerson the Lecturer," 134, 136
Encantadas, The, 120
English Novel, The, 156
English Traits, 95
Enlightenment, 41–43, 48, 53–60
Envelope structure, 162
Ephemera, The, 45
Epic, 25–26, 57, 58, 83, 118, 128
Essays (Emerson), 95
"Eternal Goodness, The," 130
"Ethan Brand," 107–108
"Ethnogenesis," 153–154
Eureka, 113, 114
"Eutaw Springs," 65
Evangeline, 124–126, 127
Evans, Nathaniel, 62
"Evening Song," 158
"Evening Star, The," 124–126
"Experience" (Emerson), 96
"Experience, The" (Taylor), 17

"Fable" (Emerson), 97
Fable for Critics, A, 135–136
Faithful Narrative, A, 28
"Fall of the House of Usher, The," 114

Fanshawe, 105
"Farewell Address at Springfield,
    Illinois," 152
Fashion, 72
Federalist, The, 50–52, 194–195
Female Quixotism, 68
"Fight, The," 143
Fine arts, 97, 111, 127, 133, 143–144,
    149, 164; and Knickerbockers, 75, 79,
    81, 86, 87
"First-Day Thoughts," 130
First Inaugural Address, 50
"Flesh and the Spirit, The," 13
Flint, Timothy, 80, 141
"Flood of Years, The," 87
*Flush Times in Alabama and
    Mississippi,* 146
Folklore, 32, 101, 128–129, 130–133
    passim, 161–162; beliefs, 36, 85, 105,
    114; customs, 115, 137, 142, 158, 165
Folktales, 76, 78–79, 132, 136, 144;
    Aarne-Thompson types, 32, 78;
    motifs, 4, 25, 78; shaggy dog, 79
Foreshadowing, 143, 164
"Forest Hymn, A," 89
Forest Rose, A, 139
"For You O Democracy," 162
Foster, Hannah, 68
"Four Ages of Man, The," 12
Frame story, 143–144, 145
Francesca da Rimini, 72
Franklin, Benjamin, 26, 33, 43–46, 139,
    191–193
Freedom of the Will, 29, 31, 32, 150
Free verse, 162
Freneau, Philip, 64–66, 88, 139, 197–198
Fuller, Margaret, 92, 93, 111, 135

"Gander Pulling, The," 142
Generall Historie of Virginia, 3–4
Genres, xi–xii, 6
George Fox Digg'd out of His Burrowes,
    18
Georgia Scenes, 142–143
"Georgia Theatrics," 142–143
"Gettysburg Address, The," 152–153
"Give All to Love," 98
"Give Me the Splendid Silent Sun," 162
Gleanings in Europe, 82
Godfrey, Thomas, 72, 88
God's Determinations, 16
"Gold Bug, The," 114
Goldsmith, Oliver, 55, 58, 139

"Good-Bye," 96
Gothicism, 14, 60, 63, 65, 76, 79, 105; in
    Brown, 69–71; Cooper, 80, 83–84;
    Poe, 111–115
"Grace," 97
Graveyard poetry, 65–66, 88–90, 127
Great Awakening, 28
Greenfield Hill, 57–58
Greenough, Horatio, 81, 166
Guardian Angel, The, 147
Guide in the Wilderness, A, 80

Hafiz, 99
Hakluyt, Richard, 2
Haliburton, Thomas Chandler, 141
Halleck, Fitz-Greene, 75
"Hamatreya," 98
Hamilton, Alexander, 50–52, 86, 195
Hariot, Thomas, 2
Harris, George Washington, 144–146,
    227
Hasty Pudding, The, 58, 59–60
Hawthorne, Nathaniel, 69, 70, 104–111,
    118, 152, 212–216
"Hawthorne," 124–126
"Hawthorne and His Mosses," 117–118
Hayne, Paul Hamilton, 151, 153, 154–
    155, 230
"Haze," 103
Headsman, The, 82
Hedge, Frederick Henry, 92
Heidenmauer, The, 82
History of New York, A, 76, 77–78
History of the Dividing Line, 36–38
*History of the Navy of the United States
    of America,* 81
Hoffman, Charles Fenno, 75
Holmes, Oliver Wendell, 95 n.4, 138,
    146–150, 155, 228–229
Home as Found, 82
"Home, Sweet Home," 72, 75
Homeward Bound, 85
Hooper, Johnson Jones, 146
Hopkinson, Francis, 54, 62
"Horse Swap, The," 143
"House of Night, The," 65
House of the Seven Gables, The, 105,
    108, 110
"House-Top, The," 121–122
Hudibrastic verse, 54, 56
Humanitarianism, 38–39, 63, 154
Humor, 4, 43–45, 66, 77–79, 126, 132,
    138–139, 146–150; Down East, 133–

136, 139–141; of the Old Southwest, 141–146
Humphreys, David, 54
"Hurricane, The," 65
"Huswifery," 17
Hutchinson, Anne, 23
Hutchinson, Thomas, 7
"Hymn to the Night," 124–126
Hyperion, 124

"Ichabod," 131
"Indian Burying Ground, The," 65–66
Indian captivity narrative, 4, 6
Indian Princess, The, 72
Indians, 8, 18–21, 49, 65–66, 71, 89–90, 128–129; Cooper's, 82–85
Informal essay, 43, 62, 75, 106, 134, 138, 147–149
Inkhorn terms, 7
"Inscription for the Entrance to a Wood," 89
"Inspiration," 103
"In the Churchyard at Cambridge," 124–126
"Inward Morning, The," 103
"Irene," 113
Irony, 9, 14, 56, 114, 120, 152; verbal, 37, 44, 69, 110, 143, 150
Irving, Washington, 69, 76–79, 123, 139, 141, 200–202
"I Saw in Louisiana a Live-Oak Growing," 164
"Israfel," 113

Jack Downing, Major, 139–141
Jack Tier, 85
James, Henry, 69, 70, 109, 111
Jay, John, 50–51, 85
Jefferson, Thomas, 48–50, 78, 86, 152, 194
Jeremiad, 25–26
"Jewish Cemetery at Newport, The," 124–126, 127
Joe Strickland letters, 139
John Lothrop Motley, 147
Journal of Madam Knight, The, 33–35
Journal (Woolman), 38–40
Judd, Sylvester, 92, 93
"Jugurtha," 124–126

Kalevala, 129
Kavanagh, 124
Kennedy, John Pendleton, 80

Key into the Language of America, A, 19
"King Witlaf's Drinking Horn," 124–126
Kirkland, Caroline Matilda, 80
Knickerbocker's *History of New York*, 77–78
Knickerbockers, 75–90
Knight, Sarah Kemble, 33–35, 190

Language, 1, 161. *See also* Diction
Lanier, Sidney, 151, 155–159, 230
Last of the Mohicans, The, 83, 84
"Last Leaf, The," 148
"Laus Deo," 132
Leatherstocking Tales, 83–85
Leaves of Grass, 161, 162
Leaves from Margaret Smith's Journal, 131
"Legend of Sleepy Hollow, The," 79
Legends of New England, 130
Leggett, William, 75
"Lenore," 113
"Letter to B——," 112 n.3
Letter to His Countrymen, A, 82
"Letter to the Town of Providence, A," 19
Letters: of Franklin, 46; of Jefferson, 50
Letters from an American Farmer, 63–64
"Letters of Jonathan Oldstyle, Gent.," 76
Lewis, Henry Clay, 146
Life and Voyages of Christopher Columbus, 76
Life and Writings of Major Jack Downing, 140
Life of Washington, 77
"Ligeia," 114
Lincoln, Abraham, 86, 90, 136, 151–153, 164–165, 166, 229
Lionel Lincoln, 85
Littlepage Manuscripts, The, 82
"Living Temple, The," 149
Local color, 57, 59–60, 79, 82, 130–133, 140–145
Locke, David Ross, 152
Locke, John, 29, 42, 47, 49, 91
London Diary, The, 36
Longfellow, Henry Wadsworth, 123–130, 155, 222–223
Longstreet, Augustus Baldwin, 69, 142–143, 227
Love poetry, 13, 89, 113–114, 158

Lowell, James Russell, 133–137, 224–225

M'Fingal, 55, 56–57
Madison, James, 50–52, 194–195
Magnalia Christi Americana, 25–26, 27, 280
Mahomet and His Successors, 77
Major Jones's Courtship, 146
"Maldive Shark, The," 121
"Man of the Crowd, The," 114
Manuductio ad Ministerium, 26–27
Marble Faun, The, 105, 111, 134
Mardi, 116
Margaret, 93
"Marshes of Glynn, The," 158
Mason, George, 49
"Masque of the Red Death, The," 114
"Massachusetts to Virginia," 131
Mather, Cotton, 7, 24–28, 188–189
Mather, Increase, 24, 26, 42
Mather, Richard, 11, 24
May-Day in New-York, 140
May Day in Town, 73
"Maypole of Merry Mount, The," 107
Meditations Three, 15; Six, 16; Eight, 16–17; Sixty-Three, 15
Melancholy, 64, 111–113
Melting-pot theory, 63
Melville, Herman, 105, 115–122, 148, 219–221
"Memories of President Lincoln," 162
Mercedes of Castile, 85
"Merlin," 96, 97
Metamora, or The Last of the Wampanoags, 72
Metaphysical poetry, 16
"Mezzo Cammin," 124–126
Michael Angelo, 124–126
Miles Wallingford, 85
Milton, John, 47, 55, 65, 109, 156
"Milton," 124–126, 129
"Minister's Black Veil, The," 106
Moby-Dick, 104, 115, 118–119
Mock epic: poetry, 56–57, 59–60, 147–148; prose, 22, 34, 35, 77–78
"Mocking-Bird, The," 155
Modern Chivalry, 68–69
Moll Pitcher, 130
Monikins, The, 82
Moore, Clement Clarke, 75
Morality play, 16
"Morituri Salutamus," 124–126, 129

Morris, George Pope, 75
Mortal Antipathy, A, 147
Morton, Nathaniel, 7
Morton, Thomas, 20–22, 187
Mosses from an Old Manse, 117–118
Motley, John Lothrop, 21
Mowatt, Anna Cora, 72
"Mrs. Yardley's Quilting," 146
"MS. Found in a Bottle," 112
"Murders in the Rue Morgue, The," 114
Music, 161; in Lanier, 156–158
"My Aunt," 148
"My Kinsman, Major Molineux," 106
"My Lost Youth," 124–126, 128
Mysteries of the Backwoods, 144
Mysticism, 30, 39, 163, 165
My Thirty Years out of the Senate, 140–141

Nationalism, 48–50, 54, 72–74
Nature, 41–42, 61, 75; in poetry, 12–13, 57–58, 64–66, 87–90, 97, 99, 132–133, 134, 136, 155, 158–159, 164–165; in prose, 30, 63–66, 71, 80, 94–95, 101, 109, 144
Nature (Emerson), 94–95
"Nature" (Longfellow), 124–126
Neal, John, 70, 80, 135
Negroes, 60, 82. See also Slavery
Neoclassicism, 53–60, 61–66 passim, 76. See also Enlightenment
New-England Primer, The, 11
"New England Two Centuries Ago," 134
New English Canaan, The, 21–22, 139
"Noiseless Patient Spider, A," 165
Notes on the State of Virginia, 49–50
Notions of the Americans, 81, 82
Novels, 67–71, 80–85, 108–111, 115–121, 147, 156
"Nuremberg," 124–126

Oak Openings, The, 85
"O Captain! My Captain!" 162, 164 n.4
Octosyllabic verse, 56, 58
Odd Leaves from the Life of a Louisiana Swamp Doctor, 146
"Ode" (Timrod), 154
"Ode: God Save the Rights of Man," 66
"Ode Recited at the Harvard Commemoration," 136
Ode to Channing, 98
Odes, 97, 125, 153–154, 157, 165

Of Plymouth Plantation, 7–9
"Oh Fairest of the Rural Maids," 89
"Old Burns's Bull-Ride," 146
"Old Ironsides," 147, 148
"Old Oaken Bucket, The," 75
Oliver Goldsmith, 77
Omoo, 115, 116
"On a Certain Condescension in Foreigners," 134
"On a Honey Bee," 66
"On Being Brought from Africa to America," 60
"Once I Pass'd through a Populous City," 160
"One's-Self I Sing," 166
Onomatopoeia, 113, 132, 158, 164
"On the Religion of Nature," 64
"On the Uniformity and Perfection of Nature," 64
"On the Universality and Other Attributes of the God of Nature," 64
"On White-Washing," 62
"Open Letter to Horace Greeley," 152
Organic form, 96, 97, 160, 166
Ormond, 71
Otis, James, 47
Our Old Home, 105
"Out of the Cradle Endlessly Rocking," 164
Outre-Mer, 123
Oversoul, 94
Over the Tea Cups, 147
Oxymoron, 30, 89, 103, 127

Paine, Thomas, 46–48, 66, 193
Paradox, 30, 101, 103, 127, 134
Parallelism, 16, 129, 158, 162, 164
Parker, Theodore, 92, 152
"Passage to India," 165
Pathfinder, The, 84
Paulding, James Kirke, 75, 76, 95, 139, 141
"Paul Revere's Ride," 124–126
Payne, John Howard, 72, 75
Peabody, Elizabeth Palmer, 92
Personal Narrative, 30
Personification, 13, 19, 58, 158
"Philosophy of Composition, The," 112 n.3
Picture of New York, A, 77
Pierre, 119
Pilgrims, 3, 5–6, 7–9
Pilot, The, 85

Pioneers, The, 80, 83–84
"Pioneers! O Pioneers!" 162
"Pit and the Pendulum, The," 114
"Plea for Captain John Brown, A," 100 n.7
Poe, Edgar Allan, 65, 87, 96, 97, 106, 111–115, 135–136, 152, 155, 158, 216–219
Poems on Various Subjects, 60
"Poet, The" (essay), 96–97
Poet at the Breakfast Table, The, 147
"Poetic Principle, The," 112 n.3
Point of view, 3, 8–9
"Politics," 102 n.11
Ponteach, 72
Poor Richard Improved, 44
Poor Richard's Almanack, 44
Pope, Alexander, 54, 55, 57, 59, 66
"Portent, The," 121
Porter, William T., 146
Pory, John, 3
"Power of Fancy, The," 65
Power of Sympathy, 67, 68
Prairie, The, 84
"Prairies, The," 89–90
Precaution, 80
"Preface, The" (Taylor), 16
Preparatory Meditations, 16–17
Preromantics, 61–66
Primitivism, 39–40, 61, 63, 64–66, 116–122, 144. *See also* Indians
Prince, Thomas, 7
Prince of Parthia, 72
Principall Navigations, The, 2
"Problem, The," 98
"Proem," 131
Professor at the Breakfast Table, The, 147
Progress of Dulness, The, 55–56
Promotional writing, 3, 4, 21
Proverbs, 44, 101
"Psalm of Life, A," 124–126
Psalterium Americanum, 27
Puns, 15, 16, 101, 115, 135
Puritanism, 5–32, 104–111, 149–150
"Purloined Letter, The," 114

Quakers, 38–39, 69, 92, 130, 160
Quixotism, 22, 69, 78, 79, 142–143

Ralph Waldo Emerson, 147
"Rappaccini's Daughter," 107
"Raven, The," 112, 113

Realism, 85, 156
Reason, the Only Oracle of Man, 42
"Reconciliation," 164
Redburn, 70, 115, 116–117
Red Rover, The, 85, 127
Redskins, The, 82
Refrains, 125, 132, 152
Regionalism, 21, 36–37, 49, 139–146
Reiteration, 15, 16, 27, 113, 152, 158, 162
Representative Men, 95
"Revenge of Hamish, The," 158
"Rhodora, The," 97
Rhyme, 14, 65, 66, 97, 98, 125–126, 130, 135, 156; elegiac, 65, 97, 127
Rights of Man, The, 46, 48, 66
Ripley, George, 92
"Rip Van Winkle," 78–79
Rogers, Major Robert, 72
"Romance," 113
Romanticism, 59–62, 64–65, 76, 80, 85, 87, 96, 123, 127, 156; analyzed, 61–62; satirized, 145, 146, 148
Rowlandson, Mary, 6
Rowson, Susanna Haswell, 68
Rules by Which a Great Empire May be Reduced to a Small One, 44

Sacramental Meditations, 16–17
"Saga of King Olaf, The," 124–126
Sale of the Hessians, The, 43
Salmagundi, 76
"Sarah Pierrepont," 28–29
Satanstoe, 82, 85
Satire, 54; prose, 20–22, 44–45, 67–69, 73–74, 77–78, 100–101, 107, 119, 140–141, 145–146, 148–149; verse, 54–60, 64, 65, 66, 98, 113–114, 134–136, 147–150, 157–158
Saturday Club, 147
Scarlet Letter, The, 104, 105, 108–110, 111
Schoolcraft, Henry Rowe, 128
Science of English Verse, 155–157
Scott, Walter, 76, 81, 85
"Sea-Drift," 162
Sea Lions, The, 85
"Seaweed," 124–126, 127
"Second Inaugural Address" (Lincoln), 153
Secret Diary (Byrd), 35–36
Secret History of the Line, The, 36
Sectionalism, 37, 154–155
Sedgwick, Catharine Maria, 80

"Self-Reliance," 96
Selling of Joseph, The, 11
"Serenade," 126
Sermons, 16, 29–32
Several Poems Compiled with Great Variety of Wit and Learning, 12
Sewall, Samuel, 9–11, 14, 185
Shakespeare, William, 78, 81, 95, 117–118, 152, 156
"Shakespeare," 124–126
Shakspere and His Forerunners, 156
Shillaber, Benjamin P., 141
"Shoemakers, The," 131
"Shooting Match, The," 142
Short story, 77, 105–106, 112, 114–115, 142–146 passim
"Sicily Burns's Wedding," 146
"Sight in Camp, A," 164
Simms, William Gilmore, 80
Simple Cobler of Aggawam, 7
Sinners in the Hands of an Angry God, 31
"Skeleton in Armor, The," 124–125, 126–127
Sketch Book, The, 76
Sketch Club, 86
Sketches of Switzerland, 82
"Skipper Ireson's Ride," 131–132
Slavery, 11, 39, 49, 63, 65, 120, 130–136, 152
"Sleeper, The," 113
Smith, (Captain) John, 2–4, 183–184
Smith, Seba, 139–141, 226
"Smoke," 103
Snow-Bound, 130, 131, 132–133
"Snow-Storm, The," 97
Society and Solitude, 95 n.3
Solitude, 101, 164
Some Adventures of Captain Simon Suggs, 146
Some Considerations on the Keeping of Negroes, 39
Song of Hiawatha, The, 124–126 passim, 128–129
"Song of Myself," 161–162, 162–163
"Song of the Chattahoochee," 158
"Songs of Labor," 131
Sonnet, 125, 126, 129, 130
"Sonnet—To Science," 113
Sot-Weed Factor, The, 54
"Sound of the Sea, The," 124–126
Sovereignty & Goodness of God, The, 6 n.1

Spanish Student, The, 124–126
Specimen Days and Collect, 166
Speech of Polly Baker, The, 43
Spenser, Edmund, 13, 59, 131
Spenserian stanza, 53, 58, 61
"Sphinx, The," 97
Spirit of the Times, 143–144, 146
Spondees, 16, 17, 149, 155
Sprung rhythm, 97, 103, 128
Spy, The, 80, 85
"Stirrup-Cup, The," 158
Stoddard, Solomon, 17, 28
Stone, John Augustus, 72
"Sunthin' in the Pastoral Line," 136
Supernaturalism of New England, The, 130
Superstition, 72
Sut Lovingood's Yarns, 144–146
Swift, Jonathan, 69, 78, 139
Symbolism, 64, 102, 105, 109, 154, 157, 165; in Melville, 116–122
"Symphony, The," 156, 157–158
Synesthesia, 30, 155

Tales of a Traveller, 76
Tales of a Wayside Inn, 124, 125
Taylor, Edward, 14–17, 186–187
"Telling the Bees," 130, 131, 132
"Tell-Tale Heart, The," 114
Tenney, Tabitha, 68
Tennyson, Alfred, 129, 155, 156, 158
Tenth Muse Lately Sprung up in America, The, 12
Tent on the Beach, The, 130
"Terminus," 99
"Thanatopsis," 87, 88–89
"Thar's More in the Man than Thar Is in the Land," 157
"There Was a Child Went Forth," 163
Thompson, William Tappan, 146
Thoreau, Henry David, 91–93, 99–103, 210–212
"Thoreau" (Lowell), 134
Thorpe, Thomas Bangs, 143–144, 227
"Three Silences of Molinos, The," 124–126
"Tide Rises, the Tide Falls, The," 124–126, 129–130
Tiger-Lilies, 156
Timrod, Henry, 151, 153–154, 229–230
"To a Caty-Did," 66
"To a Locomotive in Winter," 165–166
"To an Author," 66

"To a Waterfowl," 88
"To Cole, the Painter," 86
"To Helen," 113
"To Madame Helvetius," 43
"To My Dear and Loving Husband," 13
"To Sir Toby," 65
"To S. M. a Young African Painter, On Seeing His Works," 60
"To the Dandelion," 134
"To the Fringed Gentian," 87
"To the Memory of the Brave Americans," 65
"To the Universality of Cambridge, in New-England," 60
Tour on the Prairies, A, 76–77
Transcendental Club, 92
Transcendentalism, 29, 91–93, 100–101, 103, 104, 107, 108, 160, 164
Transcendentalists, 91–103
Travel writing, 2, 58, 81, 82
Travels in New England and New York, 58
Treatise Concerning the Religious Affections, A, 28
Tricksters, 79, 120, 128, 143
Trisyllabic feet, 87, 155
Triumph of Infidelity, The, 57
Trochaic meter, 129
True Relation of . . . Virginia, A, 3
True Travels, Adventures, and Observations of Captain John Smith, 2
Trumbull, John, 55–57, 195
Tuckerman, Frederick Goddard, 92, 93
"Turn Out, The," 142
Twain, Mark, 144
Twice-Told Tales, 105; Poe's review of, 112 n.3
Two Admirals, The, 85
Tyler, Royall, 73–74, 199–200
Typee, 115–116

"Ulalume," 113
Understatement, 148
Unpromising hero, 4, 9, 46
"Upon a Wasp Chilled with Cold," 15
"Uriel," 98
Utopia, 21

"Vanity of Existence, The," 65
"Venice," 124–126
Very, Jones, 92, 93
"Village Blacksmith, The," 124–126

Vindication of the Government of New-England Churches, 42
Vision of Columbus, The, 58
Vision of Sir Launfal, The, 134
"Visit from St. Nicholas, A," 75
Voices of the Night, 124
Voyages of the Companions of Columbus, 76

Walden, 100–102
Ward, Nathaniel, 7, 139
Warren, Mercy Otis, 72
"Washers of the Shroud, The," 136
Washington, George, 50, 77, 85
Water-Witch, The, 85
'Way down East, 140
Way to Wealth, The, 44
Ways of the Hour, The, 82
Week on the Concord and Merrimack Rivers, A, 99, 100
Weems, Mason Locke, 141, 152
Welde, Thomas, 11
Wept of Wish-ton-Wish, The, 85
"What Is an American?" 63–64
"What Mr. Robinson Thinks," 135
Wheatley, Phillis, 60, 196
"When I Heard the Learn'd Astronomer," 164
"When Lilacs Last in the Dooryard Bloom'd," 164–165
Whipple, Edwin Percy, 155
"Whistle, The," 43
Whitcher, Frances M., 141
White, John, 3
White-Jacket, 115, 116–117
Whitman, Walt, 94, 97, 100, 160–166, 231–234

Whittier, John Greenleaf, 71, 130–133, 136, 155, 223–224
Wieland, 70–71
Wigglesworth, Michael, 13–14, 185–186
"Wild Honey Suckle, The," 65
Williams, Roger, 17–20, 187
Willis, Nathaniel Parker, 75, 111
Wilson, Alexander, 62
Wing-and-Wing, The, 85
Winslow, Edward, 3
"Winter Piece, A," 89
Winthrop, John, 12
Wise, John, 42
Witchcraft, 9, 24–25, 104, 106, 110
Wolfert's Roost, 77
"Wonderful 'One-Hoss Shay,' The," 149–150
Wonders of the Invisible World, 24–25, 27, 106
"Woodman, Spare that Tree," 75
Woodworth, Samuel, 75, 139
Woolman, John, 38–40, 130, 191
Wordplay, 66. *See also* Puns
Wordsworth, William, 92, 95 n.2
"Wound-Dresser, The," 164
"Wreck of the Hesperus, The," 123, 124–126
Wyandotté, 85

Yankees, 73–74, 78, 79, 82, 139–140
Yankey in London, The, 73
"Yellow Violet, The," 87
"Young Goodman Brown," 106

Zeugma, 78